By
Jack Rosenthal

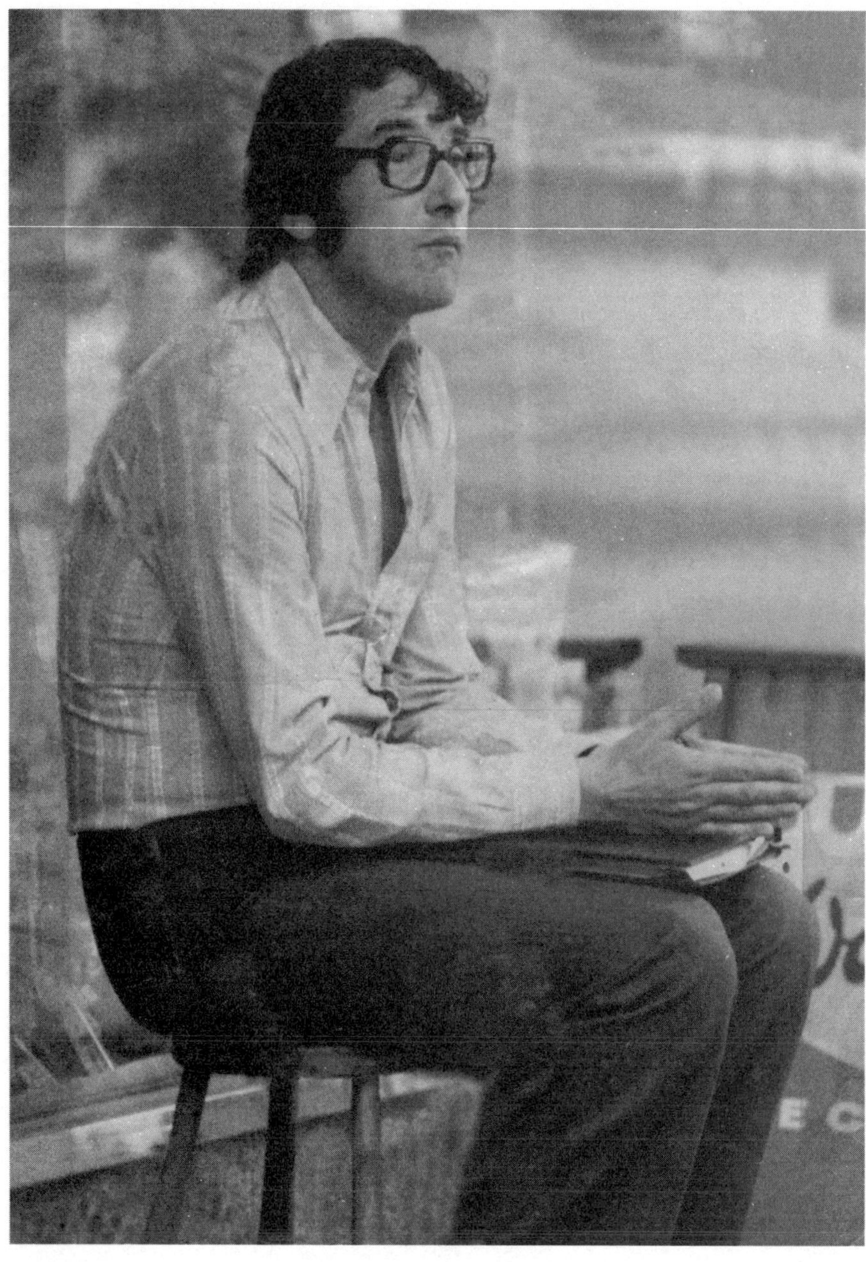

By Jack Rosenthal

An Autobiography in Six Acts

JACK ROSENTHAL

POSTSCRIPT by MAUREEN LIPMAN

Foreword by Amy Rosenthal

ROBSON

With thanks to Jeremy Robson, publisher and friend,
and Barbara Phelan, caring editor.

First published in Great Britain in 2005 by
Robson Books,
151 Freston Road
London
W10 6TH

An imprint of Anova Books Company Ltd

All photographs are from the authors' private collection, except the following images from Jack Rosenthal's works:
Yentl – Ladbroke Entertainments Ltd & MGM/UA Entertainment/BFI
P'Tang, Yang, Kipperbang – Goldcrest Films and Television & Channel Four/BFI
The Knowledge – Thames Television/BFI
Spend, Spend, Spend – BBC/BFI
Ready When You Are, Mr McGill – Granada Television/BFI
The Evacuees – BBC/BFI
Bar Mitzvah Boy – BBC/BFI
Coronation Street – ITV/Granada

ISBN 1 86105 960 4

10 9 8 7 6 5 4 3 2 1

Typeset by SX Composing DTP, Rayleigh, Essex
Printed by Creative Print & Design, Wales (Ebbw Vale)

This book can be ordered direct from the publisher
Contact the marketing department, but try your bookshop first

For all our friends, and everyone who fought so hard to keep him.

CONTENTS

FOREWORD

It was February 2003, and my parents were having dinner with their friends, publisher Jeremy Robson and his wife Carole, in a couscous restaurant in West Hampstead. My father was already suffering from back pain caused by the myeloma cancer that would soon be diagnosed.

Now, my dad didn't actually *like* couscous, but he liked my mum, a lot, and she loves it. So there they were, eating couscous, and, not for the first time, Jeremy was trying to persuade my dad to write his autobiography. Not for the first time, he was demurring.

'I wouldn't know how. It wouldn't be interesting. I wouldn't know what to put.'

'Course, you know what you *should* do, love,' said my mum suddenly, 'you should write it as a screenplay.'

'A screenplay?' Jeremy was delighted. 'That's a brilliant idea!'

'Oh, do it, Jack, it would be wonderful!' agreed Carole.

I wasn't there, but I imagine my dad gave a small, dismissive smile. *Half*-smile, half-grimace.

'You just write it like one of your plays,' my mum went on, 'you tell your own story, in your own medium. It's completely original.'

My dad seemed as unconvinced by the idea as he was by his dinner, and the conversation turned to other matters. But over the next few days, quietly and without comment, he started to make notes. The notes became scenes, the scenes became acts, which became an epic screenplay, and this completely original book.

He worked on it feverishly throughout his illness. In his first phase of high-dose chemotherapy at the Royal Marsden Hospital, he contracted pneumonia and was moved to the High Risk ward. He was desperately weak and breathless. As we stood at his bedside in the plastic aprons that we had to wear to protect him from infection, he asked me if I had a pen and paper. I did, and he removed his oxygen mask to dictate a passage of prose which you can find verbatim in this book. Later, he described a recurrent nightmare from that time in the Marsden. It was of writing; tiny spidery writing, going on and on, always picking up where it left off, never ending.

I tell you this to explain that my dad was a consummate writer, a writer to his core; and yet he wrote totally without fanfare, without show. And his writing life was so finely integrated into his *family* life that it took us all a long time to appreciate what he was doing when he sat in his study, deep in thought yet ever poised to leap up and make someone a cuppa, a sandwich or a three-course meal. It is only now, scanning his astounding list of credits, that we see how prolific was his quiet alchemy; with what dedication he spent his time spinning life into stories, spinning stories into glorious life.

And so it is the kitchen, not his study, where I miss him most. Always conscious of his own impoverished childhood, he took great pleasure in feeding people, especially his family. When we had a Chinese takeaway, he presided over the table like an anxious, loving bird, and although we were more than capable of making our own duck pancakes, he always insisted on making them for us, spreading the 'glue' (plum sauce) evenly across the thin rice pancake, adorning it with meat and a sprinkling of spring onions and cucumber, and rolling it up as delicately as if it were a Torah scroll.

What he didn't realise, as he beamed at the prospect of gluing together another duck pancake for someone who didn't need one, is that he *was* the glue. His sweetness held us together; without him we will have to try harder, we will have to learn patience and care.

During his all-too-brief remission he kept working on the book, but at the end of 2003, when his illness returned with renewed ferocity and my wonderful grandmother died suddenly of a heart attack, he too lost heart. Perhaps he'd had enough of being haunted by spidery handwriting. Perhaps after over forty years and more than 150 screenplays, in an industry changed beyond recognition from the joyful early days to today's TV drama wasteland where star-billing dictates story and 'cutting edge' has the edge on truth, he was ready to lay down his biro.

A short time before he died, my mum and I and our great friend Colin Shindler took him out in his wheelchair on Hampstead Heath. He was frail, bundled up in his herringbone coat, a rakish navy-blue sailor's cap protecting what was left of his soft black hair. It was a bright May day and the Heath was thronged with families, children, couples, cyclists, dogs. As I wheeled my dad along the path, he suddenly said:

'This is *wonderful*, you know. All these people. It's the most wonderful thing.'

I looked at the people weaving around us.

'You mean, all the different lives...?' I asked.

He shook his head, half-smiling, a bit frustrated.

'I can't explain,' he said.

And I believe that he could see something we couldn't. That he had crossed a line, and maybe he could see for real what, as a writer, he had always known was there. A goodness and humanity in people, in spite of ourselves, a fundamental decency that might not be 'cutting edge', but which ultimately most of us share. His warm, wry affection for humankind shone through his work, it shone through his life, and as I write these words, it gives me what he always gave me. Hope.

Amy Rosenthal, 2005

LIST OF ABBREVIATIONS

This book contains several abbreviations and terms traditionally found in screenplays and scripts:

INT	Interior
EXT	Exterior
VO	Voice-over
CU	Close-up
CAM	Camera
POV	Point of view
CONT	Continuous
PAN	Panning
OS	Off-screen
OOS	Out of Shot
beat	A pause in dialogue or action

I am, in fact, the best chip-maker, probably on earth; I don't want to claim too much for myself, but probably the very best.

Jack Rosenthal on *Desert Island Discs*
1998

PROLOGUE

EXTERIOR NO-MAN'S-LAND – FRANCE – DAY – 1918

A 21-year-old private in the Lancashire Fusiliers lies in the mud and slutch and stench of a shell-littered crater. His helmet is at a rakish angle – much beloved by misguided Tommies wanting to look devil-may-care and even more beloved by well-guided German bullets looking for exposed Tommy foreheads. He's bleeding and vomiting helplessly.

JACK (VOICE OVER)

His name is Sam Rosenthal and thirteen years from now – if he lasts that long – he'll be my dad.

A comrade slithers down the side of the crater, cradles Sam's neck and offers him a sip of water, then a lit Woodbine. Both make him retch.

Under the following dialogue, we hear a whistled version of 'It's a Long Way to Tipperary'.

COMRADE

Jammy bastard.

SAM

'Jammy'?

COMRADE

Wounded *and* gassed.

SAM

You're doolally-tap, you!

COMRADE

I'm right, though. You'll be back in Blighty, *dead* quick.

SAM

Bloody dead, yes. No argument.

COMRADE

Land for heroes to live in. No more dole. Maine Road every fortnight. Billy Meredith on the wing. Toothpick in his cake-hole. You'll be laughing.

(*beat*)

Shall I sing to you?

SAM

No, ta. I'm in enough pain as it is.

COMRADE

(*singing, nevertheless*)

It's a long way to tickle Mary
It's a long way to go
(Without your mother)
It's a long way to tickle Mary
To the sweetest girl I know
Goodbye, Piccadilly –

SAM

I'd get murdered.

COMRADE

Eh?

SAM

She'd be a shiksa.

COMRADE

Eh?

SAM

Bound to be. With a name like Mary. Jesus' mam was a Mary. I'm only allowed to tickle Yiddishe girls.

(*beat*)

And *they* don't let you.

He coughs painfully. His comrade plies him with another cigarette.

JACK (VO)

Throughout Sam's life, the fags and the gas ganged up on his lungs – and gunged up in them. One day they'd finish him off altogether.

His comrade was up the pole about one or two other things as well: Blighty *didn't* turn out to be a land for heroes to live in, more of a land to queue up for your dole money in.

And *Sam* was also wrong about one thing. There *were* Jewish girls called Mary. One was the sister of the girl he finally *did* get to tickle, I suppose . . .

Enough, already. This is my parents I'm talking about.

THE THIRTIES

EXT TOWN HALL – CHEETHAM HILL – MANCHESTER – DAY – 1927

Cheetham Hill Road is the bustling main thoroughfare stretching from the city centre to the heart of the working-class Jewish quarter.

Today is Sunday – not the Jewish day of rest – which means the road is a cacophonous cavalcade of bone-shaking trams, horses and carts, bikes, motor-bikes with side-cars and maybe, but only maybe, the odd car. The cacophony spills over onto the pavements . . . bearded frummers shouting the odds at girls smoking in the street on their way for pickled meat and chips in the delis, housewives pushing prams of washing (or even babies) from shop to shop, kids on roller-skates weaving between them.

This being 1927, five years or more before Oswald Mosley's blackshirts began their jackbooted marches down this road, chanting 'Jews Out!', the only march today is an out-of-step shuffle by the teenage Jewish Lads' Brigade, led by bugles and drums, half of them in unmatching football kit, two of them heading a ton-weight brown, leather football from one to the other.

Only a few yards from the nearest synagogue, the Town Hall is a popular venue for wedding receptions. A middle-aged man in overalls is standing outside the entrance under the black, wrought-iron, colonnaded canopy, pulling on a Woodbine.

Another man now slips out of the building. He's wearing a morning suit that fits where it touches, spats and cravat, and carries a top hat.

The bridegroom, in fact. Sam, in fact.

And now that he's not caked in the mud of the trenches, we can see a tall, thin man, wide forehead, curly black hair, fleshy earlobes, generous

Mr Punch nose, broken more than once, and seemingly grown all the more generous with each break. He looks round – then spots the man in the overalls.

SAM
(*hisses*)

Mickey!

The man (Mickey) turns.

MICKEY

I thought you said half past!

SAM

I couldn't get out. I'd ban bloody wedding speeches if it was up to me.

Surreptitiously (street betting being illegal), he passes some coins into Mickey's hand.

SAM

A shilling each way, Honeymoon Lass, eight o'clock tomorrow.

MICKEY

Where?

SAM

Salford Dog Track.

MICKEY

Why can't *you* put it on?

SAM

I'll be in bloody Blackpool, you shmock! I'm only the Honeymoon *lad*, aren't I?

MICKEY
(*realising*)

Oh. Yeah. Sorry. Forgot. Mazeltov, by the way.

SAM

It hasn't won yet.

MICKEY

I mean getting married.

SAM

Oh, I see. Ta.

Mickey wanders off. A last guilty look round, and Sam goes back to his wedding.

INTERIOR TOWN HALL – CHEETHAM HILL – MANCHESTER – DAY – 1927

A modest wedding reception now winding down. Waitresses in mock Joe Lyons uniforms are clearing the trestle tables of apfel strudel crumbs and crockery. A four-piece band plays 'Among My Souvenirs', absent-mindedly accompanied by a rabbi on spoon, plate and cup at a nearby table.

A few guests are sedately foxtrotting – but one couple in the centre of the dance floor, high-stepping and raucously singing, hurl themselves into it. They are the bride, Leah née Miller, now Rosenthal, and her brother Louis. Both of them are known by their childhood nicknames. Leah is Lakey. Ginger-haired Louis is Ginger.

Lakey is 21 years old, 5 feet 4 inches in high heels, slim, dark, hazel-eyed, pert, pretty and perky as they come. Her slightly buck teeth are regarded as 'showing personality'. She wears a white-lace, flapper wedding dress, cut to the knee, and a bandanna headdress.

JACK (VO)

In four years' time, Lakey would be my mam.

Sam meanders back in and starts towards the head table, which is very clearly divided into the two family groups. Into the almost opposite ends of the psychological spectrum of the human race. The two sides of the character coin. Toss it up. If it comes down heads you have the Rosenthals; tails and you get the Millers.

JACK (VO)

Maybe it was the two sides of the Russian personality. I say 'maybe' because I think both families came from Russia, but it could just as easily have been Lithuania. Who knows? No one ever said. No one ever mentioned family trees or the 'heim' or pogroms or life before they emigrated. As though life, for them, only *began* after their cattle-steamers left Hamburg. I'm going to be saying 'maybe' a lot . . .

So, heads the Rosenthals. The pessimists. (Maybe.) Dour, earnest, a little apprehensive of life. Straightfaced, straightlaced.

CAMERA *moves along the row of Rosenthals . . .*

Bernie, the patriarch, watchmaker by trade, smiling benignly over his half-spectacles, in later years letting us grandchildren peep through his magnifying glass.

His very *straightfaced wife, Leah Rosenthal Senior, her last years spent rocking to and fro, morn till night, 'davening' from a Hebrew prayer book and only acknowledging she even* had *grandchildren so that she could shush them.*

Eldest son, Abe, optician, self-made, self-assured, authoritative even. So, maybe he wasn't a Rosenthal at all. Maybe he was switched as a baby. Maybe that's why his mother prayed all the time. For forgiveness . . .

Annie, my kind, hard-working Auntie Annie. The finest piemaker the world has ever seen.

Sarah, otherwise known as Sybil. Not quite *so dour, earnest and straightfaced. Otherwise, I suppose, she'd have stuck to the biblical respectability of 'Sarah'.*

JACK (VO)

I never knew my Uncle Jack, the relative I was named after. He died before I was born. And no one ever told me anything about him.

Sam sits down at the table with the rest of his side of the family. He lights another Woodbine and watches the dancing Millers. Probably uncomprehendingly . . .

Tails, the Millers. The optimists. Funny, warm, excitable, outspoken. (Sometimes a bit too *outspoken in Jack's view, bearing in mind that he'd be a half-Rosenthal.) Always ready for a laugh, for a joke, for a bit of a knees-up.*

CAM wanders among the Miller family . . .

Head of the family, Hymie. Another gentle grandfather, looking the part with his King George V beard.

Eldest son, Harry (nicknamed Ocky). Bossy and proud of it.

Eldest daughter, Mary, who as a teenager had, by necessity, to become bossy, to become the matriarch, the little mother, when the real mother died in the rampaging post-WWI flu epidemic.

Corncrake-voiced, quick-tempered, round-shouldered Arthur (Pinky by nickname). Married to Eva, who was reputed to be the niece of the mother of Danny Kaye. Repeat, reputed. Who knows?

Corncrake-voiced, sweet-tempered, happy-go-lucky Louis, nicknamed Ginger.

Middle daughter, Florrie, maybe a little *earnest for a Miller.*

Mary is dancing with her father. After a few moments, she whispers something to him. He nods yes, and she goes over to Ginger, excuses him and starts dancing with Lakey. Ginger, Ocky and Pinky take it in ten-second turns to excuse each other and dance with Florrie.

ANGLE ON Mary and Lakey dancing.

MARY

(*urgently*)

Have you asked him yet?

LAKEY

Not yet.

MARY

Lakey! Go and ask him!

LAKEY

I can't right *now*. In *here*. It's not nice.

MARY

What's 'nice' to do with it? If you don't ask him, *I* will!

LAKEY

Bossy bugger, aren't you?

MARY

Ta, ta.

She pushes her towards the edge of the dance floor. Lakey strolls nonchalantly, or so she imagines, to Sam seated at the table and sits down beside him.

As they talk, a waitress clears the debris around them.

LAKEY

Sam? How much have you got?

SAM

How much what?

LAKEY

Money.

SAM

How d'you mean?

LAKEY

So far, like.

SAM
(*puzzled*)

In my pocket, sort of thing?

LAKEY

Saved up.

SAM
(*still puzzled*)

What am I saving up for, love?

It's now her *turn to be puzzled.*

LAKEY

Eh?

SAM

Am I saving up for summat?

LAKEY
(*beat*)

Well . . . yes. Married *life*.

A pause. This seems news to Sam.

SAM

Oh. Right.

(*another pause*)

I've got over a shilling *on* me.

He takes a handful of change from his pocket and counts it.

One and sevenpence.

LAKEY
(*beat*)

And how much for this married life caper?

SAM
(*worriedly*)

D'you fancy a dance?

LAKEY
(*even more worriedly*)

Bloody hell! *That* bad, is it?

They go to the dance floor and start to dance. She's a natural, he's a novice. He manages to tread on her toes almost at once with his size 10 centre-forward's feet. It won't be for the last time – even if they never dance together again . . .

TITLE SEQUENCE

A montage of clips or stills of, say, twenty films, each of about 5 seconds duration, cut to the rhythm of the underscored 'Among My Souvenirs'.

Superimpose CAPTION: *'By Jack Rosenthal'.*

EXT BACKYARD – NORTH MANCHESTER – DAY – 1928

Lakey is hanging out washing (nappies) on a line, while occasionally rocking baby David in his pram, softly singing a Yiddish lullaby as she does so. It's called 'Rozikin mit Mandlen' – 'Raisins and Almonds'.

Lakey's command of Yiddish, like her knowledge of Hebrew, is almost non-existent . . .

. . . 'Rozikin mit Mandlen' is consequently delivered in pure Mancunian instead, the lyrics simply consisting of the names of fruit.

Suddenly the back door of the yard is flung open – and Lakey's mother-in-law storms in. She speaks in broken English.

MOTHER-IN-LAW

You feed him plenty?

LAKEY

(*thrown*)

The baby?

MOTHER-IN-LAW

His father.

LAKEY

Sam? I'd get a right gobful if I didn't!

Her mother-in-law strides across the yard and into the scullery, slamming the door behind her. Baby David wakes up and starts to yell. Lakey gathers him up and starts for the scullery.

INT SCULLERY – NORTH MANCHESTER – DAY – 1928 (CONT)

Mother-in-law is snapping open cupboards – the pantry, the oven, the drawers – and rooting inside them. During this:

MOTHER-IN-LAW

He likes herrings. I don't see much herrings.

LAKEY

He gets plenty herrings.

MOTHER-IN-LAW

Proper dinners you make? Chicken soup, kneidlach, potato kugel?

LAKEY

Till it comes out of his ears.

David is still crying. Lakey tries to pacify him and close the cupboards at the same time.

MOTHER-IN-LAW

(*re David*)

You make too much fuss of the baby. Better you have another, then you don't spoil. I go now. This was just a friendly visit.

She sweeps out again. Fighting back tears, Lakey hugs David close to her.

INT SWEATSHOP WATERPROOF GARMENT FACTORY – MANCHESTER – DAY – 1928

Ill-lit, grimy, draughty, cold, spartan. Walls are stained by damp, windows broken.

INTERCUT between Sam (among other men) joining mackintosh seams at a wooden bench and Lakey (among other women) sewing raincoats at an industrial sewing machine. Despite their grim surroundings, the women are singing 'Side by Side'.

During this:

JACK (VO)

In the months before their wedding, Sam and Lakey sweated in the same sweatshop. Sam as a 'shmeerer' – sticking together the seams of mackintoshes with a roller gunged up with viscous varnish. Lakey as a machinist – treadling through raincoats all joined together – like a one-woman assembly line.

Their trade union, much to Sam's vociferous despair, was the toothless Transport and General Workers' – which meant wages were always half a chip-butty above starvation level and wage negotiations were unconditional surrender.

As a result, a picturesque little phrase galloped into sweatshop life with its front legs, while dragging its back legs behind it. It was a phrase that would come to haunt me throughout my childhood. Enter the 'dead horse'.

A dead horse was a sub. If there wasn't enough work to provide a liveable wage by Friday, the management, if you were lucky, subbed you a few shillings' worth. Working off the dead horse would take most of the next week. So *another* dead horse slithered out of the starting gate. And the next week, another. And so on. Dead horses ran for ever. And never won a bloody race.

After David was born, in 1928, Lakey stopped work for a while to concentrate on him. And herrings. Money got even harder to come by. Dead horses were stampeding all over Manchester.

EXT CRICKET GROUND – CHEETHAM HILL – MANCHESTER – DAY – 1929

A bowler runs up and bowls. Sam, in cricket whites, is batting. He strokes the ball beautifully to the boundary.

By the pavilion, Lakey is watching with toddler David.

JACK (VO)

Sport was everything to Sam. Both war *and* peace. He was opening batsman for a local team, Red Rose, and one day was destined to score 70 for the Lancashire Players against the Lancashire Gentlemen.

Since he was born in Yorkshire, he could never have qualified as a Lancashire Gentleman. On either count.

INT SNOOKER HALL – ARDWICK – MANCHESTER – NIGHT – 1929

Through a fog of cigarette smoke, cloth-capped punters watch anxiously as Sam and an opponent play snooker. His opponent misses the blue. The punters look even more anxious. Sam thoughtfully chalks his cue.

JACK (VO)

For Sam, sport wasn't necessarily sporting. A couple of nights a week, he'd catch a bus to some part of the city where he wasn't known in the snooker halls, and hustle. Playing badly all evening so that bets would go against him. Then when his odds were at their highest, he'd suddenly turn into Joe Davis.

Sam takes up his stance and pots the blue, pink and black in swift succession. He turns to his opponent and holds his hand out.

SAM

Half a dollar you owe me.

His opponent's eyes narrow.

OPPONENT

I like a good comedian. You'd pack 'em in at the Ardwick Hipp.

SAM

I was lucky. My hand must've slipped.

OPPONENT

I think my bleeding *fist* might an' all, bloody Sheeny!

He takes a swing at Sam. Sam ducks and wrestles his way past the punters towards the door. His opponent and one or two of the punters give chase.

EXT A CINDER FOOTBALL PITCH – CHEETHAM HILL – MANCHESTER – DAY – 1930

At the touchline, Lakey is kicking a ball to the growing David.

On the pitch, a scratch kickabout in progress. Sam has the ball. Another player tackles him – fouling him in the process. Sam swears angrily – then throws a punch at the player. They start to fight. Other players join in. It becomes a free-for-all.

Lakey stops to watch the fight. One of the men is shouting viciously, 'Dirty mamser!' (Yiddish for 'bastard'). Without looking any closer, she knows which one of them it is. She sighs, resignedly.

JACK (VO)

Sport was Sam's hot-headed way of fighting back . . . Of making himself heard, or giving himself a tattered shred of dignity, or winning a few shillings – even if he did it by cheating. 'Cheating' was just slang for 'Playing the game'.

EXT FAIRGROUND – BELLE VUE – MANCHESTER – DAY – 1930

An overweight boxer in leopardskin shorts stands with his barker outside a booth.

A sign reads 'Go one round with The White Tornado, win 2/6d. Three rounds, win 5/–. Knock him out, win 10/–'.

Sam (with David perched on his shoulders) and Lakey are in the small crowd. Sam looks at Lakey for permission. She shakes her head, no. Nevertheless he hands David down to her and goes into the booth.

INT BOXING BOOTH – BELLE VUE – MANCHESTER – DAY – 1930 (CONT)

The White Tornado is smashing rights and lefts into Sam's ribs and face. Blood pours from Sam's nose. He isn't going to win a penny . . .

EXT ELIZABETH STREET – CHEETHAM HILL – MANCHESTER – DAY – 1930

Sam and Lakey walking down the street. Lakey is pushing David in his pram.

Suddenly, terrifyingly, a rat leaps over the pram and scurries away. Sam aims a wild kick at it. Lakey screams. She pulls David from his pram and holds him tight to her breast. She stands, panting, frightened.

CLOSE-UP Mother and child.

JACK (VO)

A *rat*? In the middle of Elizabeth Street? In broad daylight? Doing the hundred yards' hurdles over prams? Could that really have happened? Well, maybe. Maybe not. Was it another of the apocryphal stories that parents and grandparents never got round to explaining?

Whether it existed or not, though, the rat was held responsible for frightening David into infantile paralysis. Could *that* really have happened?

Either way, infantile paralysis was the reason behind a renewed campaign for a sibling for David. Lakey's mother-in-law thought Abey Moses would be a good name. Lakey thought it'd be a better name for the rat and prayed for a daughter . . . a daughter she would call Jacqueline.

EXT WHITEHALL – LONDON – CINEMA NEWSREEL – DAY – 1931

Demonstrators battle violently with truncheon-wielding police. Superimpose CAPTION: *'September 8th, 1931'.*

NEWSREEL ANNOUNCER (VO)

Britain is forced off the Gold Standard. The pound is devalued. Seventeen demonstrators are arrested in Whitehall. The King gives back £50,000 to the Treasury.

EXT ST JAMES'S PALACE – LONDON – CINEMA NEWSREEL – DAY – 1931

The emaciated, bespectacled, bald-pated figure of Mahatma Gandhi, half-naked in shawl and loincloth, makes his way past policemen into the palace. Superimpose CAPTION: *'September 8th, 1931'.*

NEWSREEL ANNOUNCER (VO)

At a conference at St James's Palace, Mahatma Gandhi demands independence for India.

INT BEDROOM – TERRACED HOUSE – NORTH MANCHESTER – DAY – 1931

Three-year-old David watches Lakey rocking a newborn baby in his cot. Superimpose CAPTION: *'September 8th, 1931'.*

JACK (VO)

The newborn baby was me. Since I was another son and not the hoped-for daughter, Lakey compromised on Jacqueline – and named me Jack.

EXT JEWS' SCHOOL – DERBY STREET – MANCHESTER – DAY – 1934

Among other parents and offspring, Lakey walks towards the black, soot-stained Victorian school, round the corner from Cheetham Hill Road, six-year-old David in one hand, 2½-year-old Jack in the other.

JACK (VO)

According to Lakey, I couldn't wait to grow up. This despite a reluctance to grow up ever since I was *supposed* to. I insisted on starting school at 2½ instead of five. Not that spending

every afternoon sleeping on a camp bed or learning nursery rhymes proved of any academic advantage.

There was also a *disadvantage*: I thought my name was Jack Sprat who could eat no fat. An impossibility, of course, when you live in a ghetto in Chopped Liver Land.

Lakey, David and Jack go into the school.

INT SCULLERY – CHEETHAM HILL – MANCHESTER – DAY – 1936

Jack sits at the table, hacking chunks of hair off his head with a pair of pinking shears.

A grown-up hairstyle is a first step – although not much admired by bona fide grown-ups . . .

Lakey comes in at the door with a bag of shopping. She sees Jack's mutilated head, drops her shopping and screams.

EXT WASTE GROUND – CHEETHAM HILL – MANCHESTER – DAY – 1936

A kid in the uniform of the Jewish Lads' Brigade stands bartering with Jack.

Jack is offering a child's brand-new pedal car in exchange for a pair of stained, torn and bedraggled long trousers.

The pedal car is a birthday present from Sam and Lakey and cost £2. At most, the trousers are worth a broken clothes-peg from a rag-and-bone man.

Both boys seem satisfied with the deal. They shake hands. The kid gets in the pedal car and drives off. Jack walks away with the trousers over his arm.

INT DAVID'S AND JACK'S BEDROOM – MANCHESTER – DAY – 1936

Jack is standing on the bed, legs astride. He's wearing the long trousers, wellingtons, a scout hat and a blazer. With accompanying verbal sound effects, he's shooting a toy revolver from the hip.

Perfect. Overnight he's grown into an officer in the Royal Canadian Mounted Police – and you don't get much more grown-up than that.

David, in his half of the bed, ignores him, and turns the page of a comic.

EXT PLAYGROUND – JEWS' SCHOOL – MANCHESTER – DAY – 1937

Outside the gates, an Italian street-vendor is selling hot, roasted chestnuts.

Inside the kids are playing tag. Jack doesn't seem to be concentrating. We then see why. He's exchanging shy glances with a little girl, Shirley.

JACK (VO)

Well, of course, you *do* get more grown-up than that, once you start noticing girls. And what you do then – is invite them home to tea . . .

INT HALLWAY – TERRACED HOUSE – CHEETHAM HILL – MANCHESTER – DAY – 1937

In BACKGROUND at the far end of the hallway, the scullery door is ajar. Inside we see David and Shirley seated at the table, eating bread and jam.

In FOREGROUND, with his back to them, Jack is seated on the lower steps of the staircase, singing loudly.

JACK
(*singing*)

Look who's coming down the street
Mrs Simpson's sweaty feet
She's been married twice before
Now she's knocking on Edward's door.

INT SCULLERY – TERRACED HOUSE – MANCHESTER – DAY – 1937 (CONT)

David and Shirley, at the table, holding hands, smiling fondly at each other with jam-streaked mouths.

The song is all the rage at school. Witty, topical, constitutionally provocative – even if none of us really knows why. But Shirley reckons it's just showing off. The real truth is that David is nine and Jack is only six – and she prefers the sophisticated man-of-the-world approach.

INT FREE TRADE HALL – MANCHESTER – NIGHT – 1937

Sir Oswald Mosley, in military uniform, is at the rostrum, flanked by blackshirted thugs.

The hall is packed, the atmosphere dangerous. Here and there among the audience are hecklers. One of them is Sam.

MOSLEY

Our new party will harness modern machinery and ask for a mobilisation of energy, vitality and manhood to save the nation. We are a party of action!

SAM
(*shouting*)

A party of bloody thugs and hooligans! Fascist bastards!

Three thugs promptly storm their way down the aisle and start hammering his head, face and shoulders with truncheons.

INT SCULLERY – TERRACED HOUSE – MANCHESTER – NIGHT – 1937

Lakey is bathing Sam's wounds. David and Jack sit solemnly watching, conscious of how different life in the Wild West at the kids' matinee at the pictures is from life in Cheetham Hill. In the Wild West, if the hero's wounded, the heroine washes the blood away lovingly. In their house it isn't lovingly, it's angrily.

But, then again, to Lakey, Sam is no hero. More of a villain. With each passing payday, more and more of a villain. The Saturday morning serial is Flash Gordon and the Clay Men. *The villain is the evil Ming. Sam apparently leaves him standing.*

SAM
(*wincing*)

Ow!

LAKEY

Keep still.

SAM

That hurts!

LAKEY

Well, if you will play with ruffians . . .

SAM

I don't think they were *playing*. Sarky bugger.

LAKEY

Gay cacken!

SAM

Gay essen!

LAKEY

Gay fressen!

The brothers share an apprehensive glance. The sudden descent into scatological Yiddish insults means the next stage – the throwing of pots and pans – is imminent.

INT DAVID AND JACK'S BEDROOM – MANCHESTER – NIGHT – 1937

Half-lit by moonlight, David and Jack lie back to back, both wide awake, listening to muffled, staccato arguing coming from their parents' bedroom.

JACK

At least they've stopped chucking stuff at each other.

DAVID

Only because there's nowt to chuck in there.

JACK

In where?

DAVID

In bed. Except the pillows, p'raps. Too soft, though, pillows. No point.

JACK

What do they row about in bed?

DAVID

Don't know. That's always where *he* has the needle, though, isn't it? It's *downstairs* where *she* has it.

JACK
(*beat*)

Crackers, isn't it?

DAVID
(*beat*)

Yeah.

EXT BENT STREET – CHEETHAM HILL – MANCHESTER – DAY – 1938

Groups of schoolkids are hurling red half-bricks at each other across the street. This is the normal weekday routine. The kids from Waterloo Road (C of E) School and those from St Chad's (RC) School on their way to school. Although the brickfight is intended to be more of a warm-up for when they meet the kids on their way to the Jews' School round the corner.

Which they now do. Ambushed, David and Jack run the gauntlet of the now-allied Protestants and Catholics, dodging the hail of flint-sharp bricks coming from both directions.

EXT JEWS' SCHOOL – MANCHESTER – DAY – 1938

Outside the gates, the Italian roasted-chestnut vendor has now become his summer alter ego, *an ice-cream vendor.*

A year from now – though much loved by the schoolkids – he'll disappear in a ball of wartime red tape, interned as an enemy alien. Never to be seen again . . .

David and Jack emerge from Bent Street and make their way into the playground.

EXT PLAYGROUND – JEWS' SCHOOL – MANCHESTER – DAY – 1938 (CONT)

A terrifying iron fire escape rises from the ground along the outside of the building up to the top storey. To a bit of a kid it looks ten miles high. Jack leaves David and the others and starts tentatively, heart in mouth, up the fire escape. This is his daily nightmare.

It is the only way up to his classroom. Looking down is, of course, the worst thing to do. Come to think of it, so is looking up. Or looking anywhere. Or closing your eyes and looking nowhere.

INT JACK'S CLASSROOM – JEWS' SCHOOL – MANCHESTER – DAY – 1938

Jack and his classmates at their desks, reciting 'Cargoes' by John Masefield. A tall, willowy, balding teacher sits at the front, flicking a willowy 20-foot-long cane.

CHILDREN

Quinquireme of Nineveh from distant Ophir
Rowing home to haven in sunny Palestine,
With a cargo of ivory,
And apes and peacocks,
Sandalwood, cedarwood and sweet white wine . . .

The only consolation to the fire escape is that, once inside the classroom, things can be even more intimidating: the teacher is called Mr Whipp, and his 20-foot cane, Charlie. With which he can give the lads three of the best without anyone leaving their seats. For the really *naughty, Strangeways Prison is just a few hundred yards down the road . . .*

INT SYNAGOGUE CLASSROOM – MANCHESTER – DAY – 1938

A small Hebrew class in progress. Half a dozen boys, including David and Jack, being taught simple words from Hebrew primers by a bearded, irascible rabbi.

JACK (VO)

Schooling was briefly interrupted by a tomato sauce sandwich and a glass of Dandelion and Burdock at home before it resumed with Hebrew School, (Cheder), which was, understandably, slang for prison.

One of the boys mistranslates a word. The rabbi cuffs him across the head. He doesn't bother with a 20-foot cane. Prefers the personal touch.

INT BERLYNE FAMILY LIVING ROOM – MANCHESTER – DAY – 1938

Auntie Annie's three sons are seated at the table. Alex (fifteen) is expertly drawing a massive, intricately detailed cathedral all over the white tablecloth with an HB pencil. Neville (eleven) and Geoffrey (seven) are reading – sighing with exaggerated impatience whenever Alex pushes their hands or their books to one side in order to accommodate his drawing.

Jack sits nearby, watching all three in eye-shining admiration, while wolfing one of Auntie Annie's incomparable jam pies. This is where his schooling in everything else – General Knowledge, International Affairs, Art and Science – takes place. On his virtually daily visits to his three genius cousins round the corner in Penrose Street. Between them they know everything about everything. And love passing it on. Usually with an eyebrow raised in superiority. Academic sibling rivalry is fierce and overt.

CU Alex . . .

JACK (VO)

A few years later when Alex was teaching at the Manchester College of Art, a new student shuffled into his class. A mature student. *Very* mature student. By the name of L S Lowry. Alex nervously asked had he perhaps come into the class by mistake? Apparently not. Apparently he'd heard Alex was good at teaching feet.

Alex went on to become an artist in his own right, an incisive and humorous feature-writer with his weekly column 'With Prejudice' in the *Jerusalem Post,* and the man with the most inquisitive mind I've ever come across. Fascinated by all the barminess that flesh and blood is heir to. The master of a thousand anecdotes.

On one of his visits from Israel, I stood on my front doorstep to welcome him. As he got out of his car with his wife, Edna, I yelled my welcome. To which he promptly non-sequiturred, 'There was this feller, lived in a little village just outside Cork and he had this Siamese cat called Brobdignag and one day . . .' and launched into Anecdote One-Thousand-and-One.

CU Neville . . .

Neville, the quiet(er) one, was the peacemaker between Alex the genius and Geoffrey the genius-elect and, unsurprisingly, became a psychiatrist.

CU Geoffrey . . .

Geoffrey was my age, better than me at everything and knew it and told me so. Not only did he know what a meteorologist

was, but also how to spell it. This wasn't usual for a seven-year-old boy in 1938, when even meteorologists thought they were called forecasters.

Geoffrey became an eminent consultant at a Manchester hospital at the age of about fifteen (well, maybe sixteen) and eventually an even more eminent professor of medicine in New York . . .

All three cousins became my mentors, opening my eyes to worlds I'd never heard of. Strangely, the only really emphatic advice they gave me turned out to be . . . um . . . slightly mistaken: that if I was adamant about being a writer I should change my name. That I'd get nowhere with a name like Rosenthal. The Jack part was fine.

Auntie Annie comes in with another plate of pie. She sees the cathedral-covered tablecloth, horrified.

AUNTIE ANNIE

My Shabbos tablecloth!!

She cuffs Alex across the head. She isn't related to the Hebrew teacher. Karate-chops are regarded as an educational tool.

EXT CHEETHAM HILL ROAD – MANCHESTER – DAY – 1938

Lakey and Jack, dressed and groomed for visiting, walk along the street. More accurately, Lakey is walking; Jack is shlurrying. This is the Yiddish word describing the art of walking by scraping one foot along in front of the other, without either of them ever leaving the ground. It's not good for shoe leather or adults' eardrums, but it's highly recommended for relieving the monotony if you're eight years old and there are no puddles to tread in.

Jack's social schooling is Lakey's doing. Sunday visits to nearby friends or relatives – Bessie Cohen, ex-Tiller Girl; Gene Kaye, whose husband had been one of Fred Karno's Theatrical Troupe along with Charlie Chaplin; and Uncle Jack. Not the Uncle Jack he's named after. This one's his French *Uncle Jack . . .*

JACK

Mam? Why did Uncle Jack leave the French Foreign Legion, Mam?

LAKEY

It wasn't nice. He deserted.

JACK

Why did he join in the first place?

LAKEY

To escape from the police.

JACK

Why did he want to escape from the police?

LAKEY

Because he was a murderer. And stop shlurrying.

JACK (VO)

Murderers weren't all that run-of-the-mill in Cheetham Hill. So the legend of Uncle Jack, as handed down by my mother, was, to me, finest quality manna.

According to her, he'd been a gentle giant of a man with a ferocious red beard, who – once his murdering and Legionnairing days were done – found simpler pleasures . . .

DISSOLVE TO:

INT UNCLE JACK'S LIVING ROOM – MANCHESTER – DAY – 1914

Fifty-year-old Uncle Jack is chasing the six-year-old Lakey and nine-year-old Florrie round the room, brandishing his thick, buckled belt, then picking them up, one under each massive arm, and roaring a lot.

They love it. The more he roars, the more they scream and the more they love it.

DISSOLVE TO:

INT UNCLE JACK'S LIVING ROOM – MANCHESTER – PRESENT DAY – 1938

Uncle Jack sits at his table with Lakey and Jack, quietly drinking lemon tea.

But now Uncle Jack's old. The ferocious red beard is a wispy ginger-grey stubble. He's shrunk just about everywhere except his belly. That's still there, flopping out of his shirt above the same old buckled belt, under a threadbare matting of ginger-grey baby hairs.

JACK (VO)

He'd emitted a sort of wheezy roar of welcome just for old times' sake and made us a glass of lemon tea. Out of politeness, I didn't check for arsenic.

Many years later, I asked Auntie Mary, the only surviving member of the family to know the facts about Uncle Jack, was he really a murderer? Did he really join the French Foreign Legion? All she said was he wasn't really an uncle. He was one of those friends of families who become uncles by adoption.

I didn't pursue the facts any further. They're nothing to do with truth. And the truths of childhood are only to be tampered with at your peril.

EXT OLD TRAFFORD CRICKET GROUND – MANCHESTER – DAY – 1938

The Roses match, Lancashire v. Yorkshire. Among the spectators are Sam, David and Jack, armed with carrier bags of sandwiches and lemonade. The boys' schooling in sport was Sam's domain.

Sam calls out to Len Hutton, who's fielding on the boundary.

SAM
Can you stand a bit to leg, Len? I can't see the bloody wicket!

He laughs. David and Jack look embarrassed. Len Hutton moves a yard to his left.

LEN HUTTON
That better?

Sam laughs again. This time, David and Jack think it acceptable to join in.

EXT BALLOON STREET – MANCHESTER – DAY – 1938

Sam and Jack are walking along past the Co-operative Society Building (reputed at the time to be the tallest building in the world, or maybe England, or maybe Manchester, or, most probably, Balloon Street).

Relentless Mancunian sunshine slams down on the bleached pavement like a great flat-iron, squashing the air out of their lungs and driving the floating pee-in-beds dizzy.

Forced by Lakey, and much to his chagrin, Jack is in heatwave garb – Fair Isle pullover, short trousers and sandals, no shirt or jacket.

They bump into a pal of Sam's from work. Sam and he start chatting. Jack waits, a little impatiently. Then:

SAM
This is Javid.

He always calls both boys 'Javid' since he's never immediately sure which one of them they are.

SAM'S PAL
And is he going to be a cricketer like his dad?

SAM
I doubt it. Not with muscles like these . . .

He feels Jack's thin biceps.

. . . Like knots in cotton.

JACK (VO)

Why do we never forget a grudge, an insult, the slightest of slights? That was 1938. Sixty-five years ago. And I still haven't forgotten it, you notice. Getting a bit late now . . .

INT BOYS' BEDROOM – CHEETHAM HILL – MANCHESTER – DAY – 1939

David and Jack are taking it in turns to stick their heads up the chimney.

This is a game where muscles make no difference. The aim is to screwdrive your head as far as you can up the chimney. The winner is the one who finishes up with the sootiest head.

Jack and his sooty head emerge from the chimney. He's holding several scraps of paper. David peers at them.

DAVID

What's them?

JACK

Don't know. They were jammed in between two bricks.

They smooth out a couple of the pieces of paper.

DAVID

What d'you reckon?

JACK

(*reading*)

Irish Minstrel, 4 to 1 on, shilling each way. Crinoline Lady, 2 to 1, sixpence each way.

He shrugs, baffled.

I'll ask Mam.

INT SOLICITOR'S OFFICE – MANCHESTER – DAY – 1939

Lakey, David and Jack, all dressed in their Saturday best, sit facing a solicitor who's listening solemnly to Lakey's long, tearful list of Sam's failings as a husband.

JACK (VO)

The chimney's secrets were only the latest evidence of Sam's gambling away of pay-packets. Lakey's list went back eleven years. David and I were there to reluctantly confirm the incessant fights. Given Lakey's and Sam's complete incompatibility, the solicitor reckoned divorce was inevitable.

Then, riding to Sam's rescue came the unexpected figure of Lakey's brother, Ocky. Ocky talked Lakey out of it – the shame, the scandal, the poor, fatherless children. And Lakey relented.

A decade or so later, Ocky had no qualms about his *own* **divorce . . .**

INT BOYS' BEDROOM – CHEETHAM HILL – MANCHESTER – NIGHT – 1939

CU Jack, in bed, wide awake, listening miserably to the sounds of Lakey and Sam fighting in their bedroom.

And as their war waged on, Jack had a dead-of-night theory that Sam and Lakey were only pretending *to fight. That they were acting under orders from the Government. To toughen David and him up ready for the* other *war that was now about to start . . .*

EXT MILITARY PARADE – BERLIN – CINEMA NEWSREEL – DAY – 1939

Hitler stands at a podium saluting a march past of German soldiers. This is the famous edited clip of hundreds of German soldiers goose-stepping backwards.

JACK (VO)

As it did with everyone else on earth, September 3rd, 1939, changed my life.

And the *memory* of it, 33 years later, changed my life again . . .

INT PETER ECKERSLEY'S OFFICE – GRANADA TV – MANCHESTER – DAY – 1972

Peter Eckersley, the young, brilliant wunderkind Head of Drama sits at his desk, toying with his pen.

Opposite him sits the 41-year-old Jack, who during the last ten years has become a TV writer with 124 episodes of Coronation Street, *thirteen one-hour plays and scores of comedy and drama scripts to his credit. (More – much more – of all that, later . . .)*

PETER

What d'you want to write next?

JACK

No idea.

PETER

Why don't you have a go at a full-length TV film? Something big. Bigger than big. What's bigger than big?

JACK

Bigger.

PETER

Major. Something major.

JACK

What about?

PETER

I don't know. Something that happened to you.

JACK

Nothing's *ever* happened to me.

PETER

Alright, let's start at the beginning. You were born. *Then* what happened?

JACK

Nothing.

(*beat*)

Well, I was evacuated in the war.

PETER

There you go. There's your film. Go away and write the bugger.

JACK

I haven't got a pen.

Peter slings his pen at him across the desk.

PETER

You have now.

THE FORTIES

ANGLE ON:

Jack and David as small boys walking arm in arm with Lakey.

DISSOLVE TO:

The two young actors in The Evacuees *walking arm in arm with Maureen Lipman, who is playing her future mother-in-law.*

FILM EXCERPT: *The Evacuees*

EXT BBC SKYLINE – RADIO AERIAL – DAY – SEPTEMBER 3RD, 1939

Over this:

ANNOUNCER'S VOICE

This is London. The Prime Minister, the Right Honourable Neville Chamberlain.

EXT ENGLISH CITYSCAPES, COUNTRYSIDE, JEWS' SCHOOL – DAY – 1939 (CONT)

Over this:

CHAMBERLAIN'S VOICE

This morning the British ambassador in Berlin handed the German Government a note, stating that unless we heard from them by eleven o'clock that they were prepared to withdraw their troops from Poland –

INT CLASSROOM – A JEWISH SCHOOL – DAY – 1939

Danny (i.e. Jack) sits nervously with the rest of the boys at their desks, on each of which is parked a haversack or suitcase and gas mask. Each boy wears a luggage label bearing his name. One of the boys, Zuckerman, is peeping over his neighbour's shoulder at a comic. A teacher stands before them, in raincoat and trilby, holding a clipboard of papers detailing evacuation procedure. Over this:

CHAMBERLAIN'S VOICE

– a state of war would exist between us. I have to tell you that no such undertaking has been received, and that consequently this country is at war with Germany.

TEACHER

Now pay attention, all of you. When the bell goes, into the playground, line up next to Standard One quietly – and *how*, Zuckerman?

ZUCKERMAN

Please, sir. In an orderly fashion, sir.

TEACHER

In an orderly fashion, Zuckerman, which means *not* looking over Weisberg's shoulder at pictures of Desperate Dan eating cow pie.

Weisberg slips the comic into his haversack.

Then special tram to Victoria Station. Parents will see you off at the platform. Brothers from other standards will travel with you. When we get to Blackpool, you'll be issued with – given, that is – a tin of corned beef, for some reason. Then we'll set off and try and find ... get you fixed up with foster-parents. Right. Off we go. Best foot forward.

The boys rise and haul up their luggage.

First row, lead off and – oh, one more thing. Some of you – nearly *all* of you – will be going to people who aren't Jewish. The food won't be kosher. Now, it doesn't matter. It isn't a sin. There's a war on. Now, first row. Quietly.

The first row starts to file towards the door.

EXT PLATFORM – VICTORIA STATION – MANCHESTER – DAY – 1939

A chaotic crush of scores of parents reluctantly bustling their haversacked kids, including Neville (i.e. David) and Danny, into a train. A feeling of uncertain excitement among the children and a feeling of helpless sadness among the parents. Brave smiles, bitten lips, some tears.

Over this, Vera Lynn sings 'We'll Meet Again.' When will *they meet again?* Will *they meet again?*

EXT A BLACKPOOL STREET – SOME HOURS LATER – DAY – 1939

Danny's class trudging along in a crocodile, bent double by their luggage, clutching their tins of corned beef. They stop outside a house where the teacher is talking to 1st Housewife on the doorstep. She surveys the boys. Unseen by the teacher, Zuckerman puts on his gas mask.

1ST HOUSEWIFE
(*dubiously*)

Are they clean?

TEACHER
(*wearily*)

Oh, yes, madam. We have to evacuate the cleanest first, by Act of Parliament.

(*without turning round*)

Take it off, Zuckerman.

Zuckerman takes off his gas mask.

1ST HOUSEWIFE

You what?

TEACHER

They're all very clean.

1ST HOUSEWIFE

Go on, then. I'll have one. He'll do.

She points at Winkler. The teacher pushes him towards her.

TEACHER

Say hello to the lady.

WINKLER

Hello.

TEACHER

This is Cyril Winkler.

1ST HOUSEWIFE

That's a funny name, isn't it?

TEACHER

Say yes.

WINKLER

Yes.

1st Housewife tugs down his shirt collar slightly.

1ST HOUSEWIFE

Got a tidemark, as well, haven't you?

She ushers him in and closes the door.

EXT 2ND BLACKPOOL STREET – MORE HOURS LATER – DAY – 1939

Only the teacher and Zuckerman are left. A door closes in their face. They turn away and continue to tramp the street, ready to drop.

ZUCKERMAN

There's no houses *left.*

TEACHER

There's thousands.

ZUCKERMAN

Please, sir, can I go home?

TEACHER

No.

ZUCKERMAN

I've got a headache in my leg.

INT THE GRAHAM'S LIVING ROOM – BLACKPOOL – EVENING – SAME DAY

Mr and Mrs Graham, middle-aged foster-parents, are at the tea table.

Danny and Neville shuffle in from upstairs, scrubbed clean after their exhausting day, wearing their school caps.

MRS GRAHAM

Oh! No caps, children! Not indoors!

DANNY

We always wear –

MRS GRAHAM

I don't think so.

She takes their caps off. Mr and Mrs Graham are occupying the only chairs at the table. The two boys look round blankly, wondering where they're going to sit. Two plates have been laid for them – each bearing one cold sausage – but no chairs.

MR GRAHAM

For what we're about to receive may the Lord make us truly thankful. Amen.

MRS GRAHAM

Amen.

(*to the boys*)

Amen.

NEVILLE

Amen – what is it?

MRS GRAHAM

What's what?

He's looking at his sausage. She follows his eyes.

Silly lad. It's a cold sausage.

DANNY

We don't like cold sausage, Mrs Graham.

MRS GRAHAM

Of course you do! It's real pork!

The boys struggle through their crisis of conscience. Neville puts his hand on his head, mutters a short Hebrew prayer – then eats. Danny does the same – then gags violently.

INT BOYS' BEDROOM – BLACKPOOL – NIGHT – 1939

Danny and Neville in bed, in semi-darkness. From downstairs we hear the muted sounds of a radio comedy show. During this:

DANNY

(*quietly*)

Blessed art thou, O Lord our God, King of the Universe. Look after Mam and Dad and everyone, and let Hitler get cut up into little pieces with bayonets, and then burnt alive in boiling oil, then buried up to his neck in quicksand so's the ants eat him. And the same goes for Mrs Graham. Only double.

EXT ELIZABETH STREET – CHEETHAM HILL – MANCHESTER – DAY – 1940

It's seven months later . . .

A woman races down the street, knocking on each door, then opening each door and yelling inside . . .

WOMAN

Mrs Levy! Bananas at the Co-op! Mrs Abrams! Bananas at the Co-op! Mrs Miller!

Sarah (i.e. Lakey) comes running out of her front door, struggling into her coat.

SARAH

I heard! I heard!

She, Mrs Levy and Mrs Abrams dash out of their houses and down the street. Co-op next stop.

INT THE GRAHAM'S LIVING ROOM – BLACKPOOL – AFTERNOON – 1940

Open on Danny and Neville eating bananas. They're seated round the fire with Mrs Graham and Sarah, who is on the latest of her three-weekly visits.

A couple of games, Ludo and Snakes and Ladders, lying around.

It's late Sunday afternoon, an hour or so before Sarah is due to catch her train home. Consequently, she, Danny and Neville are in subdued mood . . .

SARAH

Another game, kids?

MRS GRAHAM

You've hardly time. Your train goes in –

SARAH

Silly Story!

DAVID

What's that?

SARAH

You get a piece of paper and everyone writes down a –

DANNY

I can't play it.

MRS GRAHAM

You don't know what it is yet, child!

She smooths down his hair maternally. Sarah notices but pretends she hasn't . . .

SARAH

(*to the boys*)

I write the beginning of a story – something silly – and fold the paper over so's the next one can't read it, then he writes *his* daft sentence and folds it over and passes it to the next and –

DANNY

It's silly.

NEVILLE

That's the idea, barm-pot!

SARAH

And when we've all finished, we read the whole thing out, and it makes a Silly Story – and we all laugh!

MRS GRAHAM

(*to the boys*)

I'll show you.

She takes pen and paper and starts writing. Danny watches solemnly and ignores Sarah's reassuring smile. Mrs Graham laughs at her own sentence, folds the paper and passes it to Neville, who starts writing.

DANNY

I don't know what to put.

SARAH

Whatever comes in your head.

And an idea is slowly coming into his head. He seems scared ... a little excited. Neville, grinning at what he's written, folds the paper and passes it to Danny. Danny looks at each of them, tensely.

MRS GRAHAM

Whatever you want, child!

He reaches a decision and starts writing thoughtfully. The others watch him, amused at his concentration. He finally folds the paper and hands it to Sarah. She starts writing. He watches nervously.

DANNY

Read it.

SARAH

In a minute.

She finishes writing and unfolds the paper.

Right.

(*reads*)

'Once upon a time there were two princes called Danny and Neville who lived in Blackpool Tower with the other monkeys.'

Sarah smiles at Mrs Graham, who smiles back, proud of her story. Sarah now reads Neville's contribution.

SARAH

(*reads*)

'And then the Spitfires attacked the Messerschmitt and the German pilot shouted, "Get off my foot!"'

She, Neville and Mrs Graham laugh. Danny watches the paper in Sarah's hands, anxiously. She starts his story ...

'She is dead cruel to us. She steals your letters and –'

She stops and stares at Danny. He sits impassively. Mrs Graham looks from one to the other, blankly. Sarah resumes reading. Slowly. Pointedly.

'She is dead cruel to us. She steals your letters and your food parcels. She makes us clean and polish the whole house every day and gives us rotten dinners we have to stand up at. She hates us. And we hate her back. All this is secret. We want to come home.'

She lowers the paper onto her lap. Everyone seems frozen to stone – except her. She speaks quietly, calmly.

Is this true, Danny?

DANNY

Yes, Mam.

SARAH

Emess?

DANNY

Emess adashem.

SARAH

Neville?

NEVILLE
(*nodding, scared*)

Yes, Mam.

SARAH

Mrs Graham?

EXT BOMBED STREETS – MANCHESTER – DAY – 1940

CAM opens tight on an embroidered sampler reading 'Home Sweet Home'.

CAM pulls back to reveal that the sampler, leaning at a slightly skew-whiff angle, is on the wall of a bedroom.

CAM pulls back to see that the wall is the only one still standing in a bombed house.

CAM pulls back to gradually encompass an entire street of demolished, devastated terraced houses. A graveyard-jagged Bosch landscape of collapsed, still smouldering ruins. And, of course, lives.

Sarah, Neville and Danny half walk, half dance through the rubble, swinging their luggage as they go.

Over this:

JACK (VO)

Three and a quarter minutes after her confrontation with our real-life foster-mother, Lakey packed our cases and hauled us onto the next train home. Or what was left of it.

Thanks to Herman Goering's sense of humour, we were just in time for a wayward Junkers 88 to dodge the pom-pom guns on the Ship Canal and, aiming for Ferranti's in Trafford Park, drop its bombs in a direct hit on the nurses' home of the Jewish Hospital across the street from our house.

We were bombed out . . . the nurses were bombed to smithereens. The next morning, a cortege of charabancs queued to take away what was left of their corpses.

And David and I were evacuated again. This time to a little cotton town in east Lancashire called Colne. But, this time, once bitten, never, ever shy, Lakey came with us . . .

EXT PANORAMA OF COLNE – DAY – 1940

CAM, hand-held, weaves its way through a small town of stone buildings, the Town Hall and parish church at its apex, built on the spine of a hill, surrounded by England's green and pleasant land and scarred by scores of dark, Satanic mill chimneys. Glowering down on it from the horizon is purple Pendle Hill, six feet too short for a mountain, notorious for its ancient witches. During this:

JACK (VO)

Although only a bus ride from Manchester, Colne was a juddering culture shock. To a city boy's eyes, a sort of *Just William* world of chickens, sheep, cowpats, gumboots, allotments, five-barred gates and stiles. (But no colonels.)

A population of 27,000, not one of them circumcised but all convinced that Jews were buried upside down. In these parts it was common parlance to use the *Oxford English Dictionary*'s alternative to the verb 'to cheat', which was, until 1958, 'to Jew'.

A sleepy little town that became the noisiest place on earth every weekday morning at half past six and in the afternoons at half past five.

We hear an almost deafening, anvil-splitting, ringing, grating cacophony of iron clashing against stone . . .

. . . This is the Clog Chorus – hammering its way to the mills and reprised on its way home. In the hours between, the silence screams with the incessant metallic thunder of thousands of looms.

EXT STEEP STREET LEADING TO COTTON MILL – COLNE – DAY – 1940 (CONT)

The cacophony continues . . .

. . . and we see hundreds of clog-shod feet scrape their iron soles down the ribbed pavements of the almost imposssibly vertical street.

PULL BACK to see half as many young women weavers and spinners on their way to work; arm in arm in rows of four or five, singing or gossiping or yawning as they go, heads turbanned over their curlers, shooting sparks with each step. L S Lowry-Land.

EXT 17 BOUNDARY STREET – COLNE – DAY – 1940

EXTREME CU Jack's eyes, watching warily.

PULL BACK to see that he's peeping out of the curtains of his bedroom window at the street below.

At the front door, Lakey is donkey-stoning the doorstep. The donkey-stone is a soft grey stone that, with elbow grease and sweat, will give you that whiter than white doorstep, which means your average housewife can hold up her head in public.

EXT BOUNDARY STREET – COLNE – DAY – 1940 (CONT)

A street of smoke-blackened two-up, two-down terraced houses.

From Jack's POINT OF VIEW a boy of about ten is delivering Daily Mirrors *into letterboxes.*

JACK (VO)

Living in Boundary Street was a bit like living in the middle of a Hogarth engraving . . .

Wally Butler, the eldest of nine brothers and sisters, didn't whistle on his paper round. He had more cosmopolitan ideas . . .

Wally starts yodelling at the top of his voice.

From Jack's POV, we see a tall, angular man in his early twenties emerge from his front door and stride briskly down the street. His jaw is set, his demeanour purposeful. This is Len Dole.

As he walks, passers-by give him a wide berth. This is because Len is notorious in the town for being a Communist *and, even more so, for being a conscientious objector. The wide berths don't bother him. He's used to worse than that – like being sworn at, spat at and put in the stocks and pelted with verbal rotten eggs.*

Everyone else has a picture of Churchill *on their living room wall. Len, being Len, has one of Stalin.*

Jack's POV of a portly, pompous Mr Pickwick lookalike coming in the opposite direction from a grocery shop.

JACK (VO)

The grocer's shop was run by Mr Beaumont. Pronounced Bewmont. I pinched it for Annie Walker's maiden name 21 years later, when I began writing *Coronation Street*. He was also our half-a-crown-a-week rent collector.

Mr Beaumont knocks on a door. No reply. He knocks on the next. No reply. And the next. Same again.

He worked on the principle that someone, someday would come out from behind their sofa.

From Jack's POV, further down the street, a knot of neighbours stand in a circle watching a woman having violent convulsions. One or two try ineffectually to help. Most just watch.

Alsace Lorraine had epileptic fits at the rate of one a week.

Jack's POV of a woman beating her teenage daughter round the head as she propels her into the house next door to the Rosenthals.

And Her-Next-Door knocked the living daylights out of her daughter for getting pregnant out of wedlock.

(*beat*)

Like *she*'d done twenty years earlier.

INT CLASSROOM – LORD STREET SCHOOL – COLNE – DAY – 1940

The female teacher is writing sums on the blackboard. Jack sits warily watching the other boys and girls drawing lines in their exercise books with rulers.

JACK (VO)

It may have been only a bus ride from Cheetham Hill, but it could just as well have been a trip in H G Wells's time-machine. I could barely understand a word of the east Lancashire accent. It was like a medieval foreign language. 'Thee's' and 'Thou's', and, on that first morning in my new school – the word 'yonder'.

He doesn't have a ruler. He raises his hand.

FEMALE TEACHER

Yes, Jack?

JACK

I haven't got a ruler, Miss.

FEMALE TEACHER

O'er yonder.

She nods vaguely towards a desk by a window. Then resumes chalking her sums. Jack looks blankly towards the window.

JACK (VO)

I didn't know what 'o'er' meant and I was completely flummoxed by 'yonder'.

He gets up and wanders tentatively over to the window, then stands there at a loss. The other kids start to titter. The teacher isn't quite so amused.

FEMALE TEACHER

Not yonder!

(*she nods towards the desk*)

Yonder.

Which leaves him just as helpless.

Na then, then, felly-'arry, tha mun shap thissel!

JACK (VO)

Which, in English, I assumed meant 'The ruler is either in the desk or outside the window.'

EXT PLAYGROUND – LORD STREET SCHOOL – DAY – 1940

Jack and another kid in a violent, punching, wrestling, no-holds-barred fight. The rest of the school surround them, cheering (and booing) them on.

JACK (VO)

So, although they were the ones who spoke in alien tongues, it was me who was nicknamed the Foreigner.

Accordingly, at dinnertime, the Cock of the School, i.e. the biggest bruiser, felt it his patriotic duty to knock the helzel out of me.

And I won. I was Cock of the School on my first day. And it all happened just there. O'er yonder.

He batters the bruiser to the ground, then leaps on top of him and pins him down. The bruiser starts to cry.

INT MUNITIONS FACTORY – COLNE – DAY – 1940

Lakey, wearing welder's goggles, overalls, turban and newly peroxided blonde hair, is welding shell cases.

JACK (VO)

While my dad stayed in Manchester from Monday to Friday slaving over his dead horses and living in miserable digs, Lakey hit Colne like a blitzkrieg. First on munitions . . .

INT GREENGROCER'S SHOP – COLNE – DAY – 1941

Lakey, in flowered apron, serves a female customer with a cabbage.

JACK (VO)

Then a greengrocer's assistant . . .

LAKEY

There y'are, chuck. That'll put hairs on your chest.

CUSTOMER

(*puzzled*)

Tha what?

LAKEY

In case you meet a Canadian airman.

CUSTOMER

(*more puzzled*)

Eh?

LAKEY

And want to put him off.

CUSTOMER

(*even more puzzled*)

Why would I want to do that?

LAKEY

What with your hubby thousands of miles away in a submarine.

CUSTOMER

(*at a loss*)

Hubby? Submarine? I've not even gorra boyfriend!

LAKEY

In that case, chuck, take a cauliflower instead.

CUSTOMER

(*blankly*)

Tha what?

INT THE ROSENTHAL LIVING ROOM – COLNE – DAY – 1942

A young woman is standing on a chair in her slip. Lakey, with a mouthful of pins, circles her, pinning paper patterns and swatches of material on her, watched by a cat called Monty (after the Field Marshal, but prettier and with more ginger fur).

JACK (VO)

Then a dressmaker – usually with fabrics her customers stole from the mill by wrapping cloth, a yard a week, round their waist under their swagger-coats . . .

INT FRESH FISH SHOP – COLNE – DAY – 1943

Lakey is slicing through a whole haddock. Two or three customers watch her, nodding in admiration. Lakey removes the filleted bone with a triumphant flourish.

JACK (VO)

Then a fishmonger . . .

The customers applaud her skill.

INT THE ROSENTHAL LIVING ROOM – COLNE – NIGHT – 1943

Lakey comes into the room, carrying a tray of mugs of hot water. Seated around the room are her colleagues from the munitions factory, and customers from the greengrocer's and fishmonger's and dressmaking (now wearing the finished frock).

JACK (VO)

And everybody's best pal . . .

The ladies add their rationed tea and sugar to their mug of hot water from twists of paper they've all brought with them. Everyone chats with Lakey. The raucous laughter filling the room tells us how risqué the chatting is getting . . .

INT THE ROSENTHAL LIVING ROOM – COLNE – NIGHT – 1943

The room is now deserted, apart from Lakey treadling away at her sewing machine.

JACK (VO)

She stayed up till midnight, many a night, sewing aprons for my dad to sell on Eccles market whenever he could rent a Saturday stall. Genuine leatherette, 1s 11d an apron bringing a profit of a *penny* an apron . . .

INT NEIGHBOUR'S PARLOUR – COLNE – NIGHT – 1943

Splattered in paint, Lakey is decorating the room.

JACK (VO)

***After* midnight, she'd scrape the paper off the walls and stipple-paint it in the contemporary style known, logically enough, as Contemporary. And when she'd redecorated our house, she'd do a neighbour's . . .**

EXT THE ROSENTHAL BACKYARD – COLNE – DAY – 1944

David is playing with a popular toy of the time: a ping-pong-style bat to the centre of which is attached a ball at the end of a length of elastic.

Jack is sprawled in a deckchair near the outside petty. Both boys are in grammar school uniform.

Lakey is hanging out washing, while referring to a Latin primer held in one hand. She speaks through a mouthful of clothes pegs.

LAKEY

No! Wrong again! It's *puer, puer, puerum, pueri, puero, puero,* you barm-pot!

JACK (VO)

And still found time to test me on my Latin. Which was, of course, all Greek to her.

INT THE ROSENTHAL KITCHEN – COLNE – NIGHT – 1944

David and Jack eating steamed cauliflower, topped with melted butter – swopped on Mr Beaumont's amateur black market in place of our bacon ration. They're loving it. It doesn't sound delicious – but it is.

JACK (VO)

She was also, needless to say, the original Best Cook in the World. Even on wartime rations. *Especially* on wartime rations.

EXTREME CU on Lakey, watching them eat . . .

To the locals, Lakey became a sort of cross between City Slicker, Agony Aunt and Earth Mother. By the time we left Colne, eight years later, to go back to Manchester, she had 27,000 people frying gefilte fish and brushing up their Latin.

I think they'd been the happiest years of her life . . .

EXT BOUNDARY STREET – COLNE – DAY – 1945

A children's victory street party. Long trestle tables covered in Union Jack bunting stretch down the middle of the street. Twenty or so over-excited kids, including Jack, David and Wally Butler, grabbing sandwiches, biscuits, cakes and lemonade. Lakey and other housewives, including Alsace Lorraine, run between their houses and the trestle tables with more goodies.

A gramophone plays the 'Victory Polka'.

JACK (VO)

VE Day and VJ Day were the pinnacles of her catering skills. Loaves, fishes, five thousand? Easy.

EXT ALBERT STREET – COLNE – DAY – 1945

CU A Labour Party leaflet urging 'Vote for Sidney Silverman'.

ANGLE ON Len Dole and Jack, armed with hundreds of leaflets, soliciting passers-by as they make their way down the high street.

JACK (VO)

Len became my political mentor. He got me into the Labour League of Youth (which increased the membership total to four) and gave me almost daily teatime lectures in his house (usually tirades on 't'grinding o' t'face o' t'workers under t'ca*pit*alist boot').

The highlight was letting me help him canvas for Sidney Silverman in the 1945 General Election. The constituency was Nelson (otherwise known as 'Little Moscow') and Colne, and Silverman was the sitting MP.

ANGLE ON Sidney Silverman, a small man with a shock of pure white-blond hair swept to one side in a tidal wave. He has his arms raised in triumph.

He was returned with a massively increased majority in Labour's famous landslide victory. Thank Len and me if you must.

He went on to achieve his life's political ambition – the abolition of the death penalty.

I once asked Sidney why politicians always evaded every question they were asked. He evaded the question.

EXT COLNE GRAMMAR SCHOOL – DAY – 1947

Scores of blue-uniformed schoolkids in an adolescent version of shlurrying make their way into the school. Among them is Jack.

JACK (VO)

The grammar school held lots of attractions for me, apart from . . .

CU 1st Girl, bathed in a golden light.

Ann Morton . . .

PAN TO CU 2nd Girl.

Jean Lowcock . . .

PAN TO CU 3rd Girl.

Peggy Wood . . .

WHIP-PAN BACK TO 1st Girl, in her golden light.

Ann Morton . . .

PAN TO CU 4th Girl.

Eunice Hartley . . ..

PAN TO CU 5th Girl.

Eileen Beck . . .

WHIP-PAN BACK TO 1st Girl, still glowing in gold.

And whatsername – Ann Morton.

CU Jack in his school cap.

One of them was our school cap, pleated at the sides, so that if you imagined it green instead of blue you could pretend it was an Australian cricket cap.

The most important of all, though, was a man who deserved a plaque on the school wall, reading 'Mr Terry Land, Genius, Taught Here'.

INT CLASSROOM – COLNE GRAMMAR SCHOOL – DAY – 1947

A class of boys and girls (including those named in the previous scene) at their desks. Among the boys are Jack and his closest pals, Pot, Shaz and Jimmy.

At his teacher's desk Terry Land – a pale, grey-haired beanpole, an even more desiccated version of Peter O'Toole in Goodbye Mr Chips *– languidly lounges, as he analyses Marlowe's Mighty Line,* while knitting a scarf.

He speaks unashamedly in a broad accent, which he identifies as closer to Elizabethan English. Whenever the headmaster pops his head in, he changes to King's English as though an east Lancashire accent wouldn't melt in his mouth. When the headmaster pops back out, he reverts again.

By way of hobbies, he plays every instrument in the school orchestra and speaks almost as many languages. He taught himself Hebrew so that he could read the 'Song of Solomon' in the original.

JACK (VO)

He was supposed to teach us English Literature. He didn't. He taught us to love it with the same passion that he did.

ANGLE ON the blackboard, on which is chalked a freehand drawing of a circle.

He spent his dinnertimes trying to draw the perfect circle. The Friday before the 1947 Cup Final between Burnley and Charlton Athletic, he changed the circle to –

Terry is now at the blackboard, chalking panels and stitching to the circle, transforming it into a drawing of a football. Underneath it he writes 'Elated'.

EXT WEMBLEY STADIUM – DAY – 1947

LIBRARY FOOTAGE of the sunlit Cup Final.

JACK (VO)

Burnley was our local team. Very local. No one else had heard of them. They were my adolescent infatuation before my life-long, true-love affair with Manchester United began the following year.

Funny, frustrating Burnley, unbelievably at Wembley in their new, silk claret-and-blue shirts . . .

INT THE ROSENTHAL LIVING ROOM – COLNE – DAY – 1947 (CONT)

A Philco wireless set sits in the middle of the table. Jack, Pot, Shaz and Jimmy kneel on chairs, crouching over it . . .

JACK (VO)

No score at half-time. No score at full-time. No score till six minutes from the end of extra-time. Then over the wireless we heard –

RAYMOND GLENDENNING (OFFSCREEN)

Hurst centres from the right . . .

EXT WEMBLEY STADIUM – DAY – 1947 (CONT)

LIBRARY FOOTAGE of the football action Wolstenholme is describing . . .

RAYMOND GLENDENNING (OS)

. . . It goes to Duffy. Duffy shoots. Duffy's scored!

JACK (VO)

Unfortunately, Duffy didn't play for Burnley . . .

The Charlton players mob Duffy in delight.

EXT BOUNDARY STREET – COLNE – DAY – 1947

Jack, Pot, Shaz and Jimmy are aimlessly, heart-brokenly kicking a tennis ball about . . .

JACK (VO)

We switched off the wireless and went out into the big, wide world of our street. At some point in life you have to grow up. We started six minutes from the end of extra-time.

POT

We didn't want the cup anyway.

SHAZ

It's only a bit of tin.

JIMMY

Bloody Duffy . . .

INT CLASSROOM – COLNE GRAMMAR SCHOOL – DAY – 1947

The following Monday dinnertime.

The drawing of the football is still on the blackboard, but Terry is changing the word chalked beneath – from 'Elated' to 'Deflated'.

A STILL OF THE BURNLEY CUP FINAL TEAM – DAY – 1947

CAM slowly zooms in on one of the players, Peter Kippax. During this:

JACK (VO)

The Burnley outside-left was the often slightly unfit, always slightly bored, Brylcreemed wizard of the wing, Peter Kippax.

To Pot, Shaz, Jimmy and me, his name became as entertaining as his dribbling . . .

So 'Peter Kippax' became 'P'Tang Kipper', which became 'P'Tang, Yang Kipper', which became 'P'Tang, Yang, Kipperbang', which finally became our password and eventually the no doubt mystifying title of one of my TV screenplays, commissioned by David Puttnam 35 years later, directed by Michael Apted and transmitted by Channel Four in its first week on the air . . .

FILM EXCERPT: *P'Tang, Yang, Kipperbang*

INT CLASSROOM – DAY – 1948

A co-educational class of fourteen-year-olds at their desks, silently reading. Among them is Ann (i.e. the golden Ann Morton).

JACK (VO)

The film is the rites-of-passage story of Alan Duckworth (i.e. me), fighting – and losing – the agonising struggles of adolescence.

Alan tumbles into the room. Everyone looks at him. He's immediately embarrassed.

ALAN

(*to the teacher*)

Sorry I'm late, Miss Land.

MISS LAND

Do you know what time school actually starts, Duckworth?

(*to the rest of the class*)

Anyone who says, 'No, it's always started by the time he gets here,' sees the Headmaster at once.

(*to Alan*)

Silent reading, *Mill on the Floss*, page 380.

Alan settles as quietly as he can (i.e. noisily) into his seat. He glances at Ann. She ignores him. He glances at Abbo, who raises his arm and bends it in a sort of rickety salute, then quietly and hoarsely moans their password.

ABBO

P'tang, yang, kipperbang, uuuh!

ALAN

(*similarly*)

P'tang, yang, kipperbang, uuuh!

MISS LAND

Who was that?

Innocent silence throughout the room. Alan turns to Shaz.

ALAN

P'tang, yang, kipperbang, uuuh!

SHAZ

P'tang, yang, kipperbang, uuuh!

MISS LAND

Duckworth, get out!

EXT SCHOOL PLAYING FIELDS – DAY – 1948

Tommy, the groundsman, is sitting on the grass, eating his sandwich lunch. Alan sits beside him on the seat of a lawnmower, watching Ann, some distance away, talking to her friends.

TOMMY

Have you got a girlfriend?

ALAN

I've got red hands.

TOMMY

Eh?

ALAN

The skin's very red and thin, like transparent, with chewed up nails. I hate my hands. And my neck – that's thin as well. And my face goes red a lot. Not blushing, I don't think. I don't blush. I just sometimes go red. It's only a phase. Bums are nothing really. Everyone's got a bum. Always have had. They're nothing to be ashamed of. Dicks neither. It's only the human torso. Tits included. They're just for feeding babies with, deep down. Not for bouncing about. Kissing's different.

(*beat*)

Anyway I don't need girlfriends, I've got my cricket.

EXT STREET – DAY – 1948 (CONT)

Alan, Pot, Shaz and Abbo walking home from school.

ALAN

... because, by ensuring victory over the Axis powers and Huns, what the British Tommies did was (a) ensure peace for all mankind full stop, (b) make all men brothers irrespective of race, colour or whatsit – doofer – creed, and (c) ended the class struggle, so that from now on, there'll never again be poverty, disease and hunger – and everyone'll be equal, with a full and rich life, probably all speaking Esperanto. The best example is Teasmaids.

SHAZ

(*blankly*)

What?

ALAN

Teasmaids.

ABBO

What about them?

ALAN

For a cup of tea when you wake up.

SHAZ

They're the best example of *what*?

ALAN

Of what I've been saying. In time, everyone on earth'll have a Teasmaid, irrespective of race, colour or creed. You can't stop progress.

(*a satisfied smile*)

I bet that's something they never thought of at Alamein.

EXT ANOTHER STREET – DAY

Alan is walking Ann home after the one and only performance of the school play, both having played the romantic leads.

JACK (VO)

The climax of the play was to have been Alan's character kissing Ann's character. And kissing Ann has been Alan's fantasy for a year. When it comes to the moment, however, he shakes hands with her instead.

Ann, who had never wanted Alan to kiss her, is bewildered – and miffed. And now, of course, she *does* want him to kiss her . . .

He tries to explain. No, he wasn't being a coward in front of the whole school. What happened was that he realised that dreaming of kissing Ann would never have been the same as really kissing her. That dreaming isn't real life. That 'Kids kid themselves'. That real men don't mess about dreaming. They grow up instead. Ann realises it's now too late . . . his rite of passage is complete.

ANN

(*sadly*)

Would you like to say, 'P'tang, yang, kipperbang'?

He smiles, shakes his head.

ALAN

Not any more.

ANN

My favourite words are yellow ochre, burnt sienna and crimson lake.

ALAN

Very nice.

(*beat*)

See you tomorrow.

He turns to go.

ANN

Alan?

He turns back. She kisses him very briefly on the cheek.

For good luck, that's all.

They both walk off, their separate ways.

EXT ALAN'S STREET – DAY – 1948

Alan is walking towards his house. Gradually his gait is beginning to change . . . becoming more confident . . . then cocky . . . then a downright swagger. He passes two workmen climbing into their lorry at the end of their day's work. He nods to them curtly – the greeting of a man among men – then goes into his house. They watch him go, impressed, despite themselves.

1ST WORKMAN

He'll be starting shaving next.

2ND WORKMAN

Then spend the rest of his life trying to stop the bleeding.

EXT COLNE GRAMMAR SCHOOL – DAY – 1948

Jack, Pot, Shaz and Jimmy come out of the building, dishevelled at the end of a school day. As usual kicking a tennis ball from one to the other.

Ever since his School Certificate results in Maths – Arithmetic 28%, Algebra 12%, Geometry 0% – Jack has concentrated on English. Encouraged by Terry Land, English has become the love of his life.

EXT ALBERT STREET – COLNE – DAY – 1948

Swinging a violin case somewhat disrespectfully as he goes, Jack is dragging his feet down the street.

JACK (VO)

Outside school hours, my principal activity was learning the violin. To look at me who would've thought that one day, after years of painstaking practice, I'd mature into very possibly the worst violinist on earth.

Why I'd even *want* to learn the violin I now put down to perversity. All my pals took piano lessons, but I had to be different, a Lancastrian Stéphane Grappelli 'who just plays the twiddly bits'. I had to stay in Saturday nights and listen to *Saturday Night Theatre,* and try and persuade my pals to go out Thursday nights, when everybody else stayed in. In later

years, I had to be the only teenager in the western world to hate Elvis Presley. Why? Because the girls all loved him. Perverse. Jealous and perverse.

EXT PLAYING FIELDS – COLNE GRAMMAR SCHOOL – DAY – 1949

Sports Day. High-jumpers, long-jumpers, 880-yard runners all in action . . .

All the non-competing pupils are massed in front of the school, cheering on the athletes representing their Houses.

ANGLE ON Jack and five other runners taking up position for a race.

JACK (VO)

Sports Day. My last day at school . . . and I was in the running, literally, to become the Victor Ludorum. I was already level on points when we came to the last event – the 100 yards.

1ST TEACHER

On your marks.

The runners take up their marks.

Get set.

They do so, and the 1st Teacher fires his pistol.

Jack and his rivals sprint off. During the race:

JACK (VO)

I'd had a mixed sporting career at school. At rugby I was as pathetic as someone not all that keen on having his balls bitten off in the scrum can be.

At cricket I knew precisely how to play every stroke in the *MCC Coaching Book* and never scored more than three. In my last game for my house, I was run out without facing a ball.

Jack victoriously breasts the tape. He stands, panting, hands on knees, revelling in the cheers of his pals.

At boxing, on the other hand, I spent sleepless nights quaking at the thought of my next bout – then won them all. Only one problem – win or lose, I always came out with a bleeding lip. Even when I'd never taken a single blow to my face. It took me a long time and a lot of bloodletting to figure out that my defensive left glove and my protruding buck teeth were colluding and colliding to give me those permanently bulging bee-stung lips.

He walks towards the 2nd Teacher, who's gaping in bewilderment at his stopwatch.

JACK

Please, sir, what was my timing?

2ND TEACHER

(*muttering to himself*)

It could be old age . . . Astigmatism, summat of that nature . . .

JACK

Pardon, sir?

2nd Teacher signals to the 1st Teacher to join him down the track.

2ND TEACHER

(*to Jack*)

Come with me.

He sets off to meet the 1st Teacher. Jack, puzzled, trundles after him.

EXT THE 100-YARD TRACK – COLNE GRAMMAR SCHOOL – DAY – 1949 (CONT)

The two teachers meet halfway, compare stopwatch readings and mutter worriedly to each other. Jack stands watching. Finally, they turn to him.

2ND TEACHER

Well, I don't know how to tell you this, Rosenthal . . . But you've broken the world record.

JACK

(*blankly*)

You mean the *school* record.

1ST TEACHER

No, lad, the *world* record, the *Olympic* record, *every* record. You're the fastest sprinter on earth.

Jack boggles at them.

JACK (VO)

Eighteen years old. Victor Ludorum of Colne Grammar School and 100-yard champion of the world.

(*beat*)

Well, for a minute I was.

1ST TEACHER

(*to 2nd Teacher*)

Happen we should measure the track.

2ND TEACHER

Happen we should.

JACK (VO)

And happen they bloody did!

Both teachers set off purposefully towards the start-line.

INT CHANGING ROOM – COLNE GRAMMAR SCHOOL – DAY – 1949

A quarter of an hour later. Jack's silver cup stands on the bench. Jack and others are changing back into their school uniforms. 2nd Teacher appears at the door. Jack throws him an anxious look.

2ND TEACHER

Sorry, lad. Eighty-seven yards, if that. Y'ave to laugh, 'aven't you?

Jack's quivering lip seems to suggest that that's debatable.

EXT COTTON MILL – COLNE – DAY – 1949

Jack is among a crowd of mill-workers clattering their clogs towards the main gate at the start of the day.

JACK (VO)

Between leaving school and starting college, I joined the proletariat to undergo a bit of face-grinding.

Come October, I was headed for University College, Leicester to do an external London Honours Degree in English, after a first year of General Studies. Why Leicester I've no idea. I imagine my school assumed Oxford and Cambridge were out of the question . . . but why Leicester? Maybe because they accepted my application. But, then again, whose application would they have rejected?

But for now I had this key job in a cotton mill . . .

INT WEAVING SHED – COLNE – DAY – 1949

Open on CU of a tray of mugs of tea.

PULL BACK to see Jack carrying the tray and distributing the mugs to weavers, all of them women, at their looms.

The noise is absolutely deafening. Jack approaches the 1st weaver and shouts at the top of his voice:

JACK

Tea up!

The shouting is inaudible.

CU 1st Weaver. As she mouths the following words, superimpose CAPTION: *'Don't try and shout. Just mouth. We all lip-read.'*

She takes a mug of tea. Mouthing and CAPTION: *'Do you fancy five minutes behind the weft basket?'*

Jack promptly goes to 2nd Weaver. As he mouths the following, superimpose CAPTION: *'Tea up!'*

CU 2nd Weaver. As she mouths the following, superimpose CAPTION: *'I'd sooner have a big one, lad, if you follow my meaning.'*

She takes a mug of tea. Jack escapes to the 3rd Weaver. As he mouths the following, superimpose CAPTION: *'Tea up!'*

CU 3rd Weaver. As she mouths the following, superimpose CAPTION: *'You want to come on nights, young Jacky, you'd learn more than you will at college.'*

Jack turns ruefully to CAM. *As he mouths the following, superimpose* CAPTION: *'I couldn't lip-read, so I never understood a word they said. But I think I got the gist.'*

EXT PLATFORM – COLNE RAILWAY STATION – DAY – 1949

David, dressed in the uniform of an army private, is seated on a bench, smoking a roll-up fag and reading the Daily Mirror.

Jack is seated beside him, dressed in green corduroy trousers, a tan jacket with elbow patches and yellow sandals. He's reading the Guardian.

Between them is a suitcase.

CAM *favours David as the train pulls in.*

JACK (VO)

David – who I thought was going to be a mathematical genius – left school at sixteen, and began his teenage rebellion. And, not quite consciously, we began to grow apart.

David picks up the suitcase, slides it into a compartment of the train and slaps Jack on the back. Jack returns the gesture then gets into the compartment.

He got work labouring in a tannery that you could locate with one nostril six streets away. At night, he and his new pals bought each other halves of mild and bitter. When he did his National Service in the Army, the halves became pints.

And me, the poncey college boy, well I was off to Leicester.

The train starts off. Jack waves from the window. David waves back, then starts to walk off down the platform.

We were going in opposite directions . . .

THE FIFTIES

INT BEDROOM – STUDENT DIGS – LEICESTER – DAY – 1949

On one of the beds is an opened box, which until a few moments ago contained a telescope. All it contains now is its instruction booklet.

Jack and two other students – Alan and Steve – are trying and failing to rig up the telescope on its tripod at the bedroom window. Each elbows the others away as tempers fray . . .

JACK

That bit *must* go in there!

STEVE

Where's the bloody instructions again, then?!

Alan glances out of the window. Sees two other students.

ALAN

S'okay. *They'll* know.

JACK (VO)

There were five of us in the digs at Leicester.

ANGLE ON Alan. Neat, dapper, slightly built, has blond hair, a limp, and an air of sagacity.

Alan was a pal from Colne Grammar School and . . .

ANGLE ON Steve. Much amused by everything – except how to set up a telescope. You have the feeling he's laughing at you even when he's in a different room.

. . . Steve was a lad from Derby, and the two Alan had spotted . . .

EXT STUDENT DIGS – LEICESTER – DAY – 1949 (CONT)

From Alan's POV, we see two bescarved students in their early thirties, wheeling their bikes up the path towards the front door.

JACK (VO)

. . . were Holmes and Horobin. Mature students. Grown-up men of the world as opposed to eighteen-year-old greenhorns. The generation whose education Hitler had snookered and who were having to start all over again.

Holmes opens the front door. They wheel their bikes inside.

INT BEDROOM – STUDENT DIGS – LEICESTER – DAY – 1949 (CONT)

Holmes and Horobin fix the telescope in seconds. Jack, Alan and Steve wait gratefully, seated in a row on one of the beds.

HOLMES

Okay, Plonks, all set.

HOROBIN

All you do now is point it at her window and drool.

STEVE

Will you be joining us in aforesaid droolery?

Holmes and Horobin share a wry smile, then transfer it to the Plonks pityingly.

JACK (VO)

Holmes and Horobin had put away childish things the minute Rommel's tanks started taking potshots at them.

They said peeping was nothing once you'd done *more* than peep. Especially in Cairo.

INT LIVING ROOM – STUDENT DIGS – LEICESTER – NIGHT – 1949

Horobin and Holmes are studying in silence.

Alan is trying to write an essay, but mostly just sucks the end of his pen.

JACK (VO)

Alan had three ambitions at college. One was to go to the pictures more often than anyone in history. Especially if it meant missing lectures.

His second, if he wasn't at the pictures, was to chase down to London to see Margot Fonteyn dance. Over the years, he graduated from giving her flowers at the stage door to getting cups of tea in her dressing room.

His third was to sip Benedictine all day, preceded by singing the single word 'Benedictine' over and over to the tune of 'Eine Kleine Nachtmusik'. At least it made Steve laugh.

One ambition he never had was to do any work. He'd been sweating over the same English essay all term, and all he'd written was half of the first cringe-making sentence: 'O Shakespeare! The very name . . .'

STEVE (OS)
(*calling*)
Alan! Zero hour!

ALAN
Damn! Just as I was getting going!

He starts for the door. Holmes and Horobin shake their heads, with indulgent resignation.

INT BEDROOM – STUDENT DIGS – LEICESTER – NIGHT – 1949 (CONT)

Steve, Alan and Jack crowd round the telescope, now pointing across the street through a gap in the drawn curtains. Steve is peering through the eyepiece.

EXT OPPOSITE HOUSE – LEICESTER – NIGHT – 1949 (CONT)

From Steve's POV, we see into the living room through uncurtained windows. A young woman goes over to a bald-headed man who's in an armchair, reading, then leaves the room. The man smiles, puts his book aside, then quickly crosses the room, switching out the light as he exits.

INT BEDROOM – STUDENT DIGS – LEICESTER – NIGHT – 1949 (CONT)

The trio as before. Steve yells excitedly.

STEVE
Okay! Countdown! One, two, three —

Jack and Alan join in, as:

JACK (VO)
This was the Leicestershire version of the Windmill Theatre. Mrs-Across-the-Road's usual Saturday night performance . . . but now magnified a bit.

EXT OPPOSITE HOUSE – LEICESTER – NIGHT – 1949 (CONT)

From Steve's POV, we see the light suddenly switched on in the uncurtained bedroom of the house across the road.

The man starts to swiftly undress . . .

INT BEDROOM – STUDENT DIGS – LEICESTER – NIGHT – 1949 (CONT)

Alan and Jack jostle for position at the eyepiece. Steve fights them off – then suddenly, like an upright, church-going spinster of this parish:

STEVE

Don't look! It's *him*!

Alan and Jack step back, mumbling manly, embarrassed apologies into mid-air.

INT BEDROOM – OPPOSITE HOUSE – LEICESTER – NIGHT – 1949 (CONT)

The man gets into bed. The woman (his wife) walks in, goes to the window and starts to strip off.

INT BEDROOM – STUDENT DIGS – LEICESTER – NIGHT – 1949 (CONT)

Alan is now squinting excitedly through the eyepiece.

ALAN

Okay! *Now!*

Jack and Steve fight for a peep.

EXT OPPOSITE HOUSE – LEICESTER – NIGHT – 1949 (CONT)

Now completely naked, facing the window, the woman stretches out her arms, holds the position for a few moments then slowly draws the curtains closed. The light goes out.

INT BEDROOM – STUDENT DIGS – LEICESTER – NIGHT – 1949 (CONT)

The three wander away from the telescope and flop down on their respective beds. An empty (putative) post-coital melancholy. A couple of sighs.

STEVE

Just a matter of getting through till *next* Saturday, really.

ALAN

That's all.

JACK

Not long. About a week, really . . .

INT LECTURE HALL – UNIV. COLL., LEICESTER – DAY – 1949

A small, bearded professor is lecturing to a hall full of students, including Jack.

JACK (VO)

Saturday nights apart, the most exciting time I had at Leicester was provided by an inspirational lecture on philosophy by Professor Leon. Not that I was reading Philosophy. Just English, History, Latin and French for the first year to qualify for the English Honours course.

Except I was then told that the Honours course was already full – and I was stuck with my four General Degree subjects. Not what I wanted.

INT LIBRARY – UNIV. COLL., LEICESTER – DAY – 1950

Students working in silence. Alan limps aimlessly in and spots Jack writing a letter. He goes over to his table, sits down opposite him, takes a page of tattered foolscap from his briefcase and sticks his pen in his mouth.

JACK (VO)

So I wrote a Dear John letter to the college telling them it was all over between us and I was leaving at the end of the academic year.

He starts writing a second letter.

Then another letter to L C Knights, my favourite literary critic and Sheffield University's Professor of English, applying to read for Honours in English Literature and Language.

I only made one mistake. I sent the Leicester letter to Sheffield and the Sheffield one to Leicester.

JACK
(*to Alan*)

How was the pictures?

ALAN

Good.

JACK

How's your essay doing?

ALAN

Marvellous.

(*reads from his tattered foolscap*)
'O Shakespeare! The very name shines like a beacon –' 'Shines like a beacon' is new. Before, it was just 'O Shakespeare, the very name . . .'

JACK

Terrific.

ALAN

Ta.

JACK (VO)

Leicester and Sheffield sorted out the letters – ***and*** **me – and I was enrolled in Professor Knight's course starting in September.**

EXT BOUNDARY STREET – COLNE – DAY – 1950

Jack is standing outside his front door. A tractor rumbles slowly along the street towards him. It's driven by a massive Man of the Earth, his face and clothes the colour of earth. It wheezes to a halt beside pasty-faced Jack. He climbs aboard, embarrassedly.

JACK (VO)

Each Christmas holiday, like most students, I worked as a postman. This summer, though, I worked for an agricultural contractor, who picked me up each day in his limo – me, a son of city streets betraying my DNA –

The tractor drives ponderously on.

– then drove me very slowly for all the neighbours to see to the middle of nowhere, to dig up whole fields on my own and, as far as I could gather, for no reason.

EXT CO-OP BAKERY – COLNE – DAY – 1950

Turbanned mill-workers scrape and spark their clogs en route to work. As they clear frame, CAM stays on the shopfront of a bakery, its window filled with huge, iced birthday cakes.

JACK (VO)

After he fired me, I worked in the Co-op bakery. By the time the Clog Chorus began at 6.30, I'd already been there an hour.

INT CO-OP BAKERY – COLNE – DAY – 1950

Two bakers are at a table, mixing dough. Two more bakers pull massive trays bearing scores of scalding hot loaves from the oven. Another baker plucks the loaves off the trays and lays them on a slab to cool. Another beckons to Jack, who's sweeping the floor, to give a hand.

Jack picks up a loaf, screams in agony, drops it to the floor and blows on his burning fingers. Everybody finds this hilarious. Not Jack though.

BAKER

Heavy, was it?

This apparently is even more hilarious.

JACK (VO)

This was my workmates' favourite joke. But they had another joke which was, literally, the icing on the cake.

EXT CO-OP BAKERY – COLNE – DAY – 1950

Through the window, we see one of the bakers take a 6 lb iced cake from the display, where it's been standing for maybe months. Its erstwhile pure-white surface is grey with dust, dirt and debris. The baker blows on it. A small dark-grey cloud billows up.

INT CO-OP BAKERY – COLNE – DAY – 1950 (CONT)

CU the muck-mottled cake on a table. The baker is painstakingly plastering a new coat of pristine icing on top of it.

EXT CO-OP BAKERY – COLNE – DAY – 1950 (CONT)

Through the window, we see the baker replace the doctored cake and change the price tag from 1s 6d to 1s 11d.

EXT SNAKE PASS – YORKSHIRE – DAY – 1950

A coach tentatively squeals its way along the tortuous hairpin bends of this notoriously dangerous road, through wild and wonderfully wooded scenery.

Through the window we see passengers staring out in trepidation – and Jack with his eyes tightly shut.

JACK (VO)

The journey to Sheffield over Snake Pass was the stomach-churning grown-up version of the climb up the fire escape at school.

INT BEDROOM – 1ST SHEFFIELD DIGS – NIGHT – 1950

Jack's now-emptied suitcase lies open on the bed. He's taking off his shirt. A tap at the door and an elderly lady comes in, carrying a large, Victorian jug of hot water. She stands it in a matching bowl on a bamboo table, then goes.

JACK

Thank you, Mrs . . . um . . . er . . .

He picks up the jug to pour the water into the bowl – and drops it. It smashes into jagged antique-pottery slivers.

JACK (VO)

My first night. And my last. The next morning, the landlady kicked me out.

INT STAIRCASE & LANDING – 2ND SHEFFIELD DIGS – NIGHT – 1950

Jack and three other students are sprawled on the stairs and landing, comatose or moaning or trying not to throw up. An attractive young woman stands, hands on hips, surveying them half ruefully, half amused. This is Mrs Wilkinson.

JACK (VO)

My next digs was at the house of the svelte Mrs Wilkinson, who liked a laugh and a joke – and us – until the night we had too many halves of shandy and apparently quote-went-too-far-unquote. We protested our innocence on the grounds of being drunk and incapable and very nice people deep down. Mr Wilkinson, purely on hearsay, disagreed and banished us.

INT LIVING ROOM – 3RD SHEFFIELD DIGS – DAY – 1950

Jack and four other *students – Phil, Matt, Ron and Hughie – sit at the breakfast table, licking their long-emptied cereal bowls. Ron looks at his watch anxiously.*

RON

I've a lecture at nine . . .

HUGHIE

I have.

MATT

Me, too.

PHIL

Maybe she's forgotten to cook anything . . .

HUGHIE

Maybe all we're getting was the Corn Flakes . . .

RON

Shall I go and ask her?

MATT

Shall I go and *hit* her?

The door opens and Mrs Thin, a walking advertisement for anorexia, sidesteps in with a tray of tinned tomatoes on toast.

MRS THIN

Sorry. I was doing one of my competitions in *John Bull* – and I suddenly thought, 'Hang on, isn't there something I'm supposed to be doing?' There blinking-well *was*! Your blinking *breakfast*. Laugh!

No one does.

JACK (VO)

My third digs. Our landlady, for obvious reasons, we called Mrs Thin. Her husband – for even more obvious reasons –

INT HALLWAY – 3RD SHEFFIELD DIGS – DAY – 1950 (CONT)

An extremely obese man strides towards the front door in his trilby and overcoat and carrying a briefcase, as Mrs Thin emerges from the living room.

JACK (VO)

– was Mr Fat.

MR FAT

(*as he passes her*)

See you tonight, dear.

Mr Fat opens the front door. Mrs Thin pulls a hate-filled face at his back, then heads back to the kitchen.

INT LIVING ROOM – 3RD SHEFFIELD DIGS – DAY – 1950 (CONT)

We hear the front door bang closed. The lads stare at their breakfasts in dismay.

JACK (VO)

We all detested tinned tomatoes. Weird, that. Considering that forty years later, I suddenly began to like them a lot. I have to eat them alone. My family leave the room.

Phil resignedly starts shovelling his tomatoes into an aspidistra's plant-pot.

Phil Radcliffe, from Bolton, became my best pal at the university, also reading English. Witty, funny, bright, he loved classical music and became a music critic, a feature-writing journalist and eventually Manchester University's Director of Communications. We still keep in touch.

Matt nonchalantly starts unloading his tomatoes into another unsuspecting plant-pot.

Matt was a school pal of Phil's. A red-headed, red-hot footballer and seemingly a red-hot lover.

We all shared a bedroom, wincing while his jilted girlfriend threw notes tied round stones at our window in the middle of the night. One of them read, 'Why are you so cruel to me?' He reckoned that was *too* cliché'd a cliché to deserve an answer. He read Maths and finally became a headmaster.

Ron angrily starts emptying his plate into the next innocent plant-pot.

Six-foot something, Big Ron was an old school pal of Phil's and Matt's. Coming from a wealthy family, he never carried money and, as though it was his birthright, cadged from the rest of us for three years. He also read Maths – but brilliantly, a genius clearly destined for a perfect 100% starred First Class degree. He also proudly claimed to have once read a book. ***Bleak House***. Years later, Ron and I fell out. Neither of us can remember why, but it still seems to rankle. With both of us. Ron became a boffin at Harwell and a professor of Maths.

Hughie regretfully starts slopping his tomatoes into the last of the plant-pots.

Hughie was a sweet-natured, gentle Geordie and a wonderful audience for the rest of us, laughing till he wept. He too read Maths, he too was a budding Einstein who became a professor. He once tried to explain to me what a harmonic pencil was. Apparently, it's to do with neither music nor with drawing, but numbers – so he never stood a chance.

Ron, Matt and Hughie grab their books and rush out of the room. Jack and Phil go round the room, carefully squashing any tell-tale tomatoes deeper into their pots.

EXT 4TH DIGS – ECCLESHALL ROAD – SHEFFIELD – DAY – 1951

Jack, Phil, Matt, Ron and Hughie are all crammed into a tiny, tinny, tenth-hand, black Austin 7, Hughie at the wheel, parked outside the digs.

They wave regally at a plump, motherly woman on her doorstep, waving back. This is Mrs Gosling. Her bosom wobbles with laughter – and pride – as her beloved boys rattle very slowly down the street towards the university.

JACK (VO)

Fourth time lucky. Mrs Gosling adored us. ***Mr*** Gosling tolerated us. At least whenever Sheffield United won a match. Whenever they lost, he hated us and the rest of mankind. While he rampaged round the house smashing ornaments, Mrs Gosling tried to mollify him with bacon sandwiches – red and white, Sheffield United's colours.

INT LECTURE ROOM – SHEFFIELD UNIVERSITY – DAY – 1951

Professor Knights, a tall, skinny, aesthetic-looking, younger version of Terry Land, is lecturing. Jack and Phil are among his note-taking students.

JACK (VO)

Once I'd got over my initial panic at realising how much I'd have to read over the next three years in the beautiful, octagonal library, the Honours course was everything I'd hoped for.

We were the first intake to be given the Labour Government's free university education, so working hard was the least we could do. And so was playing hard . . .

EXT FOOTBALL PITCH – SHEFFIELD – DAY – 1951

A match in progress. More than one player is wearing specs. (But, then again, so did the incomparable Denis Law in his embryonic days at Huddersfield Town). Jack scores a goal.

JACK (VO)

Football for the Faculty of Arts team . . .

INT BILLIARD ROOM – UNIVERSITY UNION – SHEFFIELD – DAY – 1951

Jack and Phil playing snooker.

JACK (VO)

Snooker in the Union whenever we didn't have a lecture . . .

EXT ATHLETICS TRACK – SHEFFIELD – DAY – 1951

Jack running a 100-yard race.

JACK (VO)

The hundred yards for the Faculty and University second team, once again not breaking the world record . . .

EXT CITY STREET – SHEFFIELD – DAY – 1951

Armed with a collection box and pathetically dressed as a pirate, Jack accosts passers-by.

JACK (VO)

Member of the Rag Committee. Embarrassed and embarrassing member of the Rag Committee . . .

EXT HILLSBOROUGH FOOTBALL GROUND – SHEFFIELD – DAY – 1951

LIBRARY FOOTAGE of a ginger-crowned giant of a centre-forward, hammering in goal after goal for blue-and-white striped Sheffield Wednesday.

INTERCUT with Jack, on the terraces, watching.

JACK (VO)

Gobsmacked admirer of the real-life Roy of the Rovers, virtually four-goals-a-game Derek Dooley, terrorising opposing goalkeepers for Sheffield Wednesday. Since Sheffield Wednesday is absolutely not Sheffield United, I could never confess this to Mr Gosling.

The phenomenal Derek Dooley was certain to become the highest goalscorer the game would ever know, till one innocuous day at Preston. His leg was sliced open in a tackle. Within minutes it became gangrenous. Within hours it was amputated. In one afternoon, a hero became a tragic hero.

EXT CRICKET FIELD – SHEFFIELD – DAY – 1951

The annual University v. Yorkshire match is over. Apart from a groundsman carefully uprooting the stumps, the field is now empty. Notebook and pencil in hand, Jack walks, a touch self-importantly, towards the pavilion.

JACK (VO)

I was also sports reporter for *Darts,* **the Union newspaper . . .**

He goes into the pavilion.

INT CRICKET PAVILION – SHEFFIELD – DAY – 1951 (CONT)

Jack approaches a door labelled 'Visitors' Changing Room' and knocks on the door.

JACK (VO)

. . . hoping to interview *another* sporting icon – Freddie Trueman, the Yorkshire and England opening bowler, who'd just finished skittling out the University first eleven.

One of the Yorkshire team, in his whites, opens the door.

CRICKETER

Yes?

Jack's self-importance promptly melts into schoolboy diffidence.

JACK

I wonder if I could kindly have a word with Mr Trueman, if it's not too much trouble, if that's okay, if not – not to worry, if that's –

CRICKETER

(*calls into the room*)

Freddie! For you!

He goes back inside. Jack swallows nervously. Freddie Trueman appears at the door. Not *in his whites. In fact, not in anything. Completely stark naked apart from half an orange sticking out of his mouth. Jack studies the floor.*

JACK

Hello. I'm the Union newspaper sports reporter.

FREDDIE TRUEMAN

(*through the orange*)

Oh, yes? And are you sensational?

JACK (VO)

I suppose, with hindsight, interviewing a literally bollock-naked cricket legend was a scoop.

(*beat*)

If I'd understood a word he said through his orange.

EXT ECCLESHALL ROAD – SHEFFIELD – NIGHT – 1951

Jack, Phil and Matt, in tracksuits, running along. This is their nightly routine, a two-mile jog before jogging was even invented. They run to their digs. Matt opens the door and they trot inside.

INT LIVING ROOM – 4TH SHEFFIELD DIGS – NIGHT – 1951 (CONT)

Ron and Hughie are at the table being brilliant with slide rules and calculus beyond the wit of ordinary mortals.

Matt, Phil and Jack come panting in from their run. The phone rings. Ron takes it.

RON

(*into phone*)

Hello?

(*beat*)

Hang on, Wendy.

He hands the phone to Jack, still breathless.

JACK
(*into phone*)

Hello, love.

(*beat*)

Now? I can't, honest. I'm buggered and I've got an essay to –

(*beat*)

Don't be daft! You *know* I do! But I've only just come in and I'm completely . . .

He continues weedily protesting and listening to Wendy's pleas during the following:

JACK (VO)

Wendy was the girlfriend. The very Roman Catholic girlfriend. So Roman Catholic she thought that when the Pope was dying of hiccoughs it was my fault for thinking sinful thoughts. So Roman Catholic she reckoned platonic friendship was excessively sexual.

JACK
(*into phone*)

Don't cry!

She hangs up. He sighs and replaces the phone. Then, to the others:

I'm just going round to her digs.

PHIL

Don't. Don't.

MATT

Don't.

JACK

She was crying.

RON

Jack, do not bloody go!

Jack starts wretchedly for the door.

JACK

See you in a bit.

HUGHIE

Come back!

They mumble 'Pathetic', 'What a cow', 'Crackers', 'Weedy bugger' as Jack exits.

EXT SHEFFIELD STREETS – NIGHT– 1951 (CONT)

Jack running as fast as he can, given that his lungs are bursting, his legs feel like lumps of reinforced concrete and he's got a stitch . . .

INT GIRLS' DIGS – SHEFFIELD – NIGHT – 1951

Wendy (small, mousey, serious, butter wouldn't melt in her mouth) sits with four other girls, all in their dressing gowns, having tea and toast. 1st Girl passes a slice of toast to her.

1ST GIRL

Wendy?

The doorbell rings.

EXT GIRLS' DIGS – SHEFFIELD – NIGHT – 1951 (CONT)

Jack leans against the wall at the doorway, utterly breathless. 2nd Girl opens the door.

2ND GIRL

Hi.

INT GIRLS' DIGS – SHEFFIELD – NIGHT – 1951 (CONT)

Wendy and the others sit, eyes riveted on the door. Jack appears in the doorway. All the girls – led by Wendy – explode into paroxysms of laughter.

WENDY
(*to the girls*)

See! Told you!

Jack would now like to die.

EXT COUNTRYSIDE – COLNE – DAY – 1952

A lovely summer's day. David and a red-headed girl walk, hand in hand, through picturesque scenery. She is Eileen.

JACK (VO)
I wasn't the only Rosenthal with a Roman Catholic girlfriend.

David and Eileen stop, embrace and kiss.

Eileen was originally from Larne in Northern Ireland. She was his first girlfriend, he was her first boyfriend. They planned a church wedding.

The happy couple walk on, away from CAM.

INT THE ROSENTHAL LIVING ROOM – COLNE – DAY – 1952

Lakey and Sam, the unhappy couple, sit in bleak, empty-hearted silence at the table. There are tears in Lakey's eyes.

JACK (VO)

To Sam and Lakey, it was a bitter betrayal. Of *them.* Of 5,000 years.

(*beat*)

David's middle name was Israel.

(*beat*)

Snatching him away from a jumping rat was easy. So was uprooting him to gentile Colne, escaping German bombs, escaping death. Escaping *life* can sometimes be harder.

INT UNION COFFEE BAR – SHEFFIELD UNIVERSITY – DAY – 1952

Jack, Phil and other students are arguing – not a little pretentiously – about literature.

JACK (VO)

In the early fifties, James Joyce was my generation's hero. *Ulysses* was our bible.

INT PROF. KNIGHTS'S STUDY – SHEFFIELD UNIVERSITY – DAY – 1952

A frustrated Jack faces an irritated Prof. across Knights's desk.

KNIGHTS

Are you serious?

JACK

Very.

KNIGHTS

You want to do your thesis on James Joyce?

JACK

I do.

KNIGHTS

Out of the question. *Ulysses* is a white elephant. Your thesis is one of your Finals papers. You'll jeopardise your entire degree! Think of another author.

INT PROF. KNIGHTS'S STUDY – SHEFFIELD UNIVERSITY – DAY – 1952

A month later. Jack, more frustrated, faces Knights, more irritated.

JACK (VO)

I came back a month later and said I still wanted to do my white elephant. He still said no.

INT PROF. KNIGHTS'S STUDY – SHEFFIELD UNIVERSITY – DAY – 1952

Again, a month later. Knights stares wearily across his desk at Jack, and sighs.

KNIGHTS

Are you going to come back, month after month, saying the same thing?

JACK

I am, yes.

KNIGHTS

(*another sigh, then a pause, then*)

Very well. On your own head be it.

INT EXAM ROOM – SHEFFIELD UNIVERSITY – DAY – 1952

It's packed with students answering one of their Finals papers . . . Some, Jack and Phil among them, writing quickly, confidently . . . Others, staring numbly out of the window, their hearts in their sandals.

JACK (VO)

Anglo-Saxon apart, I thought I was doing pretty well in Finals. Anglo-Saxon was my *bête noire,* if you'll pardon my Anglo-Saxon. But I'd already got a First on one paper: my thesis on James Joyce. On my own head certainly was it.

INT FIRTH HALL – SHEFFIELD UNIVERSITY – DAY – 1952

Graduation Day. In line with other mortar-boarded and gowned graduates, Phil and Jack move forward to collect their scrolls from the Chancellor, Lord Halifax.

JACK (VO)

In the end, like Phil, I got a 2:1. My tutor berated me for not swotting up for the Anglo-Saxon questions in my viva. Apparently if I'd showed the examiners the slightest improvement, or even the slightest civility, they'd've bent over backwards to give me a First. Not that I've ever been asked what class of degree I got, from that day to this. Fifty-one years.

EXT CAMPUS – SHEFFIELD UNIVERSITY – DAY – 1952

In their academic regalia, the graduates are posing for snapshots taken by their parents or siblings or friends. Phil is taking some of Jack and Wendy, arms entwined.

Watching nearby are Lakey and Sam in their best Saturday clothes.

JACK (VO)

They were torn between pride that the snotty-nosed kid from Cheetham Hill now had letters behind his name – and the sickening fear that David's history was about to repeat itself.

David became what he was through his two years in the Army. With the same bloody-mindedness that I chose James Joyce, I chose the Navy.

DISSOLVE TO:

EXT BARRACKS GATES – FILM LOCATION – DAY – 1990

A Channel 4 TV crew is positioned facing a young actor, while a make-up girl applies the last touches of Max Factor to his handsome face.

Despite the handsome face, he's playing the part of Leo, the fictional version of the 21-year-old Jack who, 38 years earlier, began his first day as a National Serviceman in the Royal Navy. He's wearing civilian clothes, circa 1952, and carries a suitcase.

SOUND RECORDIST

Sound running.

1ST ASSISTANT

Mark it.

CLAPPERBOY

Sixty-six, take one.

He 'claps' his clapperboard.

DIRECTOR

And action!

Leo starts walking towards the gates – the Art Department's reconstruction of the entrance to Victoria Barracks, the Navy's base at Portsmouth – and 'Bye, 'Bye, Baby, *the drama of Jack's two-years' National Service, begins, Drama? Um . . . well,* farce, *certainly. Plus maybe some* melodrama. *And, yes, granted, a little real-life drama, too.*

DISSOLVE TO:

FILM EXCERPT: *'Bye, 'Bye, Baby*

INT NEW INTAKE'S MESS – VICTORIA BARRACKS – DAY – 1952

Leo (Jack) is one of 24 new entries standing beside their beds, suitcases at their feet. Almost all are nervous – even frightened.

From the parade ground outside, we hear – or glimpse – a tough training instructor drilling new entries, barking commands.

During this, Petty Officer Swift – a small, weatherbeaten old salt – checks everyone's names from a clipboard.

PO SWIFT

On behalf of the First Lord of the Admiralty, the five Sea Lords, the Admiral of the Fleet and every tart from Pompey to Plymouth Hoe, welcome to the Dockyard Cavalry. Any questions?

LEO

Is it true the cooks put bromide in our tea, sir?

PO SWIFT

Put it this way – if they do, you'd wish they didn't; if they don't, you'd wish they did.

(beat)

Now. For these first few weeks you do your basic training: square-bashing, spud-bashing, a bit of cryptography, a bit of sea-time, then you learn your Russian and play at being spies, right? No one answer that 'cos it's secret.

(*beat*)

Another secret. You may all think you're clever little bastards. With your Higher School Certificates and fancy degrees. In other ways you're chalk and Chinese wedding cake. Some of you were born with a set of silver golf clubs in your mouth, others with a hobnail boot up your arse. Here, you're all the same – coder specials. Which means you're not special at all. Which means you're not such clever little bastards either. Because coder specials are the lowest branch in the Navy – and therefore the lowest known form of human life.

DISSOLVE TO:

INT TAILORS' WORKSHOP – VICTORIA BARRACKS – DAY – 1952

The real Jack is in a queue of new entrants to collect his 'fore-and-aft-rig' uniform (like a fifties postman with a peaked cap), not the usual 'square-rig' with bell-bottoms and a round cap.

Behind his counter, an elderly civilian tailor stencils each man's name ('Man's' *name? Hardly) inside the jacket. He's attending to the coder ahead of Jack.*

TAILOR

Name?

CODER

Anderson.

The tailor stencils accordingly. The coder takes his jacket and goes. Jack steps in line.

TAILOR

Name?

JACK (VO)

And that's when the curtain went up on Farce Number One. I'd been in the Navy all of twenty minutes. From then on, whenever I told anyone my surname their eyes popped, their jaw dropped and they said –

INT SICK BAY – VICTORIA BARRACKS – DAY – 1952

A sick bay attendant, filling in a form at his desk, gapes at Jack standing before him, stripped to the waist.

SBA

'Mosenthal'?

JACK

And whenever I said, 'No, *R*osenthal,' they said –

EXT PARADE GROUND – VICTORIA BARRACKS – DAY – 1952

A chief petty officer, at the head of a group of new entrants uncomfortably carrying rifles, stares at Jack, then sighs in relief.

CPO

Well, thank Christ for that! Had me worried for a minute . . .

INT GUARD ROOM – VICTORIA BARRACKS – DAY – 1952

At his window, a worried naval policeman examines the passbook Jack has just handed him.

NAVAL POLICEMAN

You didn't say '*Mosenthal*'?

INT SWIMMING POOL – VICTORIA BARRACKS – DAY – 1952

A group of new entrants, standing shivering in their trunks behind a physical training instructor, who stares at Jack dubiously.

PTI

Not 'Mosenthal'? You wouldn't be pulling my plonker . . .?

INT CORRIDOR – VICTORIA BARRACKS – DAY – 1952

Jack, in his best uniform, is being marched along by a petty officer.

JACK (VO)

The Mosenthal Mystery was solved a few days later. I'd applied to be a captain's requestman, meaning I was requesting some special consideration. In this case, three days' leave to observe the imminent Jewish New Year. It actually lasted *two* days, but since I was probably the only Jew to have served in the Navy since Francis Drake's accountant, I thought they wouldn't know that and I'd get away with *three*.

INT CAPTAIN'S ROOM – VICTORIA BARRACKS – DAY – 1952

At the end of the room is a small schooldesk. Behind it stands the captain, in full dress uniform. Fanned in a V from the desk are officers in declining rank.

The petty officer and Jack march in and up to the desk.

PO

Halt!

(*Jack halts*)

Salute!

(*Jack salutes*)

Requestman Probationary Coder Special Rosenthal D/M 930283.

Immediately on hearing the name, all the assembled eyes and jaws pop and drop respectively. The captain's most of all.

CAPTAIN

Did he say 'Mosenthal'?

1ST LIEUTENANT

(*to PO*)

Did you say 'Mosenthal'?

PO

No, sir. 'Rosenthal'.

They all visibly relax.

CAPTAIN

(*shakily*)

Not the best of starts . . .

1ST LIEUTENANT

Proceed, PO.

PO

Request for three days' leave in order to observe Jewish New Year.

A slow, gradual, triumphant smile spreads across the captain's hatchet features.

CAPTAIN

Oh, really? That's his request, is it? Is it, really? Oh, is it, indeed?

PO

(*thrown*)

Yes, sir.

CAPTAIN

Just the three days . . .

(*the smile becomes a burgeoning laugh*)

Not three weeks, then? Or three months? Three years, perhaps? Well, thanks to Mosenthal, three *hours* granted. Three hours only.

1ST LIEUTENANT

Dismiss.

PO

Salute!

(*Jack salutes*)

About turn!

(*Jack about turns*)

Quick march!

He and Jack march out of the room. The captain and his officers burst into unrestrained laughter.

JACK (VO)

I was later told that Mosenthal had been a sailor at the barracks a year or so earlier. A consummate conman. Now *he'd*

been right that the Navy hadn't a clue about Jewish rituals – and consequently requested special perks almost daily . . .

INT CORRIDOR – VICTORIA BARRACKS – DAY – 1952 (CONT)

The PO and Jack march down the corridor away from CAM.

JACK (VO)

Legend had it that he got off guard duty for Jewish festivals that didn't exist, excused drill on Mondays and Wednesdays, specially cooked desserts on Thursdays and a *fortnight*'s leave for the Jewish New Year.

(*beat*)

He finally overplayed his hand by saying there was a rabbinical law that he need only shave twice a week. Now, in the Navy, you either shave clean or not at all. And rabbis with waist-long beards are no one to talk. The captain became a whisker suspicious, phoned the Jewish chaplain to double-check and told him the whole saga. Mosenthal's life of Riley was over. And *mine,* before it'd even started. Cheers, Mosenthal, wherever you are. Mamser (bastard). *Also* with an 'M'.

EXT GATES OF THE JOINT SERVICES SCHOOL FOR LINGUISTS – COULSDON – SURREY – DAY – 1953

A lorry-load of coder specials drives through the gates. Among them is Jack, together with this latest version of the Lads. Just as Pot, Shaz and Jimmy Rye from school gave way to Phil, Matt, Hughie and Ron at university, they, in turn, have given way to Lawrie, Johnny and Jim.

Lawrie is tall, thoughtful, equable, sensible, an aggressive footballer, which he aggressively denies. A sailor's son, from Portsmouth. Later to become a radio talks and documentary producer. We still keep in touch.

Johnny is Mancunian, an enthusiastically Jewish non-Jew from Cheetham Hill, short, straightbacked, not often sober, always on the lookout for adventure and never quite finding it.

Jim is from Sale, a very talented footballer, also short but also tough, a ready laugher.

Lawrie likes the Navy and admits it, even on pain of everyone calling him Anchor-Face.

Johnny revels in the hardship of the Navy but pretends he hates it. Jimmy hates it, but it makes him laugh.

Wandering about the grounds are Russian civilians and Naval, RAF and Army personnel.

As the coders disembark:

JACK (VO)

After a few weeks in which civilisation became a bleached-out memory, the Navy then subjected us to a form of mental cruelty known as Learning Russian.

Our new base was the Joint Services School for Linguists at Coulsdon, Surrey – next door to the notoriously sadistic Guards' Camp, reverberating with the screaming of its celebrity sergeant major, RSM Brittan . . .

Suddenly they put their hands over their ears as a decibel-crunching, barking voice yells commands:

VOICE

Left, right, left, right, halt, about turn, right dress, stand at ease, stand easy!

INT CLASSROOM – JSSL – COULSDON – DAY – 1953

A Russian teacher plods through the mysteries of the cyrillic alphabet on a blackboard.

Jack and the Lads are among the coders (and RAF and Army equivalents) at their desks, poring blankly over Semeonoff's Primer.

JACK (VO)

We were taught by real-life Russians, mostly sad-faced men who'd escaped to a land that didn't bother with portmanteau verbs, packed with prefixes and suffixes, 37 syllables long – and who quickly realised that I was never going to manage Chekhov in the original. Not that we were meant to. We were training to be translators of military Russian only, or (if we were among the best 5 per cent) interpreters and packed off to Cambridge. It was clear from lesson one, I was to be one of the 95 per cent. So that was the morning routine . . .

INT CANTEEN – JSSL – COULSDON – DAY – 1953

Jack and the grimacing, nose-holding Lads slop their revolting, untouched platefuls of inedible food into a dustbin.

JACK (VO)

. . . which after a lunch in the Army canteen that only the lads who'd been at public school could stomach, was followed by a matinee performance of another farce: bayonet training.

DISSOLVE TO:

FILM EXCERPT: *'Bye, 'Bye, Baby*

EXT FIELD – JSSL – COULSDON – DAY – 1953 (CONT)

The class, including Leo, now stands in a long line, holding rifles with wooden 'bayonets' attached. Fifty yards ahead of them is the 'enemy' – bales of straw suspended from poles.

An Army drill sergeant stands facing them.

DRILL SERGEANT

At the command 'Charge!', you will charge at the enemy, yelling insults and obscenities.

(*beat*)

Present bayonets!

They all adopt a forward-leaning stance, bayonets pointed towards the bales of straw.

Yelling insults and obscenities, charge!

The class lumber forward, some strolling, some bounding like big girls, but all of them yelling the same words –

CLASS

Insults and obscenities! Insults and obscenities! Insults and obscenities!

DRILL SERGEANT

(*screaming after them*)

Come back! Get back here! You're all on a bleedin' charge!

DISSOLVE TO:

INT CODERS' MESS – JSSL – COULSDON – NIGHT – 1953

Jack and the rest of the coders stand at ease beside their beds and lockers, as a sub-lieutenant and a petty officer walk slowly from man to man, casting a cursory glance at the made beds. This is Officer's Rounds.

The sub-lieutenant stops at Johnny's bed.

SUB-LIEUTENANT

Open your locker.

Johnny does so. Everything inside is beautifully organised and stacked. The sub-lieutenant walks on.

JACK (VO)

The Navy's thrilled when its sailors keep things shipshape and Bristol fashion.

The sub-lieutenant stops at Jack's bed. He indicates that Jack open his locker.

Jack does so. Everything tumbles out and onto the floor – an avalanche of boots, shirts, underpants, pyjamas, socks, shaving gear, books, pencils, bars of chocolate, photographs of Wendy (and, in a somewhat different pose, Marilyn Monroe).

If they're not, they tend to get a bit upset . . .

The sub-lieutenant fixes Jack with a beady eye.

And *you* tend to get put on a charge. I seemed to upset them a lot . . .

EXT PARADE GROUND – JSSL – COULSDON – DAY – 1953

A motley squad of coders, RAF men and soldiers standing to attention. An Army RSM strolls down the line, stops at Jack and sighs heavily.

Jack's uniform is creased, stained, frayed and a bit short of buttons; his grommetless cap is folded à la Victor Mature as a GI; his boots are unpolished.

RSM
(*Scottish accent*)
You know what you are, Coder?

JACK
(*pondering*)
Um . . .

RSM
I'll help you. What you are is dirty and slovenly on parade. What are you?

JACK
(*he's learning*)
Dirty and slovenly on parade, Sergeant Major.

RSM
Correct. Now, unfortunately, the Geneva Convention forbids me to hang, draw and quarter you, then boil what's left in oil and kick it off the top of Ben Nevis.

JACK (VO)

In the end, though, he wasn't *too* disappointed –

IMMEDIATE CUT TO:

EXT COOK-HOUSE – JSSL – COULSDON – DAY – 1953

Armed with a long-handled stiff brush and a hosepipe, Jack is climbing up a stepladder propped against an enormous black cauldron.

A grossly overweight sergeant-cook, in white tunic, blue-and-white check pants and a chef's hat – all of them grubbier than Jack's uniform was when on parade – is grimly supervising. He gestures Jack to get inside the cauldron.

JACK (VO)

My punishment was to scrub off lumps of cold porridge inside cauldrons that cannibals could've used to feed an entire World Cannibal Convention.

ANGLE ON cauldron interior as Jack clambers in and starts scrubbing.

EXT FOOTBALL PITCH – JSSL – COULSDON – DAY – 1953

Jack is staggering, exhausted, round the perimeter, holding a rifle horizontally above his head with both hands.

JACK (VO)

Added together I must've spent eighteen months of my two years under punishment. Always for misdemeanours that anyone normal would regard as fleabites, but spotty army corporals who'd failed their eleven-plus regarded as having your face chewed off by crocodiles.

EXT NISSEN HUTS – JSSL – COULSDON – NIGHT – 1953

The dead of night and bitterly cold. The camp is fast asleep.

Wearing a greatcoat and carrying a truncheon and torch on a belt around his waist, Jack wanders aimlessly around, shivering and blowing on his mittened hands.

JACK (VO)

A less sadistic punishment was extra guard duty. Not so effective at ripping your shoulders out of their sockets, granted. But fun just the same if you like freezing and don't like sleeping.

It was on one of those nights that I read and re-read and re-read a letter from Wendy . . .

He pulls a well-worn letter from his pocket and reads by the light of his torch, although he knows it by heart.

WENDY (VO)

I don't know how to tell you this, but something's happened. With a capital 'H'.

(*beat*)

You remember Don who was in the year before us doing French and got a First or a 'premier' as he calls it – he has this really potty sense of humour. Well, I'm *his* little Teddy Bear now.

(*beat*)

Please don't feel bitter and twisted and get tattooed or anything. I will, of course, pray for you. As will Don. Yours sincerely, Wendy.

JACK (VO)

I thought maybe I could sort it out when I went home for Christmas leave. But then *this* happened. With a capital 'H'.

DISSOLVE TO:

FILM EXCERPT: *'Bye, 'Bye, Baby'*

INT COMMANDER'S OFFICE – JSSL – DAY – 1953 (CONT)

Lt Comm. Bourgat is seated at his desk. Leo stands before him.

Bourgat is in his fifties, a little down at heel, with an air of resigned world-weariness, disappointment and futility. Ending his career in an army backwater in charge of coder specials is hardly the Captain Hornblower glory he once dreamt of.

BOURGAT

Now, laddie, what mob are you?

LEO

(*puzzled*)

'Mob', sir?

BOURGAT

Religion. Church of Turkey?

LEO

Jewish, sir.

BOURGAT

That the mob that don't eat meat on Fridays?

LEO

That's the Catholics, sir.

BOURGAT

Ah. So you're the ones who don't have Christmas, correct?

LEO

Yes, sir.

BOURGAT

Good. Well, here's the thing ...

He locates a memo on his desk.

Pongo standing orders. In its wisdom, the Army considers it vital to National Security to maintain a token force here – even though there's a public footpath running through the place and possibly a bloody picnic site, too, I shouldn't wonder – while everyone else is on Christmas leave, This force, for want of a better word, will comprise –

(*checks the memo*)

– all those under punishment, or no home to go to, or Jewish. I.e. the criminals, the vagrants and you.

A miserable silence.

LEO

My girlfriend was expecting me, sir.

BOURGAT

She should've joined the Wrens, then, lad. Dismiss.

As Leo salutes and goes ...

JACK (VO)

So I never did sort it out. A year or two later, she and Don got married. At the last count, I think, they had seven kids. I don't think the Pope has hiccoughed since.

EXT HMS ROYAL ALBERT LAND-BASE – CUXHAVEN – GERMANY – DAY – 1954

A snow-covered, frozen wasteland of an ex-U-boat base. Scores of aerials and radio masts sprout from a large watchroom.

A group of coders make their way into the watchroom, among them Leo and the Lads.

JACK (VO)

In addition to our hammock-rigging and insults-and-obscenities-yelling skills we were now blithely considered experts in Russian (i.e. just scraped through), cryptography (a three-day course), and Atomic, Biological and Chemical Warfare (a one-day course: atomic mastered in the morning,

biological and chemical in the afternoon) – and were shipped off to Germany.

INT WATCHROOM – HMS ROYAL ALBERT – CUXHAVEN – DAY – 1954 (CONT)

The walls are covered with maps of the Baltic and North Sea, charts of Soviet ships and submarines, and blackboards bearing Russian call signs.

Leading coder specials are seated three to a row at four benches of bays. Each of them is operating a B40 radio receiver and Ferrograph tape recorder. Before them are logging pads and pencils. They wear bulky headphones.

They've been on watch for almost four hours, swivelling their tuning dials through the manic wavebands, befuddled by listening to, recording and logging Russian naval messages through a welter of Polish weather forecasts, atmospherics, interference and Eartha Kitt.

A midshipman is explaining watchroom procedure to Leo's group of new-boy coders.

MIDSHIPMAN

... one man per bay in four-hour watches, 24 hours a day, covering all Soviet radio transmissions from sea and air centred on the Baltic and North Sea.

(*beat*)

If you want a reason why, suffice to say the Soviet Navy has 550 submarines and we have three. And we chaps, you and me, are the only ones stopping them marching down Oxford Street.

LEO

The *submarines*?

MIDSHIPMAN

Sorry?

INT TRAIN (TRAVELLING) – GERMANY – DAY – 1954

Leo and three other leading coder specials loll about in the compartment. Two of them have a sack of mail on the seat beside them, the other (and Leo) wears a white belt, a gun-holster and gaiters.

JACK (VO)

After six months watch-keeping, just as our brains were beginning to curdle, two of us were given new jobs. One was made the courier and I was the courier's guard. Each day the courier was to collect the mail in Hamburg, take it to HMS *Royal Albert* in Cuxhaven then go back to Hamburg. And I was to guard him – with my empty gun-holster.

(*beat*)

On our first day, the courier and guard we were replacing came with us to show us the ropes.

The train begins to slow down.

EXT PLATFORM – VILLAGE STATION – GERMANY – DAY – 1954 (CONT)

The train comes to a stop and three schoolgirls, satchels on their backs, board the train, in the coders' compartment.

INT TRAIN – GERMANY – DAY – 1954 (CONT)

As the schoolgirls come in, smiling:

LEO

Oy! Hoppit. This compartment's reserved.

The girls' smiles fall.

1ST CODER

No, s'okay, this is Emma and Helga and Elke. This is Mickey and Leo.

Mickey, the new courier, shakes their proffered hands. Leo avoids them.

2ND CODER

Come on, time for work. German to English first.

The girls take textbooks from their satchels, hand one of them to the two coders to share, then turn to an exercise.

ELKE

'Tomorrow if it will be rain, Johann to the zoo cannot go.'

1ST CODER

Hang on, hang on! 'Tomorrow, if it rains' or 'If it rains tomorrow.'

2ND CODER

'Johann cannot go to the zoo.' Remember, the object comes *after* the verb.

Leo watches, bewildered and ill at ease.

LEO

What's going on?

MICKEY

It's obvious.

HELGA

(*to 1st and 2nd coders*)

Your turn.

The coders concentrate on the text-book.

1ST CODER

Um ... *Aber was kann wir sonst machen, wenn es regnet? Sagt die Junge.*

The girls double up, laughing.

EMMA

Können wir! Not *Kann wir!*

ELKE

Also *'der' Junge*! *Die Junge* is not possible!

LEO

(*curtly*)

Would someone like to explain before I pull the communication cord?

2ND CODER

It's the routine. On their way home for dinner. They live a couple of villages down the line.

1ST CODER

The couriers before us did it, and the ones before them, and the ones before them. Always have.

2ND CODER

Ever since the end of the war. With these and the kids before these. And so on. Ten years.

1ST CODER

Non-stop.

LEO

(*brusquely*)

Want to bet?

1ST CODER

It's a tradition. Twenty minutes each day. We help with their English, they help with our German –

LEO

(*bitterly*)

Not with mine, they don't! Mine's perfect. *Sieg Heil, Donner-und-Blitzen, Arbeit Macht Frei verstunkene Juden!*

MICKEY

Leo, they weren't even bloody born!

LEO

They were lucky! Ask the poor sods who were!

Oblivious to the argument, Elke resumes her translation exercise.

ELKE

'Do not do a noise.' her father laughing said ...

1ST CODER

Stop there. 'Do not *make* a noise.' *Make*, not *do*. And 'laughing' should be 'laughingly', the adverb.

LEO

Ask her what *her* father did.

They all turn to stare at him. A pause.

1ST CODER

What?

LEO

In the war.

MICKEY

For Christ's sake, Leo!

LEO

(*to Elke*)

What did your father do in the war, little girl?

Elke is puzzled and frightened by his hostility.

ELKE

Bitte?

LEO

What did your father do in the war?

ELKE

(*a beat – then simply*)

Er starb. He died.

(*beat*)

Have I said correctly?

Leo's world turns inside out. Poleaxed by the opposite half of the truth. He stares at her.

INTERCUT between his face and hers.

ELKE

Are *you* a father? You have beard as father have.

Leo faces an agonising choice. Fighting tears, he then does what he doesn't want to do; but what, in the end, there's no alternative to doing. A pause, then quietly:

LEO

That should be: 'You have a beard like a father *has*.' 'Has' is singular, 'have' is plural. *Nein, ich nicht habe Kinder . . .*

The girls laugh at his bad German.

HELGA

'*Ich habe* keine *Kinder*!'

LEO

Ich habe keine Kinder. Ich bin selbst noch ein Kind.

The girls laugh.

EMMA

Nein! You are not yourself a child! *Du bist ein Mann*. You are a man!

A slow, sad smile from Leo. His eyes glisten with tears.

LEO
(*quietly*)

Danke.

EMMA
(*laughs*)

Bitte.

LEO

Thank you.

GIRLS

Please.

INT COMMANDER'S OFFICE – HMS DRAKE – PLYMOUTH – DAY – 1955

The last day of National Service. Leo and his fellow leading coders stand to attention in front of the commander, who's reading from a document. As CAM pans across their faces, trying to control their laughter:

COMMANDER

On behalf of the Admiralty and Her Majesty's Government, I would like to express their appreciation of your valuable contribution to the defence of the nation and its NATO allies and to world peace, in the branch of the Royal Navy in which you served.

The ex-coders embarrassedly mutter, 'You're welcome, me old mucker,' 'Not at all,' 'Don't mention it,' 'Our pleasure.'

JACK (VO)

And so we were demobbed. All with tears in our eyes because the happiest two years of our lives – that we'd hated every

minute of – were finally over. The freezing cold, the hunger, the bullying by idiots with stripes on their arms, the boredom, the inanity, the utter waste of two years of young men's lives . . .

(*beat*)

. . . Although, to be fair, on the other hand, not one Russian submarine ever did make it down Oxford Street . . .

DISSOLVE TO:

EXT 211 WOODSEND RD, FLIXTON, MANCHESTER – DAY – 1955

Home is Manchester again. Not the bleak streets of Cheetham Hill any more but the leafy suburb of Flixton.

An estate of uniform, quite attractive semis. At the end of it flows a stretch of the Manchester Ship Canal. Ocean-going cargo ships steam serenely past people's gardens.

Being a sunny summer Sunday afternoon, all the neighbours are out, the air filled with the rattle of lawnmowers and the slap of soapy chamois leathers on Morris Minors parked in each driveway.

In the Rosenthal garden, Sam sits snoring in a deckchair, his face covered with the Reynolds News. *His system for getting a suntan is to avoid the sun. Lakey's system is more technical. Fortified by her favourite midday snack of slices of orange, sprinkled with sugar – in a sandwich – she's on her hands and knees weeding a flower-bed, her upraised bottom aimed at the heavens. Both systems produced deeply burnished faces.*

Jack, in civvies, is mowing the lawn. David is a permanent absentee; now married to Eileen, his Irish girlfriend, they've stayed behind in Colne.

The newspaper blows off Sam's face. Jack picks it up. On the back page is a photograph of Taylor of Manchester United scoring a goal.

EXT MAINE RD FOOTBALL GROUND – MANCHESTER – NIGHT – 1955

LIBRARY FOOTAGE of a Manchester United floodlit football match in progress.

Flixton is only three miles or so from Manchester City's football ground, which United shares while its bomb-damaged Old Trafford is being rebuilt.

Jack is on the terraces, resuming his love affair with United – the joyous Busby Babes, teasing, caressing the (then) beautiful game with a Brazilian brio, a playful panache. Eleven kids having the time of their lives beating the opposition, irresistibly, cockily and, above all, entertainingly. Demolishing

First Division teams, FA Cup opponents and famously, a year from now, the Belgian champions, Anderlecht, in the European Cup, 10–0.

It's hard not to wax lyrical about them – as the bizarre Manchester United Calypso proved . . .

WEST INDIAN SINGING (VO)

Manchester, Manchester,
Manchester United,
A bunch of bouncing Busby Babes,
They deserve to be knighted,
Whenever they're playin' in your town,
Go 'long down to the football groun',
Take a lesson, go to see,
Football taught by Matt Busby,
And Manchester, Manchester, Manchester United,
The team that gets me excited, Manchester United!

JACK (VO)

No, not Richard Rodgers, but, to me, as stirring as *Oklahoma*! And the memory of those players still stirs – Byrne, Edwards, Blanchflower, Colman, Berry, Whelan, Violett, Taylor – well, all of them. Artists, all of them.

EXT MARKET STREET – MANCHESTER – DAY – 1955

Jack walks down the busy shopping street.

JACK (VO)

For the last year of National Service, I'd had this ambition. To buy myself the perfect symbol of Civvy Street. No more dirty and slovenly naval uniform to wear on parade. Instead the most civilian of *civilian* uniforms.

He goes into a shop: Dunne's, Hat-Makers.

INT DUNNE'S SHOP – MANCHESTER – DAY – 1955 (CONT)

Jack is trying on a bowler hat. Dark brown, curly brim, jaunty as hell. But still a bowler. In 1955, it isn't considered an old man's hat. More a young *man's old man's hat. And he looks absolutely ridiculous.*

The counter is littered with bowlers he's already tried on and rejected. Behind the counter, a young salesman is going through agonies trying not to laugh. His veins throb, his face turns puce, he looks as if he might burst. Jack sighs in defeat.

JACK

P'raps I'll not bother, eh?

He takes the bowler off and puts it with the others. Years later – after A Clockwork Orange *and* The Avengers *– he could say he was years ahead of his time. But he'd still have looked ridiculous.*

Thanks for your help.

He goes. The salesman clutches the counter and squeaks in relief.

INT OFFICE – OSBORNE PEACOCK'S – MANCHESTER – DAY – 1955

Jack sprawls at a desk, dividing his time between doodling on a foolscap pad and looking at his watch.

JACK (VO)

To pay for the mortgage on our Flixton house (£5 a week), I got my first job the minute I was demobbed. In those days you could. High unemployment belonged to different decades. In the fifties you took your pick.

I was now a junior copywriter in an advertising agency. Which meant, on that first morning, that I'd nothing to do.

He checks his watch again, gets up, collects his raincoat from a coat stand and leaves the office.

So, at ten to twelve, I went to lunch.

INT LANDING OUTSIDE OSBORNE PEACOCK'S – MANCHESTER – DAY – 1955 (CONT)

Struggling into his raincoat, Jack comes out of a door bearing a plaque reading 'Osborne Peacock Ltd'.

A young woman is coming up the stairs from the street. She sees him.

YOUNG WOMAN

'Scuse me. Do you work there?

JACK

Um . . . yeah.

YOUNG WOMAN

Only I need an advert doing.

JACK

Uh-huh.

YOUNG WOMAN

Just a sentence in *Popular Gardening* to sell my garden gnomes.

JACK

Um . . . well, the thing is I don't think agencies do little ones like that. They talk in hundreds of pounds. Thousands, even. This'd be about twelve and six. They'd get about one and thruppence commission.

YOUNG WOMAN

(*disappointed*)

Oh, flip.

(*beat*)

Will *you* do it for me? The wording and that. For one and thruppence?

JACK

S'alright. I'll do it for nothing.

He takes out a pen from his top pocket and a folded copy of Advertiser's Weekly *from his coat. As they discuss the ad, he jots down notes on his magazine. During this:*

JACK (VO)

It wasn't *quite* for nothing. I wrote her sentence and sent it to *Popular Gardening*. They sent me a free copy for the next eight years. Not bad for my first morning. Not that I ever read them.

INT KARDOMAH CAFE – MANCHESTER – DAY – 1955

Jack at a table, eating an eggs-on-toast lunch. He's reading an article on the front page of Advertiser's Weekly *propped up against a cruet.*

JACK (VO)

***This* magazine had a bigger impact on my life. The biggest. In it was a piece about something called Granada TV that was planned to go on the air in a year or so, in Manchester, as part of the commercial ITV network.**

EXT WASTE GROUND – WATER STREET – MANCHESTER – DAY – 1955

A rubbish dump tip in a derelict bombsite of muddy puddles, scrap iron and nettles.

Looking forlorn in the middle of it is a small, wooden green hut.

JACK (VO)

But, for now, this hut was all there was of Granada. Inside it was Granada's sole employee, Jim Phoenix, its Northern Administrator.

The article said that Jim was getting a hundred letters a week from people applying for jobs – as anything from typists to transmission controllers. I wrote and asked him did he mind getting letter 101 . . .

INT GREEN HUT – WATER STREET – MANCHESTER – DAY – 1955 (CONT)

Jim Phoenix, late forties, tall, dark, bespectacled, with a rich, Deryk Guyler Scouse voice, sits at one side of a primus stove, Jack at the other. On the stove is a boiling kettle. Jim pours two mugs of tea.

JIM PHOENIX

So how's that sound, son? You join our graduate training scheme, called 'Getting to Know Granada'. You go down to London for a year. Work in the theatres – which is posh for cinemas – then come back for when the TV station goes on the air. Fancy it?

JACK

Yeah. Okay. Thank you.

JIM PHOENIX

Good. Now, then, do you take milk and sugar?

JACK (VO)

Like so many future Granada colleagues, Jim became a mate and a mentor. A man to look up to in both senses. Ten-foot tall executives seemed compulsory at Granada.

EXT CLAPHAM JUNCTION STATION – LONDON – DAY – 1955

Jack, suitcase in hand, disembarks from a train.

JACK (VO)

The day Granada offered me a job at £8 a week, Vantona Textiles offered me one as a shirt salesman for a pound more. I said yes to Granada and started work at Clapham Junction. No, not the station –

EXT GRANADA CLAPHAM JUNCTION THEATRE – LONDON – DAY – 1955

Jack and a smartly besuited middle-aged man, the manager of the theatre, Mr Longthorn, are fixing posters into the wall display cabinets. The film is Love is a Many-Splendored Thing . . .

JACK (VO)

– the cinema. Acting Trainee Manager to Mr Longthorn.

MR LONGTHORN

Now, Jack. Job for you. Watch this tonight with the audience. Then tell me what happens seven minutes from the end.

JACK

In the picture, like?

MR LONGTHORN

In the *audience*. I *know* what happens in the picture, I saw it this morning. I also know what'll happen in the audience, but I want you to see for yourself. Okay? Seven minutes from the end.

INT AUDITORIUM – GRANADA CLAPHAM JUNCTION – LONDON – NIGHT – 1955

Jack sits in the stalls of a packed house. The film is playing. He looks at his watch – seven minutes to go.

On the screen Jennifer Jones stands on a hill . . . then, suddenly, she 'sees' William Holden – even though he's been killed earlier. Just as suddenly he vanishes again.

At that moment the music of Love is a Many-Splendored Thing *heartbreakingly swells . . . and also at that moment, among the audience, scores of handbags snap open for scores of handkerchieves to come rustling out, then snap closed again. Scores of female eyes are patted, scores of female noses are blown and scores of male throats are harrumphingly cleared. The noise almost drowns the music.*

INT AUDITORIUM – GRANADA CLAPHAM JUNCTION – LONDON – DAY – 1955

The auditorium is now filled with screaming, wrestling kids scrambling over seats at the children's matinee. All of them ignoring Jack, onstage, wearing an allegedly funny hat and jacket.

JACK (VO)

Another of my jobs was being Uncle Mac at the kids' matinee; another was queue-organiser-in-chief outside the theatre, another was having to come up with ideas to save the theatre £10 a week expenditure (then an additional £10 the next week, then the next, then the next – till expenditure was down to zero and it cost nothing to run a theatre). I was also expected to inspect the theatre's public facilities and report on them once a quarter to Mr Cecil (Bernstein) at Granada's head office in Golden Square . . .

INT GRANADA BOARDROOM – GOLDEN SQUARE – LONDON – DAY – 1955

Immaculately groomed Mr Cecil, short, balding, hook-nosed; two or three executives and a nervous Jack are seated at the boardroom table.

Tasteful, avant-garde works of art are on the walls.

MR CECIL
Public facilities. Clapham. Any of them impressed you?

JACK
(*overdoing it several tads*)
Oh, absolutely, Mr Cecil! Tons.

MR CECIL
For example?

JACK
The gents' toilets. The redecoration in the gents' is terrific!

He's on safe ground here. The gents' toilets have been very recently redecorated to a typically high Granada standard.

MR CECIL
(*pleased*)
Good. I agree. Any criticisms?

JACK
Um . . . I don't think so . . .

It occurs to him that they'd like *him to be critical. Being critical shows true executive material.*

Well, yes, I suppose. Just one.

He invents one out of nothing.

The *ladies'* toilets. Pity they haven't been redecorated as well.

He's on somewhat shakier ground now. He's never even seen the ladies' toilets. They're all staring at him, puzzled. He starts to protest too much.

They're a bit of a disgrace, actually.

Yes, he's gone too far.

MR CECIL
(*now not so pleased*)
Really? Interesting. Since they were redecorated at the same time as the gents', in exactly the same style.

JACK (VO)
Which gave rise to the old proverb, 'If you've nothing to say, keep your trap shut.'

EXT GRANADA TV STUDIOS – MANCHESTER – DAY – 1956

The green hut has gone. In its place, an office block and the world's newest, shiniest, state-of-the-art six-studio TV complex.

JACK (VO)

May 1956. As promised in the *Advertiser's Weekly* two years before, commercial television's baby was born – and I was back in Manchester for the circumcision.

INT OFFICES AND CORRIDORS – GRANADA TV STUDIOS – DAY – 1956

Arguably, the most exciting place on Earth.

Bright young things bustle in and out of the offices, clipboards clutched in hand and stopwatches bouncing on bosom.

The air clangs in a babel of colliding accents – Cambridge, Cockney, Canadian, Knightsbridge, with the odd bit of Ardwick thrown in.

The corridors shimmer with legendary, yellow-corduroyed whizzkids of West End stage and Silver Screen discussing Life and Art.

Phones ring everywhere. Typewriters clatter.

From one office a voice yells, 'But that's how we always did it in Toronto!' From another, swell the sweeping strains of a violin being played by a director who hasn't to be disturbed because he's 'thinking'.

EXT NEW THEATRE PUB – MANCHESTER – NIGHT – 1956

Employees make their way across the road from Granada to the pub.

JACK (VO)

And the excitement went on well after hometime.

INT NEW THEATRE PUB – MANCHESTER – NIGHT – 1956 – (CONT)

It's packed with Granada employees, hormones running riot. Jack stands at the bar, agog.

JACK (VO)

The New Theatre pub crackled with passions and ideas and anecdotes. But mostly with passions. Like a sort of Mancunian Club Med with clothes on. Everyone threw parties for everyone else. Romances blossomed and withered. *Songs for Swinging Lovers* had a hell of a lot to answer for.

EXT GRANADA TV STUDIOS – DAY – 1956

A taxi is parked outside. Jack is heaving boxes labelled 'Toilet-roll holders' out of it, and onto the steps of the main entrance.

JACK (VO)

After completing the Granada graduates' course – the only one to do so, since I was the only one ever to even start it, since, as I later found out, it didn't really exist – the job I was given was in the Buying Department. I lasted for one day. And at lunchtime . . .

INT CANTEEN – GRANADA TV – DAY – MAY 6TH, 1956

Original contemporary works of art adorn the walls – yes, even of a canteen. The room is filled with every Granada employee. Standing facing them is Granada's chairman, Sidney Bernstein, otherwise known as Mr Sidney, but mostly as SLB.

He's a leonine, silver-haired, giant of a man, bursting with ferocious energy, radiating charisma. A strong, chiselled face with a boxer's broken nose. Beautifully groomed. (Rumour has it he changes his entire outfit twice a day.)

He's in mid-speech, a rallying cry – and threat *– to the troops before Agincourt. Today is Day One, the day Granada goes on the air for the first time.*

SLB

. . . and, together, starting tonight, we'll make Granada the best TV station in Britain. The best programmes, the best progamme-*makers*. That means every one of *you*.

(*beat*)

Now. You'll find that Granada has a way of doing things. If you don't like it, tell us *your* way. If we reject it, hard luck, we'll continue doing it our way, whether you like it or not. And so will you.

(*an ominous beat*)

If any of you are unhappy with that, you can leave right now.

He pauses. No one moves a muscle.

AN OFFICE DOOR – GRANADA TV – DAY – MAY 7TH, 1956

The morning after the night before, Granada's first night on the air.

CAM tracks slowly towards the door.

JACK (VO)

The next morning when we all turned up for work, there was a card Sellotaped to the door of every office, every department. On it, in Mr Sidney's handwriting was –

CAM reaches a CU of a card on the door. It reads: 'Thanks. It was a wow! SLB'.

INT JIM PHOENIX'S OFFICE – GRANADA TV – DAY – 1956

The green hut is now a spacious, executive office. The primus stove a spacious, executive desk. Jim and Jack talk across it, affably as ever.

JIM PHOENIX

Okay, you leave the Buying Department as of now, and you split your week between *two* jobs. One's the Promotion Department, writing programme trailers for the announcers to read over slides, beginning with the station call sign.

A SLIDE of Granada's logo – an arrow pointing upwards to the words 'Granada TV'.

ANNOUNCER'S VOICE

From the North, this is Granada.

JACK (VO)

That took 3½ seconds to speak. With every second of a commercial break costing fortunes, every half-second counted.

INT PROMOTION DEPT – GRANADA TV – DAY – 1956

Jack sits at a desk typing promotion scripts. The door opens and Geoffrey Lancashire comes in, hangs up his coat and sits at another desk to start typing. They exchange greetings.

CU Geoff.

JACK (VO)

Geoffrey Lancashire was an ex-journalist, and was now head of the two-man Promotion Department. This meant he could start work when he felt like it, and since he didn't often feel like it, that's what he did.

(*beat*)

Like me, Geoff was buck-toothed, but somehow, unlike in my case, girls seemed to find that attractive. He was red-hot at his job . . . and with girls, too. Again like me, he later became a *Coronation Street* writer and the writer of comedy series and plays.

(*beat*)

From the first day we became best pals. And stayed best pals for many years. For five of them I was a lodger at his house in Oldham, where he lived with his wife, Hilda, their toddler son, John, and newborn twins, Simon and Sarah. Apart from

lodger I was also official Uncle Jack to the kids – particularly Sarah. Eventually, five-year-old Sarah used to play at being my secretary. I don't want to sound over-critical but she was a lousy secretary. Okay, okay, I know she was only five, but she was as thick as a *forest* of short planks.

(*beat*)

On the other hand, maybe it was all a brilliantly clever act. She was the same Sarah Lancashire who became the successful TV actress.

INT RESEARCH DEPT – GRANADA TV – DAY – 1956

Barrie Heads, sprightly energy in every move, is speaking crisply into the phone. Jack is wearily skimming through all the day's newspapers.

JACK (VO)

My other job was in the Research Department which was run by Barrie Heads, another ex-journalist, fast-talking, fast-working. Me, I was as slow as my five-year-old secretary. Researcher seemed to be a posh word for dogsbody. And research seemed to mean whatever Granada's producers and directors wanted it to mean . . .

THE SCREEN SPLITS INTO SIX MINI-SCREENS:

ON SCREEN ONE:

A glider aircraft takes off from Barton Airport.

JACK (VO)

Research meant me writing naive little scripts for afternoon outside-broadcast documentaries on fascinating, exotic subjects like Barton Airport and –

The shot of the aircraft mixes to a shot of a canal.

Manchester Ship Canal, narrowboats and Liverpool Docks.

Meanwhile . . .

ON SCREEN TWO:

Jack is buying a book in a St Anne's Square bookshop.

JACK (VO)

Research also meant buying a book on Chinese neck-rests, for which I got a bollocking for spending £2 when I could've got it at the library for nothing. Meanwhile . . .

ON SCREEN THREE:

Jack is buying a ticket at a Manchester railway station ticket office.

JACK (VO)

Research meant travelling to Aberystwyth to interview a Welsh Nationalist – for which I got a bollocking for going by train when, for about ten times the cost, I could've gone by taxi. Meanwhile . . .

ON SCREEN FOUR:

A studio audience is firing angry questions at a big TV screen on which they can see a politician in a London studio. Robin Day is the chairman. Robin Day, bespectacled, bow-tied, at the height of his powers as a political interviewer.

JACK (VO)

Research meant finding rational, articulate, responsible citizens to question politicians on burning issues of the day.

Suddenly a man leaps up from his seat in the audience, runs up to Robin Day and starts punching him violently in the face. His trademark bow-tie squirts skew-whiffily to his ear. Stagehands and other members of the audience race to both men's aid, and it becomes a free-for-all. Meanwhile . . .

ON SCREEN FIVE:

Jack is chatting to Derek Dooley, walking with a crutch around Sheffield Wednesday's ground.

JACK (VO)

Research also meant preparing a dossier for a documentary on Sheffield – since I was regarded as the Sheffield expert. It did give me the chance to meet my erstwhile hero, Derek Dooley, but Barrie rejected the dossier on the grounds that it was about as exciting as the ship canal. And meanwhile . . .

ON SCREEN SIX:

A coach is driving through the Welsh countryside.

CUT TO:

The COACH INTERIOR, *which is packed with men, women and children. Jack stands in the aisle at the front addressing them fervently.*

JACK (VO)

Research meant going to Capel Celyn, a tiny village in north Wales, which was threatened with drowning by Liverpool City Council building a reservoir on its land. I got the entire population to come to Granada to confront the reservoir planners – no passing burglars seemed to notice.

The villagers start singing.

Barrie told me to whip them into a frenzy by getting them to sing martial, patriotic songs. My suggestion of 'Men of Harlech' got nowhere. It seemed there was only me who knew the words. They finished up singing 'You are My Sunshine', and on the programme they were sweetness itself to the life-threatening Liverpudlians. On the journey home, I whipped them into another frenzy singing 'Mairzy Doats and Doazy Doats'.

THE SIX SCREENS SPLINTER INTO 24:

JACK (VO)

Research, of course, meant anything and everything. Since it was obvious I wasn't a natural, I moved across the fifth-floor corridor to be full time in the Promotion Department.

(*beat*)

To take my place came two fresh-faced young turks. Two. One was Dave Plowright, who would go on to become Granada's managing director. The other was Jeremy Isaacs, who would go on to become chief executive of Channel 4. Maybe I wasn't all that bad.

EXT WEMBLEY STADIUM – LONDON – DAY – 1957

LIBRARY FOOTAGE of the Aston Villa v. Manchester United Cup Final.

From the terraces, Jack watches Aston Villa cheat the Babes out of a League and Cup double. McParland splinters the United goalie's cheekbone in a ferocious misjudged shoulder charge early in the game.

Substitutes aren't allowed, so centre-half Jackie Blanchflower goes in goal, and Wood, the goalie, concussed, in pain, and barely able to walk let alone run, stands uselessly on the wing.

United play superbly, heroically – and, football being football, lose 2–1.

Then, eight months later:

INT CORRIDOR – GRANADA TV – 1958

Jack is walking down the corridor. Striding purposefully towards him is a squarely built, young German woman, Ursula. She's a senior programme assistant who works on Granada's news programmes. She looks solemn. As they're about to pass each other:

JACK

Hi, Ursula.

URSULA

(*a trace of a German accent*)

I've just had a call from ITN. They're extending their news programme. Something about a football team in an accident.

JACK
(an ominous beat)
What kind of accident?

URSULA
Aircraft. In Munich. A couple of them dead, they think.

She walks on. Jack stands, shaken.

JACK (VO)
It was February the 6th, 1958. Ursula was wrong about a couple being dead. Almost the entire Manchester United team – *my* team, the Busby Babes – was dead.

INT WEDDING RECEPTION – MANCHESTER – DAY – 1958

Johnny, Jack's pal from their National Service days, drink in hand, carnation in buttonhole, stands talking solemnly to Jack, Jimmy and other male guests. His bride, Margaret, in her white gown, stands talking to her bridesmaids. An air of deep sadness.

JACK (VO)
A few days later, my Navy oppo, Johnny, got married. Like almost everyone at the wedding, he was a fanatical United supporter. And those who weren't were still Mancunians. We were all still stricken, still in shock. Devastated. Poor Johnny's wedding was like a wake.

EXT CITY STREETS – MANCHESTER – NIGHT – 1958

A cortege of coffins drives slowly from Ringway Airport to Old Trafford – six or more miles – past pavements crammed deep with silent Mancunians, men, women and children, United supporters, City supporters, people who've never watched a game in their lives.

Silent as silent tears fall, as throats tighten, as strangers' eyes meet bleakly, briefly, hoping somehow for comfort that doesn't exist.

JACK (VO)
Tears from me, too, now, half a century later. Tears for what? The pointless waste? The grotesque mutilation of something beautiful? Transience? Mortality itself? The loss of their youth? The loss of ours?

EXT OLD TRAFFORD – MANCHESTER – NIGHT – 1958

Jack stands on the terraces before the kick-off of a rearranged cup tie against Sheffield Wednesday.

It's only a matter of days since the Munich tragedy. Jack looks at the programme.

ANGLE ON programme. On one page it lists all the names of the Sheffield Wednesday players. The facing page, intended to list the United players, is heartbreakingly blank.

DISSOLVE TO:

EXT GRANADA TV STUDIOS – DAY – 1958

Geoff is standing outside the entrance to the building talking and laughing with an eighteen-year-old girl – except she only gives an impression of being a real girl: she's blurred and out of focus, a hazy, two-dimensional cut-out.

Jack comes down the street towards the studios. As he reaches Geoff and Geoff's companion:

GEOFF

Hello, mate.

JACK

Hi. Been for some fags.

GEOFF

(*to the girl*)

This is Jack. Pal of mine.

(*to Jack*)

This is Maxine.

DISSOLVE TO:

INT CHINESE RESTAURANT – LONDON – NIGHT – 1989

Thirty-one years later. Jack is 58. He's eating a Chinese meal with his wife, Maureen, and his children, Amy, fifteen years old, and Adam, thirteen.

AMY

In my class at school, I'm almost the only one whose mum and dad haven't been married before. Or one of them.

JACK

Really?

Pause. Maureen looks at Jack. He continues eating.

Almost the only one? Fancy.

Another pause. She looks at him again. Coughs.

MAUREEN

Er . . . Daddy was.

JACK

Who?

MAUREEN

You.

JACK

Was I?

(*beat*)

Bloody hell! You're right!

Amy and Adam stare at him in shock.

MAUREEN
(*to the kids*)
Your dad's been married before, pass the seaweed.

AMY
(*tears pricking*)

He hasn't!

ADAM

I don't believe it!

AMY
He was married to someone else?

MAUREEN
(*amused*)
He was married to someone else. Maxine.

Amy screws up her face in disgust.

AMY

'Maxine'?

ADAM

What was she like?

JACK

I can't remember.

AMY
You must remember *something*.

JACK

Not much.

AMY
You've never, ever mentioned her!

JACK
There's never been anything to mention.

ADAM

What did she look like?

JACK

Reddish hair . . . It's all a bit vague. It's a long time ago. It was only for a couple of years.

AMY

You married this Maxine woman?

JACK

I believe I did, yes.

AMY

And you can't remember her?

JACK

I will. I'll try.

MAUREEN

(*enjoying every minute*)

Come on, kids, eat up.

ADAM

I don't want to now.

AMY

I feel sick.

(*to Maureen*)

I could understand it if *you* were the one who'd been married before.

Maureen laughs and tucks into her duck. Amy, Adam and, most of all, Jack have lost their appetites.

DISSOLVE TO:

EXT WILSON ADVERTISING – MANCHESTER – 1958

Jim Phoenix, briefcase in hand, walks into the entrance of a Victorian building, the home of Wilson Advertising.

JACK (VO)

The fifties frogmarched us to a close, in our all-the-rage Italian shoes, strolling down Deansgate to Manchester's only nightspot, the Mokarlo Coffee Bar (yes, coffee bar). And Jim Phoenix left Granada to become the managing director of an advertising agency. He promptly offered me a job as a copywriter. Negotiating my salary was like an Abbott and Costello comedy sketch.

INTERCUT between:

INT JIM PHOENIX'S OFFICE – WILSON ADVERTISING – MANCHESTER – DAY

Jim, at his desk, speaking into his phone . . .

AND:

INT PROMOTION DEPT – GRANADA TV – DAY – 1958 (CONT)

Jack, at his desk, speaking into his phone . . .

JIM PHOENIX

Eighteen quid a week.

JACK

(*unable to believe his luck*)

Eighteen?

JIM PHOENIX

(*thinking Jack's disappointed*)

Okay, then, bugger. Twenty.

JACK

(*ecstatic*)

Are you kidding?

JIM PHOENIX

(*again misunderstanding*)

22, then. And not a penny more. You're going to whinge again, aren't you? Alright, then, 24.

JACK

Done!

INT PROMOTION DEPT – GRANADA TV – DAY – 1959

Geoff is typing away, Jack is showing promotion slides to his replacement in the department, a fortnight before he is due to clear his desk so that he can show him the ropes. The replacement has exploded into the office – and into our lives.

He is young, tall, willowy, outrageously witty, bubbling with infectious energy. And simmering and shimmering with something more. A couple of years later we found out what. Genius.

JACK (VO)

His name was destined to be seen more times than any other on British television screens. Say, at a rough guess, 5,000 times and climbing.

(*beat*)

His screen credit would read 'Created by Tony Warren'. What he was soon to create was *Coronation Street.*

(beat)

Shortly afterwards he and his street would change my life completely.

(beat)

And Maxine would try her damnedest to.

THE SIXTIES

A BLACK-AND-WHITE TV SET – 1960

On it we see a scene from episode 1 of Coronation Street: *Ena Sharples haranguing Florrie Lindley in the corner shop.*

The programme is unique. It explodes on the consciousness of its millions of viewers – and on the nation itself.

Real, rooted, three-dimensional characters, vivid dialogue, comedy and drama sculpted out of ordinary (i.e., as ever, extraordinary*) lives.*

The most colourful black-and-white pictures television has ever seen . . .

INT WILSON ADVERTISING – MANCHESTER – DAY – 1960

Jack paces the office, excitedly dialling a number on his phone. Jim Phoenix pops his head round the door.

JIM

Tell him 'Well done' from me. *Bloody* well done.

He goes.

JACK

(*into phone*)

Tony?

(*beat*)

Jack.

INT PROMOTION DEPT – GRANADA TV – DAY – 1960 (CONT)

Geoff is working at his desk. Tony Warren is taking Jack's call.

TONY

Hiya.

INTERCUT between the two offices, as required.

JACK

Listen. I watched it last night. Bloody brilliant. Sensational.

TONY

Did Lakey like it? Sod everyone else.

JACK

Lakey, Sam, the dog, Jim Phoenix, everybody. Are Granada pleased?

TONY

Chuffed to little mint balls. I've just come from a meeting with Harry Elton and all the bigwigs. They reckon it might run for more than the thirteen episodes I've written. P'raps.

JACK (VO)

They were right. It's been running for almost 5,000 episodes . . . over forty-odd years.

JACK

Fingers crossed.

TONY

So the thing is – they may want a whole team of writers apart from me. They'll have to do a fifteen-minute trial script and if Harry Elton likes it, and Harry Kershaw and *me*, they'll commission a full episode. Do you fancy having a go?

JACK (VO)

Did I! **He was handing me the biggest, luckiest break a hopeful writer could've dreamt of. If I'd never worked at Granada . . . If I'd never met Tony . . . If I'd never known the two Harrys. If. It's a big word alright. No wonder Kipling wrote a poem about it.**

INT STATIONERY SHOP – MANCHESTER – DAY – 1960

Jack is at the counter buying a typewriter. It's a £25, cast-iron, manual, Olympia portable. Forty-three years from now, though slightly pitted with rust, it'll still be in almost *working order.*

EXT GRANADA TV STUDIOS – DAY – 1960

Jack runs into the building, typewriter (in its case) in hand.

INT TYPING POOL – GRANADA TV – DAY – 1960

A large open-plan office where seven or eight typists sit at their desks, clattering away at their typewriters.

Mrs Dickson, in her forties, the doyenne of the typing pool, is a maternally indulgent pal of Jack's from his Granada days. Jack is cadging foolscap paper from her. She gives him an old-fashioned look.

MRS DICKSON

A fifteen-minute pretend *Coronation Street*. That's about eighteen pages.

She starts counting out sheets of foolscap.

JACK

Hang on, though. Plus two carbon copies and one for me. That's three times eighteen, that's . . . um . . .

MRS DICKSON

Fifty-four.

She starts counting out 54 sheets.

JACK

Except that I may make typing errors and bugger up a few pages.

MRS DICKSON

You're trying to cadge a whole ream, aren't you?

JACK

If the truth were told.

She drops a packeted ream onto the desk.

MRS DICKSON

You know you don't work here any more, don't you?

JACK

Um . . . The carbon copies that were mentioned . . .

MRS DICKSON

What about them?

JACK

I haven't got any carbon paper.

She slams a packet of carbon paper on top of the ream of foolscap.

MRS DICKSON

You wouldn't like me to write it for you, by any chance?

Jack seems to consider this. She slaps a packet of paper clips on top of the carbon paper.

With the compliments of the management. Before I get fired.

INT JACK'S BEDROOM – FLIXTON – NIGHT – 1960

Jack is at a desk, lit by a desk lamp. He pulls a title page of foolscap and three of carbon from his brand-new typewriter. They read Coronation Street: Trial script.

He threads four more sheets of foolscap interleaved with carbon paper into the typewriter. He sits, deep in thought, then suddenly seems about to attack the keys. At the last second, he pulls his hands back and resumes his deep thinking. Again his fingers shoot towards the keys, then stop again. More thinking.

Then, finally, very tentatively, he starts typing the first scene . . .

EXT GRANADA TV STUDIOS – DAY – 1960

Jack walks soberly out of the entrance and starts up the street towards St Peter's Square.

JACK (VO)

Tony's street was right up *my* street. His fictional characters were the factual ones I'd lived with all my life. I passed the trial.

Abruptly, he leaps in the air and clicks his heels.

And got my reward. Episode 30, to be transmitted in January 1961.

He breaks into a half-run, half-tap dance, chanting to himself:

JACK

I'm a writer, I'm a writer, I'm a writer . . .

Passers-by give him a wide berth. Modesty forbids him chanting, 'And they're paying me a hundred pounds.'

INT JACK'S BEDROOM – FLIXTON – NIGHT – 1960

Jack, at his desk, types the last page and the word 'End'.

JACK (VO)

I thought I'd written a masterpiece. A minor, if not as near-as-dammit major, work of art. I was wrong. I read it now, and it's truly terrible. There's one good line in it: Ena says –

IMMEDIATE CUT TO:

FILM EXCERPT: *Coronation Street*

TV SCREEN: INT THE STUDIO SET OF THE SNUG – ROVER'S RETURN – NIGHT – 1961

Ena, Minnie and Martha at their table, with their glasses of stout.

ENA

Folk round 'ere know nowt. One walk down t'canal bank and they think they're charting the Ganges.

IMMEDIATE CUT TO:

INT JACK'S BEDROOM – FLIXTON – NIGHT – 1960

Jack, at his desk. He collates his copies, straightens the bottom one (i.e. the least legible, i.e. his), clips the pages together and puts them on an empty shelf above the desk.

JACK (VO)

The line was suggested by Geoff Lancashire who later became a prolific *Coronation Street* writer himself. In it went.

INT CORRIDOR – GRANADA TV – DAY – 1961

Jack almost sleepwalks along, his now-printed script in hand. He's trembling with nerves and excitement. His face twitching between panicky apprehension and cocky anticipation. He *thinks he looks nonchalant. He opens a door to a rehearsal room.*

INT REHEARSAL ROOM – GRANADA TV – DAY – 1961 (CONT)

The first day of rehearsals of episode 30.

In Jack comes. Seated in a semi-circle before him, watching his distinctly chalant entrance, is the cast of Coronation Street. *A matter of weeks after Tony's initial episode, theirs have become the most famous faces on television, the most famous in the land: Violet Carson (Ena Sharples), Pat Phoenix (Elsie Tanner), Philip Lowrie (Dennis Tanner), Eileen Derbyshire (Miss Nugent), Doris Speed (Annie Walker), Lynne Carol (Martha Longhurst), Margot Bryant (Minnie Caldwell) . . . all of them. Jack's legs turn to water.*

He sits at a table with the director and his PA, facing the cast. The director introduces him. He pipes, 'Good morning,' a couple of octaves above his normal speaking voice. The director then nods to his PA.

DIRECTOR

Start the watch.

Click. She starts her stopwatch. This is it. The read-through. The real thing. For Jack, the world stops spinning. The most beautiful words in the language are about to be breathed into life . . .

DISSOLVE TO:

INT REHEARSAL ROOM – GRANADA TV – DAY – 1961

Roughly 26 minutes later.

The last line of dialogue is spoken.

DIRECTOR
(*to his PA*)

Stop the watch.

Click. It's all over. For Jack, the world starts creakily spinning again. He smiles diffidently at the cast, wondering whether they'll break into applause and shout, 'Author!' They manage to restrain themselves.

DIRECTOR
(*to his PA*)

How was it for time?

Each episode has to last 24½ minutes.

PA

A bit too long.

DIRECTOR

How *much* too long?

Jack Haworth, who plays the curmudgeonly misery-guts Albert Tatlock, wobbles his jowls . . .

JACK HAWORTH

About 24½ minutes.

INT JACK'S BEDROOM – FLIXTON – NIGHT – 1961

In FAST MOTION Jack types and adds more Coronation Street *scripts to the one on the shelf.*

JACK (VO)

Misery-Guts was wrong. More *Coronation Street* commissions followed. Then more and more.

He adds six Bulldog Breed *scripts to the others on the shelf. This is a comedy series, suggested by a* Coronation Street *producer, Derek Granger, so bad (or 'before its time' according to Derek) that it was taken off the air after four episodes.*

LIBRARY FOOTAGE – *THAT WAS THE WEEK THAT WAS* – 1962

In a BBC studio, Millicent Martin sings the title song.

JACK (VO)

Absolutely *of* its time was the iconoclastic satirical show *TW3*. Every Thursday, I telephoned a sketch down the line to David Frost at the BBC. Saturday night the show was transmitted live.

The sketches were all a spin-off of monologues for Kenneth Cope, who played Minnie Caldwell's nephew in 'the Street'.

Twenty-five years later Ken brought a script of his own round to show me in Muswell Hill. I said what I thought were encouraging words and made some suggestions and he went away. I never heard from him again until I received word that because of my 'treatment of his script' he had given up writing for ever. He would never forgive me. I was utterly nonplussed.

INT HARRY DRIVER'S LIVING ROOM – MANCHESTER – DAY – 1962

A modest semi-detached house.

Harry Driver, in his late twenties, sits in a wheelchair. He's been paralysed for some years. His thumb and head are the only parts of his body he can move.

Jack sits opposite him, writing in pen on a page of foolscap.

Seated beside Harry is Jack Ripley, in his early thirties, his loyal, hard-working secretary, nurse and amanuensis.

Harry is a storyline writer with Coronation Street, *shaping all the ideas dreamed-up at the three-weekly story conferences into synopses of twelve scenes for each episode.*

*An ex-stand-up comedian, he's a funny, courageously cheerful, gag-a-minute, lovable man. He and Vince Powell (gag-a-*second*) were the comedy-writing team who created* The Harry Worth Show *and, eventually,* Never Mind the Quality, Feel The Width *and many more.*

Jack stops writing to have a smoke. He takes a cigarette from its packet – and taps the end of it twice on the back of the packet.

HARRY
(*yelling*)

Don't! I can't stand it!

JACK
(*blankly*)
Can't stand what?

HARRY
Watching you do what you do!

JACK
What do I do?

HARRY
Don't you *know*? When you light a fag.

JACK
I just light it.

HARRY
No, you don't.

JACK RIPLEY
If only. If only.

JACK
Don't *you* start!

HARRY
Go on, light it. Do what you do – just once more. After you've tapped it on the packet . . . Twice.

Still bemused, Jack taps the end of his cigarette twice on his box of matches, then taps it twice on the point of his chin, then twice on the tip of his nose. All absolutely automatically – and much to his own bewilderment.

HARRY
That's it. That's what you do. Every time.

JACK
I don't, do I?

JACK RIPLEY
Every single time.

HARRY
And I can't stand it.

JACK RIPLEY
Me neither.

With a bit of a struggle, Jack manages to light his cigarette by just lighting it. Harry sighs in relief.

HARRY
Good lad.

JACK RIPLEY

We're proud of you.

JACK (VO)

Apart from cigarette-lighting lessons, I worked with Harry writing half-hour comedy scripts –

INT JACK'S BEDROOM – FLIXTON – DAY – 1962

*Again in ferocious FAST MOTION, Jack types three separate scripts – '*BBC Comedy Playhouse: *by Harry Driver and Jack Rosenthal' – and puts them on the shelf.*

JACK (VO)

– interspersed with other sixty-minute scripts of my own . . .

A CLOSE SHOT of the shelf as two thrillers entitled The Odd Man *and two courtroom dramas entitled* The Verdict is Yours *are added . . . followed by more episodes of* Coronation Street.

JACK (VO)

So much so that Jim Phoenix told me to stop coming to work half-asleep each morning, go freelance and start writing full-time . . . And if it all dried up I could pop in to the agency now and then and he'd pay me as a consultant.

Grateful, of course, and petrified, of course, I did as I was told.

EXT BUNGALOW – BLACKPOOL – DAY – 1962

A beautiful morning. In the garden is a greenhouse – and in the greenhouse is Lakey, singing contentedly and tunelessly, in her element, fertilising cucumbers and tomatoes. We've never seen her so happy.

JACK (VO)

The script fees provided Lakey with a dream-come-true. A bungalow at the seaside, a flourishing garden and, best of all, a greenhouse.

For Sam it meant retirement and fresh sea air for his long-suffering bronchitic lungs.

Carrying his raincoat and a carrier bag (containing greaseproof-papered sandwiches and a bottle of lemonade), Sam pops his head out of the back door and calls to Lakey.

SAM

See you tonight.

Lakey sings on.

EXT OLD TRAFFORD CRICKET GROUND – MANCHESTER – DAY – 1962

Sam approaches the gates to the ground. An hour-and-a-half train journey from Blackpool to Manchester Victoria, then a bus ride to Old Trafford, and he's just in time for the opening overs of Lancashire's county cricket match.

He's vaguely puzzled by the absence of any other cricket-lovers making their way to the ground . . .

He arrives at the gates. They're locked.

On them is a large notice reading: 'Lancashire v. Notts to be played at Blackpool' – which, of course, is an hour-and-a-half train journey back to where he's just come from.

He takes a sandwich from his carrier bag and a swig of lemonade from the bottle for an early lunch . . . and starts back to Blackpool.

EXT BUNGALOW – BLACKPOOL – DAY – 1962

Late afternoon, and Lakey, singing away, is now watering her flowerbeds.

Sam appears at the back door in his raincoat, carrying his now-empty, folded-up carrier bag.

SAM

Hello, kid.

LAKEY

How was your cricket?

SAM

Um . . .

She resumes singing. And Sam avoids having to confess his wasted day.

JACK (VO)

Lakey's singing, however, was soon to drift into silence, and her dream-come-true to sour into nightmare – when she discovered that Maxine was also coming to live in Blackpool.

(*beat*)

Who?

(*beat*)

Oh, yes, Maxine . . .

INT AN EXTRAVAGANT STYLISED 'HOLLYWOOD MUSICAL' SET – 1962

Jack, dressed in white tie and tails and top hat, whisks and whirls Maxine – still a blurred two-dimensional cut-out *and dressed in flowing chiffon and tulle – around the set in an absurdly exaggerated pastiche of Fred Astaire and Ginger Rogers.*

An unseen string orchestra swells in lush accompaniment.

JACK (VO)

Maxine was good at following me.

He twirls her round in an intricate tap-dance . . .

But not as good as *I* was at following *her*, I suppose. Like with Wendy, only even more pathetically.

(*beat*)

Three weeks after our first date, I'd wanted to call it a day. And didn't. Thereafter, I'd wanted to call it a month, then six, then a year, then two and so on.

(*beat*)

And the longer I didn't, the more she wanted us to get married . . . and the more she threatened to kill herself if we didn't.

With beaming smiles, their danse macabre *swoops into a sweeping stylised tango . . .*

No one much liked Maxine – including her friends. Although I suppose I must've done. Telling the truth wasn't her forte, nor was concern for others. Selfishness was her most outstanding feature. Stupidity and cowardice were mine.

They gently lunge into a free-falling, flowing, billowing waltz . . .

A day or so before our first date, I later discovered, she'd slept with Geoff. On the other hand, to mollify Lakey (and me), she took religious lessons so's we could marry in a Reform synagogue. She was no more sincere in this than in anything else – but, credit where it's reluctantly due, she did it.

INT LAKEY'S AND SAM'S BUNGALOW – BLACKPOOL – DAY – 1962

Maxine (blurred) and Lakey are staring each other out with screwed-up eyes and pursed lips across the table. Jack sits between them, looking from one to the other, helplessly. Over this:

JACK (VO)

There was no love even mislaid between Lakey and Maxine. I, of course, was in the middle, just as I'd always been with Lakey and Sam when I was a kid. The perennial peacemaker, the gutanashomma, the referee buffeted about, weedily flailing . . . and failing.

FILM EXCERPT: ***Bar Mitzvah Boy***

INT A LIVING ROOM:

Harold (a fictional gutanashomma version of Jack), is seated in between Victor and Rita, his intended parents-in-law, who are in the middle of a screaming match. Much to Harold's discomfort.

RITA

Harold, am I right or am I wrong?

HAROLD

(*scared at suddenly being involved*)

What?

RITA

Who's right?

VICTOR

What's it got to do with him?

HAROLD

Nothing.

VICTOR

Sticking his bloody oar in . . .

RITA

Harold?

HAROLD

(*wriggling*)

Um . . . well, actually it's not for me to say . . . um . . .

RITA

It is if I ask you. You have my permission.

VICTOR

And mine. Go on: who's right?

They both look at Harold. He looks from one to the other, petrified of offending either.

HAROLD

Well, in some respects, there seems to be some truth in what –

VICTOR

Which respects?

HAROLD

(*hastily*)

Not *all*. I didn't say *all*.

RITA

Which?

Harold is speechless with fear. A pause.

VICTOR

Well, *speak*! For once in your life *upset* someone!

HAROLD

Um ... well, actually, in many respects, you're *both* right. I think there's a lot to be said for ... um ... for what you both said. I agree with you both.

(*beat*)

Wholeheartedly.

INT A STYLISED 'HOLLYWOOD MUSICAL' WEDDING SET – DAY – 1963

Jack, dressed as in the previous scene, and Maxine, now with a bridal head-dress and a bouquet, dance their Fred Astaire and Ginger Rogers grand climax. The orchestra's violins go beserk.

JACK (VO)

So. Of course. Naturally. Needless to say. Eventually. In the end. What did you expect? Instead of calling it a day after three weeks, we were married in Blackpool, and she didn't have to throw herself off the top of the Tower.

INT JACK'S STUDY – BUNGALOW – THORNTON – DAY – 1963

Jack is typing scripts at a desk. He now has metal stacking shelves, carrying all his scripts.

JACK (VO)

Thanks to my script fees, we moved into a bungalow of our own in Thornton Cleveleys and Maxine opened a model agency. Which was a very good way of meeting young businessmen . . .

EXT THE A1 – DAY – 1963

Harry's Volvo speeding along the road to London. Jack Ripley driving, Harry in the passenger seat, Jack squashed in the back.

In 1963, The Army Game *is TV's top comedy show. To their amazement Jack and Harry are commissioned to write an episode. They're on their way to the read-through of what they believe to be the definitive* Army Game *script. The read-through and the cast would seem to confirm it.*

However – watch this space.

The show is scheduled to be transmitted at 8 p.m. on November 22nd, 1963.

Something else was scheduled for that day:

EXT DALLAS – TEXAS – DAY – 1963

LIBRARY FOOTAGE of President Kennedy being assassinated in his motorcade.

JACK (VO)

British TV observed the tragedy by cancelling its programmes and playing dirges over a blank screen throughout the afternoon and early evening until eight o'clock, when, to my horror, on our screens – on the worst night for comedy since the Battle of Passchendaele . . .

A TV SCREEN – JACK'S BUNGALOW – THORTON – NIGHT – 1963 (CONT)

The Army Game *titles appear, backed by the jaunty, komic-with-a-k, orky-duck theme tune . . . cancelling out the dirges – and our mourning – in about ten seconds.*

Jack watches, open-mouthed.

JACK (VO)

Even I, co-writer though I was, didn't want to see the bloody thing. Instead of being proud that this was the peak of my comedy career, I was ashamed.

Shame sank into mortification when the show reached part 2 . . . when I saw that the cast had jettisoned every single word of the script, which now seemed to be about a sausage and what each character wants to do with it. Which I wished they would . . .

Forty-odd years later, *Sitting Pretty,* a comedy by Amy Rosenthal, starring Maureen Lipman, would open in Southampton. The date: September 11th, 2001.

INT JACK'S STUDY – BUNGALOW – THORNTON – DAY – 1964

CAM pans along the metal bookshelves. Jack's hand adds more Coronation Street *scripts, plus a one-hour play called* Pie in the Sky *– a title plagiarised in the 1990s for a drama series – and another called* Green Rub *about a sailor on a weekend's leave.*

The only review for Green Rub *is in the* Daily Mirror, *written by Ken Irwin, one of show-biz's least savoury or talented critics. It reads: 'Last night Granada showed a stupid play called* Green Rub.*' Just that.*

EXT A1 – DAY – 1964

Jack Ripley drives Harry and Jack in the Volvo past a signpost pointing towards London.

JACK (VO)

Ted Willis devised a drama series called *Taxi* with Sid James . . .

The Volvo drives in the opposite direction past a signpost pointing towards Manchester.

He asked us to write the second series . . .

The Volvo drives back to London.

So we wrote twenty of them.

The Volvo drives to Manchester.

This meant twenty trips to London and back.

INT JACK'S STUDY – BUNGALOW – THORNTON – DAY – 1964

Jack is adding the twenty Taxi *scripts to the shelf. The phone rings. He drops the scripts and takes the phone.*

JACK
(*into phone*)

Hello?

(*beat*)

Who?

(*beat*)

Michael who?

A beat. He tenses, excitedly, incredulously.

Hello, Mr Winner . . .

The door opens and Maxine blurs in with a mug of tea. She puts it on the desk.

JACK (VO)

A year after our wedding, Maxine gave me an anniversary card thanking me for the happiest year of her life. No, don't say Aaah! Wait. Six months later more would be revealed. Six months after that, even more.

EXT REGENT STREET – LONDON – DAY – 1964

Jack and Jack Ripley wheeling Harry in his wheelchair approach an office block, trying not to look too excited. Jack checks Michael Winner's plaque at the entrance. He holds the door open for Jack Ripley to wheel Harry in.

Harry wriggles his nose irritatedly.

HARRY

Nose.

Jack Ripley takes a handkerchief from his pocket.

No. Scratch.

Jack Ripley replaces the handkerchief and scratches Harry's nose. Harry nods his thanks.

They go into the building.

INT MICHAEL WINNER'S OFFICE – LONDON – DAY – 1964

The office reflects its owner's standing as a successful film-maker. Michael Winner lounges at his desk, finishing a cup of coffee. Jack finishes his. Jack Ripley feeds Harry his. A pause. Michael leans forward and puts his palms together.

MICHAEL

So. What can I do for you gentlemen?

A vaguely puzzled beat.

JACK

Sorry?

MICHAEL

What've you got to tell me?

HARRY

(*puzzled*)

Tell you?

MICHAEL

Why you asked to see me.

An uncomfortable pause.

JACK

Um . . . actually, our agent said *you* wanted to see *us*.

MICHAEL

Um . . . no. He told me *you* wanted to see *me*.

JACK

Ah.

HARRY

Uh-huh.

Everyone smiles awkwardly at each other.

MICHAEL

So, you haven't an idea to pitch? For a movie?

No, they haven't. Not one. Undeterred, Harry launches into a burbling, nonsensical slab of black seam tripe, making it up as he goes along . . .

HARRY

Well, yes, there's this . . . it's about this, well, girl, really, and she . . . what she does is . . . she sort of works in the canteen of this factory . . . in . . . well, it's in Ramsbottom in Lancashire . . . and she, well, when I say *she*, she and some others join this amateur . . . um, this non-professional . . . um . . .

He turns to Jack.

You carry on.

Wheelchair or no wheelchair, Jack would like to kill him.

JACK

Um . . . she joins this, well, *group*, really . . . group of . . .

He turns to Harry.

You tell it. You tell it better.

HARRY

(*now quite enjoying himself*)

. . . dancers, really, and eventually, after a –

JACK

– lot of adventures . . .

HARRY

Hilarious adventures . . .

JACK

She . . . um . . .

HARRY

. . . finishes up in this palace belonging to this Middle Eastern potentate and . . .

MICHAEL

Is it a part for Audrey Hepburn?

HARRY

Oh, absolutely. That's who we were going to suggest.

MICHAEL

Carry on.

HARRY

Um . . .

Finally, even Harry slithers into a quicksand of silence and he and his fellow imposters say their goodbyes.

Harry's movie idea gets no further. Audrey Hepburn goes on to other things.

INT TRAIN COMPARTMENT (TRAVELLING) – DAY – 1964

Jack is seated, flicking through a typed script. The title page reads The Villains.

JACK (VO)

While on my way back from a Granada script conference about my latest scripts – two episodes of a thriller series called *The Villains* – an old pal from my Navy days called at home to see me.

This was six months after Maxine's card thanking me for the happiest year of her life.

And something happened.

Actually, it may not have. It may *not* have been hand-on-heart fact, but I *suspected* it did. How strong does a suspicion have to be before it's a fact? Well, that's how strong it was. If not stronger . . .

EXT JACK'S BUNGALOW – THORNTON – DAY – 1964 (CONT)

George, handsome, easy-going, rings the doorbell. Good old blurry, two-dimensional cut-out Maxine opens the door.

CU his eyes, looking deep into hers.

GEORGE

Hello. I'm George.

CU her eyes, deeply searching his.

MAXINE

Hello, I'm Maxine.

CU his eyes, boring intently into hers.

CU her eyes, piercing his.

Then, abruptly, they fling themselves into each other's arms. She pulls him across the threshold and slams the door closed behind him.

INT LIVING ROOM – JACK'S BUNGALOW – THORNTON – DAY – 1964 (CONT)

Locked in their passionate embrace, George and Maxine whirl each other across the room towards the open door of a bedroom – and the bed visible inside.

They revolve through the door. With a powerful back-heel she kicks it shut.

IMMEDIATE CUT TO:

INT TRAIN COMPARTMENT (TRAVELLING) – DAY – 1964 (CONT)

Jack promptly sits bolt upright in his seat. He looks puzzled, troubled.

JACK (VO)

When I got home, they were sitting at opposite ends of the living room, speaking over-politely, a little stiltedly. Looking so innocent, they could only be guilty.

INT JACK'S STUDY – BUNGALOW – THORNTON – DAY – 1965

The parting of the ways. No, not with Maxine. With Harry. Jack is at his desk, Harry in his wheelchair. They're about to write their fifth episode of a comedy series – Pardon the Expression *with Arthur Lowe – when it suddenly dawns on them that their comedy styles are very different. Maybe not all that suddenly. Despite the mounds of scripts they've written together, maybe it's something they've known all along.*

At the start of the episode, page 1, scene 1, neither of them has an inkling of what Arthur Lowe should say or do when he opens the door to a 'veritable Kilimanjaro of a woman standing on the threshold'. (A 'Kilimanjaro of a woman' is comedy-writer-speak for a character who'll be played by a slightly plump, not-all-that-tall actress. More a sort of 'minor hillock of a woman'). They flail in silence for an opening line . . . Whenever Harry suggests one, Jack pooh-poohs it. And vice versa.

They're clearly trying to say something. If only goodbye.

A glum silence.

HARRY

Shall we pack it in?

JACK

We're only on page 1!

HARRY

I mean *us*.

JACK

Oh. I see.

So they do – and Harry resumes his partnership with his real soulmate, Vince Powell.

INT DENIS FORMAN'S OFFICE – GRANADA TV – DAY – 1966

Another little heart-to-heart. Granada's managing director, Denis Forman, looking sober if not outright grim, faces Jack across his huge, executive desk.

Jack wonders why he's been sent for. Is he about to be made Head of Comedy? Head of Drama? Head of anything? No. He's going to be told off.

DENIS

I watched TV last night, Jack.

JACK

Oh, yes?

DENIS

I saw Kathleen Harrison in an episode of a drama series, *Mrs Thursday*.

JACK

Right.

DENIS

You wrote it.

JACK

(*beams*)

Did you like it?

DENIS

(*even grimmer*)

It's produced by ATV.

JACK

That's right.

DENIS

(*his grimmest*)

You work for Granada! Not ATV!

JACK

Not exactly, Denis. I'm freelance.

DENIS

But you're a Granada man! Always have been! You can't work for other companies!

JACK

Well, actually, since I'm freelance –

DENIS

Granada's a family. You're a member of it.

(*he smiles warmly*)

End of discussion. Good morning.

INT CORRIDOR – 5TH FLOOR – GRANADA TV – DAY – 1966 (CONT)

Jack comes out of Denis's office, wryly shaking his head. John Birt is coming down the corridor towards him. They nod as they pass. John Birt knocks on Denis's door.

DENIS (OS)

Come!

John Birt goes in. Jack continues down the corridor.

JACK (VO)

That was John Birt, another Granada man. I'm not sure what he was producing in 1966. Probably giving us his light magazine programme, *Nice Time*.

(*beat*)

Which is more than he gave us when he ran the BBC. Into the ground.

INT BEDROOM – JACK'S BUNGALOW – THORNTON – DAY – 1966

Blurry Maxine is packing a suitcase. Jack leans against the doorpost watching, with his bewildered Eric Morecambe face.

JACK (VO)

A year or so after the happiest year of her life, Maxine seemed to want an even happier one – and told me she was going.

JACK

(*ever-so-slightly fatuous*)

Why?

MAXINE

Funny, isn't it? As soon as I got what I wanted, I realised I didn't want it at all.

JACK (VO)

QED. It's a common complaint. She probably wasn't the first, nor the last, to suffer from it.

INT JACK'S STUDY – BUNGALOW – THORNTON – DAY – 1966

On top of his more conventional clothes, Jack's wearing a red and white England football rosette the size of his chest. The ribbons reach down to his shoes. On his head is a red fez with the word 'England' inscribed on it.

He's typing a script.

JACK (VO)

Life, of course, goes on. And did. Despite Denis Forman's lecture, my next TV play – *The Night Before the Morning After* – was writtten for ABC TV.

We hear a blast of a referee's whistle from the living room. He immediately leaps up, grabs a wooden football rattle from the desk and races out of the door.

TV SET: LIBRARY FOOTAGE – 1966 (CONT)

England and Germany playing in the World Cup Final at Wembley.

INT LIVING ROOM – JACK'S BUNGALOW – THORNTON – DAY – 1966 (CONT)

Jack sits on the edge of the settee, intently watching the match on TV, swooping up and down from delight to dismay and back again, rattling his rattle.

JACK (VO)

Life for the England football team – and its supporters – also went on. To victory in extra-time.

(*beat*)

I have no explanation for the floor-length rosette, other than Lakey insisted on making it, as a patriotic gesture. The Egyptian hat, of course, made no sense at all.

Until I hit on this hilarious hoot the following Monday. *Intended* hilarious hoot . . .

INT A CONFERENCE ROOM – GRANADA TV – DAY – 1966

A Coronation Street *story conference in progress. Six or seven writers, including Tony Warren, Geoff Lancashire and Peter Eckersley, the producer, two directors, two storyline writers and a casting director, seated round a table, trawling ideas for the next six episodes.*

CASTING DIRECTOR

So we need a four-episode story for Ena before –

The door opens and Jack walks in wearing the red fez and the rosette and rattling the rattle. They all look at him, impassively. Then return to their notes. He sits at the table, slightly thrown.

JACK

Morning. Sorry I'm late.

(*chanting*)

England! England!

There's no reaction whatever from anyone.

CASTING DIRECTOR
(*continues*)

– for Ena, Minnie and Martha before Violet goes on holiday.

Jack rattles his rattle again. And again, no reaction.

TONY

How long has she got off?

CASTING DIRECTOR

A week. Two episodes.

PRODUCER

So we need a story that'll take her away . . .

CASTING DIRECTOR

Visiting someone, p'raps.

Jack glumly takes off his fez and puts it on the table.

STORYLINE WRITER

We could put her in hospital for two episodes.

GEOFF

No. If we put her in hospital, we'll want to see her there.

Jack takes his rosette off and puts his rattle down.

PETER

How about we play a big hospital story for the four, then let her recuperate for the two?

JACK

Good idea.

PRODUCER

Morning, Jack.

The others likewise greet him as though he's only just come in.

JACK
(*wryly*)

Morning.

Some hoots are more hilarious than others.

EXT BUNGALOW – BLACKPOOL – DAY – 1966

An ambulance waits outside Sam's and Lakey's home. Two ambulance men carry Sam out on a stretcher. A worried Lakey follows them.

JACK (VO)

Life, of course, doesn't always go on. Sam's time in the trenches and the years of bronchitis finally caught up with him.

INT WARD – VICTORIA HOSPITAL – BLACKPOOL – DAY – 1966

Sam lies in bed, wearing an oxygen mask. Lakey and Jack sit on either side of the bed.

JACK (VO)

All I could think was there goes another wasted life. Another anonymous life that never stood a chance. Another 'shmeerer' struggling from payday to payday, from dole queue to dole queue.

Eaten up with bitterness against the system that made sure a week's wages could only last a week. Against the bosses who enforced it and the unions that accepted it.

A simple man of simple pleasures – really not all that much more than cricket and herrings.

Sam, who was given so little life story to tell, to pass on. But, without him, *I* wouldn't have had either.

I sometimes catch a glimpse of myself in the mirror – and see Sam. And feel grateful. I'm glad this man was my dad.

He died quietly and in peace.

I smile when I remember how smart he always looked in a bowler hat. Dashing. Debonair. A real toff.

EXT MIDDLEGATE – OLDHAM – DAY – 1966

Jack unloads suitcases, files and his typewriter from the boot and backseat of his mini outside Geoff Lancashire's imposing house.

On the doorstep stand Hilda and the twins, Simon and Sarah. Geoff and their eldest, John, go to the car to help Jack lug his luggage into the house.

Over this, we hear the Beatles singing 'Eleanor Rigby'.

JACK (VO)

These were the Swinging Sixties. The King's Road. Carnaby Street. Me, I swung down the East Lancs Road to Oldham. To lodge with Geoff and his family.

Mind you, just like Swinging London, even Oldham could hear the Beatles on the radio, see Twiggy on the cover of magazines and wear kipper ties, cuban heels or mini-skirts like pelmets. So, no surprise that I got bitten by the transcendental meditation bug . . .

INT GURU'S LIVING ROOM – OLDHAM – EVENING – 1966

Jack and a middle-aged guru (an Oldham lad, born and bred) sit on two facing chairs. Jack gives him a flower, a white handkerchief and an envelope.

JACK (VO)

As requested, I gave my guru two spiritual symbols and one rather more material one – a week's salary. In return he gave me my Maharishi Mahesh Yogi mantra and a quick lesson in how to use it.

INT GEOFF'S STUDY – OLDHAM – EVENING – 1966

Jack sits in Geoff's leather chair at one end of the room, eyes closed, hands on his knees, in deep meditation.

JACK (VO)

I meditated twice a day in twenty-minute spells, one of them in Geoff's study. Often I just nodded off – but sometimes mysterious, almost magical things happened . . .

He opens his eyes as Geoff pops his head in.

GEOFF

Sorry.

JACK

It's OK, I've finished.

GEOFF

Sure? I only came in for a book.

JACK

Carry on.

Geoff starts towards the bookcase that fills the wall at the far end of the room, then stops in his tracks, staring incredulously ahead.

GEOFF

Good God! What's happened?

JACK
(*puzzled*)

How d'you mean?

Geoff points at the bookcase.

GEOFF

I can read the titles on the spines!

JACK

So?

GEOFF

But I *can't*! I sit where you are every day – and I *can't* read the titles! Not from there. I have to go right up to them. Till now. Now I can read them all! How's it happened?

He turns to Jack. They stare at each other.

INT GURU'S LIVING ROOM – OLDHAM – EVENING – 1966

Jack and his guru sit facing each other. Jack, eyes closed, is laughing joyfully. He snaps his eyes open.

GURU

Something happened?

JACK

I'll say!

GURU

Tell me.

JACK

I don't know if I can . . . It was this feeling . . . Total happiness. Bubbling. And colours. Orange. A sunburst. A sort of mental orgasm.

GURU

Good. You've reached the First Stage. You now go on till you reach the Seventh, perfect spiritual bliss. Go on. It's the easiest thing in the world.

Jack closes his eyes and concentrates. And finds it's the hardest. *Anticipating the wonders of the First Stage, he can't relax – and, if you can't relax, you can't meditate. So he never again would cure myopic mates or giggle himself into the lowest level of bliss, let alone the highest.*

But he does the next best thing. Like everyone else in long hair and hipsters, he writes a Swinging Sixties poem . . .

JACK (VO)

'I dreamt that when I grew up,
I'd win the World Cup
For England. Single-handed.
I even imagined
Rockefeller cadging
From me. A million quid.
I dreamt that ev'ry girl's whim
Was to go for a spin
In my Ferrari. Painted purple.
But I never once dreamt
I ever was meant
To wake up. But I did.'

Sorry about the flaws. But this was the sixties. Rules didn't apply.

INT OFFICE – GRANADA TV – DAY – 1966

Peter Eckersley and Jack sit at their desks facing each other. Following a Cecil Bernstein directive, they're trying to devise a new comedy show.

Their pretty, vivacious secretary, Margaret Ogden, is busy at her filing cabinets.

Like everyone else who knows him, Jack is in awe of Peter; although younger than Jack, he's the man Jack always says he'd like to be when he grows up. Behind Peter's massive, dome-like forehead is an equally massive encyclopedia. Really half-encyclopedia, half-Bumper Fun Book. He's the most knowledgeable man Jack's ever met. And, at the same time, warm, witty and all the wiser for being taken with a pinch of Eckersley salt.

He's a unique, seminal producer, eventually Head of Drama, a superb writer, a prodigious man of television. A triumph.

Margaret looks at her watch and gives a sudden yelp.

MARGARET

Lunchtime!

Peter and Jack's faces crumple in dismay.

PETER

Oh, no!

JACK

Please not lunchtime!

PETER

Anything but lunchtime!

Lunchtime has a different meaning in this office. It's nothing to do with egg and chips. It means it's time for a lesson in Greek Dancing. This is a daily, sadistic aberration of Margaret's that, in an indulgent moment, they agreed to. Something to do with getting exercise . . .

She puts 'Zorba's Dance' on the record-player, then drags them both to their feet and starts teaching. Jack's pathetic, and Peter, the genius, is worse.

PETER

It'll end in tears.

He's right. He watches his legs being silly and laughs and laughs till he cries.

INT THE PINEAPPLE PUB – SALFORD – NIGHT – 1966

A dingy, Dickensian room in a moribund pub in a ghostly, ill-lit street.

This is the monthly meeting place, ideal for nineteenth-century opium-smuggling Lascars from Salford Docks – but, on this occasion, it's for a cobbled-together band of seven writers called Group North. (Which inspired Marty Feldman to call himself Group South.)

The seven writers – including Peter and Jack, John Finch, Harry Driver and Vince Powell – sit crouched round the single, spluttering bar of an ancient electric fire.

The idea of Group North had been to offer its services to broadcasters; to devise drama series with contributions from each, or at least some, of the seven. After an initial flurry of minor success (a series called Catch Hand*), the broadcasters have lost interest – and so have the seven. They've decided to disband.*

This meeting is to decide what to do with the £300 of combined subs left in the kitty.

JOHN FINCH

How about giving it to an old couple for Christmas?

HARRY

What about a *young* couple, just starting out in life?

VINCE

I've a better idea. We rent a little flat in Chorlton where we can put up chorus girls from the Opera House – and *we* take it in turns to –

THE OTHER SIX

No, Vince.

PETER

(*solemnly*)

How about this . . .?

He speaks in quiet, measured, thoughtful tones.

Portrait of the artist as a *very* young man: Jack aged 18 months.

'Sam, Sam – pick up tha' musket': Jack's dad, Sam Rosenthal, in uniform during the Great War.

Jack's mother, Leah Miller, aged 19 – Cheetham Hill's answer to Dorothy Parker.

Lakey Miller marrying Sam Rosenthal in 1927. 'The two sides of the character coin ... If it comes down heads, you have the Rosenthals; tails, and you get the Millers.'

'Her real-life dialogue was heaven sent to a budding writer': Jack and Lakey.

David's National Service: Jack's brother in arms.

Rosenthal, pugnacious, on the wing …

Scoop! Rosenthal smashes world record … or does he?

Either Jack at university or a Russian poet in the Gulag.

Ten green bottles … Yes, it's Jack at university.

Not quite Cap'n Jack yet, but leading Coder Rosenthal.

They joined the navy to see … Portsmouth.

Who says size doesn't matter? Lakey with sister Mary and friend, displaying her home-grown cucumbers in the Blackpool version of the Le Corbusier chair.

Sam Rosenthal: 'A simple man of simple pleasures'.

We set up a writing school, or *pretend* to, advertise it and get little old ladies from Newton-le-Willows who fancy themselves as budding Chekhovs to send us their stories and postal orders.

Then we send back the stories, saying they're rubbish and cash the postal orders. We could make a bomb.

Everyone stares at him in disbelief. Peter of all people. The most iniquitous suggestion imaginable from the kindest, most human of men. A babel of scandalised voices as all six writers argue vociferously against it . . .

DISSOLVE TO:

INT THE PINEAPPLE PUB – SALFORD – NIGHT – 1966

Two hours later.

Group North – apart from Peter – is exhausted. He's still cynically, adamantly and eloquently promoting his idea. The other six are disillusioned with him and fed up with the whole evening.

LANDLADY
(*behind the bar*)

Time, gents. Ta.

PETER

Shall we put it to the vote? All those in favour?

Three of them wearily, shamefacedly, raise their hands. Anything to call it a day.

HARRY

Him and silver tongue . . .

PETER

Against?

The other three raise their hands.

Right. I have the casting vote.

He begins to chuckle . . .

Well, *I* think it's the most disgraceful, appalling idea I've ever heard.

The chuckle begins to bubble into laughter.

I'm ashamed of all of you for even *considering* it. Disgusting. Grown men.

Everyone stares at him.

I therefore vote against.

Once again, it's ending in tears.

Motion defeated. 'Night, 'night.

He starts for the door, shaking with laughter and drying his eyes.

HARRY

You sod!

VINCE

Lousy pig!

JACK

Two hours arguing the toss . . .

A pause.

JOHN FINCH

So what'll we do with the three hundred quid?

FILM EXCERPT: *Coronation Street* – Script by Jack Rosenthal

INT *CORONATION STREET* STUDIO – GRANADA TV – DAY – 1967

A dress rehearsal in progress. Cameras and boom-microphones move into the Tanners' living room set. Dennis Tanner is reading a comic at the table. Elsie Tanner strolls in. Stands for a moment, pensively taps a fingernail against a tooth, then:

ELSIE

(ominously gentle)

Dennis, chuck.

He looks at her warily.

I think it's time we had one of our little chats.

(beat)

Why is there a gorilla sitting in my sink?

INT GALLERY – GRANADA TV – DAY – 1967 (CONT)

The director, his PA and technical crew sit at the bays before their control consoles.

Jack sits behind the director, white-faced, alternating between anxiously chewing his lip and chewing his nails, inwardly (and, no doubt, outwardly) despairing that people (i.e. actors) are only human. This is what he's always been like when watching his work being done – and what he'll always be like, to the end of his career. Naively believing that no one notices.

On a bank of TV monitors, we see the shot of the wryly grimacing Elsie after her 'gorilla' line.

DIRECTOR

Cue grams. Fade to black. Roll credits.

His PA throws switches. The programme's signature tune starts to play and the monitors replace the shot of Elsie with a roller caption of actor and technical credits.

During this:

JACK (VO)

In 1967 I became a respectable *senior* member of Denis Forman's (really SLB's) Granada family. For six months I was *Coronation Street*'s reluctant producer. They became the most nerve-wracking six months I'd ever had at Granada. Here I was – able to hire and fire, able to reject scripts written by erstwhile close friends and colleagues. Not only able to, *expected* to.

INT ST ANN'S CHURCH – MANCHESTER – DAY – 1967

Jack sits alone in the beautiful, white-walled, elegantly timbered – above all, peaceful *church. Breathing in its therapeutic tranquillity.*

JACK (VO)

Every Friday before the two *Coronation Street* episodes were videotaped, this is where I, Yiddishe boy, escaped to. Breathing deep, forgetting for an hour the afternoon's traumas lying in wait at the other end of Deansgate.

The one Friday I needed my haven most of all, I couldn't go. I was trapped in the studio. This was the day we recorded the programme's biggest story to date, a story I'd inherited from the previous producer, a story I hated. The wedding of Elsie Tanner and her US master-sergeant.

The madness had begun a few weeks earlier . . .

IMMEDIATE CUT TO:

INT PRODUCER'S OFFICE – GRANADA TV – DAY – 1967

Jack, harassed, is at his desk. The phone rings. He takes it.

JACK
(*into phone*)

Yes?

INT RECEPTION – GRANADA TV – DAY – 1967 (CONT)

The commissionaire is at his desk, speaking into the phone. A salesman, carrying a small case, stands before him.

COMMISSIONAIRE
(*into phone*)
Jack? Reception here. There's a chap come to see you. He says Pat Phoenix told him to. He's from H Samuels, the jewellers.

INT PRODUCER'S OFFICE – GRANADA TV – DAY – 1967

Jack faces the salesman, nursing his case in his lap, across the desk.

JACK
(*bewildered*)
Pat Phoenix told you?

SALESMAN
(*an ingratiating smile*)
To pick her wedding ring.

Jack stares, gobsmacked.

JACK
She's not getting married! Her *character* is!

SALESMAN
(*an understanding smile*)
Same difference, int'it?

He puts the case on the desk and opens it. Rows of rings sparkle in their red velvet mounting.

Now the one she fancies is –

JACK
Hang on. It's the one *I* fancy that matters. How much are they?

SALESMAN
(*a businesslike smile*)
They kick off at a thousand.

Jack closes the case.

JACK
The one *I* fancy is in our Props Department. It costs nothing. Sorry.

This time the salesman gives us his philosophical smile. Jack shakes his hand and watches him go.

JACK (VO)

That was just the start. 546 viewers sent wedding presents, hundreds cancelled their holidays so's not to miss the Happy Day and one nutter threatened to knife Pat, the bridegroom Paul Maxwell – and *me* – if the wedding went ahead.

Total lunacy was achieved the day it was to be recorded . . .

INT STUDIO – GRANADA TV – DAY – 1967

The massive set of a church interior fills the studio. Cameras and mikes move among the regular Street *characters all in their pews. Paul, in his best dress-uniform, stands before the vicar. The organ thumps out Mendelssohn. Goosepimples burgeon.*

INT GALLERY – GRANADA TV – DAY – 1967 (CONT)

The director, his PA, all his technicians and Jack are glued to the monitors.

DIRECTOR
(into mike)

Cue Pat.

Nothing happens.

Cue Pat's entrance!

Still nothing happens.

Stop the tape!

(into mike)

What the hell's going on?

INT STUDIO – GRANADA TV – DAY – 1967 (CONT)

The floor manager, wearing a headset, dashes in front of a camera.

FLOOR MANAGER

I don't know!

INT GALLERY – GRANADA TV – DAY – 1967 (CONT)

The director et al, as before, now boggling at the floor manager on the monitor.

DIRECTOR
(into mike)

Where is she?

FLOOR MANAGER
(on monitor)

In her dressing room. She says she's not coming out.

DIRECTOR
(*into mike*)

What?

Jack leans towards the director's mike.

JACK
(*into mike*)
She's *got* to come out! She's getting married!

FLOOR MANAGER
(*on monitor*)
She says she's not. She says she's changed her mind.

For a moment, Jack contemplates slitting his wrists, then leaps to his feet and races out.

INT CORRIDOR – STUDIOS – GRANADA TV – DAY – 1967

Jack knocks on Pat's dressing room door.

PAT (OS)
(*inside*)

There's no one home.

JACK

Pat, it's me. Jack.

PAT (OS)
(*inside*)

I'm not budging.

JACK
You must! We're ready to shoot! Your wedding!

PAT (OS)
(*inside*)

Exactly.

JACK

What d'you mean?

PAT (OS)
(*inside*)

I'm not getting wed.

JACK

Pat. Let me in.

PAT (OS)
(*inside*)

No.

JACK

Please, Pat!

She opens the door. She's in her wedding dress and looking sensational. Jack goes in.

INT PAT'S DRESSING ROOM – GRANADA TV – DAY – 1967 (CONT)

Pat sits down in front of her mirror, the light bulbs making her dress shimmer all the more. Jack sits down beside her and takes her hand.

PAT

Save your breath, lad. I'm not doing it.

JACK

Pat, millions of viewers are –

PAT

You're a man, you don't understand. It's the biggest day of a girl's life, her wedding day.

For a moment, Jack thinks he's going mad. This isn't *Pat's wedding day, it's a fictional* character's *wedding day. Isn't it? It's Elsie bloody* Tanner's. *And Pat Phoenix isn't Elsie Tanner. Or is she?*

JACK

It's just that you look so beautiful . . . and radiant . . . and it's going to be the most fabulous –

A pause.

PAT

Really beautiful?

JACK

(*reverently*)

Mmm? Yeah. Very. I've never seen such a beautiful bride.

Another pause. Unbeknownst to him, Jack has just whispered 'Open sesame'. Pat stands up.

PAT

Is my mascara smudged?

JACK

(*smiles weakly*)

It wouldn't dare.

PAT

Come on then.

She takes him by the hand, the drained and haggard father of the bride, and they leave the dressing room; she to the studio, he to the gallery.

INT GALLERY – GRANADA TV – DAY – 1967

On the monitors Jack and the others watch Pat and Paul, i.e. Elsie and Steve, finally say, 'I do.'

JACK (VO)

After three months I begged my boss, Julian Amyes, to let me off my remaining three months. I pleaded increasingly unsound mind. He winced, said, 'Join the club,' and refused.

EXT PARIS STREETS – DAY – 1968

LIBRARY FOOTAGE of running battles between students and baton-wielding police.

JACK (VO)

For three or four weeks in 1968 it looked as though the world was going to change; that young people were going to have a voice apart from on LPs. The students of Paris, then the workers, were sitting in and striking and manning the barricades and charging other barricades.

(*beat*)

And then, just as Flower Power eventually failed to blossom, the seeds of the new French Revolution were blown away. Life returned to normal.

INT JACK'S BEDROOM – GEOFF'S HOUSE – OLDHAM – DAY – 1968

Jack, once again, at his desk, typing away. For him 'normal' means writing the next play – Compensation Alice *with Sheila Hancock – for ABC (when Denis isn't looking), followed by his first ninety-minute TV film.*

EXT BACKSTREETS OF SALFORD – DAY – 1968

Jack is slaving away with a gang of dustbinmen, hauling ton-weight metal dustbins down back-entries to empty into the waiting dustcart.

The film – for Granada – is called There's a Hole in Your Dustbin, Delilah, *a fragrant tale of dustbinmen, for which he has done a week's muscle-wrenching, spine-crunching research. It's directed by Mike Apted. He and Jack have worked together often on* Coronation Street, *and would much more on TV films in the future. Very much on the same wavelength, they share the same sense of humour and sense of irony. An intelligent, perceptive director, Cambridge-educated; he and Jack become close pals – and, in time,*

Mike becomes a successful director in Hollywood: Coalminer's Daughter, Triple Echo, Gorky Park, The World is Not Enough.

As we watch Jack and his (temporarily) fellow dustbinmen manhandle the bins down the backstreets:

JACK (VO)

For years directors accused me of setting *all* my plays in grimy northern backstreets, and never Hawaii. It isn't true, of course. Very few are set in northern backstreets.

(beat)

But, I suppose, even fewer in Hawaii.

EXT WEMBLEY STADIUM – NIGHT – 1968

LIBRARY FOOTAGE of the Manchester United v. Benfica European Cup Final. As we watch United scoring their four goals . . .

JACK (VO)

Ten years after the Munich Disaster, United won the European Cup. I wasn't at Wembley to revel in it, but I did see the semi-final at the awesome Bernabeu Stadium in Madrid – where we heroically came back from 3–1 down to nick a draw and win on aggregate.

(beat)

After the match, a Real Madrid fan offered to swap his beautiful, solid, enamelled Real Madrid badge for my bedraggled, tuppence-ha'penny cardboard United rosette. I refused on grounds of loyalty. I'd like to think I've never regretted it. I'd *like* to.

EXT SKIES ABOVE SPAIN – DAY – 1968

A BEA plane in flight. We hear Manchester United fans raucously, tipsily singing . . .

JACK (VO)

The next day the plane home was full of United fans – all still high as a kite from the night before.

Just before we landed in Manchester . . .

INT PLANE (IN FLIGHT) – DAY – 1968

A fan, bescarved, red-and-white-bonneted, much the worse for wear, shoulders his way down the aisle, thrusting a carrier bag at each of the hooligan passengers, who drop coins into it. For all the world as though they're on a charabanc day-trip to Morecambe, it's a whip-round for the pilot.

EXT MANCHESTER AIRPORT – DAY – 1968

The plane is about to land.

JACK (VO)

When we landed, they showed their appreciation in their own traditional manner . . .

INT PLANE – DAY – 1968

As it lands, the fans stand, clap and cheer. The pilot comes out of the cockpit and bows.

INT – REHEARSAL ROOM – GRANADA STUDIOS – MANCHESTER – DAY – 1969

Rehearsals are in progress for one of Jack's TV plays.

Jack is crouched in the habitual pose of a writer in the rehearsal room: ashen-faced, frozen shoulders closely aligned with earlobes, lower jaw protruding, fingernails locked over lower teeth. Every now and then, barely perceptibly, he flinches.

The director, a flowery-shirted young man who regards the writer as a necessary evil, contrives to ignore the hunched and twitching figure in the corner.

JACK (VO)

The scene they were rehearsing was a key moment in the script, when the daughter has to tell her mother that she's pregnant. I watched in increasing consternation as the actress who was playing the mother gave no reaction whatsoever to this explosive piece of news, but merely continued washing up as though nothing had happened. After some consideration, I decided not to say anything and mention it quietly to the director at lunchtime.

INT – CANTEEN – GRANADA STUDIOS – MANCHESTER – DAY – 1969 (CONT)

Jack stands in the queue in the buzzing, bustling canteen with his tray of food and his glass of lemonade. He spots the flowery shirt of his director a little further up, by the desserts. Jack wriggles his way through until he is beside him.

JACK

Er . . . sorry, mate . . . Have you got a minute?

The director fixes him with a withering look.

It's just, um, when she confesses. About the pregnancy. Well, at the moment, it's sort of going for nothing, isn't it? I mean, it's supposed to be the most momentous, earth-shattering revelation. Don't you think her mother would have more of a reaction?

Before Jack has time to register what's happening, the director draws back his arm, clenches his fist and delivers a powerful uppercut blow to his jaw. Jack flies through the air and lands on the floor some way away, gravy down his shirt front, mashed potato all over his trousers, custard dripping gently down his glasses. He sits there, blinking.

All conversation has ceased in the canteen. A roomful of Granada employees leap to the simultaneous conclusion that they have just witnessed a gay lovers' tiff.

DIRECTOR
(calmly)
Either she does that, or she does nothing. There is no in-between.

EXT FILM EXCHANGE PUB – MANCHESTER – EVENING – 1969

With his long hair, hipsters, Marks and Spencer's waisted shirt and heavy-rimmed glasses, i.e. looking a bit of a dick, Jack walks towards the entrance – unaware that the lines from his poem – 'I never once dreamt I ever was meant to wake up/But I did' are about to happen.

In the nicest possible way . . .

INT FILM EXCHANGE PUB – MANCHESTER – EVENING – 1969 (CONT)

It's a hundred yards from the studios and packed with Granada staff and a few members of a troupe of actors. The troupe are known as the Stables Theatre, an offshoot of Granada TV; the idea is to present stage plays in Granada's own small theatre with the intention of then adapting them for TV. Among its members are Richard Wilson, Fiona Walker, Ann Rye, John Shrapnel and veteran actors Maureen Pryor, Andre von Gyseghem, John Fraser and John Flanegan.

And one Maureen Lipman.

Jack greets a few mates en route to the bar. Then sees the aforementioned Lipman. And something happens. It needs a better poet than him to describe it. But it's something to do with a sudden, surging feeling of happiness – and of certainty. A bubbling sunburst of fun and pleasure and excitement that leaves the First Stage of transcendental meditation apologising for its pretentiousness. A feeling of coming home – and finding himself there. But a new *himself. One he actually* likes. *It's something at first sight, alright.*

They exchange a glance, maybe a word, en passant, and he moves on to one of the Film Exchange's regulars, a ginger-haired and -bearded ex-wrestler, as wide as he's tall, Tommy Mann.

TOMMY

Cut it out, Buggerlugs. I've seen you gawping.

JACK

Who?

TOMMY

'Who?', he says. Gawping and slavering. Give up before you start. You'll get nowhere with her.

JACK

Wanna bet?

TOMMY

Certainly. A quid says, 'Nowhere'.

JACK

No. A quid says, 'Everywhere'.

TOMMY

You're on.

They shake hands. Jack throws her another look.

JACK (VO)

Our first date was at Fulda's Kosher Restaurant. We started talking, then laughing, and we never stopped for the next 35 years.

INT THE STABLES' REHEARSAL ROOM – GRANADA TV – DAY – 1969

Maureen and her fellow actors are squirming on the floor on their stomachs, hollowly chanting, 'Blue, green, ultramarine', under the appreciative eye of their director. To him, seemingly, it makes sense.

Jack wanders into the room with a script under his arm – as though this will fool anyone that he's passing through on urgent business. (To where, for God's sake?) What with this being a short-cut. Which it isn't.

Maureen notices and gives him a glance in between 'green' and 'ultramarine'.

INT ADULT EDUCATION CLASSROOM – MANCHESTER – EVENING – 1969

A teacher stands at a blackboard teaching elementary Hebrew to a class of two nuns, three housewives and Jack.

Two years earlier, at the start of the Arab–Israeli Six Day War, Jack had enrolled in a Hebrew class in case the Royal Navy poached him for his services as part of a peacekeeping force. Six days later it was all over and the second week's classes were cancelled.

Now it had all flared up again and this time it was going to last longer, at least as far as conjugating verbs.

INT FILM EXCHANGE PUB – MANCHESTER – NIGHT – 1969

Maureen, Tommy Mann and Jack are chatting at the bar.

JACK (VO)

To ingratiate myself a bit with Maureen, I modestly went on at some length about my Hebrew classes and how I was the only man in a classful of middle-aged women.

INT JACK'S OFFICE – GRANADA TV – DAY – 1969

Jack is busy writing at his desk, a comedy series called The Dustbinmen, *a spin-off from* There's a Hole in Your Dustbin, Delilah. *The phone rings. He takes it.*

JACK
(*into phone*)

Hello?

CROAKY FEMALE VOICE

Is that Mr Rosenthal?

JACK
(*into phone*)

Speaking. Who's that?

CROAKY FEMALE VOICE

Mrs Schwartzkopf.

JACK
(*into phone*)

I'm sorry?

CROAKY FEMALE VOICE

Mrs Schwartzkopf. You know me. I'm the lady with grapes in her hat.

JACK
(*into phone*)

Sorry?

CROAKY FEMALE VOICE

In your Hebrew class. The one on the front row with the hat. The hat with the grapes. You must've noticed the hat even if you didn't notice the grapes!

Jack begins to panic.

JACK

(*into phone*)

Um . . . I'm sorry . . . I don't quite . . .

CROAKY FEMALE VOICE

The reason I'm ringing is you seem a nice young man on your own in Manchester. So I thought maybe you'd like to come to dinner, Friday night.

Jack panics even more.

JACK

(*into phone*)

The thing is, Mrs . . .

CROAKY FEMALE VOICE

Schwartzkopf.

JACK

(*into phone*)

. . . Mrs Schwartzkopf, I go to Blackpool Friday nights.

CROAKY FEMALE VOICE

Every Friday?

JACK

(*into phone*)

Yes. To my mother . . . she gets very upset if I –

CROAKY FEMALE VOICE

Every Friday night! You couldn't spare one lousy Friday night?

He's now getting desperate.

JACK

(*into phone*)

The thing is –

CROAKY FEMALE VOICE

I've got a daughter, Mr Rosenthal. Jacky – I've got a daughter – beautiful. She's what you'd call a catch. A figure on her . . .

JACK

(*into phone*)

I'm afraid I –

CROAKY FEMALE VOICE

Listen! Don't do me any favours! You don't want to come, you don't want to come. Lig en dred!

The owner of the Croaky Female Voice slams down the phone. Jack sighs in relief, replaces the phone, mops his brow and lights a fag.

Later that evening, Jack enters the Film Exchange. Maureen is at the bar with fellow actors.

JACK

Hello, love. I need a drink. I've had a very unusual . . . Jesus! Mrs Schwartzkopf! . . . It was you!

THE SEVENTIES

INT 2ND FLOOR CORRIDOR – GRANADA TV – DAY – 1970

Jack and Maureen stand waiting for the lift – a discreet silence and discreet distance between them. A particularly hammy performance of perfect-strangers-waiting-for-a-lift from both of them. Maybe Maureen plays it a touch more convincingly than Jack.

The lift arrives. Going down. The doors open.

INT LIFT – GRANADA TV – DAY – 1970 (CONT)

Jack and Maureen go in. Standing inside is a secretary with an armful of files. She and Jack share a polite nod. Then he and Maureen station themselves at opposite sides of the lift. The doors close.

INT 1ST FLOOR CORRIDOR – GRANADA TV – DAY – 1970 (CONT)

The lift arrives. The doors open. The secretary comes out. The doors close.

INT LIFT – GRANADA TV – DAY – 1970 (CONT)

Maureen and Jack promptly leap across the lift and hurl themselves into a passionate embrace, violently clashing their glasses in the process.

INT GROUND FLOOR FOYER – GRANADA TV – DAY – 1970 (CONT)

Two white-overalled decorators (who work permanently at Granada doing a Firth of Forth painting job, starting again at one end of the building as soon as they've finished at the other) stand waiting with paint and brushes.

The lift arrives. The doors open. Maureen and Jack are once again a lift-width apart.

The decorators pile in, and stand, faintly puzzled that neither Jack nor Maureen is getting out . . .

1ST DECORATOR
Um . . . We're going *up* . . .

JACK
Yeah. *We* are.

2ND DECORATOR
But you've just come *down*.

JACK
Yeah, but . . .

MAUREEN
By mistake, really . . . um . . .

JACK
Pressed the wrong whatsit.

MAUREEN
For the ground floor instead of for the whatsit.

JACK
Third.

1ST DECORATOR
(*a puzzled beat*)
Right.

The doors close. The lift goes up.

INT 1ST FLOOR CORRIDOR – GRANADA TV – DAY – 1970 (CONT)

The lift stops. The decorators come out.

INT LIFT – GRANADA TV – DAY – 1970 (CONT)

Jack and Maureen fling themselves back into their embrace. During this:

JACK (VO)
Granada's lifts became synonymous with stolen kisses. Although the most spectacular stolen kiss of all happened in Hull . . . on a weekend visit to Maureen's parents' house.

INT SPARE ROOM – THE LIPMANS' – HULL – NIGHT – 1970

Jack is climbing into his pyjamas.

JACK (VO)

After a traditional Friday night dinner (roasted-over chicken, i.e. chicken roasted, then roasted over. And over. And over. And over. It's Maureen's mum's speciality. The cooked-chicken version of hanging, drawing, quartering, then drowning, then electrocuting, then burying in quicksand), I was billeted in the traditional spare room.

INT MAUREEN'S BEDROOM – THE LIPMANS' – HULL – NIGHT – 1970 (CONT)

Still a cheerful shrine to Maureen's childhood, adorned with pictures, toys and teddy bear. Maureen is wrestling into her nightie.

JACK (VO)

Maureen was back in her old room.

INT MASTER BEDROOM – THE LIPMANS' – HULL – NIGHT – 1970 (CONT)

Maureen's mum, Zelma, is at her dressing table, cramming rollers into her hair. Maurice, Maureen's dad, is sitting up in bed, scouring the Jewish Chronicle *for possible photos of people from Hull.*

JACK (VO)

Zelma and Maurice were, of course, in their own bedroom. All was as it should be.

But wait . . .

INT MASTER BEDROOM – THE LIPMANS' – HULL – NIGHT – 1970

ZELMA
(*calling*)

Maureen!

MAUREEN (OS)
(*in her bedroom*)

Hello?

ZELMA

Are you there?

MAUREEN (OS)

I must be. I'm the one who said hello.

ZELMA

Come and have a chat before you go to sleep.

Maureen goes into her parents' bedroom – sits on edge of bed and chats.

MAURICE
(mumbling through broken sleep)
Chat in the morning . . .

ZELMA
Only for a few minutes.

MAURICE
I want to gay shloffen (go to sleep).

ZELMA
Two minutes, Maurice! We've hardly seen her.

MAURICE
We'll see her in the morning, woman!

ZELMA
(*to Maureen*)
Take no notice. He's only being awkward.

They continue chatting. Maurice's eyelids begin to droop. The newspaper slips from his fingers.

INT SPARE ROOM – THE LIPMANS' – HULL – NIGHT – 1970 (CONT)

Jack pulls the overhead cord to put out the light and settles down to sleep.

INT MASTER BEDROOM – THE LIPMANS' – HULL – NIGHT – 1970 (CONT)

Maureen and Zelma are still swopping their news with, if anything, increasing gusto. Maurice sighs with exaggerated impatience and makes a big performance of pulling the eiderdown over his head on the pillow.

Maureen slips into bed beside Zelma for more titbits of gossip.

MAURICE
Right! That's it! You win!

(*to Maureen*)
You stay here. I'll sleep in *your* room.

(*to Zelma*)
Otherwise you'll have me up all night.

He clambers out of bed.

So don't argue.

ZELMA
Who's arguing? We'd *like* you to go.

Maurice tramps irritatedly out of the room. Zelma shifts to one side to give Maureen more room in the bed. The chatting continues.

INT SPARE ROOM – THE LIPMANS' – HULL – NIGHT – 1970

Jack is fast asleep, oblivious, of course, to the French farce enacted earlier in the master bedroom.

A chink of daylight creeps through the curtains. Jack peers bleary-eyed at his bedside clock. It reads ten past six.

A moment to get his bearings, then he decides to go walkabout to Maureen's bedroom and slides out of bed.

INT MAUREEN'S BEDROOM – THE LIPMANS' – HULL – NIGHT – 1970 (CONT)

Maurice is in dreamland, lying on his side in Maureen's single bed, her teddy bear on the pillow beside him. Just the crown of his head is visible.

The doorknob silently turns. The door slowly opens. Jack creeps in. He closes the door gently and levers himself gingerly into bed, snuggling up behind Maurice.

He slips his arm round him, respected proprietor of a city square tailoring establishment, respectable pillar of Humberside society, president of the local synagogue, Freemason and his girlfriend's father, *for God's sake, and – now here comes the stolen kiss – tenderly kisses the nape of his neck.*

Maurice jack-knifes out of dreamland and leaps up as though he's been shot. By a couple of dozen howitzers. Fists already clenched, he swivels round and sees Jack – the one with the pursed lips. Just as horrified, Jack sees him.

MAURICE

What the bloody hell fire are you doing?

A beat. Jack tries to come up with a sensible reply. And fails.

JACK

I was wondering if you fancied a cup of tea?

EXT BLACKPOOL PROMENADE – DAY – 1970

A dustcart – its name, 'Thunderbird 2', amateurishly painted at the back – is careering haphazardly along. Half hanging out of it are its crew: Cheese and Egg (played by Bryan Pringle), Heavy Breathing (Trevor Bannister), Eric (Tim Wilton) and Winston (Graham Haberfield).

JACK (VO)

As well as writing the first two series of *The Dustbinmen,* I also produced it. Which meant I could give the cast a little

treat, a week's filming well away from Salford's grimy backstreets – in *Blackpool*'s grimy backstreets.

EXT GRIMY BLACKPOOL BACKSTREET – DAY – 1970

A Granada TV film crew are shooting Graham Haberfield hauling a dustbin down the entry. Behind the camera are Les Chatfield, the director, young and handsome, curly-haired, bearded (and often less appreciated than he deserved, especially by Jack), Jack and a small crowd of holidaymakers in their Kiss Me Quick hats who've stopped to watch.

CU Graham:

JACK (VO)

Young Graham Haberfield was one of my most favourite actors. Heart-warmingly vulnerable, sensitive, perceptive, intelligent, brilliant at playing embarrassment, a real pleasure to work with.

And playing Winston was a real pleasure to *him.* It meant he could lay to rest the ghost of 'Jerry', the character he'd been playing for years in *Coronation Street.* If there was one thing that shattered his gentle demeanour and tore his vulnerabilty wide open, it was members of the public calling him 'Jerry'.

In the middle of the shot, a man in the watching crowd calls out.

MAN IN CROWD

Hello, Jerry! How's Ena?

Les, Jack and members of the crew swivel angrily round to 'shush' him.

Graham, a thousand times more angrily, slams his dustbin into the ground.

GRAHAM

(*with little of the aforementioned sensitivity*)

Piss off!

LES

Cut!

EXT BLACKPOOL HOTEL – NIGHT – 1970

A small group of uniformed policemen stroll into the entrance.

JACK (VO)

One night, a Police Federation dinner was being held in the hotel where *The Dustbinmen* cast were staying.

A grim-faced Graham marches out, dressed for a night on the town.

And Graham, sick to death of being called 'Jerry' all day by the entire population of the Fylde coast, went out to get sozzled.

EXT BLACKPOOL HOTEL – NIGHT – 1970

The previous shot of Graham leaving the hotel flips into the reverse image of Graham returning to the hotel some hours later. Although, instead of marching, he's tottering drunkenly.

INT BAR – BLACKPOOL HOTEL – NIGHT – 1970 (CONT)

A posse of policemen are rowdily drinking and laughing. Graham comes staggering in.

JACK (VO)

It didn't take many sniffs of the barmaid's apron to make Graham legless – and that's exactly how many he'd had. Drowning 'Jerry' with each one. On his way to the bar for one more –

He passes out and crashes in a rag-doll heap to the floor. The room falls silent, then the policemen gather round him in concern. Someone throws a glass of water into his face.

He opens his eyes . . .

CAM pans round a circle of policemen's faces from Graham's POV, bobbing and wobbling into view. All staring down at him.

1ST POLICEMAN

You alright, Jerry?

2ND POLICEMAN

Jerry? You okay?

3RD POLICEMAN

Good lad, Jerry, lad.

He closes his eyes again . . . trying to suck the teardrops back inside.

INT JACK'S OFFICE – GRANADA TV – DAY – 1970

Jack and Les Chatfield are poring over a script. At least, Jack *is. Les is* purporting *to. Difficult for him with Margaret in the same room. She's busying herself at her filing cabinet. Not very convincingly, since she's much busier sharing longing glances with Les . . .*

LES

Male or female ants?

JACK
(*stares at him*)

Sorry?

LES

The ants. For the scene with the ants. Do you want little boy ants or little girl ants?

JACK

Have you gone *pot-shop*? There *aren't* any ants!

Les riffles through the script to the relevant scene. He points at a line of stage directions.

LES
(*reading*)

'She pours boiling water from a kettle into the cracks in the pavement to kill the ants.'

JACK

But we don't *see* any ants, Les! It's just explaining what she's doing. There aren't any *actual* ants.

A rueful beat.

LES

Pity.

JACK

Why?

LES

I've ordered a hundred from the Oxford Film Unit. I was going to shoot them through glass.

JACK

Jesus!

LES
(*patting Jack's head*)

Half male, half female. They'd run out of hermaphrodites.

He and Margaret smile at each other. The phone rings.

JACK (VO)

At which point I was subjected to another trick in the Mrs Schwartzkopf tradition.

He picks up the receiver.

JACK
(*into phone*)

Jack Rosenthal.

TIGHT CU MIRIAM MARGOLYES – DAY – 1970 (CONT)

A sweet-faced, plump(ish) young woman, seemingly dressed in fringes, woolly-haired – but most definitely not woolly-headed. She's speaking into a phone. Beautiful, cut-glass intonation.

MIRIAM
(*into phone*)
Oh, good. I'm Miriam Margolyes. I'm an actress. Rather a good one. In fact, a *very* good one. Certainly good enough to be in your comedy series. I'd be marvellous.

INTERCUT between Miriam and Jack, as required:

JACK
(*into phone*)
Um . . . right . . . fine. The only thing is the series is fully cast.

MIRIAM
(*into phone*)
Not one teeny part?

JACK
(*into phone*)
None. Sorry.

MIRIAM
(*into phone*)
You should still meet me, though. In case anything crops up for the future.

JACK
(*into phone*)
Fine. When you're next in Manchester, pop in.

MIRIAM
(*into phone*)
Thanks, I shall.

INT JACK'S OFFICE – GRANADA TV – DAY – 1970 (CONT)

Jack sighs wearily and replaces his receiver.

LES
Who was –?

There's a knock at the door.

JACK
Come in.

Miriam pops her woolly-haired head round the door.

MIRIAM

Hi. Miriam Margolyes. *Has* anything cropped up?

Jack stares at her gobsmacked. As does Les.

JACK

Where were you? When you rang?

MIRIAM

(*smiling sweetly*)

The office next door.

JACK (VO)

If I'd had a part to offer her, I would have. Even Richard III. For sheer chutzpah.

(*beat*)

Or maybe not.

EXT GEOFF'S HOUSE – OLDHAM – DAY – 1970

A grand, imposing, detached Edwardian house in Middlegate – the right side of the Oldham tracks.

In the drive, Jack's Triumph TR6 sports car (in French Navy as opposed to Royal Blue, which he thought *he'd ordered) is parked.*

Jack is loading it up with suitcases, files and his typewriter. Geoff and his son, John, are helping with bits of small repro pieces of furniture – and little Simon with very *small pieces.*

Sarah watches from the window of Geoff's study, crying helplessly as she waves Jack goodbye. She punches the window in frustration – and cries all the more, the bitter tears of childhood.

JACK (VO)

I was moving to Didsbury, a leafy Manchester suburb. Clothorn Road.

I may have been losing a lousy secretary but I was gaining a spacious, sunny Arts and Crafts flat round the corner from Maureen's digs in Fog Lane.

EXT FOG LANE – DIDSBURY – NIGHT – 1970

Maureen and Jack, hand in hand, approach the front door. Maureen opens it.

INT HALLWAY – MAUREEN'S DIGS – DIDSBURY – NIGHT – 1970 (CONT)

Maureen and Jack come in the front door. Maureen closes it quietly behind them.

They start up the stairs.

MRS NIVEN (OS)
(*in living room*)
Is that you, dear?

Maureen judders to a halt.

MAUREEN
(*grimacing*)
Yes, Mrs Niven.

MRS NIVEN (OS)
Let's have a look at you, then, dear.

Maureen and Jack exchange resigned grimaces and start back down the stairs to the living room.

INT LIVING ROOM – MAUREEN'S DIGS – DIDSBURY – NIGHT – 1970 (CONT)

Mrs Niven is Maureen's landlady. Middle-aged, physically a sort of softer version of Tommy Mann – as wide as she is short. Almost entirely globular in fact. Her buttocks seem to begin at the nape of her neck.

She's perched in an armchair in her bare feet. A man, some fifteen years her junior, is on his knees, cutting her toenails. This is Frank, another lodger, her boyfriend and loyal slave.

Maureen and Jack pop their heads in. Mrs Niven's face falls a little on seeeing Jack's.

MRS NIVEN
Oh . . . *Both* of you. Never mind.

(*beat*)
Frank's just going for some fish and chips, aren't you, Frank?

FRANK
If you're fancying, Mrs Niven.

He gets up.

MRS NIVEN
Cod and chips for three, then.

(*as though struck by a sudden thought*)
Unless Jack's not going home *just* yet . . .

(*to Jack*)
Were you planning on staying a minute?

JACK
Well, yes, as a matter of –

MRS NIVEN

For four, then, Frank.

MAUREEN

Actually, we've just eaten, Mrs Niven. In town.

FRANK

(*staunchly, pointedly*)

I think Mrs Niven thought you might appreciate her company.

MAUREEN

Oh.

FRANK

It's not everyone who's given the honour.

MAUREEN

No. Right. Thank you.

JACK

Ta.

They stand in silent defeat.

INT THE STABLES' GREEN ROOM – GRANADA TV – DAY – 1970

Assorted Stables actors lolloping around . . . reading, writing letters, brewing tea, drinking tea, snoozing.

Maureen is showing three or four of them one of her 'telepathy' party tricks: 'The Wizard'. She shuffles a pack of cards, then offers the pack to Richard Wilson.

MAUREEN

Okay. Pick a card. Any card.

He does so. Looks at it.

RICHARD

Four of Hearts.

MAUREEN

Right. I now phone the wizard and he'll tell you the four of Hearts.

She starts to dial a number on the payphone.

INT JACK'S OFFICE – GRANADA TV – DAY – 1970 (CONT)

Jack is dictating a letter to Margaret. Les is once again trying to look as though he's got a valid reason for being there apart from ogling Margaret.

Jack's phone duly rings. He grabs the receiver.

JACK
(into phone)
Hello?

INTERCUT between the Green Room and Jack's office:

MAUREEN
(into phone)
May I speak to the wizard, please?

JACK
(into phone)
Clubs, Diamonds, Hearts –

MAUREEN
(immediately, into phone)
Because I have someone who wants to talk to him.

JACK
(into phone)
Ace, two, three, four –

MAUREEN
(immediately, into phone)
Oh, hello, Wizard. I have someone who wants to talk to you.

She hands the phone to Richard.

RICHARD
(wryly, into phone)
Hello?

JACK
(croaking as per an ancient wizard into phone)
Your card is the four of Hearts.

He slams the phone down. Richard stares at his dead phone, incredulously, then at his fellow actors, then at Maureen.

RICHARD
(bewildered)
Jesus!

INT LES'S BEDROOM – NIGHT – 1970

Les is grimly packing a suitcase. As he puts each item in, his wife bitterly hurls it out again and onto the floor. This leads to a violent tug-of-war with each one.

JACK (VO)
Things had been bad between Les and his wife for a long time. Now that he and Margaret had found their perfect

partner in life, he decided to move out . . . and share my flat in Didsbury.

On his last night in the marital battlefield –

The bedside phone rings. They both lunge across the bed to grab it. Les wins.

LES'S WIFE
If that's your lousy tart, you bastard –

LES
(*a beat, then into phone*)
Pardon?

(*beat*)
Oh. Sorry. Right. Ace, two, three, four, five, six –

His wife grabs whatever she can and throws it at him – pictures from the wall, books, an alarm clock . . . Les tries to dodge the barrage while disentangling himself from the phone flex.

LES
(*into phone*)
Hearts, Diamonds, Clubs –

LES'S WIFE
I'll club you alright, you dirty swine!

LES
(*into phone; croaky wizard voice*)
Your card is the six of Clubs.

A flying hairdryer hits him on the head.

INT GEOFF'S LIVING ROOM – OLDHAM – NIGHT – 1970 (CONT)

A very puzzled Sarah, holding a six of Clubs, is replacing the phone. Seated around are Geoff, Hilda, Simon, John and their visitors Maureen and Jack.

LES (OS)
(*via phone*)
Ow!

HILDA
(*to Sarah*)
Did he tell you your card?

SARAH
Yes. Then he screamed at me . . .

INT CORRIDOR – GRANADA TV – DAY – 1970

Jack, in something of a muck-sweat, is tentatively knocking on the door of a dressing room.

JACK

Just let me in! I'll explain what happened.

From inside, we hear the voice of the actor Alfred Lynch.

ALFRED LYNCH (OS)

(*curtly*)

I *saw* what happened, thank you.

JACK

Alfred! It was a misunderstanding!

ALFRED LYNCH (OS)

I've nothing more to say.

JACK

You've got it all wrong!

ALFRED LYNCH (OS)

(*livid*)

The *character*?

JACK

Not the character! You got what *happened* all wrong!

(*pause*)

Alfred?

(*no answer*)

Alfred. Talk to me.

He gives up, sighs and walks disconsolately away.

JACK (VO)

The actor doing an Elsie Tanner on me was Alfred Lynch, playing Edgar in my play *Your Name's Not God, It's Edgar*. And playing it superbly. Unfortunately he caught me whispering to Mike Apted, the director, on the studio floor – whispering about how brilliant Alfred was. One look at my haunted, ashen face and he assumed I was whispering about how *bad* he was. What he didn't know, of course, was that I *always* looked like that – even when I was delighted. Which I was. He never believed me. I even wrote to him explaining how my face is my misfortune. He still didn't believe me.

Both of us, of course, within our rights to mutter, 'There ain't no justice,' through clenched teeth. No justice. Only injustice. One way or another, we all trudge to the gallows (manned by

our schoolteacher, or boss, or partner or shop assistant or whoever) – entirely blameless – almost every day. Fairness and unfairness were (still are) hobbyhorses of mine and I ride them in virtually every play I've written . . . *Another Sunday and Sweet FA* made no bones about it . . .

FILM EXCERPT: ***Another Sunday and Sweet FA*** **(1971)**

EXT FOOTBALL PITCH – DAY

Various shots of a Sunday morning match in progress in front of the two managers, the two trainers and the odd girlfriend. About seven spectators all told, and a dog. The two teams (wearing only approximate versions of their colours) are CWS Albion 2nd XI and Parker Street Bus Depot. The idea seems to be that victory goes to the team that inflicts the most grievous bodily harm on the other.

JACK (VO)

Another Sunday and Sweet FA – also directed by Mike Apted – was the story of Eric, a football referee, beautifully played by David Swift, officiating at a Collyhurst and District Third Division League Match.

To Eric, life is an Immorality Play. Right never triumphs over wrong. Good never vanquishes evil. No one knows the meaning of 'fairness'. Which is why he's a Sunday morning referee – hoping that in his own small way, in a foreign field that's for ever Manchester, he and his whistle might change the world.

He blows his whistle for a foul. The victim, Ronnie, rolls on the ground. The opposing players profess their innocence.

At the touchline, his girlfriend, Denise, her pal Shirley and the manager, Colin, are watching.

SHIRLEY

Who's down?

COLIN

Ronnie. Right in the doings.

DENISE

(*alarmed*)

What?

Colin picks up his trainer's bag and dashes onto the pitch, water dripping from his magic sponge. Eric sternly waves him away.

ERIC

Alright, back you go.

COLIN

He's in bloody agony!

ERIC

Yes. Actress of the Year Award, 1971.

COLIN

The lad's in pain.

ERIC

Childbirth's never pleasant. Off!

COLIN

Be fair, ref!

At the touchline, Denise shouts angrily:

DENISE

Dirty foulers!

(*to Shirley*)

Kicked him right in my engagement present.

Colin returns to the touchline. Ronnie gets to his feet. Eric whistles for the free kick, and the game resumes. Now Brian, Colin's trainer, yells at Eric.

BRIAN

Be fair, ref!

ERIC (VO)
(*to himself*)

Oh, hello. First cuckoo of spring. He got a free kick. What more did he want? The British Empire Medal and a visit to Match of the Day when it's in his area?

COLIN AND BRIAN

Fair's fair, ref!

ERIC (VO)
(*to himself*)

Same old song. Second verse same as the first, bring on the dancing girls. Slice it for a goal kick and scream for a corner. Boot it into touch and claim a throw-in. One day a player'll come up to me and say – ''Scuse me, Ref, you probably didn't see it, busy as you are, but I've just kicked their striker in the calf. It's preying on my mind so would you care to take my name? Please.'

In the CWS penalty area, Graham, the Parker Street captain, weaves past three defenders, draws the goalkeeper and gently strokes the ball towards goal. It rolls nearer and nearer ... then stops two inches from the line. A defender races up and boots it out of play. Graham turns away, miserably. Eric is nearby.

GRAHAM

We should have a cricket score.

ERIC

That's life, lad.

GRAHAM

(*frustratedly*)

Can't you just give us one?

ERIC

And that's wishful thinking.

GRAHAM

I think there's a jinx on that ball.

ERIC

You can't blame the ball. Blame the patron saint of football.

GRAHAM

Who's that?

ERIC

Mephistopheles.

GRAHAM

Who's that?

The game continues. Tight on Eric as we follow him about the field, refereeing with concentration, grimacing, shaking his head, gesticulating . . .

ERIC (VO)

Nice ball, son! Now use it! Be a decent player, that kid, if he wasn't so . . . That's a foul! Oh, forget it! *He* clobbered *him* a minute ago. Mind you, he deserved it for *calling* him what he did, but then again, he got called it himself in the first half. Vicious circle.`

(*pause*)

So where do you start? Tell them to play the game?

(*he blows his whistle for an infringement*)

Play to the rules? Half of them's probably been on the dole for eighteen months . . . Find the space, lad! Now *shield* the ball! Hard luck. Of course they should have a cricket score. But that *is* life, I wasn't wrong. Not that it ever sinks in.

(*pause*)

And all you can do is tell them to be fair. It's never won a football match yet, mind you. It's never won anything. They might not know Mephistopheles, but they know *that* all right. Been out of nappies long enough.

(pause)

So what do they do? Blame the ref. Yes, lads, I know being fair isn't fair. *Any* day of the week. That's why we turn out on Sundays – hoping this time it will be. It never is, but we *hope*. The beauty of football they used to call it . . .

The game continues.

Then in the ninetieth minute, as Eric looks at his watch, ready to blow the final whistle . . .

. . . a Parker Street player beats his full-back and makes to centre the ball.

CUT to Eric, watching. He suddenly sprints into the CWS penalty area as the ball is centred. As it soars into the goalmouth, Eric leaps into the air like a latter-day Dixie Dean and heads the ball like a rocket into the back of the net.

EXT FOOTBALL PITCH LOCATION – MANCHESTER – DAY – 1971

The Granada Film Unit are shooting the scene with two cameras, one operating at normal speed, one at slow motion. Mike, Peter Eckersley, the producer and Jack stand watching.

JACK (VO)

At least, according to the *script,* he 'heads the ball like a rocket into the back of the net'.

There was only one problem. Which David somehow forgot to mention. He was physically incapable of heading a football. At all. Let alone like Dixie Dean.

Mike tells the actor to centre the ball again. And again. And again. And again. And each time, he either misses it completely or lets it bounce like a big, daft girl's blouse, with his eyes shut, uselessly onto his ear, or shoulder or nose.

There are usually five or six takes allowed shooting a TV film. Sometimes seven. The number of David's takes are now in the thirties. With two cameras running, and twice the film stock being wasted, Peter is getting edgy.

Finally, Mike comes up with a solution. A kid watching David's pathetic attempts in open-mouthed disbelief, has a light, plastic toy football. Mike borrows it. He shoots the actor centring the real ball, then cuts to a single shot of David. Out of vision, he tosses the toy ball gently in the air – and David heads it.

So, therefore, in the edited film, it finally did look like this:

FILM EXCERPT: ***Another Sunday and Sweet FA***

EXT FOOTBALL PITCH – DAY

Eric heads the ball like a rocket into the back of the net. He whistles for a goal, points to the centre-circle and thrusts his arm in the air in a Denis Law triumphal salute.

The impossible has happened. On a quiet Sunday morning in Manchester, the earth has spun to a stop and started rotating in the opposite direction.

The 22 players stare at Eric, dead-eyed, in utter incomprehension. Eric strides back towards the centre-spot, noting the goal in his book and checking the time on his watch.

All the players are standing stock-still: motionless since the moment he headed the ball.

As he passes Graham:

GRAHAM

Er . . . What er . . .

ERIC

Mmm?

GRAHAM

I don't . . . er . . . exactly . . .

ERIC

Get your team back in your own half, laddie, for the kick-off.

GRAHAM

Kick-off?

ERIC

We always kick off after a goal's been scored. Otherwise we'd die of exposure.

GRAHAM

A goal's been scored?

ERIC

A goal's been scored.

GRAHAM

Are we winning 1–0?

ERIC

You're winning 1–0.

Graham throws his arms in the air and yells in jubilation. His team-mates follow suit and race about congratulating and kissing each other.

On the touchline the Parker Street supporters cheer deliriously.

It slowly dawns on the CWS team what's happened. They converge on Eric in a jostling, pushing, angry mob – screaming, threatening and pleading their protests.

In response, he takes from his pocket a copy of the F.A. Laws of Football. *He finds the relevant page.*

ERIC

Law 9, paragraph B of *The Laws of Football* published by the Council of the Football Association, Patron Her Majesty the Queen, states as follows: 'The ball is in play if it rebounds off either the referee or linesman when they are in the field of play.' Satisfied?

He replaces his booklet.

CWS CAPTAIN

Are we hell-as-like! It *didn't* rebound off you!

The rest of his team angrily yell their agreement.

ERIC

(*calmly*)

Don't argue with the referee, lads. I don't want to send you all off. They'd only stroll upfield and tap another in, wouldn't they?

CWS MANAGER

(*murderously*)

Ref. The ball didn't rebound off you. You jumped up and headed the sodding thing in. Deliberate.

ERIC

There's eleven players over there wouldn't agree with that interpretation. And neither would the referee, acting in accordance with the Rules of the Game. And that's all that counts. Be fair.

He blows his whistle.

Full time!

He walks off the pitch, vindicated. MIX from his beaming face to a slow-motion re-enactment of his goal. The words 'Action replay' superimposed over the picture.

INT THE BEVERLY ARMS HOTEL – HULL – NIGHT – 1971

It's one of Maurice's Masonic Ladies' Evenings. Dinner has been dined upon, speeches spoken. Wine glasses have been charged to the east and – for all non-masons know – possibly to the west as well.

A photographer is now taking pictures of family groups, the men in their black ties, the ladies in their sequins. One of the groups is the Lipmans. Maurice and son, rugby-playing, air-transport expert Geoffrey (two or three years Maureen's senior), Zelma, Suzy (Geoffrey's wife), Maureen (hair up à la Audrey Hepburn) and Jack, though not officially a family member.

The photographer keeps trying to position them in what he thinks is the best arrangement. And Zelma keeps overruling him . . . each time firmly shuffling Jack to the end *of the line. The photographer's puzzled by her insistence. So's Jack. Maureen* isn't. *She knows that if Jack never* does *become a member of the family, if he and Maureen split up, if, as Zelma's friends would tut-tut, 'Nothing comes of it,' with one snip of her scissors he would never have existed, history would be rewritten and, most importantly, the photo would look none the worse.*

Three years later, she would actually succeed *in blatantly vandalising another – more significant – photograph. All will be revealed shortly . . .*

INT LIVING ROOM – THE LIPMANS' – HULL – DAY – 1971

Open on the now silver-framed group photo on the sideboard. Jack is still on it, of course. Just. *Still vulnerable, perched at the end.*

CAM pulls back to see Zelma setting the table with cups, saucers, plates and biscuits for two. Jack nicks one of the biscuits.

ZELMA

Will he want a sandwich, do you think?

JACK

No. He's an actor. He's lucky to be getting a biscuit.

ZELMA

I could easily make him a salmon paste sandwich.

JACK

Zelma! He won't *want* a –

The doorbell rings.

I'll go.

He starts for the hall.

ZELMA

Just one little salmon paste sandwich for him, then.

She starts towards the kitchen.

Or two.

INT LIVING ROOM – THE LIPMANS' – HULL – DAY – 1971

An hour or so later . . .

Jack and Richard Beckinsale, a tall, dark and very handsome young actor, are seated in armchairs opposite each other, scripts in hand, reading a scene aloud.

JACK (VO)

I was auditioning Richard for the male lead in a comedy series I'd written, called *The Lovers*.

Set in Altrincham, not exactly the hub of the Permissive Society. And it's about a boy and girl in their early twenties, Beryl and Geoffrey (or 'Geoffrey-Bobbles-Bon-Bon' in Beryl's more romantic moments, and 'Percy Filth' in his*). It's about the games courting couples play. And invariably lose.*

Beryl is prim, proper and with one ambition: to marry Geoffrey without him having got her into bed. And one dream: to share the wildest orgy in the history of orgies with Paul McCartney.

Geoffrey also has one ambition: to get Beryl into bed without *marrying her. And one dream: to marry Brigitte Bardot.*

The only trouble is neither Paul nor Brigitte come to Altrincham all that often.

Almost thirty years before *The Royle Family,* the initial idea of *The Lovers* was for the characters to talk their way through each episode, their backsides rooted to Beryl's mum's settee. Unfortunately, unlike *The Royle Family,* it didn't work and the settee element was abandoned. The concept of *The Royle Family* was much more adventurous and groundbreaking. Cleverer. Much.

Richard was being auditioned in Zelma's house because it was more convenient to meet in Hull – which is a phrase that can't have been said often in life – since Hull was where he was appearing in a stage play.

The reason he was being auditioned at *all* was also unique: every actor who'd so far read the script had said, 'There's only one actor for this part. Richard Beckinsale. Tailor-made for him.' One actor talking himself out of a job is unusual enough. But six?

Zelma comes in to collect the crockery, the remains of the biscuits and the untouched salmon paste sandwiches.

ZELMA

(*brightly, to Richard*)

Has he given you the part?

RICHARD

(*embarrassed*)

Oh, I don't . . . I mean . . . um . . .

JACK

(*also embarrassed*)

We haven't yet . . . We're still . . .

ZELMA

(*to Richard, indulgently*)

He *will*. I've no qualms. You'll take a marvellous part.

(*confidentially*)

He *listens* to me.

She goes. Jack and Richard tug their sideburns (a characteristic of both Jack and Geoffrey-Bobbles-Bon-Bon) uncomfortably.

JACK (VO)

I hate to say it, but she was right. He got the part. And *was* marvellous. As he was in later years in *Porridge* and *Rising Damp* and everything he played. He died suddenly, shatteringly, still so young, from a heart attack. I'm certain he would have become one of our very finest actors, comic, romantic or tragic. His delicacy of touch had already become a trademark. Though it wasn't all that delicate when he played football in the rehearsal room. I had the bruises to prove it.

EXT OXFORD ROAD – MANCHESTER – DAY – 1971

Jack is driving his Triumph GT6. The traffic lights go to red. He stops, then glances out of the passenger window. The glance suddenly becomes an intense, excited stare . . .

EXT SHOP WINDOW – OXFORD ROAD – DAY – 1971 (CONT)

From Jack's POV, we see the window stocked with artists' materials.

EXT OXFORD ROAD – MANCHESTER – DAY – 1971 (CONT)

Jack is still staring – coming to what seems like an earth-shattering decision.

The lights change to green. He continues to stare. The cars behind start to honk.

He drives around the corner and parks. He gets out of the car and strides resolutely back to the shop.

INT KITCHEN – JACK'S FLAT – DIDSBURY – NIGHT – 1971

Jack is at the kitchen table, building a skeletal aluminium armature of an action figure about ten inches high. At hand are a couple of clay-modelling manuals and wooden tools.

He then starts bedding layers of modelling clay to the armature. Gradually the model begins to take the shape of a footballer in mid-shot.

JACK (VO)

When I was little, half the pleasure of visiting my Auntie Mary in Heaton Park was being given apfel strudel. The other half was stroking her white, marble (maybe alabaster) lion squatting ominously on her sideboard. I grew up loving figurative sculpture – bronzes most of all. And for all my adult life, I'd had this pricking urge to try my hand at making one. I promised myself that, one day, I'd buy some clay and do a Rodin.

Then, that day, I did. Buy some clay, that is. Not quite do a Rodin, unless he made an as yet undiscovered bronze of Bobby Charlton.

In a developing series of rapid shots, the model becomes more and more identifiable as the Manchester United and England footballer.

JACK (VO)

From the minute I got my clay home, I got more and more obsessed. (My obsessiveness is well known to those who know me and have to suffer it. The obsessions are often short-lived, but nonetheless intense while they last. And often, as with the sculpture, they do return even if half a lifetime later.) I started work on Bobby at four o'clock that first day. By midnight, I noticed I hadn't drunk a single cup of coffee (most unusual) or smoked a single Silk Cut (unheard of).

INT KITCHEN – JACK'S FLAT – DIDSBURY – DAY – 1972

Months later.

Les sprays four or five J-Cloths with water, then gently drapes the cloths over an aluminium cage to cover the now much more detailed clay model.

JACK (VO)

Making Bobby took, in all, over two years (I think Rodin took the odd Thursday afternoon), having to make way a little for other obsessions – writing and Maureen.

Maureen had by now moved back to London, working for the National Theatre at The Old Vic, cycling between there and her Kentish Town digs every day.

I used to drive down to see her at the weekends, and Les was landed with the essential chore of keeping Bobby moist. Our social lives (mostly *his*) were governed by always having to race back to the flat 'to stop Bobby cracking'.

INT JACK'S OFFICE – GRANADA TV – DAY – 1972

Jack is dictating a letter to Margaret. The phone rings. She takes it.

MARGARET
(*into phone*)
Jack Rosenthal's office.

INT RECEPTION – GRANADA TV – DAY – 1972 (CONT)

The commissionaire is speaking into his phone, somewhat guardedly, as though – for Jack's sake – not wanting to be overheard. Facing him impassively across his desk are two broad-shouldered gents who could be nothing else but police detectives. And are.

COMMISSIONAIRE
(*into phone*)
I've two chaps here want to see Jack.

INT JACK'S OFFICE – GRANADA TV – DAY – 1972 (CONT)

A beat, then Margaret stares, gobsmacked, at her phone. Jack stares, gobsmacked, at Margaret.

JACK
From *where?*

MARGARET
The Vice Squad.

INT RECEPTION – GRANADA TV – DAY – 1972 (CONT)

Commissionaire and detectives, as before.

COMMISSIONAIRE
(*into phone*)
No, love, I don't *think* they're kidding.

A beat, then to the detectives.

He's on his way.

INT LOUNGE AREA – RECEPTION – GRANADA TV – DAY – 1972 (CONT)

Jack sits tensely hunched – hoping it gives the impression of appearing languidly at ease – between the two policemen on settees. Whatever crime they're about to accuse him of he's already convinced he's committed. If anyone wanted to make a sculpture entitled Guilt, Sweat and Remorse, *he'd be a perfect model.*

1ST DETECTIVE

Morning.

JACK

Morning.

1ST DETECTIVE
(*shows ID*)

Detective-Sergeant Cartwright.

2ND DETECTIVE
(*shows ID*)

Detective Constable Marsh.

JACK

How de do.

1ST DETECTIVE

We're making enquiries apropos of the murder of a young woman at Mere Corner in Cheshire.

JACK

'Murder'. I see. Uh-huh. Right.

He rifles, panic-stricken, through his memory for any young women he's murdered.

2ND DETECTIVE

We're interviewing men who drive blue sports cars.

1ST DETECTIVE

I.e. possible suspects.

JACK

Quite right. Good thinking.

2ND DETECTIVE
(*checks his notebook*)

Are you the owner of a blue Triumph GT6, Registr–

JACK
(*interrupting*)
Yes.

1ST DETECTIVE
Actually, we're interviewing men who drive blue sports cars and who make a habit of picking up blondes in miniskirts and giving them lifts.

JACK
I don't.

2ND DETECTIVE
(*checks his notebook*)
You did last Thursday. Palatine Road, Didsbury, 11.25 a.m.

A beat. Jack furrows his brow and ponders.

JACK
Did I?

1ST DETECTIVE
We have a witness.

Another beat. Jack's brow unfurrows. He relaxes.

JACK
Correct. I did. She's a producer. Pal of mine. She works here. Fifth floor. He didn't happen to mention what she was carrying did he – your expert witness?

1ST DETECTIVE
Carrying?

JACK
Carrying. He didn't mention when he was clocking her miniskirt and her blonde hair that she was carrying the biggest electric fire you've seen in your life – did he?

The detectives look slightly disappointed.

Shall I get the commissionaire to tell her to come down?

1ST DETECTIVE
S'okay, *we* will.

(*beat*)
In which case, you can tootle off back to your office.

JACK
Thanks.

He gets up to go, then stops and turns back.

Incidentally, who was it shopped me, this witness?

2ND DETECTIVE
A gentleman who happened to be looking out of the window of his flat. Nice man. President of the Spanish and Portuguese Synagogue.

JACK
(*laughs*)
Perfect.

1ST DETECTIVE
(*checks notebook*)
He doesn't seem to have noticed the radiator. Just that she was blonde. And wearing a miniskirt.

JACK
Of course.

He continues on his way towards the lifts. Ten minutes older and wiser.

EXT WEST END STREETS – LONDON – DAY – 1972

Jack is strolling along, whistling contentedly to himself.

JACK (VO)
With a growing list of TV shows to my credit, I was in the market for a new agent.

My first agent had been Liz Evett, a good agent, a good pal and a quite superb healer – using transcendental meditation. So superb she began to scare herself, and stopped doing it.

She also stopped being an agent, and joined Granada TV.

My next agent was Kenneth Ewing – mostly because he represented the whole of Group North. The closest *we* got was sharing a bed when I was staying overnight from Thornton Cleveleys and Kenneth from London, and Harry Driver put us up in his house. We both spent the night flat on our backs on the edges of the bed. No reason.

But now I was promenading round the West End looking under stones for agents to audition.

First on the list was Anthony Jones.

INT ANTHONY JONES'S OFFICE – LONDON – DAY – 1972

Anthony, very tall, very slim, bright with bonhomie, is at his desk, speaking into his phone.

ANTHONY JONES
(*into phone*)
How about lunch tomorrow, then?

INT LIVING ROOM – JACK'S FLAT – DIDSBURY – DAY – 1972 (CONT)

Jack is flopped in an armchair, speaking into his phone.

JACK
(*into phone*)
Fine.

INT ANTHONY JONES' OFFICE – LONDON – DAY – 1972 (CONT)

Anthony, as before.

ANTHONY JONES
(*into phone*)
Anywhere special?

INT LIVING ROOM – JACK'S FLAT – DIDSBURY – DAY – 1972 (CONT)

Jack, as before.

JACK
(*into phone*)
Anywhere but Joe Allen's. I can't hear myself think in Joe Allen's.

EXT WEST END STREETS – LONDON – DAY – 1972

Jack strolls along with a slightly cocky, independent air.

JACK (VO)
Whereupon he booked a table for two at Joe Allen's.

Okay, maybe he misheard. Maybe he didn't catch the 'anywhere but' bit, but I decided to work my way further down the list.

I may have been too presumptuous jilting Anthony. He's proved himself to be one of the best agents. Though one day I found him just a touch too sycophantic . . .

[Flash forward to:]

INT UNIVERSAL STUDIOS SCREENING ROOM – HOLLYWOOD – DAY – 1982

In darkness, a screening of Mike Apted's latest film is just coming to an end. It's Continental Divide *– John Belushi's last film before his death – written by Lawrence Kasdan and rewritten by me. The film is not good.* Very *not good.*

The final credits fade. The house lights go up. The four or five studio executives sit in numb, dumb silence. So do Mike and his LA agent and Anthony. So does Mike's wife, Jo. And so do I. Then, suddenly –

LA AGENT

Magical!

ANTHONY JONES

Absolutely magical!

And they start to clap.

JACK (VO)

I suppose, for their client's immediate sake, that may have been the right thing to do. For his future sake, maybe telling the truth would've been smarter. Sorry, am I being naive?

INT CORRIDOR – FIFTH FLOOR – GRANADA TV – DAY – 1972

Jack walks past an open office door. Inside is a young woman, Judy Daish. They wave at each other. Jack walks on.

JACK (VO)

Judy Daish was a PA down the corridor from me at Granada in my *Another Sunday and Sweet FA* days.

CAM *stays on the open door, as Judy works at her desk.*

She eventually became a very successful agent, and I often felt she may have been the right one for me but, pally though we'd always been, I couldn't even suggest it. Her 'friendship' (in quotes) with Mike Apted, and my friendship (without quotes) with his wife, Jo, made it impossible. I think Jo would never have spoken to me again. What's a career between friends?

EXT GOODWIN'S COURT – WEST END – LONDON – DAY – 1972

Jack rounds the corner into the narrow, picturesque alley. He goes to number 14a, opens the door and starts up a steep staircase.

JACK (VO)

So here I was, on my way to see the most legendary agent of all, the agent even other agents recommended, like actors did

with Richard Beckinsale. The doyenne of the West End – Peggy Ramsay.

INT PEGGY RAMSAY'S OFFICE – LONDON – DAY – 1972

Jack is perched on the edge of a fairly worn settee, as though worshipping at the feet (one of them shoeless) of the master. The wall behind him parades a row of Evening Standard *Award programmes, commemorating the theatrical successes of various of her clients. The other walls are covered with framed theatre posters of more of their triumphs, the floor and every surface a mass – and mess – of scripts from hopeful unknowns and even more of her clients.*

The office, and Peggy, are colourful, chaotic and eccentric to the point of barminess.

Peggy, in her fifties, is a slim, willowy, reddish-fair-haired woman in floating organdie, her legs (of which she's clearly, and probably justly, proud) stretched out, crossed, on her desk. As she talks, she occasionally heaves her behind off her chair to flail her legs in the air like the sails of a windmill and cross them the other way.

JACK (VO)

I fell for her – and her office.

In 2002, she was played onstage to absolute perfection by Maureen in Alan Plater's play ***Peggy for You.*** Although Maureen had never met her, she got every tic, every twitch, every billowing swoop of her undulating body, every over-long stride, the sharpness of her voice, the angularity of her stance.

Peggy the First prattled on for about an hour and made me feel I was the best writer in the land. She always did, over the years, even when I suspected she didn't think much of me at all.

(Years later, I discovered I was right to be suspicious . . . That's a whole other story for the 1990s.)

So I went with the eccentric. She had no idea about fees, about what her clients were worth, what the going rates were, no interest in money, ***our*** money. When Universal asked me to rewrite ***Continental Divide,*** they were three weeks away from shooting. In trouble. I told her she could therefore get whatever she asked for. To me she said, 'Are you being greedy, dear?'; to billionaire Universal Pictures she said, 'How do I know if you ***have*** any money? Where do you keep it? In a cardboard box under your desk?'

She accepted their first offer after getting it into her head that since I said I ***wasn't*** being greedy, I had a private income. Forget 'eccentric', just read 'barmy'.

EXT LAKE HOUSE – SOUTH HILL PARK – HAMPSTEAD – DAY – 1973

A steep hill of tall, terraced Victorian houses. Wedged between two of the terraces is a small, sixties block of flats. This is Lake House.

The record of Carly Simon's 'You're so Vain' is playing OS.

Jack's car is parked outside. On the ground beside the boot are his suitcases.

He's gingerly carrying the finished clay model of Bobby Charlton inside its aluminium cage, swathed in J-Cloths, towards the entrance to the flats.

Maureen is holding the door open.

JACK (VO)

Now that I'd changed agents, I did what all the agents I'd met told me to do – move to London.

I came to live with Maureen in Jennie Stoller's flat – Jennie being a fellow actress friend of Maureen's from the sixties. At the time my absentee landlady was touring the world in Peter Brook's *Midsummer Night's Dream.*

For a decade, I'd been reluctant to move from Manchester. Isn't it painful pulling up roots? Would I ever write again?

The pain lasted about twelve seconds – once I'd discovered that nobody in London came from London – and I wrote up a storm . . .

INT JENNIE'S LIVING ROOM – LAKE HOUSE – HAMPSTEAD – DAY – 1973

Jack sits at a white formica, circular dining table, busy typing. Facing him is a wall-length picture window looking out onto the spectacular Hampstead Heath and its ponds.

JACK (VO)

With Maureen onstage at the Old Vic, for my next trick I was writing a new play, called *For My Next Trick.*

It's a TV studio play about a young woman who, each evening, goes to look round houses for sale in readiness for her imminent marriage. We discover at the end, that not only is her marriage not imminent, she doesn't even have a boyfriend. What she doesn't discover is that the house she visits isn't for sale. The 'vendor' is only using the For Sale sign to lure in passing strangers for a cup of tea, a biscuit and a natter. A tale of two lonely people. For 89 of its 90 minutes, though, a comedy.

The doorbell rings. Jack goes to the door and opens it.

JACK (VO)

I had a few strangers of my own popping in for cups of tea, friends of Jennie's or Maureen's.

Philip Sayer greets him and strides in. Philip is a tall, shoulderlength-haired, strikingly handsome young Welshman, with the aquiline profile of a Red Indian. 'Heap Big Charismatic Chieftain'.

JACK (VO)

Philip was another graduate of LAMDA. The long white dress he was sporting was apparently a kaftan. To those of us from Cheetham Hill, it was a dress.

INT JENNIE'S LIVING ROOM – LAKE HOUSE – HAMPSTEAD – DAY – 1973

Philip and Jack stand at the window, looking out over the Heath, sipping cups of tea.

JACK (VO)

Philip was a witty, fun-loving, often outrageous man of rare beauty – inside and out. I've known no one more excitingly alive than Philip. 'The good die young' could so aptly, and so sadly, have been his epitaph.

INT JENNIE'S LIVING ROOM – LAKE HOUSE – HAMPSTEAD – NIGHT – 1973

Jack is again writing at the table. Again, the doorbell rings. He gets up and opens the door. A young black man – Toby – is standing there.

JACK (VO)

Not all calls were purely social . . .

TOBY

Hi. Toby. Jennie home?

JACK

She's away for six months.

TOBY

Damn. I usually supply her once a month.

JACK

With what?

Didsbury folk were a bit innocent in 1973.

TOBY

Usually about £5 worth.

JACK

What of?

TOBY

(*a puzzled beat*)

You're joking, right?

INT JENNIE'S LIVING ROOM – LAKE HOUSE – HAMPSTEAD – NIGHT – 1973

Some weeks later.

Jack is at his usual station, working. Once again, the doorbell rings. He answers it. A second young black man is on the threshold. This is Patrick.

JACK

Hi.

PATRICK

Hi. Jennie home?

JACK

In Africa or somewhere. Back in October.

PATRICK

Okay. October. No sweat.

He turns to go.

JACK

Would you like me to take some, say £10 worth, for when she gets back?

PATRICK

(*turns back, puzzled*)

Some what?

A beat. It slowly dawns on Jack that not all black men are the same person.

JACK

Ah. You're not Toby, are you?

PATRICK

Patrick. An old pal of hers. If she phones, tell her the police cadet called to say hi.

JACK

Police cadet?

PATRICK

Right.

JACK

(*sucks his teeth, embarrassedly*)

All that gubbins about £10 worth . . . Only joking.

EXT WEST LONDON SYNAGOGUE – DAY – 1973

Guests arrive for a wedding at the Moorish-styled entrance of the synagogue. Zelma is in her finery, maybe a little incongruously laden with shopping bags.

JACK (VO)

It's February 18th,1973. Jack's position at the end of the line in the photograph in Hull is now secure. Zelma has put away her scissors, fried 300 salmon patties and taken them to her daughter's wedding in case the caterers are suddenly afflicted with a communal migraine and fail to turn up.

INT ANTE-ROOM – WEST LONDON SYNAGOGUE – DAY – 1973

Maureen is wearing a petrel-blue dress, leg o' mutton sleeves, sweetheart neckline, an extra piece of material sewn in to make it less décolleté and looking a picture in a large picture hat.

Maurice is standing beside her.

From the other side of the door, we hear the 'Wedding March'.

MAURICE

Mammele, I'm the proudest father in the whole world. You should only be happy – I love you. See you inside.

He goes inside – leaving her OUTSIDE. Incredulously, she watches him. Then snaps to attention, wedges her specially dyed satin shoe in the door and hisses down the aisle.

MAUREEN

Dad! Dad! You're supposed to come *with* me! To walk me down the aisle! It's supposed to be the moment you've been waiting for for twenty years!

MAURICE

(*looks back, puzzled*)

Oh. Fair enough, Mammele – you should've said.

He takes her arm and they walk sedately in time to the music.

INT WEST LONDON SYNAGOGUE – DAY – CONT – 1973

A synagogue of richly ornate, exotic, quixotic architecture.

The guests – friends, relatives and seemingly half the actors and actresses in Spotlight *– in their pews.*

Maureen and Maurice make their way down the aisle. Jack (in a dark brown suit, its matching tie bought the previous day minutes before the shops closed) is waiting under the bimah, flanked by Zelma and Lakey.

Instead of the shul's rabbi, Hugo Gryn – who eventually became a great friend – Rabbi Percy Goldberg of the Manchester Reform Synagogue is officiating. He's been officially (and, as it turns out, mistakenly) requested by Jack.

Mistakenly, since he knows Jack very well indeed, and Maureen not at all. In his eulogy, therefore, he praises Jack, for what seems like three hours – mostly for writing Coronation Street *– and seems unaware that there's this young woman in this picture hat standing next to him. Who is also getting married.*

EXT HAMPSTEAD STREETS – DAY – 1973

Hundreds of pages of A4 paper, covered in typewritten lines, swirl and dance crazily through the air, swooping and buffeting in what seems like a monster snow-storm.

JACK (VO)

No, not confetti. This was the storm I mentioned I was writing up. The storm became a blizzard, then a whirlwind, then a hurricane. Tornado may be going a bit too far.

As page after page splatters into CAM, we see some of them bear titles . . . The Lovers/Feature Film *– but that one quickly and silently blows away; then* Hot Fat, *a BBC* Play for Today . . .

JACK (VO)

. . . which was distinguished by the lead actor being knocked over by a car on his way to the studio on recording day. Not fatally, thank God, but bad enough for him to go to hospital. A replacement was swiftly found. I went through his lines with him in his dressing room for an hour, poor soul, then bundled him in front of the cameras. It was a brave try, but we didn't quite get away with it. He managed to get *some* of his lines right – but clearly didn't know what the hell they were talking about . . .

FILM EXCERPT: ***Hot Fat***

INT SAUNA CHANGING ROOM – DAY

Mrs Lane, the receptionist, is pointlessly giving the deceased Mr Pate mouth-to-mouth resuscitation. Mr Holland is equally pointlessly massaging Pate's heart.

JACK (VO)

It was a play about three strangers in a sauna. Not so much about people not being what they seem, more about what they'd *like* to have been. The lead character dies in the sauna. In his wallet, the others find a scrap of paper . . .

MR TORTOISESHELL

(*reading it*)

'G Pate Esq. c/o The Salvation Army Hostel, Corn Street, SW14, Obituary Notice.'

MR HOLLAND

What?

MR TORTOISESHELL

That's what it says.

MR HOLLAND

He's walking around – *was* – with his own obituary?

MR TORTOISESHELL

(*reading*)

'In the event of my death, please send the following information to the newspapers. G Pate, born Willesden, London, 1919. BA Oxford, MA Cambridge and also a PhD into the bargain. First Lieutenant Grenadier Guards 1939 to 1944, VC. Author of several books of political, sociological and philosophical content. Awarded Order of Merit but declined to accept. Original thinker and man of action and opening batsman for Yorkshire Cricket Club heading the batting averages for three seasons. Much admired, loved and respected, he will long be remembered with admiration, love and respect. RIP'

A numb silence.

MR HOLLAND

You *can't* play for Yorkshire if you're born in Willesden.

JACK (VO)

Appearance versus reality, as Terry Land used to say . . .

EXT HAMPSTEAD SKYLINE – DAY – 1973

The next sheet of A4 to skitter past CAM reads Polly Put the Kettle On, *the story of a determinedly excited, desperately sad woman who, bit by bit, tries to commandeer her daughter's wedding reception as her own . . . As though she's the bride. Celebrating the happiest day of her life. A day that, unbeknown to her daughter, she herself never had.*

This is followed by Mr Ellis Versus The People, *a (partially) romantic comedy set in a polling station on election day and starring Ron Moody. It begins with his character (the Returning Officer) leaving his house to go to the polling station.*

INT REHEARSAL ROOM – GRANADA TV – 1973

Ron and his fellow actors, Jack and the director sit at a trestle table leafing through their scripts.

After the read-through, Ron insists on knowing whether his house has a porch or not. No one knows; no house has yet been picked for filming. He says he can't play the scene till he knows.

JACK (VO)

Was I going potty? He wouldn't *have* to play the scene till he's being filmed actually leaving the house. And he'd *know* then if it had a porch or not. By . . . er . . . *looking* at it.

(*beat*)

I'm not very *au fait* with the subtle differences between porch and non-porch acting . . .

EXT HAMPSTEAD STREETS – DAY – 1973

Pedestrians' feet shuffle through piles of A4 falling and sticking to the pavements.

One of the pages carries the title There'll Almost Always be an England. *The inhabitants of a street are threatened by a gas-leak and are evacuated to their village hall for the night. During it they start new friendships, tentative romances and new enmities.*

As they dust themselves down to go home the next morning, believing the danger is over, there's supposed to be an enormous explosion down the street. In the context of the relationships, it's a deliberately cynical, sour ending. Pessimistic and unpatriotic. However, a Union–Management dispute has led to the studio technicians refusing to work overtime. At nine o'clock precisely they pull the plug – and there's no explosion. The play ends optimistically and patriotically. The very opposite of what's intended. The next day the Daily Express *review is delighted.*

CAM picks out another title – Big Sid. *Starring Ronald Lewis, it's a tale of a Lancashire League cricketer at the end of a distinguished career. Grateful club directors offer him future security – then renege on their promises. The one-time hero faces poverty. Invited to be the guest speaker at his local grammar school's Speech Day – and now deeply embittered – he decides to tell a few home truths about life . . .*

FILM EXCERPT: *Big Sid*

INT SID'S BEDROOM – NIGHT

Sid stands with the notes of his speech before the full-length wardrobe mirror. Throughout the entire speech, from first word to last, he speaks reasonably and pleasantly . . .

The MUSIC of Forty Years On *creeps in.*

SID

School Governors, Headmaster, Members of Staff, School. It's a great honour to be here today to present prizes to those who've been successful on the field of play.

(*beat*)

Just over twenty years ago, I was sat where you are now. In this same hall. In them same chairs. P'rhaps with the same lumps of chewing-gum stuck underneath. Half listening to some old fogey like me droning on with the same old clichés you hear every Speech Day.

(*beat*)

Only this time, lads, I'd like you to *really* listen. Because *this* time, for the *first* time, someone's going to tell you summat worth knowing. Specially those of you leaving today.

(*beat*)

Twenty years ago – I knew nowt. Happen a bit about litmus paper and Palmerston and the square on the hypotenuse and the other two sides. What I *didn't* know was everything else. I didn't know that everybody was just as scared of everybody *else* as *I* was. I didn't know we were all the same. That, that big successful feller stood up there on Speech Day was just a feller whose pyjama bottoms rolled up in the night like mine did, and who – and now we come to the really funny bit – told *lies* like I did.

(*beat*)

I didn't know that that feller up there was a liar. Like your headmaster. Like your teachers. All liars. Because the one fact of life they never teach you is what bastards people are. And that the only way to live with them is to be a bigger bastard. You come first. Remember that. Kick them before they kick you. Kick them where it hurts. Above all, kick them when they're down.

(*beat*)

Here endeth the first, last and only lesson worth knowing. Of course, one or two of you have already mastered the basic principles. And you're the ones – the Bastards – it's my privilege to present prizes to. So I'd first like to call on ...

He turns slowly, aware that he's being watched. His wife, Sheila, is at the door, staring at him, having heard every word. And horrified.

DISSOLVE TO:

INT SCHOOL ASSEMBLY HALL – DAY

The entire school is assembled in the body of the hall. The governors, headmaster, staff – and Sid – are seated on the platform.

MUSIC OVER: 'Lord, Dismiss Us with Thy Blessing'.

On his way into the school, Sid has been offered a job out of the blue by one of the governors, to manage a sports centre. His future is now assured, gift-wrapped and tied in a bow with the old school tie ...

He's called on to give his speech. He goes to the podium and takes his notes from his pocket. Sheila watches ...

SID

School Governors, Headmaster, Members of Staff, School. It's a great honour to be here today.

(*beat*)

Just over twenty years ago, I was sitting where you are now ... and I learnt something here that was true for me then and has been ever since. And that is ...

He puts his notes back in pocket.

... always keep a straight bat. Always abide by the umpire's decision. Always play the game.

As he continues, Sheila stares at him in relief and disbelief. The headmaster and governors beam with pleasure. The MUSIC reaches its climax.

EXT HAMPSTEAD STREET – DAY – 1973

The gale-force wind has dropped. A streetsweeper is sweeping the scattered sheets of A4 along the gutter and into his bin. A woman cleans the inside of a bin she's just emptied.

CAM floats gently onto a page entitled Sadie, It's Cold Outside – Comedy Series, 6 Episodes.

JACK (VO)

The series dealt with a long-married couple, expertly played by the delightful Rosemary Leach (Sadie) and equally delightful Bernard Hepton (Norman), at a loss what to do with their lives in the icy, hostile, threatening world that began in the seventies, now that their offspring have sprung off . . .

FILM EXCERPT: *Sadie, It's Cold Outside*, Episode 1

INT SUPERMARKET – DAY

Sadie, in big CU.

ANNOUNCER'S VOICE

This is Sadie. She is one of the five out of every five housewives who can't tell Stork from Blue Band, Summer County and Flora.

When she was a little girl, her one ambition was to be a housewife. She thought how exciting it would be to cook, clean and go shopping every day.

She has now cooked, cleaned and gone shopping 8,279 times.

Her one ambition now is to take all her clothes off in the middle of Tesco's, stick a Green Shield stamp on her navel and scream herself sick.

CASHIER

Next!

Pull back to see that Sadie is next in line in a queue of women, waiting to be dealt with by a young, foul-tempered cashier.

I haven't got all rotten day!

SADIE

Sorry.

CASHIER

(*ringing up the total*)

£3.89. D'you want a carrier bag?

SADIE

(*pathetically grateful*)

Oh, yes, please.

CASHIER

That'll be £3.99. *Next!*

Sadie pays and looks puzzled that the cashier isn't packing the carrier with her purchases. She realises she has to pack them herself, and does so.

SADIE

Good afternoon.

CASHIER

(*suspiciously*)

What do you mean?

SADIE

When?

CASHIER

Then.

SADIE

Nothing. Just 'Good afternoon' . . .

CASHIER

I don't get paid to get insulted. If you've any complaints see the manager. He's in Tenerife.

Sadie wanders bemusedly off.

CASHIER

(*to herself*)

All the same. No bloody respect. Next!

CUT TO:

EXT FACTORY YARD – DAY

Norman in big CU.

ANNOUNCER'S VOICE

This is Norman, Sadie's husband. Norman was a Marmite baby in the days when bread used to taste of bread. At fourteen and a half they started courting.

During those long, hot, perfect summer evenings we've heard so much about, they'd shelter from the pouring rain in the bandstand in the park; he'd hold her hand and whisper what he was going to do when he grew up. Open the batting for England, harness the power of the sun, lead the workers to revolution, nationalise the monarchy, unite the whole of mankind in brotherhood and love – and be a millionaire. Norman was special. A man of destiny. One thing he'd never be was one of the crowd.

A factory hooter sounds.

Pull back to see that, throughout the CU, he's in the midst of a seething mass of factory workers making their way out of the gates at the end of the day.

ANNOUNCER'S VOICE

He hasn't yet, however, got round to doing *any* of those things. He would've done but he's been busy every Monday, Tuesday and Wednesday night watching television. The same goes for Thursdays, Fridays and Saturdays. And Sunday, of course, is his day of rest. So he watches television. His favourite programme is the weather forecast.

DISSOLVE TO:

INT BEDROOM – NIGHT

Sadie pulls the cord to switch off the light. She and Norman settle down to sleep. Suddenly Norman switches the light on again.

NORMAN

The traffic was better this morning.

SADIE

Norman! You've had all evening to talk! And all you did was nod off in front of the telly!

NORMAN

There were only eleven traffic jams. The bus driver started crying with joy. Big, strong lad. Pakistani. A traffic warden had to slap his face and tell him to pull himself together. He'd only go through the traffic lights when they were at green. Must be a learner.

An empty silence.

SADIE

This is it, isn't it, Norman. Life. What it was all for. Why I slept with bitter aloes on my fingernails and Victor Mature under my pillow. And had to wear National Health glasses through eating dried eggs. And let you put your hand up my dirndl skirt at the Festival of Britain while my mother thought I was potato-picking with the Young Conservatives. And married you. And brought up a daughter without a single fishfinger. And taught her the hula hoop and a sense of values. Then watched her run off with the first spotty-faced hooligan who showed her his Roy Orbison.

She switches off the light. The room is half-lit by moonlight. All is quiet, then, with a deep sigh . . .

P'raps I'll change the living room furniture round tomorrow.

NORMAN

Righto.

SADIE

I changed it round yesterday.

NORMAN

Did you?

SADIE

You only didn't notice because I changed it round the day before.

NORMAN

That's the idea, love. As long as you're happy.

EXT 31 ROSSLYN HILL – HAMPSTEAD – DAY – 1973

A tall, imposing house in a grand Victorian terrace, white globes at the gate, white pillars at the front door. Jack and Maureen have moved into their own marital flat on the ground floor. Out of the scores of flats they'd tramped round, this is the one they always wanted. Their dream flat. Mortgaged for £21,500.

Outside is parked a van. On its side are the words 'Dry Rot Specialists'. Two men, with their heavy-duty rot-fighting equipment, get out and make their way up to the front door.

INT LIVING ROOM – HAMPSTEAD FLAT – EVENING – 1973

Open on a tray bearing two plates of baked beans on toast and two mugs of tea.

CAM pulls back to see that it's being carried to the oval, glass table with much ceremony by Maureen. She's in full evening dress.

Jack is seated at the table, knife and fork at the ready. He's in a tuxedo, bow tie, cufflinks, shiny black shoes. Maureen serves their dinner with a flourish.

For some arcane reason they seem to think that wearing evening dress while chunks of their walls are being hacked out would somehow show the exposed dry rot that they're too suave to care. The fact that dinner is Heinz Baked Beans perhaps spoils the effect.

EXT 31 ROSSLYN HILL – HAMPSTEAD – DAY – 1973

Jack comes out of the flat – now untuxedo'd *– carefully carrying the now completed, cast and patina'd bronze of Bobby* Charlton.

After Jack's two years of fiddling with clay and Les's two years of wet J-Cloths, Bobby the bronze is about to be given to Bobby the man.

Close on the sculpture as it's carried to the car.

INT LOUNGE – THE INN ON THE PARK – LONDON – DAY – 1973

Open on the sculpture being passed from Jack's hands into Bobby's.

Jack had written to Bobby, with some embarrassment, a few weeks before, introducing himself, confessing his hero worship and offering him the bronze.

Bobby is in London for a stint of Cup Final punditry with the BBC, and they arrange to meet. Two shy, diffident men; Bobby modestly flattered and Jack in total awe.

Bobby looks at the bronze – and he's pleased. As a thank you he offers Jack a ticket to any of United's matches. For life. (Jack takes advantage of this just once – two tickets, one for himself, the other, of course, for Les).

DISSOLVE TO:

INT MANCHESTER UNITED MUSEUM – DAY – 1974

After a few months in pride of place in Bobby's home, the bronze goes to Old Trafford.

The United Museum curator places the figure in a display case among the club's shimmering trophies. For Jack it's as though he's scored a Cup-winning goal for United. Maybe even a hat-trick. One with his right foot, one with his left and one with his head.

CU A PHOTOGRAPH OF MAUREEN – DAY – 1974

She's lying supine, very naked and very, very pregnant, tastefully, lovingly, even quite artistically photographed by Jack a couple of weeks before the birth of their baby; the idea being that it'll be the first photo in the baby album, the frontispiece.

Unfortunately that was reckoning without the insatiable, clandestine, East Yorkshire photo-vandal they know and love. A pair of hands pick up the photo.

CAM pulls back to see that the hands are, of course, Zelma's. She's horrified at the sight of the naked Maureen and, without even a suspicion of any ado, ferociously rips the photo into shreds. No scissors necessary.

Coronation Street's Ena (Violet Carson), Martha (Lynne Carol) and Minnie (Margot Bryant) in't snug. Jack Walker (Arthur Leslie) looks on.

If a picture paints a thousand scripts …

'Ey – Mam. It's the Dustbinmen!': Trevor Bannister, Bryan Pringle, Tim Wylton, Graham Haberfield.

Stephen Serember and Gary Carp play 'The Evacuees'.

Right: The real ones: Jack and David get on their bike for home.

wo 'yarmulkes' kullcaps) and a ird's nest: Bernard pear, Jeremy Steyn nd Maria Charles *Bar Mitzvah Boy* 976).

xtra, extra, read all bout it ...' Jack hepherd and Joe lack play director nd extra in *Ready Vhen You Are, Mr. IcGill* (1976).

usan Littler icks winning tips om the real iv Nicholson *Spend, Spend, pend* (1977).

Agent Peggy Ramsay, slightly unstrung!

Left: Nigel Hawthorne as 'The Vampire' Mr Burgess in *The Knowledge*: 'You don't have to be brilliant. Perfect will do fine.'

Below: Abigail Cruttenden as Ann (second row, left) and Alison Steadman as Miss Land: *P'Tang, Yang, Kipperbang* (1982).

'You've to pull your socks up, lad!' *P'tang, Yang, Kipperbang* director Mike Apted, John Albasiny and Jack on location in Wimbledon (1982).

Below: Mandy Patinkin schmoozes his director, Barbra Streisand.

'Everyone's got a horror story about moving house'. Director Jack Gold and Jack on location for *The Chain* (1985).

Working with Maureen on *Bag Lady*. Then he had to go home with her!

Distinguished, but boom-laden writer with Maureen and David Ross on location in Cambridge for *Eskimo Day* (1996).

Tom Wilkinson – a traitor to his Alma Mater in *Eskimo Day* with Anna Cartaret, Maureen Lipman and David Ross (Queen's College, Cambridge).

Jack, Bill Nighy, director Paul Seed, Phil Davis, Amanda Holden, Sam Kelly and Sir Tom Courtenay as Mr McGill, the extra, in *Ready When You Are, Mr McGill* – the remake (2003).

Rosenthal's Bronze Age. Clockwise from left: Don Bradman, Bobby Charlton, Ryan Giggs and Eric Cantona.

There's no negative. Our baby's ante-natal moment in history is lost for ever.

ANGLE ON A DUSTBIN: Zelma drops the torn remnants inside and replaces the lid. She beams – a job well done.

For a decade or so she'll deny any knowledge of the missing photo, then finally, proudly and defiantly she confesses. With irrefutable Talmudic logic:

ANGLE ON JACK AND ZELMA face to face.

JACK

You'd no right! It was a picture of my daughter-to-be!

ZELMA

(*smiles*)

No. It was a picture of *my* daughter-as-*is*!

EXT GARDEN – 31 ROSSLYN HILL – HAMPSTEAD – DAY – 1974

A beautiful baby girl, a few days old, lies solemnly gurgling in her pram, seemingly enjoying the summer sunshine; but probably – in hindsight – actually working out a plot for a play.

Inadvertently six weeks dysmature (small-for-dates), she's induced on June 7th, because the consultant was keen to scarper off on holiday. Born after 23 hours of labour, after giving her parents-to-be heart failure when the machine monitoring her heartbeats conks out and they thought she *had.*

Jack drives her home from the St John's Wood clinic at a steady three miles an hour, the most precious cargo held tightly in Maureen's arms. The bundle of pure joy is Amy. Who has, in fact, two more names. One of them a mystery . . .

EXT HAMPSTEAD TOWN HALL – DAY – 1974

Jack walks down Rosslyn Hill and up the steps to the Town Hall entrance.

JACK (VO)

She was only supposed to have *one* more name. Maureen and I thought 'Amy Samantha' – Amy Sam – would be perfect, following the Jewish tradition of keeping alive the name of a member of the family now passed away, in this case my dad.

But once inside the Town Hall . . .

INT REGISTER OFFICE – HAMPSTEAD TOWN HALL – DAY – 1974 (CONT)

Jack faces the registrar across the counter.

REGISTRAR

(*writing*)

So that's 'Amy Samantha Rosenthal', right?

A beat – then inexplicably, for no reason, with no forethought, out of Jack's mouth tumbles:

JACK

No. 'Amy Samantha *Rachel* Rosenthal'.

REGISTRAR

(*stops writing*)

You want 'Rachel' in there, as well?

JACK

Yes, please.

REGISTRAR

(*inserts 'Rachel'*)

As you wish.

INT LIVING ROOM – 31 ROSSLYN HILL – HAMPSTEAD – DAY – 1974

Maureen stares, gobsmacked, at a somewhat sheepish-looking Jack.

MAUREEN

'*Rachel*'?

JACK

In a sense.

It's even more inexplicable to Maureen. Decades later she's still bemused. As is Jack. He's no idea why he said it – and no one's ever said it since.

INT MASTER BEDROOM – 31 ROSSLYN HILL – HAMPSTEAD – DAY – 1974

Amy's arrival means Jack's departure from the second bedroom, which has been his study hitherto.

Consequently, he's carrying his typewriter across the master bedroom towards a walk-in wardrobe – always referred to as 'The Cupboard' – which has been decorated by Francine, Maureen's dresser at the Old Vic, with a handpainted mouse and ear of corn.

INT THE CUPBOARD – 31 ROSSLYN HILL – HAMPSTEAD – DAY – 1974 (CONT)

It measures about 5 feet by 4 feet, virtually filled by a small, mirrorless dressing-table, a chair and a single bookshelf.

Jack brings in the typewriter, puts it on the dressing table, sits down and starts typing.

His visit to Hampstead Town Hall leads to his next play, Well, Thank You, Thursday, *the story of a Registrar of Births, Marriages and Deaths. Her day's clients are a young couple who can't agree on a name for their newborn child, another young couple about to marry that day – and who don't know if they want to – and an old man who's having the most self-important (and seemingly enjoyable) day of his life registering the death of his wife.*

The Registrar weaves between them, between the three most significant moments in life, while preoccupied with the one matter of supreme importance to herself – the arrival of a new desk. And there, with the grace of God, go we all.

INT CONFERENCE ROOM – GRANADA TV – DAY – 1974

Peter Eckersley, Jack, a director – Kevin Billington – a production manager, a designer and a costing clerk sit round the table, scripts, notes and figures in front of them, in glum silence.

The 'big' play on Jack's experiences as an evacuee that Peter prised out of him is written and ready to go into production at Granada – then hits a snag. It's going to cost £45,000 to make and Granada are getting twitchy. No one will actually say the words – that the project is going to be cancelled. Well, in the end, one *of them does . . .*

JACK

It's going to be cancelled, isn't it?

The answer is 'Yes'.

EXT RAILWAY STATION – KEIGHLEY – DAY – 1974

The station is the location for a scene supposedly set in Victoria Station, Manchester, in The Evacuees. *Keighley Station is one of a small handful of stations equipped with 1939 trains and gauges.*

A film unit is shooting the scene on the platform, where crowds of haversacked, labelled kids are being shooed by their mothers onto the Blackpool train. Maureen (as Sarah) and Margery Withers (as Grandma) are bravely fighting back tears as they bundle Gary Carp (as Danny) and Steven Serember (as Neville) aboard.

The cameraman is one of the industry's finest – Brian Tufano. The director is the current TV film whizzkid, destined to be the future feature-*film whizzkid, the uniquely talented Alan Parker.*

JACK (VO)

I gave Granada back the £900 they'd paid for the script and sold it to the BBC as a *Play for Today*.

They costed it and shot it for twice Granada's prohibitive budget . . .

INT THE CUPBOARD – 31 ROSSLYN HILL – HAMPSTEAD – DAY – 1974

The writing storm is welling up again, howling round in a flurry in the confines of the cupboard, as Jack types at his paper-strewn dressing table.

Next out of the typewriter comes Ready When You Are, Mr McGill. *A TV film about a TV film. A satire perfectly acted by Jack Shepherd and beautifully directed by Mike Newell (later to achieve fame, fortune and feature-film offers from Hollywood for* Four Weddings and a Funeral.*)*

FILM EXCERPT: *Ready When You are, Mr McGill*

EXT FILM LOCATION – DAY

JACK (VO)

It's the story of an elderly film-extra (Mr McGill) who has one line to speak – and, after thirteen takes, over a whole day, he fails. This leads to a savage attack on him by the young director (Phil). The most important person on the set against the least consequential. The attack leads to a ferocious confrontation; and Mr McGill's defence of himself and what really matters in life.

The one line is: 'I've never seen the young lady in my life before, and I've lived here fifty years.'

PHIL

That, Mr McGill, was the most terrible, appalling, disgusting performance in the annals of acting history. Congratulations. It was wooden, incomprehensible and the worst bloody mess I've seen in my bloody life! And I feel as though *I've* lived here fifty sodding years!

(*beat*)

You're just no good, Mr McGill. And that's why you're an extra. A stupid, lousy extra! Stupid old bugger!

Mr McGill speaks quietly, very simply.

MR McGILL

You don't know me. You know nothing about me. You don't know if I'm stupid. Or no good. Or anything. You've only really met me today.

(*beat*)

I've been going for a lot of days before this one. Hell of a lot. I might be very good for all you know. I might be a very interesting person. I might have been acting since before you were born. I may have been on the landings at D-Day when I was your age. I might have done all sorts of *really* important things. Like bringing up a family. Like –

PHIL

Mr McGill. You'd *one* important thing to do. And you couldn't.

MR McGILL

(*erupting, exploding*)

That's not real *life*, lad! It's *pretend*! It's *all* pretend! *You're* pretending. The damn-fool *play's* pretending!

Long pause

PHIL

(quietly, almost regretfully)

Real life is how *well* you pretend, isn't it, Sir? You, me. Everybody in the world.

INT THE CUPBOARD – 31 ROSSLYN HILL – HAMPSTEAD – DAY – 1974

Jack punches holes in the next script, then staples the pages together. The title page reads Bar Mitzvah Boy.

According to Jewish tradition – law, in fact – thirteen is the age at which a Jewish boy 'becomes a man' and takes on a man's responsibilities. To do this, after a year of tuition, he goes to the synagogue and reads his portion of the Law (the Torah) before the rabbis, the congregation and his family. To them it's the proudest day of their lives.

But a thirteen-year-old is, after all, thirteen. The age when he knows everything and no one else knows anything. Particularly his parents. And, in this *boy's case, also his grandad and his sister's boyfriend.*

Comes the big day. Our Bar Mitzvah Boy, Eliot, is called by the rabbi up to the bimah to recite his portion. With his family beside themselves with excitement, pride and pleasure (known in the trade as 'shlepping nachas'), he gets up from his pew, is about to walk to the bimah – then suddenly turns and walks straight out of the synagogue, and runs like hell down the street, swallowed up by Saturday morning shoppers.

JACK (VO)

So far so good. Except that now I was stuck. Blocked. Written myself into a hole. I'd no idea what should happen next. Where he'd go.

EXT ROSSLYN HILL – HAMPSTEAD – DAY – 1974

Jack trudges worriedly down the street towards the cab drivers' shelter. Two or three cabs are parked outside and two or three cabbies lean against the railings, swigging pint pots of strong tea. Jack stops at the shelter and buys himself a sausage sarnie, comfort food. Then carries on trudging.

JACK (VO)

Every day for three weeks I walked down to the cabbies' shelter trying to figure out what should happen next, where Eliot would go.

Maureen freewheels on her bike down the street towards Haverstock Hill, Amy Sam (not to mention Rachel) strapped snugly in a sling on her chest. Maureen and Jack wave at each other as she cycles off to the park.

JACK (VO)

Then, finally, eureka! The solution, as ever, lies in the character. The character would do what his character would do.

If he runs out of the synagogue, he clearly doesn't want to be a man. Which means he wants to stay a kid. So where would a kid go?

IMMEDIATE CUT TO:

FILM EXCERPT: ***Bar Mitzvah Boy***

EXT CHILDREN'S PLAYGROUND – DAY

Eliot is seated on a swing now wearing a Mickey Mouse mask, swinging gently, aimlessly to and fro. His twenty-year-old sister, Lesley, has discovered (circuitously) where he is. She approaches; acknowledges the mask.

LESLEY

(*bitterly*)

I should always wear it. It's a hell of an improvement.

INT ELIOT'S PARENTS' BEDROOM – DAY

Eliot's grandad can be heard downstairs, heartbrokenly sighing and 'oy, oy, oying'.

Eliot's mother, Rita, lies distraught on the bed. His father, Victor, sits beside her. Lesley's boyfriend, Harold, stands at the other side, an ignored bowl of bean and barley soup to comfort Rita in his hands. All still unaware where Eliot is.

All silent. There's nothing to say. The happiest day of the family's life is in ashes. Then, in a voice like death:

RITA

At this moment ... on their way ... are 117 guests. They're on the train. In cars. Queuing for buses. All on their way. At half past six, Victor, 117 people from Bournemouth, from Manchester, Leeds and Glasgow, from Birmingham, everywhere, are going to turn up at the Reuben Shulman Hall expecting a dinner-dance. All dressed up. Your Uncle Zalman. My cousin Freda. Your brother we don't talk about from Cardiff.

VICTOR

Ssshhh. Don't upset yourself.

RITA

(*oblivious*)

117 people. 117 portions of chopped liver. 117 mushroom vol-au-vents, 117 chicken with croquette potatoes and helzel, French beans and coleslaw. 117 lockshen cuggles, a three-piece band – and no bar mitzvah boy. No bar mitzvah. No nothing.

VICTOR

It's no help upsetting yourself.

RITA

(*oblivious*)

So, tell me, how do we cancel? How do we stop trains and cars and tell everyone to go home again? Do we stand on the M1 with a noticeboard? Do we stand outside the Reuben Shulman Hall and tell them Eliot's gone for a walk and they've got no dinner? Ring the caterer and tell them we accidentally made a mistake – it was *next* year? What do we say? Do *we* go? Do *we* turn up? Do we ever show our face *again*? You're a clever man, you read the newspapers, you argue politics, tell me. I'd like to know.

A helpless silence. Rita's eyes fill up. Victor and Harold stare uselessly down at their shoes.

HAROLD

Shall I ring the police again?

They ignore him. Silence.

RITA

117 guests. All in their evening suits. Long dresses. Sequin handbags.

A pause.

VICTOR

(*calmly, matter-of-fact*)

They *say* they break your heart. It's an old saying. My *father* said it. 'Children break your heart.'

(*beat*)

I'll break every bone in his body.

EXT CHILDREN'S PLAYGROUND – DAY – CONT

Eliot and Lesley are at the swing. Lesley demands to know what his flight was all about. Eventually, unhappily, he explains that it's to do with the men in his life. That Victor is a selfish, oafish, utterly insensitive man; that Harold is a feeble twerp, scared of everything and everyone; that Grandad is an attention-seeking baby. And if they're examples of what being a man is, he doesn't want to be one.

Lesley retorts that it's just an excuse; that he was chicken, that he'd forgotten what he'd learnt. Eliot scoffs back; he knows his portion by heart – he could do it standing on his head. Which he then, literally, proceeds to do. He does it perfectly from start to finish.

INT LIVING ROOM – ELIOT'S PARENTS' HOUSE – DAY

The whole family – and the rabbi – surround Eliot, persuaded by Lesley to come home, that, being a grown-up, she'll lie *his way out of trouble.*

She explains to everyone that he recited his portion in the playground on the right day. To everyone's relief, the rabbi confirms that if he did it, he did it, wherever he was, and that he's now legitimately barmitzvah'd. All is well – except that Grandad prods that little bit further. Why did he run out of the synagogue? Eliot and Lesley exchange an anxious glance. He can't confess the truth – so Lesley twists it into her promised lie ...

LESLEY

He thought ... he thought he couldn't be the man ... well, the sort of man you'd expect him to be ... a man like *you*. And Dad. And Harold.

A silence. All are touched by this. Victor goes to Eliot, sits on his haunches in front of him and takes his hands.

VICTOR

(*tenderly, expansively*)

Eliot. Barm-pot. To you I seem like a god ... a hero. It's only natural. Natural but stupid. We're not all that wonderful. We've all got faults. *Little* ones, maybe. But we've got them. Sometimes I've been a bit of a lobbos. When I was younger perhaps – I wasn't all that perfect. Nor Grandad here ...

GRANDAD

'Course not.

VICTOR

A fine man. But not every second of the day! And Harold. A fine boy. A gutanashomma, certainly. But sometimes – not often – a bit of a shlemiel.

HAROLD

Now and then.

VICTOR

We've all got little faults. You just haven't noticed them, that's all. Only because we've learnt to hide them. In the fullness of time.

INT REUBEN SHULMAN HALL – EVENING

The bar mitzvah dinner-dance. The three-piece band is playing 'Always'. Dinner now over, the guests are dancing. Eliot is dancing with his now kvelling (joyful) mother . . .

JACK (VO)

I had a feeling *Bar Mitzvah Boy* would go down well with viewers and critics, when, before I ever started writing it, I mentioned the idea to Valerie Hyams, an old school pal of Maureen's from Hull. She was horrified. Scandalised. Almost traumatised. Disgusted. *A boy running out of his bar mitzvah?* Unheard of! She felt sick at the thought. Terrific. The next day I picked up my pen and started.

After it was transmitted, it was rabbinically lambasted in a Manchester pulpit. And word was that after it was shown in Australia, a Melbourne rabbi's son also did an Eliot.

Another man not too happy was an actor – an extra playing one of the guests. At the rehearsals of the dinner-dance scene over a hundred of them had to sit at tables already laid with plates of chopped liver. The first assistant forbade everyone to eat it at the rehearsal – they would, of course, do so when the scene was actually being filmed. The actor ignored him and polished off his liver. Another plateful was provided and the first assistant repeated his embargo. Whereupon our actor repeated his eating. The first assistant then announced that if he ate the *next* helping, he'd be fired. Our man duly did. And was duly fired. The only actor ever to be fired for eating chopped liver. He should've put it in *Spotlight*.

The MUSIC ends. Eliot bows to his mum.

INT HEALTH CLINIC – HAMPSTEAD – DAY – 1976

Amy, on Maureen's knee, is being 'assessed' by a doctor to see how she's developing. Maureen and Jack think she's developing pretty good. Breaking records, in fact. Not to put too fine a point on it, they're fairly convinced she's 'gifted'. A mini-genius in the making. She's begun talking whole sentences while her contemporaries are struggling with 'Mamma' and 'goo-goo'. Her first sentence at fifteen months was, 'Is everybody Jewish?' Soon afterwards 'She's *stupid' to Maureen's hapless pal, Val. One way or another, Val considers curtailing her visits.*

The doctor holds a picturebook in front of Amy. She points with a spatula at a picture of a house.

DOCTOR

What's that, Amy?

AMY

Unintelligible noise.

DOCTOR

And that?

AMY

Blargh foo.

A longer pause. Maureen is disconcerted – and embarrassed. The doctor points to a picture of an apple.

DOCTOR

And that?

AMY

Mana-la-pa.

Maureen's beginning to think maybe Amy's not quite as gifted as she thought. The doctor sighs, then points her spatula at an elephant.

DOCTOR

And that, Amy. Now try hard. What is this, eh? What do you think this is?

AMY

(sigh)

A spatula.

EXT 124 DUKE'S AVENUE – MUSWELL HILL – DAY – 1976

A removal van is parked outside. Removal men are lugging furniture from the van into the house.

Much to her chagrin, Amy is about to have a little brother. This means – apart from competition for Amy for her parents' attention – that the

Rosenthals need an extra bedroom, or a house instead of a flat. It seems the only areas in London where a three-bedroomed house can be bought for the price of the sale of the Rosslyn Hill flat (£24,500) are Chiswick or Muswell Hill. Muswell Hill is nearer. They move to Muswell Hill . . . only slightly worried that virtually everyone they meet tells them that they *once lived in Muswell Hill's bedsit-land till they'd earned enough to get the hell out.*

INT HALL – 124 DUKE'S AVENUE – MUSWELL HILL – DAY – 1976 (CONT)

The hallway is piled high and wide with teachests, packing cases, suitcases and, balanced vertically on one of its ends, a tan leather settee.

Maureen is trying to organise their dispersal into their various intended rooms. Two removal men pretend to listen to her while clacking cleverly dried mouths, hinting, none too subtly, that it's time for another brew . . .

The phone rings. Jack, holding a stack of books, dashes in, drops the books and starts clambering over teachests, trying to locate where the ringing's coming from.

JACK

The phone! Where's the phone?

Maureen and the removal men start hauling packing cases away from the walls in search of the telephone point.

Some weeks earlier, Jack had been commissioned by Granada TV to adapt the Stanley Houghton classic stage play Hindle Wakes, *in the series* Sir Laurence Olivier's Best Play of—, Hindle Wakes *being his choice as the best play of 1912; and it was to be directed by the great man himself.*

One of the removal men finds the telephone wall-point, the cable and the phone itself. He hands it to Jack and licks his dry lips in Maureen's direction. She takes the point and starts off towards the kitchen.

JACK
(*into phone*)

Hello?

EXT A BEACH IN THE BAHAMAS – DAY – 1976 (CONT)

The sun blazes down on –

– Sir Laurence Olivier, in swimming trunks, stretched out in a deckchair, a long, cool drink in one hand . . . a phone in the other. On his knees is the TV script of Hindle Wakes.

SIR LAURENCE
(*into phone*)

Is that the genius?

INTERCUT between the Bahamas and Muswell Hill . . .

JACK
(*into phone*)
Sorry?

SIR LAURENCE
(*into phone*)
Is that Jack Rosenthal?

JACK
(*into phone*)
Yes.

SIR LAURENCE
(*into phone*)
It's Laurence Olivier. I'm in the Bahamas.

JACK
(*into phone*)
Oh. Right.

SIR LAURENCE
(*into phone*)
I've just read your adaptation. It's brilliant. You're a genius, dear boy. Just thought I'd let you know. Glorious weather here. See you soon. Absolutely brilliant script. I love it. Sheer genius.

He hangs up. So does Jack.

JACK
Bloody hell . . .

(*calls*)

Maureen! Guess what!

MAUREEN (OS)
Hang on! I'm just making a cup of tea.

The removal men beam.

1ST REMOVAL MAN
(*to Jack*)
Just making a cup of tea.

INT LIVING ROOM – 124 DUKE'S AVENUE – MUSWELL HILL – DAY – 1976

Three weeks later – and another phone call. This time it's from Peter Eckersley, Head of Drama, overseeing the Laurence Olivier series.

JACK
(*into phone*)

Yes, Peter?

PETER (OS)
(*into phone*)

What are we going to do about this script of yours?

JACK
(*into phone*)

What do you mean?

PETER (OS)
(*into phone*)

He hates it.

JACK
(*into phone*)

Who does?

PETER (OS)

Sir Laurence.

JACK
(*into phone; incredulously*)

He *loved* it!

PETER (OS)
(*into phone*)

Now he hates it. We'd better have a meeting.

INT CONFERENCE ROOM – GRANADA TV – DAY – 1976

Sir Laurence, Peter, Jack, a casting director and a production designer around a table. The meeting begins amicably . . . then grows more spirited . . . then dis*pirited.*

Sir Laurence appears to have cold feet about the changes a TV production would mean to the play. Jack and Peter would welcome *them. Jack is delighted with his adaptation (well, yes, he would say that); he's convinced that had Stanley Houghton been writing in the 1970s, he would've written it as Jack has done. The TV version has precisely the same plot and characters, just as powerful, just as moving – but much more visual, economical and pacey. The original play has five acts; four of them begin with a painstaking recap of what happened in the previous ones. All the incidents cumbersomely revealed in reported speech in the stage play are enacted in scenes filmed on location.*

But it seems that Sir Laurence wants to change nothing – and simply point a camera at the stage play. Everyone thinks this is wrong. He then suggests interspersing some of the TV scenes with those of the original. Everyone thinks this would be a mess of conflicting styles and knocks the idea on its already misshapen head. He repeats the suggestion. Everyone repeats their opposition. He insists. They give way.

Jack begins to see the writing on the page also giving way. To the writing on the wall.

The rest of the meeting deals with casting. Despite his lifetime in the theatre, it seems the only actor Sir Laurence has heard of is Donald Pleasance.

INT LIVING ROOM – 124 DUKE'S AVENUE – MUSWELL HILL – DAY – 1976

In a black dress and with a white lace doily on her head, Amy toys with her breakfast. After months of barely eating at all, she now only deigns to if she's dressed as Queen Victoria – with Maureen (speaking in a Danish accent as Princess Alexandra) and Jack (in a German accent as Prince Albert) honoured to serve her.

This has been the daily routine ever since she was completely overwhelmed by Annette Crosbie's TV portrayal.

The phone rings. Jack takes it, leaves Amy to Maureen and sits beside Adam in his high chair and feeds him his baby food while he speaks. Adam isn't bothering being any historical figure at all.

JACK
(*into phone*)
Hello?

INT PETER ECKERSLEY'S OFFICE – GRANADA TV – DAY – 1976 (CONT)

Peter paces the room, dragging the phone cable around with him as he goes . . .

PETER
(*into phone*)
Hi, it's Pete. Listen. He's adamant about doing the hotchpotch, bloody patchwork quilt of a script. Bits of yours, bits of the original.

INTERCUT Between Peter and Jack:

JACK
(*into phone; sighs*)
Okay. But take my name off it, Pete.

PETER
(*into phone*)
Are you sure?

JACK
(*into phone*)
Positive. And good luck with it all.

PETER
(*into phone*)
Thanks.

JACK
(*into phone*)
Who's playing the lead?

PETER
(*into phone*)
Donald Pleasance.

INT SPARE BEDROOM – 124 DUKE'S AVENUE – MUSWELL HILL – DAY – 1976

Jack sits at his old dressing table from The Cupboard, typing. The family's mad tabby cat, Pushkin, much loved by the kids on account of her bony elbows and also variously known as Eelii, Dog, Stoat, Fiend, The Youthful Eel and, not surprisingly, Pushkinos Bambinos Aliinos Go-Toe, is seated on pages of script, critically watching him.

JACK (VO)

Once he'd heard I'd withdrawn my name from the script, Sir Laurence suggested that *he* be given the writer's credit. Peter pointed out that he hadn't written a word and that Sellotaping bits of stage play into bits of TV script didn't qualify for Writers' Guild approval.

Sir Laurence graciously relented. The mess of a play went on the air as 'Based on the stage play by Stanley Houghton'. Based by no one.

Pushkin continues to eye Jack's typing fingers . . .

They tap out Michael the First. *This is a composite film – adapted from a novel – consisting of three screenplays, one by Willis Hall (who later becomes a close mate), one by Tom Stoppard and one by Jack. None of them knows the others. The film is never made . . .*

Then an episode of a TV drama series, The Duchess of Duke Street . . .

Pushkin yawns.

JACK (VO)

Then a TV play, *Spaghetti Two-Step*. As happened in *There'll Almost Always be an England,* the last scene was changed into the exact opposite of what was intended. Set in a London

restaurant, the idea was to get to know, and be amused by, four groups of diners and their problems. A comedy. Then suddenly, in the last minute, the restaurant was to be demolished by an IRA bomb through the window. The characters we'd hopefully grown to know and love – *because they'd made us laugh* – are killed. The principle was to lull, then shock the audience by turning the genre upside down with the violent deaths of *comic* characters at a time when the public were becoming blasé about the deaths of real, *unknown* people through IRA attacks. The management, however, Yorkshire TV, claimed they'd recently made another film about the IRA and wanted the ending changed. I rewrote a new scene that takes place a year later – and shows how life has changed the four groups of diners. Not quite the original intention . . .

Then a TV biopic of Lilian Baylis (played by Amy's heroine, Annette Crosbie), Auntie's Niece . . .

Pushkin stretches out and falls asleep on the scripts.

Then a TV film adaptation of the biography of the notorious pools winner, Vivian Nicholson, *Spend, Spend, Spend* . . . eventually played, magnificently, by Susan Littler.

I heard about Vivian Nicholson a few hours before the rest of Britain. In 1961, working for Jim Phoenix in the advertising agency, I shared an office with Tony Iveson, a PR man. Tony was the one who went chasing off to Castleford, on behalf of Littlewoods Pools, to interview Vivian and her husband, Keith, the day they got the eight draws that brought them their record £152,000. And to talk them into allowing publicity . . .

From that day on, I followed her wild, seemingly stupid adventures in the papers – and believed every snide, snooty, biased word the relentless publicity said. All adding up to *one* word – that she was a cow.

Then producer John Goldschmidt brought me a copy of her biography, *Spend, Spend, Spend*; and I saw *why* she behaved as she did. I did a complete U-turn. I became a fan.

When I was asked to write the screenplay of her life story, I couldn't wait to put the record straight . . .

DISSOLVE TO:

FILM EXCERPT: *Spend, Spend, Spend*

EXT BACK ALLEY – CASTLEFORD – EVENING – 1950

An extremely poor, working-class street of terraced houses. Along it, Vivian is exhaustedly pushing a rusty, decrepit bike towards her parents' house, at the age of fourteen. The bike is laden with sacks of coal-slack. Vivian is filthy and dressed in ill-fitting, worn clothes.

VIVIAN (VO)

I was born in 1936, in Castleford, Yorkshire. You'll find it on the map. *I'm* the bugger that put it there.

(*beat*)

Where we lived, all the fellers were coalminers. Except my dad. *He* was a full-time, fully paid-up bastard.

(*beat*)

I wish we'd've won the pools in *them* days. I'd have bought him a bloody punchbag and had a day off.

DISSOLVE TO:

INT SPARE BEDROOM – 124 DUKE'S AVENUE – MUSWELL HILL – DAY – 1976

Jack is typing away.

JACK (VO)

Winning the pools brought her even more pain than her childhood.

For weeks before the big win she'd been virtually starving.

Two days before, all the money she had in the world amounted to a shilling. The next day, nothing at all. *After* the win, her husband, Keith, was killed in a horrific car crash, she had another three vicious, violent, terrifying marriages – and then numbing poverty again.

The story of Vivian Nicholson is a cautionary tale and a morality tale. It becomes a triumph of courage and survival; and the finding of a sad wisdom . . .

DISSOLVE TO:

FILM EXCERPT: ***Spend, Spend, Spend***

EXT KERSHAW AVENUE – CASTLEFORD – DAY

Vivian surveys the street.

VIVAN (VO)

Not long ago, I went back to Kershaw Avenue, where we lived when we came up on the pools, just to see what it felt like ... looked like.

Silently, gently, she begins to cry.

I looked. And I remembered everything. I thought if Motherwell had got another goal and Stockport not drawn with Oldham ... we'd still be there. Happen we'd have had the front room furnished by now. With its nice glass doors. To let the sunshine in.

I understand why everything went wrong: because there's no other way it *could've* gone. People like me aren't much good. A bit sick. But there's others as bad. Bank managers and newspapermen – only *they* make a living out of it.

Money's a mystery to people like me and Keith. We only understand a week's wages at a time. Happen that's all some folk *want* us to understand.

Newspapers, of course, are newspapers. The more you bugger up your life, the more they like it.

(*beat*)

Do you like a good laugh? Here's one for you. When we won the pools, we put a cross on the coupon for 'No publicity'.

(*beat*)

I had some bad times in that street. *Bloody* bad. So bad I wanted to die.

(*beat*)

They were the best times I ever had.

DISSOLVE TO:

INT SPARE BEDROOM – 124 DUKE'S AVENUE – MUSWELL HILL – DAY – 1976

Jack stops typing in mid-thought and strokes Pushkin's belly. She gurgles contentedly in her sleep.

JACK (VO)

I met Vivian many times while I was writing the screenplay – and later a stage version – and became an even bigger fan. Her rough-diamond barminess was no obstacle; in fact, it was one of the principal reasons.

The last time we met, we had lunch in a café. She told me she was now a Jehovah's Witness. She didn't mind coming off the booze, but she wasn't keen on giving up men. But she'd succeeded. While she was telling me this she had her hand on my thigh under the tablecloth.

INT A WARD – ST ANN'S HOSPITAL – TOTTENHAM – DAY – 1977

Lakey lies in a bed. Jack by the bedside.

LAKEY

If anything happens to me you mustn't give my lawnmower away to your Uncle Pinky.

JACK

Nothing's going to happen to you.

Back home in Blackpool, Lakey had complained of stomach pains and sickness. Her doctor, for want of a better word, thought there was nothing wrong. So in the absence of medicines, she sucked mints and downed hideous teaspoonfuls of a tonic called Devil's Claw.

Jack brings her to London and she's put in hospital for observation – to see if there are 'any nasties'. No, there aren't. Good.

INT LIVING ROOM – 124 DUKE'S AVENUE – MUSWELL HILL – DAY – 1977

Lakey is lying on the settee, Amy beside her, Adam crawling on the floor. Her pain is getting worse.

Jack's incompetent, smug little GP announces she's merely suffering from 'depression'. Keep her occupied, get her to walk about a lot, distract her – make her watch TV.

INT NORTH LONDON STREETS – NIGHT – 1977

An ambulance is racing through the dark, deserted streets.

JACK (VO)

In the middle of the night, in agony, her ankles suddenly, alarmingly swollen, I rang emergency. A doctor came and whipped her straight back into hospital. It wasn't depression, it was cancer of the pancreas.

EXT ST ANN'S HOSPITAL – TOTTENHAM – DAY – 1977

Jack comes out of the hospital, carrying a small suitcase containing Lakey's clothes, her handbag, her glasses and her watch.

JACK (VO)

Early the next morning the hospital rang. Lakey was dead. A week after her 71st birthday. The ward sister told me that during the night a rabbi came to her bedside and prayed. She must've been terrified. A strange black-hatted man, the beard, the incomprehensible Hebrew. All of a sudden. When here she was in hospital, probably going to get better. And I hadn't been there to . . . To what? . . . Maybe hold her hand.

I asked the sister hopefully, stupidly, 'Was she okay when the rabbi came?' She's dead, and I'm asking was she okay in the night. A woman dying of cancer, my mother of all people, and I'd been dragging her round supermarkets to fight off non-existent depression, keeping her up chatting, exhausted, while I watched *Match of the Day*.

EXT CEMETERY – BLACKPOOL – DAY – 1977

David and Eileen, Jack and Maureen, Rabbi Zalud, Lakey's brothers Ginger and Pinky, cousins, other relatives and friends shovel small mounds of earth onto the coffin deep inside the grave. Over this, their voices recite the Hebrew Prayer for the Dead . . . 'Yitkadal, v'yitkadash, shemay, rabba . . .'

INT HALLWAY – LAKEY'S BUNGALOW – BLACKPOOL – DAY – 1977

Jack's Uncle Pinky is struggling towards the front door, his arms overflowing with souvenirs pillaged from the bungalow, greenhouse and garden shed. Jack, following behind, has already disobeyed Lakey's instruction and given him her lawnmower. His biggest coup is scavenging a single elastic band he finds nestling in a corner of a kitchen drawer.

Jack goes to open the front door for him, just as Uncle Pinky is passing a truly appalling ornament (much admired by Lakey just to be awkward) hanging on the wall. It's the grotesque glass face of a clown. Despite having his hands full, he contorts himself trying to unhook it to add to his loot.

Suddenly it lurches loose and falls, smashing in pieces on the floor, together with everything else he's carrying. Jack looks up to heaven and grins congratulations to Lakey.

Pinky goes home empty-handed, apart from the elastic band.

In her life Lakey had been a godsend to anyone wanting to write comedy. She'd been a godsend, full stop.

EXT HEATHROW – DAY – 1977

Jack is boarding a plane bound for New York. Trundling busily along beside him is the man who's bought his ticket. A small, crumpled, balding man of about sixty, this is Peter Witt, a theatre producer, ex-Hollywood agent, one-time Californian tennis champ, Viennese-American. A sometimes alarming mixture of Sachertorte *softness and Tin Pan Alley toughness.*

EXT PLANE (IN FLIGHT) – DAY – 1977

Jack and Peter are seated beside each other. Peter is babbling excitedly about how Jack is about to join 'the best creative team in the world – bar none!' Jack's also beginning to get excited. Almost as much as Peter.

JACK (VO)

Over the years, several of my plays had won awards, but *Bar Mitzvah Boy* – joyously directed by Mike Tuchner – was not just showered with them, it was drenched.

As a result, Peter had offered to mount it as a stage musical.

EXT SKIES – DAY – 1977

The plane zooms west over the ocean. In the distance lies the New World – and, sadly, what turns out to be an old story . . .

EXT KENNEDY AIRPORT – NEW YORK – DAY – 1977

Jack and Peter, even more crumpled, disembark.

JACK (VO)

Since I'd never written the book for a musical before, Peter had hired Martin Charnin, the director of the staggeringly successful hit show *Annie*, as our director and my tutor – who'd tell me what to write.

Londoner Don Black, already an established and admired lyricist (who'd initially suggested the play to Peter), and Jule Styne, the great composer of roughly a thousand great shows

and a million great songs – great! – would be scoring the show. What could go wrong?

Say hello to the best creative team in the world.

EXT HOTEL PIERRE – NEW YORK – DAY – 1977

Peter fussily wafts his prodigies into the entrance . . .

First Jule . . . late sixties perhaps, small, squat, stiff, a bit like a toad with a big, black fedora on its head.

Next, Martin, in his thirties, supremely self-assured, neatly bearded, expensively groomed, fashionably bescarved down to his ankles.

Next, Don, also in his thirties, good-looking, easy-going, witty, Beatle-fringed, life-and-soul.

Next, Jack, being slightly nudged to one side by Peter as he extravagantly kowtows Jule into the foyer.

INT RESTAURANT – HOTEL PIERRE – NEW YORK – DAY – 1977 (CONT)

Now elevating shmoozing into an art form, Peter bows and scrapes Jule through the doors ahead of the others. Jule, after all, is 'the money'.

Jule strides in – and the waiters break into applause!

They're clapping a small, squat, toad-lookalike for walking into a restaurant for breakfast!

Or, on the other hand, maybe it's because he's a Broadway icon, a theatre legend, a musical genius. Or, on the other *other hand, maybe Peter Witt has paid them.*

If Jack doesn't get a glimmer now of what lies in store, he soon will . . .

INT JULE'S APARTMENT – NEW YORK – NIGHT – 1977

Jule is tinkling the keys of his breathtakingly beautiful, ebony, billion-dollar grand piano. A large gin and tonic to one side.

Peter, Martin, Don and Jack are seated around the piano.

JACK (VO)

I'd delivered the first draft of the scenario the day before. Martin loved it. Don loved it. Peter waited till he heard what *they* thought, then said *he* loved it.

Jule, bless his size-one cotton socks, *loathed* it.

Jule has invited the team round to his apartment to play four tunes he says he's already written for the show. Before *he's even read the script. In other words, they weren't written for the show; they were lying rejected and dejected in his bottom drawer, written for other long-gone shows. The icon was telling fibs.*

CAM pans round the faces as they listen to the relentlessly minor-keyed tunes. They all look profoundly moved. Except Jack, the musical novice, who looks profoundly numbed. At the end of the first tune, again excepting Jack, they all leap into rapturous applause. Jack agonises: should he, too, congratulate Jule, even though the tune leaves him stone-cold? Too late; he agonises too long, Jule has started his second tune.

Again, Peter, Martin and Don are ecstatic. And Jack isn't. Again he leaves it too late to wriggle out of it.

It happens a third time. Same story – only this time, Jack thinks of a way of making up for his embarrassing silences. When Jule finishes his fourth tune and the others are whooping in delight, he'll lean across to him, grasp him by the wrist, like they do in showbusiness, and mumble, hoarse with raw emotion, 'Jule . . . Thank you . . . All four are fantastic.'

The tuneless tune dribbles into silence. The others enjoy a good, sycophantic whoop. Jack leans forward for wrist-grabbing – and knocks Jule's large gin and tonic into the inside *of his breathtakingly beautiful, billion-dollar piano.*

Aghast, Jack stares at the clinking ice cubes swimming around inside . . . then at Jule.

Jule stares back through heavy-hooded Al Capone eyes. War is declared.

INT SUITE – THE ALBANY HOTEL – LONDON – DAY – 1977

A 'creative meeting', comprising Jule, Peter, Martin, Don, Jack, the production designer, the choreographer, the musical director and the stage manager.

All are silent – except Jule. 'Creative' has had its neck twisted. It's now a 'destructive' meeting. With language rarely heard outside a stoker's mess, with eyes bulging and veins throbbing, Jule is screaming, violently, viciously, about how terrible the script is, too clever, too subtle, impossible to score, how we should sling it in the trashcan and start all over again: instead of this crap, he'll *plot the story . . . he'll base it on Al Jolson. No, that isn't a misprint. Al Jolson, the bar mitzvah boy.*

He finally rants himself into exhaustion. Everyone stays silent. Jack bleakly wonders if anyone *has ever been so insulted in their life. He looks at all the others.* All *of them loved the script. And not* one *of them says a dickey-bird. Nothing. Not a whisper in his defence. Total, feet-shuffling silence.*

Jack agonises again. He hasn't yet signed a contract. The rights in Bar Mitzvah Boy *are his. He can get up, give Jule a V-sign, bid everyone a not-so-fond farewell, go home and cancel the musical.*

Or – *and here's where he makes his mistake – he can behave 'professionally'. He can smile and say, 'Okay, let's see how we can make it work so that Jule's happy.' He reckons this might be the British way to handle it. The civilised way. Mature. So that's what he does. And, of course, he's wrong. He should've said goodbye. It's a lesson he'll learn for next time – with Ms Streisand: if you think you should walk away, walk away.*

The meeting fizzles out. No further business. The threatened power struggle between Jule and Martin is over before it starts. He with the loudest voice is crowned the victor. Jule's the boss, Don's his willing lieutenant, Martin's a necessary evil, Peter's a pain in the arse and Jack . . . sorry, who?

Jack goes home, mulling over what Tom Stoppard told him just before the New York trip: 'Always remember, you know better than they do.'

INT REHEARSAL ROOM – KENNINGTON – DAY – 1978

In their leotards and leg-warmers, 25 or so chorus boys and girls frighteningly thunder across the floorboards like stampeding rhinos. The MD is accompanying them on the piano. Peter Gennaro, the choreographer, watches a little distantly. Unusually, he's an almost completely deaf choreographer.

Martin, the mentor, stands watching the dancers. Jack, the pupil, stands beside him. Martin clicks his fingers. Jack leaps to attention.

MARTIN

I need a line.

JACK

Sorry?

MARTIN

Now.

JACK

A line?

MARTIN

Of dialogue. For the girl next to the end, playing one of the customers in the hairdressing salon. Gimme a funny line.

JACK

What about?

MARTIN

I don't know. You're the goddamn writer.

EXT KENNINGTON ROAD – DAY – 1978

Rehearsals have broken for lunch. Martin and Jack walk along, looking for a likely restaurant.

MARTIN

Somewhere where they do mashed potato.

JACK

Uh-huh. What with?

MARTIN

Nothing. On their own'd be fine. With ice-cream to follow.

He grins at Jack and claps him on the back.

I've got a good feeling about this show. I figure it'll make you about a million in the West End. Pounds not dollars.

JACK
(*swallowing*)

Really?

MARTIN

And, say three million on Broadway. Again, pounds not dollars.

Jack's beginning to think he may like musicals after all, Jule or no Jule . . .

EXT OPERA HOUSE – MANCHESTER – DAY – 1978

Manchester changes Jack's mind.

Outside the theatre, a stone's throw from Granada's studios, display posters advertise the forthcoming musical production of the TV hit play Bar Mitzvah Boy.

Inside, the show is playing for its out-of-town run, three weeks for ironing out problems and 'getting it right' for the West End.

Jack is racing down the street fom the Midland Hotel to the theatre, swinging a briefcase packed with rewrites. These are demanded by Martin every day, sometimes twice a day, sometimes three. Although Don assumes Jack doesn't like doing the rewrites, he's wrong. That is until it dawns on Jack that each one seems to make the show worse. More creases, less ironing out. More contortions from Martin trying to make it more like Annie*; more panics from Peter; more self-justifying harangues – 'This is the best goddamn, motherfuckin' song I ever wrote!' – from Jule; more sitting on the fence before sliding off onto Jule's side from Don.*

More under-breath muttering from Jack as he runs into the stage door.

INT OPERA HOUSE – MANCHESTER – DAY – 1978 (CONT)

The cast are rehearsing on stage, the orchestra playing in the pit. Jule is bursting a blood vessel all over the MD. Don stands loyally nodding by his side. Martin watches the rehearsal, ashen-faced and ashen-mouthed in disbelief. In the otherwise empty stalls, Peter is enviously quizzing a chorus girl about exactly why Martin keeps giving another chorus girl extra lines to say, an extra few bars of song to sing, an extra few feet further downstage to stand . . . could something be maybe going on?

Jack comes running in with the rewrites.

JACK (VO)

Everything was out of kilter. Whatever could be wrong with a musical was wrong with this one. What had begun life as a (forgive me) truthful, delicate, poignant comedy had become a brashly broad, crassly banal, schmaltz-sodden, on-the-nose mess. It was rumoured that Peter, like Jule a big-money gambler, had gone into it underfunded, which is probably illegal.

EXT OPERA HOUSE – MANCHESTER – DAY – 1978

Jack strolls along, circling the theatre, deep in thought. Strangely, he seems quite serene.

JACK (VO)

To keep sane, I walked round and round the theatre, thinking of Amy and Adam.

Adam had broken his nose while I was away. No, Amy hadn't caught him with a straight left. It was *my* fault. During one of my phone calls home, he'd escaped Maureen's hands and fallen nose-first onto a wooden coffee table. It ironed itself out okay.

INT OPERA HOUSE – MANCHESTER – NIGHT – 1978

A performance on stage before an audience. The queasily pseudo-Kletzmerish number 'It's a Simcha' in progress.

Jack is standing at the back of the stalls, ready for a quick getaway should the punters turn nasty and beat him to death with their programmes. He starts to walk despondently towards the door to the gents', when his foot bumps into something.

It's our director, lying on the floor at the back of the centre aisle, crying.

INT BAR – OPERA HOUSE – MANCHESTER – NIGHT 1978

An hour or so after the curtain has come down. An emergency meeting of the best creative team in the world to see if anyone *has any idea how to make the show work. Martin suggests changing the characters of the Hendon kosher caterers who are purveying the bar mitzvah dinner – into Sicilian Mafia gangsters. Everyone looks at their shoes. Then:*

MARTIN

Okay. Now here's the thing. Another idea. How about we turn Eliot's family into *animals*? Wearing animals' heads – lions, tigers, chimpanzees – and redesign the living room into a circus and they're all sitting on their haunches on those animal-stool things and Eliot is the ringmaster with a –

PETER

I have only one thing to say. And here I speak with my producer's hat on and I will allow no argument. That whatever people do with what they got inside their pants is nobody's business but theirs.

After which, on to the West End.

EXT HER MAJESTY'S THEATRE – LONDON – NIGHT – 1978

Outside, posters proclaim the show, fresh from its Manchester triumph.

A small trickle of theatregoers wander in.

JACK (VO)

The show came into town and closed ten weeks later. Neither public nor critics – nor, I suspected, even Jule – liked it. I also began to suspect he never had. The thought made me warm slightly to him. Slightly.

The musical was a year's work. And it was over. Peter, Martin and Jule go back to New York. Don back to Mill Hill. And Jack back to real life.

Martin was wrong about the million pounds in the West End, and the three million on Broadway. He was wrong to the tune of four million.

DISSOLVE TO:

FILM EXCERPT: *The Knowledge*

INT WAITING ROOM – THE PUBLIC CARRIAGE OFFICE – DAY

Seven men and a woman are seated in hard-back chairs. All applicants to be cab-drivers.

Mr Burgess strides in. He's in his late forties, an ex-policeman, the chief examiner. Big and very intimidating. He launches into his speech. He's given it a hundred times before: every word, every pause, every expression is now second nature.

MR BURGESS

Good afternoon. My name is Mr Burgess – no applause please – and this little chat is called your acceptance interview. It means you're now, starting today, officially on The Knowledge. Which, by a remarkable twist of logic, brings us to Question Number One, namely, what exactly *is* The Knowledge?

FREEZE FRAME:

One evening Jack takes a phone call from the director, Bob Brooks, an American who'd lived and worked in London for many years, making a string of award-winning commercials. He wanted to offer a tribute to his adopted city – to make a film about something exclusive to London. Would Jack be interested in writing a screenplay about The Knowledge?

RESUME Mr Burgess at a wallmap.

MR BURGESS

As laid down by the London Hackney Carriage Act – a bit before my time – all The Knowledge means . . .

(*beat*)

. . . is that you commit to memory . . .

(*beat*)

. . . every street within a six-mile radius of Charing Cross.

He circles the radius on the map.

Every street – and what's *on* every street. Every hotel, club, hospital, department store, shop, government building, theatre, cinema, restaurant, art gallery, park, church, synagogue, mosque, etcetera, etcetera, etcetera. And etcetera. In the words of the poet, John Keats, 'That is all you know on earth and all you need to know.'

(*a bleak smile*)

Keats *House*, for the uninitiated, is halfway down the right-hand side of Keats Grove, leaving on right Downshire Hill, leaving on right Hampstead High Street, NW3.

FREEZE FRAME:

Verity Lambert at Euston Films commissions the screenplay. Jack goes to her office to deliver it – then, as she takes hold of one end of it, he doesn't let go of the other. Suddenly he's decided he wants to rewrite it.

VERITY

Well, can't I read it first?

JACK

It isn't right. Let me redo it.

They both tug at the script.

VERITY

You've brought it in specially, though!

JACK

There's a way of doing it better.

VERITY

You can't bring it in, then take it away again!

JACK

It's not right, though.

They continue their tug-of-war. Verity gives up. He goes away, rewrites it and hands it over like a normal human being.

RESUME Mr Burgess:

He picks up a small booklet.

MR BURGESS

Now, this . . . is your bible. It's called the Blue Book . . . probably because it's coloured pink. A bit like Life in a way.

On page one, you'll find a list – which we call a page – of routes – which we call runs. Run number one on page number one is Manor House Station to Gibson Square. Not that anyone has ever *wanted* to go from Manor House to Gibson Square. But *you've* got to know *how* to. All the one-way systems, traffic lights, roundabouts, streets – what's *on* every street. Right?

Everyone stares at him, blank and bemused.

So far – piece of pudding. Except for one little thing. There's not one page – there's 26. And there's not one list on each page – there's eighteen. So that's 460 runs altogether, with say fifteen streets on each one. A grand total of five and half thousand streets . . . and the umpteen thousand buildings on them. And that, lady and gentlemen, is only the first part of The Knowledge. There are *three*.

FREEZE FRAME:

Both Bob Brooks and Jack are warned they'll never get on together. That they're both implacably opinionated on every detail of filming. As it turns out, they enjoy an entirely harmonious – and fruitful – partnership.

RESUME Mr Burgess:

MR BURGESS

Now, The Knowledge sounds impossible. It isn't. Otherwise there'd be no such phenomenon as the London cabby. It's true that no taxi-driver in no other city in the world has to know a *fraction* of what you have to know. And not many brain surgeons neither. But there we are. That's how we built an Empire – and, no doubt, how we knocked the bugger down again. We live ... We learn ... What we, in our ignorance, call Knowledge.

Passing it is different from everything else in the world. It's unique. It's not *who* you know, it's *what* you know.

(*a bleak, chilling smile*)

Know what I mean?

FREEZE FRAME:

Nigel Hawthorne, such a lovely man, such a lovely actor, heads a superb cast and gives a superlative, unforgettable comic performance as Mr Burgess – based on a real-life, notoriously sadistic examiner. Overnight, the 13,000 London cabbies become Nigel's, the cast's and Jack's biggest fans . . .

EXT GARDEN – 31 ROSSLYN HILL – HAMPSTEAD – DAY – 1979

Bryan and Edith Butler, from Bolton, one-time childhood sweethearts, now in their fifties, live in the flat below the Rosenthals' old one.

Maureen, Jack, Amy and Adam are visiting them. Cups of tea and Ribena in the garden.

EDITH

I got a right shock the other day. I thought the radio said Jule Styne had died.

Jack and Maureen stare at her.

MAUREEN

What?

EDITH

S'alright, I got it wrong. It wasn't him. It was Somebody-Else Styne.

JACK

(*beat*)

Oh. Right.

ANGLE ON Amy and Adam playing on the lawn with the Butlers' virtually human Yorkshire Terrier, Emily.

JACK (VO)

What we didn't know was that Amy had half heard what Edith said about Jule – and for months afterwards nursed a secret worry that I'd killed him.

I'd never thought of killing Jule. *Maiming* him, yes. But neither rat poison nor strangling him with piano wire nor pushing him under a bus had ever crossed my mind. And now, of course, it was too late. He was back in New York, no doubt getting a standing ovation for breaking wind.

Damn.

EXT A DISCREET GRAND HOUSE – PARIS – EVENING – 1980

Two beefy bouncers stand at the door, arms folded, legs astride. An expensively dressed middle-aged couple get out of a chauffeur-driven Mercedes and walk to the door. They show a letter to one of the bouncers. He promptly opens the door and ushers them inside.

INT THE DISCREET HOUSE – PARIS – EVENING – 1980 (CONT)

We hear an intermittent breath-squashing sound like the air brakes of a hundred heavy lorries, as CAM *opens tight on the smiling, anticipating faces of the middle-aged couple now entering a spacious drawing room.*

CAM *pulls back to see they're no longer expensively dressed – they're completely naked.*

There are no heavy lorries. Just heavy-breathing swingers. The room is a writhing, wriggling mass of similarly naked, or half-naked, men and women in every copulating position possible, plus a few not quite *possible, in chairs, on sofas and on the Persian carpets. No one's yet swinging from the chandeliers, but the night's still young.*

In the midst of the sea of bouncing breasts, buttocks and the odd testicle, a naked man is seated on a settee, reading a book, a briefcase on his knees. He closes the book, thinks for a moment, takes a notebook out of his briefcase and checks a number. He then picks up a phone on a table beside him and dials. The man is Max Fischer. He speaks in a faintly Continental *accent.*

MAX
(*into phone*)
Is that Peggy Ramsay?

INT PEGGY RAMSAY'S OFFICE – LONDON – EVENING – 1980 (CONT)

Peggy is seated at her desk, her legs levitating somewhere above it.

PEGGY

That depends slightly on who *you* are.

INTERCUT between Max in Paris and Peggy in London.

MAX

(*into phone*)

My name's Max Fischer. I'm in Paris. We're an hour ahead of you. I was hoping Madame Ramsay was still in her office.

PEGGY

(*into phone*)

She's *always* in her office. What do you want?

A passing hand grabs his penis. He gives a strangled yelp.

PEGGY

(*into phone*)

Are you having a heart attack?

MAX

(*into phone*)

No, no. I'm at a swingers' party.

PEGGY

(*into phone*)

Swingers? Saxophone players?

MAX

(*into phone*)

No, no . . . um . . . different swingers. An orgy.

PEGGY

(*into phone*)

I see.

MAX

(*into phone*)

I hope you aren't offended.

PEGGY

(*into phone*)

'Offended'? I'm delighted for you. Most civilised. Personally, I'm making do with a lukewarm cup of Nescafé. Now what is it you want?

As they continue their conversation . . .

JACK (VO)

What he wanted was me. To write a feature film based on the short story he was reading, 'La Belle Etoile'. Max was an Egyptian-Dutch film director who'd so far only made commercials – and had clearly no idea what fees writers commanded. A couple of years later he confessed that he thought I'd be about a hundred quid. I think I was a few thousand. Not all that many, but a few.

EXT VILLAGE SQUARE – HOLLAND – DAY – 1981

Max's film unit is shooting the final scene from La Belle Etoile *(*The Lucky Star*). Strutting by the Town Hall in front of the camera is Rod Steiger, in the uniform of a German Army officer in 1942. Standing nearby is Louise Fletcher, who was such a critical success in* One Flew over the Cuckoo's Nest, *her arm around the shoulders of a teenage boy – the hero of the film.*

JACK (VO)

In the story, he's a Jewish kid in Amsterdam when the Germans invade. He escapes from the city, still wearing his yellow star. He's given refuge by the Louise Fletcher character, a farmer. Crazy about Westerns, he believes the yellow star makes him a sheriff. He captures the local Wehrmacht commanding officer (Rod Steiger) and locks him in a shed behind bars. Oddly they become almost friends and eventually, when the officer is released, he's a man solemnly changed by his experience. In the final scene, the boy goes to the village to see him . . .

MAX

(shouting)

Action!

The boy runs forward. The German guards see him.

GUARDS

Halt!

Rod Steiger turns in surprise. The boy continues running to him. Louise Fletcher tries to grab him back. Too late – the guards gun the boy down. Rod Steiger kneels beside him and cradles his head, but the kid's dead. His erstwhile prisoner is devastated.

JACK (VO)

That's how the film ended – and very moving it was, too. Rod had argued hard for a different ending: *he* wanted to be the one to be killed, then he could do his 'dying' acting. It made no sense, of course, in the context of the story, and he was diplomatically dissuaded.

We had another actor keen on changing his lines and his part – the veteran Canadian, Lou Jacobi, who did himself, and the audience, no favours with a particularly unsubtle performance as a Yiddishe cabaret clown.

INT A CONFERENCE ROOM – DAY – 1981

Around a boardroom table sit the eminent director Jack Gold; eminent playwright Willy Russell; eminent theatre director Mike Ockrent; eminent businessman Kiffer Weiselberg; Victor Glynn, not so eminent anything; and Jack. These are the members of Quintet Films (five in number before Victor Glynn slithered his way in), a hopeful production company. It was a golden era for independent production companies.

As opposed to making hard-nose business decisions, they all seem to be having a good laugh. Lots of them. The fact is – they're actually enjoying *the whole enterprise. Certainly rather more obviously than company directors usually do.*

But Victor isn't laughing. Victor seems deeply pensive. Could he be plotting the downfall of the Relatively Famous Five even though he's their managing director? Surely not.

DISSOLVE TO:

INT A CONFERENCE ROOM – DAY – SOME YEARS LATER

Assuredly yes. This is some years and some pretty profitable productions *later.*

But now no one seems to be enjoying himself. No one's laughing any more. It doesn't feel *like a profitable company. Maybe no rats scuttle across the floor or vultures cling to the bare-bulb electric cable hanging from the ceiling but there's no doubt times have changed. Everyone looks pretty grim. Apart from Victor, who seems quite chipper . . .*

He has just informed his co-directors that Quintet Films isn't healthily – very healthily – in the black, as they thought. Instead, it's unable to pay outstanding VAT, which means it's unable to trade, unable to make any more films.

The company faces bankruptcy and its directors very possibly beheading. All except Victor, of course, are gobsmacked. What happened to all his grandiose schemes for expansion? They all lost money and shrank to nothing.

He hands each of them documents to sign. And they sign the company over to him. For free. He promises, almost convincingly, to pay its debts. He stuffs the signed documents into his briefcase, and starts for the door. To the Victor the spoils. He turns and waves goodbye. It seems he was *an eminent something after all. An eminent Machiavellian shyster.*

The others look at each other, balefully. Ever been had? In a blazing tangle of celluloid, Quintet Films burns to nothing.

WILLY RUSSELL

Hang on. There's *something* we can do. To feel better.

They all look at him . . . their faces filled with hope.

WILLY RUSSELL

I'll get some of my muckers down from Liverpool. They can fuckin' kneecap him.

Everyone nods, sighs, then gets up and goes out, back to their work and their lives.

JACK (VO)

It was because of Victor that I decided to bank at Coutts. Or rather because of the wallet Coutts gave you. In a richly glowing yellow leather, very beautiful. So I joined. The yellow leather had been discontinued. In its place was fairly crappy, maroon leatherette. I don't suppose I can blame Victor, but I'd like to.

INT BEDROOM – 124 DUKE'S AVENUE – MUSWELL HILL – NIGHT – 1981

Jack is twitching in his sleep, tortured by whatever he's dreaming . . .

JACK (VO)

Ever since the nightmare of the *Bar Mitzvah Boy* musical, I'd dreamt of getting revenge on Jule, Martin and Peter . . .

DISSOLVE TO:

EXT 5TH AVENUE – NEW YORK – DAY – 1981

DREAM SEQUENCE:

Through binoculars, from the roof of a skyscraper, Jack sees Jule strolling along. He promptly raises a shotgun and takes aim. But suddenly the air is filled with thousands of tiny ribbons of paper, catapulted out of the windows of office blocks, drowning 5th Avenue in a billowing snowstorm – no, they're not Jack's rewrites for Martin, torn to shreds, they're a traditional New York ticker-tape parade for Jule. For putting one leg in front of the other. And it obliterates him from Jack's view.

Frustrated, Jack lowers the gun – then spots Martin walking along, wearing his trademark ankle-length scarf. Jack takes aim again and fires – just as Martin trips over his scarf and falls headlong. Jack's shot pings harmlessly on the sidewalk.

He then sees Peter, trundling along. He raises his shotgun again and fires again – just as Peter half-swivels, half-stumbles 360 degrees to try and ogle the back view of a passing girl. Again, the shot misses.

INT BEDROOM – 124 DUKE'S AVENUE – MUSWELL HILL – DAY – 1981

Jack emerges, sweating, from his dream, as Amy, now aged seven, and Adam, five, both in pyjamas, stick their heads round the door.

AMY

Dod!

— which is Amy-speak and Adam-speak for 'Dad'.

Wake up!

ADAM

Time for school!

EXT 124 DUKE'S AVENUE – MUSWELL HILL – DAY – 1981

Amy and Adam pile into the back seats of the Rosenthal Honda. Jack, unshaven, climbs blearily into the driver's seat.

JACK (VO)

Maureen was having her lie-in after performing onstage the night before. My turn for the school run – all of roughly 400 yards.

EXT RHODES AVENUE SCHOOL – MUSWELL HILL – DAY – 1981 (CONT)

The Honda stutters through the traffic jams towards the entrance.

The kids are doing their Ethel Merman impersonation singing 'There's No Business Like Show Business' in the back. Only louder.

JACK (VO)

And it was on the school run that it dawned on me that to get revenge on my American allies, I didn't need a pop-gun. As ever, the solution lay in the answer to the question: 'What would the character do?'

INT STUDY – 124 DUKE'S AVENUE – MUSWELL HILL – DAY – 1981

Jack is ferociously typing at his desk.

JACK (VO)

He'd do what he *does,* i.e. in my case, he'd *write.* So I did. A stage play about the whole lousy *Bar Mitzvah Boy* musical

experience. I'd put Jule, Martin and Peter on stage and tell the truth; wherever dramatically possible putting the words in their mouths that they'd actually spoken. Virtually verbatim.

CU the page in the typewriter as Jack types the title: Smash!

INT QC'S OFFICE – THE INNS OF COURT – LONDON – DAY – 1981

In the gleaming, mahogany-panelled room, Jonathan Lynn, Michael Codron and Jack sit glumly listening to a solemn-looking QC *across his desk, his hands church-steepled in front of his face.*

Jonathan is the future writer of Yes, Minister, *the actor who gave such excellent performances in two of Jack's TV films – Harold in* Bar Mitzvah Boy *and Ted Margolies in* The Knowledge *– as well as in scores of other TV and stage plays. He's also a pal whose family – wife, Rita, and son, Edward – share bagels and smoked salmon with the Rosenthals every Sunday morning. He's now the artistic director of the Arts Theatre in Cambridge. He wants to tour* Smash! *and eventually bring it into the West End.*

Michael is one of the West End's most prolific, experienced and cultured producers. He wants to produce the play but he's uneasy about the legality of its treatment of Jule, Peter and Martin. Hence the involvement of a QC.

QC

To sum up . . . I enjoyed reading the play. Very interesting. Entertaining. However, I'm afraid it's skating on scarcely any ice at all.

A beat. He smiles ruefully at each of them in turn.

QC

It's totally defamatory. If Messrs Styne, Charnin and Witt saw a performance and concluded the characters were intended to represent themselves, they could apply for an immediate injunction, get the play taken off and sue you –

(*peers at Jack over his bifocals*)

– particularly *you* – for defamation. Americans enjoy doing that. And they'd win. The three lawsuits could cost you three million dollars. Or many years in jail. Sorry to be the bearer etcetera, etcetera.

That appears to be that. Michael, Jonathan and Jack wearily unbend themselves upright. They share shrugs, defeated smiles and sighs. They mutter their thanks to the QC, *shake his hand and start for the door.*

At the exact moment they reach it – as in a hundred plays and films, perfectly timed for full corny, dramatic effect – the QC *calls out:*

QC

Or, on the other hand . . .

The trio turn back to face him.

If you send the play to each of them with a letter asking their *permission* to stage it and, in exchange, offering them one dollar plus 1 per cent of the play's West End profits – and they say 'Yes' . . .

(he beams at them, triumphantly)

Well, the show must go on, as you people say.

Michael, Jonathan and Jack stare at each other . . . daring to dare to hope.

INT RICHMOND THEATRE – LONDON – NIGHT – 1981

On stage, playing Act I, scene 1 from Smash!, *are Nigel Hawthorne as Theo (i.e. the fictional Peter Witt), John Bluthal as Bebe (i.e. the fictional Jule Styne), Stephen Moore as Stacey (i.e. the fictional Martin Charnin) and Maureen Lipman as Liz (i.e. the fictional Jack Rosenthal, who's undergone a sex change for the purposes of the play since he was too cowardly to write himself).*

The scene they're playing, to a packed house, is the fictional (but virtually 100 per cent factual) depiction of the scene in the Albany Hotel when Jule lambasted Jack – and everybody else mysteriously lost their voice.

JACK (VO)

All three defamed men (Don is amicably treated in the play) accepted the dollar and the potential 1 per cent and gave wholehearted and enthusiastic permission.

Jule thought the play had been very kind to him, but harsh on Martin and Peter.

Martin thought it had been kind to *him,* but tough on Peter and Jule.

Peter thought it had been generous to *him* ('Maybe you have me doing a little too much effing and blinding. I don't eff and blind so much, do I?' 'Yes, Peter, all the effing time.'), but hard on Jule and Martin.

All three of them loved the play and didn't seem to notice how incompetent they'd been painted. Martin asked if he could direct it on Broadway; Jule and Peter asked in all seriousness if they could produce it.

DISSOLVE TO:

STAGE EXCERPT: *Smash!*

THEO'S HOTEL SUITE – NEW YORK – EVENING

The creative team are meeting to discuss Liz's script. Bebe and Liz have never met before. She stands offering her hand to be shaken. Bebe sits stiffly in an armchair very pointedly ignoring her.

THEO

Bebe, allow me. This is your author, Liz. Liz – your esteemed composer, the one and only Bebe Kaiser.

LIZ

I'm honoured to meet you, Mr Kaiser.

He ignores her. An uncomfortable silence.

STACEY

Bebe. Liz said she was pleased to meet you.

BEBE

Yeah? That pleases her, does it? Well, fine, I'll roast a turkey, we'll have a parade! You know what'd please *me*? Knowing how to put flesh and blood into those cardboard asshole characters of hers! She got any ideas? 'Cos sure as hell, *I* ain't!

An embarrassed silence.

LIZ

(*meekly*)

What cardboard characters?

THEO

Okay, Liz, cool it! You want violence, get the elevator, there's a streetful of it down there.

LIZ

Mr Kaiser, if you don't like the script, let's discuss what you –

BEBE

I ain't *seen* no script!

STACEY

Okay, Bebe, simmer down.

Bebe leaps ferociously to his feet.

BEBE

'Simmer down'? *Me?* And what'll *you* do, Golden Boy? You just stand there and wear your scarf. In the middle of summer.

THEO

(*gently*)

Bebe. You got the script yesterday. Hand-delivered. First draft.

BEBE

I did not get no first draft delivered! I got a fancy packet of *crap* delivered! You guys ain't had the privilege of working with me before, you don't know my nature. My nature is to be helpful. Twenty-eight Broadway shows, so what's a shmock like me know? Twenty-eight Broadway smasheroos.

(*to Stacey*)

How many you done? Two? Three? So that gives you the right under the Constitution to wear a scarf down to your ankles and tell *me* to simmer down?

He turns to Liz for the first time.

You. The broad. You'd like to discuss what's wrong, right? A discussion.

He raps out his words with staccato intensity.

You got no conflict. You got no characters. You got no love interest. You got no narrative drive. You got no climax. You don't even got a happy ending. All you got is crap.

THEO

Nobody said the first draft was perfect.

LIZ

You did. This morning.

BEBE

A show's gotta have conflict.

All look at Stacey. He looks at Liz.

STACEY

We'll have conflict.

All look at Bebe. He looks at Liz.

BEBE

Conflict is essential.

All look at Stacey. He looks at Liz.

STACEY

Conflict there'll be.

All look at Bebe. He looks at Liz.

BEBE

Without conflict you're dead.

All look at Stacey. He looks at Liz.

STACEY

We can promise you conflict.

All turn to Bebe. A pause.

BEBE

Okay, let's get this goddamn show on the road.

Everyone sags, washed in relief. Except Liz.

DISSOLVE TO:

EXT RICHMOND THEATRE – LONDON – NIGHT – 1981

Michael, Jonathan and Jack are seated on the steps leading to the entrance, deep in conversation. From inside the theatre we hear encouraging bursts of laughter.

The play is doing well, although it has had its problems. Barry Davies is initially the director, but flounders helplessly from day one of rehearsals and, unsurprisingly, loses the confidence of his cast. A rescue job is needed, and quickly. No one moves more quickly than Jonathan Lynn. He takes over the direction.

Larry Adler is initially cast to play Bebe. He tries valiantly – but, unfortunately, a brilliant virtuoso musician does not necessarily an audible actor make, who can take his fingers out of his mouth for long enough to walk and talk at the same time. He's succeeded, halfway through rehearsals, by John Bluthal.

Who proceeds to give Jonathan and Jack another *problem . . .*

INT RICHMOND THEATRE – LONDON – NIGHT – 1981

On stage are all the principal actors, playing the scene at the end of act I.

John has decided to give two diametrically opposite versions of the character. When he has no friends in the audience, he plays Bebe meanly, beadily and viciously (which is how he's supposed *to be played, i.e. as written and directed). When he* does *have friends in the audience, he plays him sweetly, jovially and avuncularly (a travesty of the play's intentions).*

Whichever of the two versions he delivers, he does do one *thing consistently at every performance when the director's not present. Which gives Nigel a particularly* painful *problem . . .*

The act ends with Bebe prodding Liz in the chest, which leads to a punch-up between Bebe and Theo, while Stacey, Mike and Liz try to pull them apart. Since this is a play and not real life, it's a pretend *punch-up. John doesn't seem to quite grasp this. So each night, sweet or vicious John flings himself on Nigel and punches hell out of him. His punch in the kidneys, hidden from the audience, is his speciality. Nigel's in agony. Jonathan warns him again and again, 'Once more and you're fired.' It makes no difference. Whenever Jonathan isn't in the theatre, Nigel's back gets thumped. Shame, Bluthal's a good actor. He could've been an even better, if dirty, boxer.*

INT DRESSING ROOMS – RICHMOND THEATRE – LONDON – NIGHT – 1981

Nigel, Stephen, Peter and John in their dressing rooms, and Maureen in hers, are packing away their belongings at the end of the Richmond run, which is the end of the tour.

JACK (VO)

The play had been a success, commercially and critically. It was destined to go into the West End – then, minutes later, it wasn't. Michael Codron had suffered a sudden and very major personal tragedy and had to withdraw. I tried hard to get other managements interested. Half a dozen of them came to see it in its final week – and *all* of them sang its praises. 'The best time I've had in the theatre for years' was their theme song.

Unfortunately, for an encore, they sang 'But the punters don't like plays about showbusiness.'

They do, of course. Punters *love* showbusiness. That's *why* they're punters. (And a year later, Michael Frayn's hilarious *Noises Off* became the best and most successful showbiz play of all).

And then . . . and then . . . after all the West End producers had given a final though seemingly reluctant thumbs-down . . . one of them had sudden second thoughts. And something weird happened . . .

EXT GOODWIN'S COURT – WEST END – DAY – 1981

After their lunch, two men – with their backs to CAM – come out of Giovanni's restaurant and walk down the narrow alley. One is a West End producer, the other a writer.

Further down the street, Peggy is pacing up and down on one of her daily patrols outside her office, having a private, if public, ponder about Life and Art.

She and the producer greet each other.

FADE UP the music and lyrics of 'Whispering Grass'.

The producer tells Peggy he's interested in bringing Smash! *into town.*

ANGLE ON Peggy, as she immediately becomes more and more agitated, arms semaphoring and legs akimbo, and emphatically starts talking him out *of it. Repeat: an agent passionately* dissuading *a producer from bringing her client's play into the West End. It's the equivalent of . . . no, there probably* is *no equivalent. Except maybe in the world of* double-*agents.*

Jack knows he's no favourite of Peggy's. A disappointment, in fact. He's far too conventional – married, a TV writer rather than a theatre writer, never phones her at three in the morning to be bailed out of a Peruvian prison or helped into a Bratislavan brothel. But this? Isn't this going too *far?*

INT LIVING ROOM – DUKE'S AVENUE – MUSWELL HILL – DAY – 1981

The phone rings. Jack takes it. The caller is the writer from the previous scene, telling him of Peggy's betrayal in Goodwin's Court.

JACK
(*into phone*)

What? Never!

INT PEGGY RAMSAY'S OFFICE – LONDON – DAY – 1981

The phone rings. Peggy takes it. The caller is Jack. After a couple of weeks of shock and a couple of months of sulking and not speaking to her, he now tells her what he was told.

PEGGY
(*into phone, incredulously*)

What? Never!

INT THE OFFICE OF HARBOTTLE AND LEWIS, SOLICITORS – LONDON – DAY – 1981

The phone rings. A solicitor takes it. The caller is Peggy, a client of Harbottle and Lewis. She tells him of Jack's call and how she has consequently decided to stop being an agent and commit suicide. She doesn't say in which order.

SOLICITOR
(*into phone, incredulously*)

What? Never!

Needless to say, she does neither. Maybe she has her fingers crossed behind her back. What she does *do, however, is this:*

INT PEGGY RAMSAY'S BEDROOM – LONDON – NIGHT – 1981

A no doubt very feminine boudoir. Peggy is in bed, propped up on her pillows, a stack of books and scripts by the bed, pen and writing pad in hand. She's fiercely writing ferociously scathing (as yet unpublished) letters . . .

She writes: 'Jack is a bit worried about Stephen [Moore]. This shows he simply doesn't understand actors.'

JACK (VO)

I've worked with actors since 1961. Hundreds of them. One of them I *married*. I was worried about Stephen in rehearsal under our hapless, initial director. Throughout that period, I was Stephen's ally. When the play opened, I was *very* happy with his performance.

Peggy writes: 'Jack has totally deluded himself into believing everyone thinks it's a wonderful play.'

No, not everyone, and not wonderful. But many people believed it deserved a West End run – Michael Codron, with an enviable reputation for good taste; Jonathan Lynn, an established West End director; Sir Peter Hall, who later wanted to mount it at the National Theatre; Sheridan Morley, who nominated it Best Comedy in *Plays and Players*; Michael Grade, in his LWT office, after hours, addressing envelopes containing the play to potentially interested parties; and thousands of theatregoers throughout its tour. But, by then, it was I who'd lost heart.

Peggy writes: 'Maureen Lipman is becoming impossibly ambitious for the play to come in.'

Maureen phoned Peggy *once,* on behalf of the rest of the cast, who were in a quandary about turning down other offers of work if *Smash!* didn't come in – to ask did Peggy have any hope?

She did this believing that Peggy felt as passionately about the play as the cast did. Peggy *never* told me, or Maureen, that she didn't like it.

Peggy writes: 'The play was a financial disaster from the start.'

A lie. According to Michael and Jonathan, it was, on the contrary, a financial success.

Peggy writes: 'Jack arranged for pro "cliques" to see the play in Richmond.'

Another lie. There were no cliques at all. None. Pro's went to see the play, of their own accord, because it was about their world.

Peggy writes: 'Managers were embarrassed to talk to Jack.'

Yep. Another lie. They *did* talk to me. At length. Some invited me to lunch, *specifically* to talk.

Peggy writes: 'The play is a vintage, pseudo-thirties view of showbiz.'

The woman clearly didn't understand the play at all. It was a truthful dramatisation of events that occurred *three* years earlier. The *character* of Peter Witt (Theo), played by Nigel, *is* precisely an old Hollywood, Tin Pan Alley shyster – as was Peter, himself.

Peggy writes: 'Theo's sadness and innate loneliness are missing.'

Or, on the other hand, present all the way through – *between* the lines, under the lines, and, very often, *in* the lines.

Peggy writes: 'Jack was frantic to get the play on.'

Passionate, yes. Which *she* should have been. It was Peggy, my agent, who was frantic – to get the play off.

INT 2 BRYDGES PLACE – COVENT GARDEN – LONDON – DAY – 1999

This is Simon Callow's very cosy, very exclusive club looking out towards Trafalgar Square.

Simon and Jack are eating lunch, although, most of the time, Simon is laughing as uproariously as only Simon can. Jack has read his enthralling book, Love is Where It Falls, *in which he tells of his and Peggy's unique and fascinating 'love affair' and – en passant – mentions a letter from Peggy asserting that* Smash! *was a financial flop.*

Jack has invited him to lunch to put the record straight – that it was a financial success. Too late, of course, since her words are lying (i.e. lying) there in black and white. Simon, being Simon, generously invites Jack to lunch instead at his club. He listens solemnly to the whole saga of Peggy and Smash! *– then bursts into even more uproarious laughter. Apparently,* Smash! *wasn't the only little oeuvre Peggy put the mockers on. Far from it. She had almost as big a reputation (albeit secret) for strangling healthy plays at birth as giving sick ones the kiss of life.*

JACK (VO)

Enough about bloody Peggy.

Except for one thing: Simon tells Jack what Peggy had written about some of her other *clients. Some of the most prolific, original and brilliant playwrights of our time. She thought they couldn't actually write a decent play. Jack feels in prestigious company.*

Almost two decades later Maureen gave her aforementioned searing performance as Peggy Ramsay in Alan Plater's Peggy for You. *She was scheming, manipulative and deadly. Peggy would not have wanted this play to 'come in'. Maureen made her hilarious and Alan made her soft centred. She was neither. When Act II was in trouble I told Maureen about the time I'd gone into the office with a grievance and Peggy somehow got me to lay a carpet which had just been delivered. Alan wove it skilfully into Act II and it became a sort of symbol of Peggy at her most physical and most perverse.*

A CHANNEL 4 LOGO CAPTION

CAM pulls back to reveal that the caption is on the screen of a TV set.

JACK (VO)

Attended by the brightest midwives, television gave birth to an exciting new channel. Exciting to its viewers and certainly to writers.

CAM pulls back, and we see that the TV set is in the corner of:

INT BOARDROOM – CHANNEL 4 – CHARLOTTE ST – LONDON – DAY – 1982

Around the table sit Channel 4's chief, Jeremy Isaacs, David Rose, David Puttnam and Jack. Jeremy is the same Jeremy who succeeded Jack in Granada's Research Department 26 years ago – and has continued succeeding ever since.

JACK (VO)

To launch the new channel and its drama ambitions, David Rose, the head of Film on Four, commissioned Goldcrest Films, who commissioned David Puttnam of Enigma Productions to make a series of films under the umbrella-title *First Love*. David, generous to me as ever, commissioned me to write one of them and script-edit the rest.

EXT A WIMBLEDON STREET – DAY – 1982

A film unit is shooting a scene from P'Tang, Yang, Kipperbang, *the first of the* First Loves. *Mike Apted, taking a break from Hollywood, is directing it with his usual relaxed style and skill. He and Jack stand in their habitual shooting positions when working together – literally shoulder to shoulder.*

JACK (VO)

An excellent, edgier film called *Walter*, starring Ian McKellen, opened the Channel. *P'Tang, Yang, Kipperbang* was transmitted the night after.

The film, which also had a run in cinemas both here and in the States, was a success. As was most of the *First Love* series.

INT ENIGMA PRODUCTIONS' OFFICE – LONDON – DAY – 1982

A relaxed, informal meeting between David Puttnam, Jack and Philip Saville – who's directing another of the First Love *series,* Those Glory, Glory Days, *written by Julie Welch.*

Jack had phoned David earlier to say he'd be half an hour late – he needed to talk to a builder at home.

The meeting ends. Philip and Jack make their way to the door to take their leave, when –

DAVID

Can you hang on a minute, Jack?

Jack stops.

JACK

'Course.

Philip goes. David waits till he's sure Philip is out of earshot – then explodes.

DAVID

Are you crazy?

JACK
(*thrown*)

Am I?

DAVID

You 'need to talk to a builder'?

JACK

What?

DAVID

You've more important things to do than talk to builders! Like being on time for meetings, for example! Like writing, or filming, or *thinking* every second of the day! You could be the most prolific, *terr*ific writer in Britain if you hired *other* people to talk to builders! You need a Margaret!

JACK (VO)

Margaret was David's (and his wife Patsy's) brilliant amanuensis.

DAVID

For God's sake, get yourself a Margaret!

(*he simmers down*)

Okay, that was it. Just a quiet word of advice. See you tomorrow.

Jack wanders out of the office, a little shaken.

JACK (VO)

Actually, I thought I already *was* the most prolific writer in Britain . . . but I suppose he was right.

(*beat*)

Except it was people like builders who peopled my scripts. If I didn't talk to builders and people like builders I wouldn't have all that much to write about, and I wouldn't have written half the things I already had.

(*beat*)

Needless to say, I didn't think of this till I was in the car on my way home. To talk to a plumber.

INT A LONDON UNDERGROUND STATION – DAY – 1982

A film unit, under the direction of Brian Gilbert, is shooting a scene on the crowded platform: a man and girl kissing.

JACK (VO)

***First Love* gave me only one regret. Posy Simmonds, the exceptionally talented *Guardian* cartoonist, had written an exceptionally talented screenplay, called *Frog Prince* – perceptive, elegant, delicate, witty and touching.**

(*beat*)

Brian Gilbert wanted to put his stamp on it – and stamped it into the ground. The producer, Susan Richards, didn't, or couldn't, stop him. Posy, in dismay and disbelief, threw away her typewriter and went back to her drawing board.

(*beat*)

And an extremely promising writer was lost to us.

EXT A MANSION – BEL AIR – CALIFORNIA – DAY – 1983

Jack gets out of a taxi, pays the driver, doesn't get a thank you, but, being British, mutters, 'Don't mention it,' just the same, then goes to the massive electronic gates and presses an intercom button.

A VOICE

Yes?

JACK

I'm Jack Rosenthal. I've an appointment with Miss Streisand at two-thirty.

His voice is an octave or two higher than intended.

A VOICE

Okay.

A buzzer sounds. The gates glide silently open, and Jack walks into the driveway, populated by five parked cars.

INT LIVING ROOM – BARBRA'S HOUSE – BEL AIR – DAY – 1983

Jack stands in the middle of a huge, sumptuously furnished room – white leather sofas, Charles Rennie Mackintosh fittings. Barbra Streisand walks in.

BARBRA

Hi.

JACK

Hi.

They shake hands.

BARBRA

You don't look anything like I thought you'd look.

JACK

You look *exactly* like I thought you'd look.

Which Jack thinks is an hilariously witty, impromptu line. But Barbra doesn't laugh. This is something Jack's going to have to get used to . . .

INT CONSERVATORY – BARBRA'S HOUSE – BEL AIR – DAY – 1983

Barbra and Jack sit opposite each other in the tastefully-appointed room. Everything in it is either pink or green. On the table is a porcelain objet d'art *dish, a green lizard snaking across the pink lid. Inside are pink and green bon-bons.*

JACK (VO)

I'd had a call a week or so before from an executive producer telling me to expect a call, two days later, from Barbra Streisand. In the meantime, would I read the Isaac Bashevis Singer short story 'Yentl', to see if I'd be interested in adapting it for a feature film. Barbra was to produce it, direct it and star in it. So here I was.

It transpires that Barbra has a Yentl *screenplay already written – in fact, she has* nine, *all written by different writers. Seems I wasn't the first choice, then.*

Each screenplay is a modification of the one before. The last one modified by Barbra herself.

Barbra reads it aloud, while Jack follows in his copy. When she comes to a song – the film is to be a musical – she sings it.

The hairs rise on Jack's neck.

Here he is, alone with probably the most famous singer on earth – and she's singing. With that voice. That glorious voice. Just to him. From two feet away.

The hairs on his neck begin to sway to the rhythm.

As long as the song lasts, he can ignore how inexpert the script is. When it ends Barbra takes a minute to wonder whether the builders doing alterations to the conservatory are ripping her off . . . She clearly needs a Margaret. And she has one. A perfect one called Renata.

INT BEACH HOUSE – MALIBU – CALIFORNIA – DAY – 1983

Barbra and Jack sit with their backs to what Californians, quite logically, call 'the ocean', and what Blackpool-brainwashed Mancunians call 'the water'. Barbra decides to commission him to write his *version of the story. This'll be the tenth.*

As they talk, Jon Peters, Barbra's ex-hairdresser-now-movie-producer husband, strides in and out, shouting into a phone. He seems narked about something. Or someone. Barbra? Me?

EXT STREET – ST TROPEZ – DAY – 1983

JACK (VO)

First Malibu, now St Tropez. Just one swanky sunkissed location after another, isn't it? Whatever happened to those grimy Salford backstreets? Don't worry, they're still lurking round the corner.

A parade of promenading bronzed bodies – bikini'd, bum-bagged and sandalled – dodging the Vespas.

From an open first-floor window, we hear a typewriter – or, maybe, by now, a more softly-spoken word-processor.

INT FLAT – ST TROPEZ – DAY – 1983 – (CONT)

Jack is at a desk at the window, typing his version of Yentl.

He's on holiday with Maureen, their friends Julia McKenzie and her husband, Jerry, Louie Ramsay and Derek and Bobby Cartiledge, whose flat this is.

Jack's happy with what he has written.

EXT 5-STAR HOTEL – LONDON – DAY – 1983

Barbra is unhappy *with what he's written. More than unhappy. Traumatised. Paralysed. Culture-shocked.*

Jack drives up to the hotel entrance, parks his car, takes a deep breath – and goes in.

INT BARBRA'S SUITE – 5-STAR HOTEL – LONDON – DAY – 1983

Barbra, Jack and Barbra's assistant on the film, Rusty Lemorande, a tall, young, slightly balding, immensely patient film buff and future movie director, sit on settees, scripts in hand, looking glum.

Pouring their room-service tea is Barbra's aforementioned Margaret: Renata, her long-serving, fiercely loyal, 24-hours-a-day, hard-working, Jill-of-all-trades, young, Romanian personal assistant.

It slowly dawns on Jack that what Barbra wanted wasn't his version of the story at all – but confirmation that the one before, hers, *couldn't really be improved on.*

It's finally decided that they take all the best elements of the previous, say, five screenplays, together with Barbra's and Jack's, and that he and Barbra do an entirely new rewrite together. *From now on, they're co-writers . . .*

INT BARBRA'S SUITE – 5-STAR HOTEL – LONDON – DAY – 1983

The next morning.

Barbra paces the room, making her scene suggestions. Jack sits at a table, making notes. Occasionally arguing. And losing. Always *losing.*

INT STUDY – 124 DUKE'S AVENUE – MUSWELL HILL – NIGHT – 1983

That night. Dead of.

Jack sits at his desk, typing away. If we could see the moon, it'd be full. If there were wolves, we'd hear one howling. If we could afford wolves.

INT BARBRA'S SUITE – 5-STAR HOTEL – LONDON – DAY – 1983

The following morning.

Barbra and Jack, pages in hand, are enacting one of the scenes Jack wrote the night before. They reach the end. Barbra looks at him, impressed.

BARBRA

Hey! You're not bad! I'd like to cast you in the movie! In all the roles!

JACK

Including yours?

BARBRA

(*one slowly raised brow*)

C'mon. Back to work.

He obeys. But they don't often see eye to eye. Usually eyeball to eyeball. In the film, Hadass, Yentl's wife, bakes him (actually her, *i.e. Barbra, disguised as a man) a plate of biscuits. Barbra wants her, in the dialogue, to refer to them as 'cookies'.*

JACK

Barbra, this is Poland in 1900. Not Brooklyn in 1983. They can't say 'cookies'.

BARBRA

What then?

JACK

'Biscuits'.

BARBRA

(*horrified*)

Are you *kidding*? There's no such word.

JACK

Alright, 'cakes', then. Cuchen.

BARBRA

Uh-huh.

Which means they're going to be called 'cookies'. Barbra wins (well, of course, she does. She's the producer, the director, the star and co-writer. She's also Barbra). She wins again, over the inclusion of a song, 'Tomorrow Night'.

Like all the songs in the film, the music is by Michel Legrand and the lyrics by Marilyn and Alan Bergman. It's to be sung over a very long montage covering all the preparations for Yentl's wedding . . . right from being measured for a suit by a tailor through to the wedding night.

Jack dislikes the song and excludes it from every new draft of the script. Barbra simply reinstates it. In the penultimate draft, he deletes it again and, in its place, writes a list of bona fide London heart specialists in case he's given Barbra a heart attack. Without a word, in the final draft, Barbra deletes the list and puts the song back in.

JACK (VO)

And she was right. The song and its montage turn out to be one of the best things in the film. She was right, and I was wrong.

(*beat*)

And that's a sentence very few people have heard me say before. If any. Especially directors.

(*beat*)

Actually, I'm not sure I've *ever* said it before . . .

INT LIVING ROOM – 124 DUKE'S AVENUE – MUSWELL HILL – DAY – 1983

For the umpteenth time, Jack is rewriting the umpteenth draft of Yentl. *The phone rings. He sighs and takes it.*

It's Max Fischer in the middle of editing The Lucky Star *in Montreal. Can Jack come over for a few days and help? The film is also having distribution troubles. It needs Canadian tax-shelter finance – and therefore a bigger involvement in the film by people of Canadian nationality or connection. Would Jack mind if Max (he's applied for Canadian nationality) took a shared credit for the screenplay?*

JACK

(*into phone*)

Max! You didn't write one syllable of it!

INT EDITING SUITE – MONTREAL – DAY – 1983

Max agitatedly fiddles with the Steenbeck as he speaks into the phone.

MAX

(*into phone*)

It's either that or the film will never be shown.

(*beat*)

Your wonderful script will never be shown . . .

INTERCUT between Jack in Muswell Hill and Max in Montreal.

JACK

(*into phone*)

That's blackmail, Max.

MAX

(*into phone*)

You're our only hope, Jack . . .

A long pause.

JACK

(*sighs, then into phone*)

Okay.

(*beat*)

How long have you known this, Max?

But Max has hung up. He starts whistling as he spins the Steenbeck turntables.

EXT 5-STAR HOTEL – LONDON – DAY – 1983

A harassed Maureen and an actress friend, Karen Craig, are shepherding Amy and Adam into the entrance.

INT FOYER – 5-STAR HOTEL – LONDON – DAY – 1983 (CONT)

Karen holds the kids by the hand while Maureen approaches the concierge.

MAUREEN

Can I talk to Mr Rosenthal, please. He's on extension 316.

CONCIERGE

Miss Streisand's suite?

MAUREEN

That's right. I'm his missus.

CONCIERGE

No, you're not, you're Maureen Lipman.

MAUREEN

Either way.

INT BARBRA'S SUITE – 5-STAR HOTEL – LONDON – 1983 (CONT)

Barbra and Jack are making notes for more rewrites on the pages Jack wrote the previous night. The phone rings. Barbra takes it.

BARBRA
(*into phone*)

Hello?

(*beat*)

One second.

(*beat*)

For you. Reception.

Jack takes the phone.

JACK
(*into phone*)

Hello?

INT FOYER – 5-STAR HOTEL – LONDON – DAY – 1983 (CONT)

Karen is trying to stop the kids grilling Maureen as to what their father's doing here anyway.

MAUREEN
(*into phone*)
Hi, love. It's me. Sorry to interrupt. I'm on my way to the theatre and Karen's taking the kids back home and I've come out without a key.

(*beat*)
Okay. Thanks.

She hands the phone back to the concierge.

INT BARBRA'S SUITE – 5-STAR HOTEL – LONDON – 1983 (CONT)

Barbra takes a punnet of strawberries out of the fridge and puts them on the table, then picks up the phone.

BARBRA
(*into phone*)
Hi. Suite 316. There's a Mr Rosenthal just about coming into reception. Can I have a word with him?

(*pause*)
Jack? Me. Listen, tell your wife to bring your kids up here.

INT FOYER – 5-STAR HOTEL – LONDON – DAY – 1983 (CONT)

Jack holds the phone. Maureen emphatically shakes her head.

MAUREEN
No. I'm not ready to meet her. I've got to be ready. I can't just . . . not without being ready.

INTERCUT between Maureen and Jack in reception and Barbra in her suite.

BARBRA
(*into phone*)
Tell her I have strawberries for Amy and Adam.

MAUREEN
(*shaking her head at Jack*)
No! I've got to get to the theatre!

BARBRA
(*into phone*)
Tell her I'll play her my record.

MAUREEN

(*to Jack*)

I'm on my way! Come on, kids!

She scoops them up and races to the lifts. Jack and Karen follow, with a little more dignity.

The record in question is 'Memories', the Trevor Nunn/Andrew Lloyd Webber hit song from Cats, *recorded by Barbra a few days ago. She'd played it to Jack the day before – and, unusually for him apropos* any *record – he'd raved about it. When he'd got home he'd raved about it to Maureen all over again. Hence the unseemly dash to the lift, with a child almost under each arm.*

INT BARBRA'S SUITE – 5-STAR HOTEL – LONDON – 1983 (CONT)

The cassette of 'Memories' is playing. Maureen is enchanted. Karen, Amy and Adam are eating strawberries.

Barbra is watching them all keenly. Jack is watching Barbra a little suspiciously.

The song comes to an end. A pause, then:

BARBRA

Well, Adam? Did you like it.

The world's most phenomenal superstar is asking a seven-year-old boy his opinion. Adam ponders, then:

ADAM

Youra voice-a is very louda.

In recent weeks Adam has affected an Italian accent. It's a mystery to the whole family.

BARBRA

You think it's too loud?

ADAM

Yes. It's terrifyingly louda. Youra voice-a, it hurtsa my ears.

BARBRA

Uh-huh. Okay.

She turns her gaze on Maureen, a hardening, slightly defiant gaze.

Maureen?

This presents Maureen with a dilemma. She desperately wants to like Barbra, and wants Barbra to like her. *She'd like to be her best friend in the universe. And that means telling the truth. In this case, it won't be easy. She thinks Barbra sings the song superbly, better than anyone else in the world – except for a few bars in the middle section, which Maureen thinks is too low.*

MAUREEN

It's wonderful. Beautiful. You sing it magnificently.

But Barbra can feel a 'but' coming on. And here it is . . .

But you don't think the middle's too low, do you? Not *low*, exactly, sort of low*ish*, not low*ish*, more well, not as high as –

Barbra's blue eyes have narrowed, two laser beams converging on Maureen's face. The one thing you don't *do to a superstar is tell the truth.*

She waits in silence, giving Maureen no chance to avoid continuing digging her own grave. All Jack's warning throat-clearing, tics and sniffs are too late.

MAUREEN

Not that it matters. It's *nice* low. Not *low*, that is. Low*ish*. Well, not really lo . . . .

She finally peters into silence. Almost.

But it really is beautiful. Gorgeous.

A long silence, then:

BARBRA

What play are you doing in the theatre?

MAUREEN

(*still burbling*)

Chapter Two. Neil Simon. Lyric, Hammersmith. Matinee. It's really lovely that cassette, I really –

BARBRA

Do you play it American?

MAUREEN

Yes.

BARBRA

Do some for me.

Is this an audition for Yentl *or a sophisticated way of getting revenge? Maureen leaps into one of her New York character's speeches from the play. It comes out pure Yorkshire.*

INT CORRIDOR OUTSIDE BARBRA'S SUITE – 5-STAR HOTEL – LONDON – DAY – 1983 (CONT)

Maureen ushers Karen and the children out, then lies down full-length, moaning, 'Oh, God, oh, God, oh, God . . .'

Amy and Adam pluck worriedly at her sleeves . . .

ADAM

Whatsa da matter?

INT BARBRA'S SUITE – 5-STAR HOTEL – LONDON – DAY – 1983 (CONT)

Barbra rips the cassette from the player and hurls it across the room.

BARBRA

I *told* Andrew the middle section was too low! I *told* him!

Now why couldn't she have said that when Maureen was in the room?

EXT GARDEN – 124 DUKE'S AVENUE – MUSWELL HILL – DAY – 1983

Amy is conducting a heated, fairly melodramatic argument between two stones and a broken plant-pot at the end of the garden. The dialogue could well be a scene from The Carnells, *a soap-opera saga she's been writing every day for months.*

Adam is leaping fearlessly from one side of his junior goalpost set to the other, fingertipping away full-blooded volleys from his father ('bending it' hasn't quite been invented yet – apart from the odd Brazilian and Johan Cruyff).

Over Adam's formative sporting years, Jack proves to be the worst kind of coach – forcing a seven-year-old to be two-footed at football, and, at cricket, forcing him to bat absolutely straight-batty-Geoffrey-Boycotty-correctly. Forgetting to let him just enjoy *kicking hell out of a football with either foot and slogging a cricket ball right through the kitchen window.*

Maureen appears at the french windows, phone in hand. She calls out, excitedly:

MAUREEN

Amy?

Amy lets the plant-pot subside into a sulky silence.

AMY

Yes, Mod?

MAUREEN

I've got Bernard Krichefski on the line.

Bernard is a TV producer, friend and neighbour.

He wants to know if you'd like to be in an episode of *Nanny* with Wendy Craig.

Amy sizes this up for a moment. Then:

AMY

Tell him I only do musicals.

Not only does she not *only do musicals, she's never, of course, 'done' anything.*

MAUREEN

He thinks you'd be good. It's to play an autistic child. You just have to look sad . . . sort of suffering inside.

AMY

Tell him I'll have to see a script.

MAUREEN

(*into phone*)

Did you hear that, Bernard?

(*beat, then to Amy*)

There are no lines to learn.

AMY

Okay, then.

(*beat*)

I'll think about it.

She accepts Bernard's offer without too much negotiation over the contract.

INT/EXT CAR (TRAVELLING) – DAY – 1983

Jack is driving through Hyde Park en route to Barbra's hotel.

Each night when he gets home, Maureen is agog for snippets of news, gossip, anything . . . Did Barbra mention Ryan O'Neal? Did she get any phone calls from Hollywood? He's spending all day with her – has he nothing *to report? Well, no, he hasn't. Well, what was she wearing? He didn't notice. Was it a dress? Trousers? A bikini? A suit of armour? He doesn't know. P'raps something grey. Maybe.*

He drives up to the hotel entrance.

INT BARBRA'S SUITE – 5-STAR HOTEL – LONDON – DAY – 1983

Jack is alone on the settee, flicking through the pages he's written the previous night, and mouthing the lines. He glances at his watch. The delay in starting work is very un-Barbra-like. He always arrives each morning at eleven on the dot. Renata has always ordered room service coffee, also for eleven on the dot.

But not today. No coffee. No Barbra. After letting him in, Renata – in her overcoat – has disappeared back into Barbra's bedroom.

Ten minutes later, she and Barbra emerge. Barbra – in her dressing gown – seems agitated. Renata carries a small package. They both start towards the door.

BARBRA

Any drugstore pharmacist. The nearest.

Renata goes. Barbra starts back to her bedroom. En route:

Morning.

JACK

Morning.

BARBRA

Order coffee.

Then comes back.

Is the brown line supposed to be above the green? Or below? Which is positive, which is negative?

JACK

Sorry?

Flustered, she exits again.

She goes into her bedroom. Jack sits staring, unseeing, into space. Does all that mean what he thinks it means? Is he going to be the only person in the world apart from Renata who'll know Barbra's pregnant? Will Yentl *have to be cancelled? For the only time in his life, he'll be privy to information the tabloids would kill for. Who's the father? Will they think it's* him*? He lifts up the phone. But only to call room service.*

Renata comes back. Barbra appears at the bedroom door. Renata smiles. Negative. Barbra smiles. Without quite knowing why, Jack smiles. Maybe it's because all the rewrites and drafts aren't going to be in vain. Renata goes back to her work. Barbra and Jack start on the next scene. All's right with the world.

And Jack'll have some gossip to tell Maureen at last.

INT LIVING ROOM – 124 DUKE'S AVENUE – MUSWELL HILL – NIGHT – 1983

Another phone call from Max Fischer. He's very *excited – 'Terrific news.' The screenplay of* The Lucky Star *has been nominated for a Canadian 'Oscar'. Jack feels a little surge of pleasure – tempered by a tiny twinge of annoyance. Because Max has officially co-written it – without, of course, writing a word – the nomination is* shared *between them. The tiny twinge quickly turns into a punch in the solar plexus.*

The picture Maureen carried to every dressing room in England.

Below: The happiest day of my wife (West London Synagogue, 18 February 1973).

Hampstead: Horn-rims, Habitat furniture and shag pile rugs – could it be the Seventies?

A night on the tiles in casual dress with friend Astrid King.

Below: … Yes, and every night Mummy, Daddy, Amy and baby Adam all gathered around the typewriter …

One of those ma'amy evenings at BAFTA.

Right: 'Lads, you can't learn the game of life until you learn the game of football.' David Shindler and Adam, aged 7, get a pep talk at half time.

Below: This bar mitzvah boy stayed in the synagogue throughout.

Jack holds himself at arm's length: The artist and her dad.

Playmates and playwrights stand shoulder to shoulder.

'If there's one thing I can't bear,' said Zelma once, 'it's silence.' Jack smiles bravely on.

Jack, the lad and the lass, at Adam's graduation (King's College, Cambridge, 1999).

'1946 was also the year of the invention of the biro, which could write over 200,000 letters … and still not get a reply from Alan Yentob at the BBC.' Jack wowing the guests at Maureen's 50th birthday party (the late Hugo Gryn and Louie Ramsay laugh on).

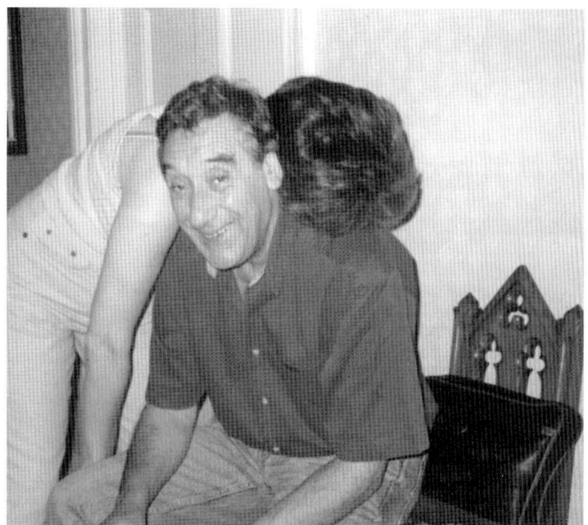

Top left: A mug's game: Teaching screenwriting at Hebdon Bridge, Yorkshire.

Top right: That's it – we're packing in this packing lark!': Mo and Jack about to go on holiday.

Above: Goodbye chemo, hello Guinness: Jack by Loch Hyne, Skibbereen.

Left: Now they've started calling me a 'veteran playwright', I'd better grow a beard!

'Yes, Zelma? What is it?'

INT GARDEN SHED – 124 DUKE'S AVENUE – MUSWELL HILL – DAY – 1983

In the half-darkness, among the garden tools and rusting paraphernalia, we see a cardboard box on the floor. On it is felt-tipped the word 'Zuckerman'. And the box appears to be moving*, a hardly discernible irregular, side-stepping dance.*

The door opens. Daylight bursts in. As does Jack. He searches along the shelves for an oilcan – then freezes. He can hear rustling. Puzzled, he looks around, then down – and sees the gently rocking box.

ANGLE ON *Zuckerman – who is a tortoise – inside the box among scattered straw. His eyes are open and his jaws clamped tightly shut.*

He's woken up too soon from hibernation. Jack gingerly lifts him out.

The whole Zuckerman saga, of which this is the beginning, will later be dramatised in a TV film (imaginatively called Tortoise*) that incorporates other, rather more conventional themes like love and marriage between humans.*

It will be written in 1990. Thirteen years later, as part of a trilogy of TV films, it will still be awaiting production. The real-life drama of tortoise-paced indecision by a tortoise-brained executive – will be told later . . .

In the meantime . . .

DISSOLVE TO:

FILM EXCERPT: *Tortoise*

INT REPTILE SPECIALIST'S SURGERY – DAY

The walls are decorated with medical illustrations of various species of reptiles.

Mr Lebone, the specialist, is injecting the tortoise (the fictional counterpart of Zuckerman, called Merlin). Roy Palfrey (the fictional counterpart of Jack) sits watching, concerned. Merlin had apparently woken up too early because he was hungry*. A week before, his local vet had told Roy to inject tomato soup into Zuckerman's clamped mouth – and he'd failed.*

ROY

Is that tomato soup?

LEBONE

Tomato soup's off. The chef recommends the cock-a-leekie.

ROY

Pardon?

LEBONE

It's a saline solution, Mr Palfrey. Emergency action, I'm afraid.

(*sighs*)

In a civilised society, of course, the *real* action'd be taken the minute they disembark at our ports. Personally, I'd favour machine-guns. Line the buggers up and mow them down.

ROY

(*aghast*)

Shoot them?

LEBONE

Not the tortoises. The sadists who bring them. Every man-jack.

He puts the tortoise down and measures it. During this:

Would you keep a camel in the back garden, Mr Palfrey? A polar bear? A crocodile?

ROY

(*defensively*)

It was a birthday present . . .

LEBONE

Tortoises can only survive in England with very special attention. They have only one thing in common with the English: they can't stand the climate. It kills them – just as it's killing this one.

ROY

(*shocked*)

'Kill'?

(*beat*)

He's not dying, is he?

LEBONE

'She'.

ROY

Sorry?

LEBONE

Female. About 45 years old.

ROY

Merlin's a *girl*?

LEBONE

And Greek. Perhaps Merlina would be more apt. After Melina Mercouri. We stole a lot more from the Greeks than the Elgin

Marbles, Mr Palfrey. Hundreds of thousands of *these*. And condemned them to death.

ROY

She really is dying?

LEBONE

If she doesn't eat by Thursday morning, at the latest, you've got liquid tortoise.

ROY

He *won't* eat, though!

LEBONE

She.

ROY

She. She won't. She turns her nose up . . . well, not up. Inside.

LEBONE

Correct. She'll only unlock her jaws and eat when she's at a certain temperature. When you leave here, Mr Palfrey, you go and buy a 300-watt infrared lamp. At once, Mr Palfrey. Every single minute counts. Position the lamp exactly 12 inches or 30.5 centimetres above the centre of her shell. Keep it there, day and night. Leave fresh food in front of her. Real food – fruit, vegetables, fish. No lettuce. That's how she got in this mess in the first place. Lettuce can't feed an anorexic ant.

Roy looks at the tortoise – wracked with compassion, worry and guilt.

ROY

The amazing thing is, I was going to try her on a bit of moussaka tonight, and I didn't even *know* she was Greek.

LEBONE

Not moussaka, please, Mr Palfrey.

He takes the straw from the box, screws up pieces of newspaper and puts them in the box instead.

And paper in here, not straw. Straw *chokes* them to death.

He puts the tortoise back in the box.

ROY

300 watt, infrared . . . What if I can't get one?

Lebone looks at him severely.

LEBONE

Mr Palfrey, in the human breast there stirs passion. *Com*passion. Our most human attribute. You suddenly have the opportunity to save the life of a living creature. The noblest act any *other* living creature can perform. You have, at this moment, the power of life and death. Our most *god*like attribute.

He hands Roy the box.

We are as gods, Mr Palfrey. My receptionist will give you the bill on your way out. No credit cards, please.

DISSOLVE TO:

INT CELLAR – 124 DUKE'S AVENUE – MUSWELL HILL – DAY – 1983

Maureen and Jack carefully lower the immobile Zuckerman onto a patch of carpet on the concrete floor, beneath a 300-watt infrared lamp. Ranged before her is a buffet of herring, peaches, grapes and carrots. The point of no return.

Saving Zuckerman's life has almost become their reason for living. They take it in turns to keep watch in the cellar, which seems to become slowly infrared radioactive, and to clean up the mess that appears at the one end of Zuckerman that often opens, even though the other end stays shut.

Once he's learnt that Zuckerman is a 45-year-old Greek female, Jack plays her 'Never on a Sunday', 'Zorba's Dance' and World War II ballads on his violin. It doesn't seem to be making much difference. Maybe she's deaf.

INT STUDY – 124 DUKE'S AVENUE – DAY – 1983

A final phone call from Max Fischer. The Lucky Star has won the Canadian 'Oscar' for best screenplay. Or as Max sensitively puts it:

MAX (OS)
(*into phone*)

I won!

Jack stares in disbelief at the phone in his hand. 'I'? Meaning him? Max? As in 'he' won? Well, yes. Grammatically, at least, he's right. As he goes on to say, because he has Canadian 'points' and Jack hasn't, he 'had to take sole credit' for the screenplay.

So on Max's mantelpiece is a proudly polished trophy for a screenplay he never wrote. The punch in the solar plexus has become a knife in the back. Jack never hears from him again.

INT LIVING ROOM – A KENSINGTON HOUSE – NIGHT – 1983

After eight tortuous and tortured months of drafts and rewrites and rewrites of the rewrites, the last Yentl *script meeting is taking place. Shooting is to begin in three weeks' time.*

Present in Barbra's rented house is a group of United Artists executives, producer Larry de Waay (an ally of Jack's and an unruffled stalwart since day one), Barbra and Jack.

Jack's lying full-length, on his stomach, on the floor, the penultimate draft under his nose, pen poised, ready to make notes. Every line, if not every word, has been discussed and analysed and usually rewritten over and over again, throughout those eight months. All Jack now expects is a few, last-thought, minor changes.

He's wrong. Barbra asks everyone to turn to page 1, scene 1, line one. Should the opening shot of the film be the bird flying through the sky to land on the cross on the church steeple, or should it be already *there? Jack doesn't understand . . .*

JACK

Barbra, all you have to do is shoot the first alternative. Then, in editing, decide whether to use the bird in flight or simply start with the bird perched on the cross. They're both the same shot.

BARBRA

Uh-huh.

She's unconvinced. The logic means nothing. She'll probably shoot two separate openings. Barbra is often, almost always, labelled a perfectionist. Jack would disagree. What she is (sometimes touchingly, sometimes maddeningly), is insecure – in herself and her judgement – unsure and indecisive. She thinks nothing of asking the elevator man, who has no inkling of the story, which of two versions of a scene he prefers.

Suddenly the phone rings. An executive grabs the receiver.

EXECUTIVE

(*into phone*)

Yeah? . . . Who? . . . Uh-huh . . . One second.

(*beat*)

Jack. For you. Your wife.

JACK

Oh, right.

He takes the phone.

Sorry.

(*into phone*)

Yes, love?

INT LIVING ROOM – 124 DUKE'S AVENUE – MUSWELL HILL – NIGHT – 1983 (CONT)

Maureen, almost beside herself with excitement, makes a commendable stab at appearing cool, calm and – no, she doesn't quite *make it . . .*

MAUREEN

It's Zuckerman! She's, no, he's, no, she's eaten! A piece of peach! I saw her do it!

INT LIVING ROOM – A KENSINGTON HOUSE – NIGHT – 1983 (CONT)

JACK

(*into phone*)

Great. Fantastic. Thank God. Have you tried her on the herring?

INT LIVING ROOM – 124 DUKE'S AVENUE – MUSWELL HILL – NIGHT – 1983 (CONT)

Maureen bounces up and down . . .

MAUREEN

(*into phone*)

For God's sake! Sod the herring! She's eaten *something*! She's going to live! Zuckerman is going to live!

INT LIVING ROOM – A KENSINGTON HOUSE – NIGHT – 1983 (CONT)

Jack slowly replaces the receiver, a man at peace with the world. He beams at the blank faces turned towards him.

JACK

It's Zuckerman . . . He's a tortoise. Well, *she*, rather . . . She's a she, now . . . and she'd woken up . . . bloody ravenous . . . but her jaws were locked because her brain thought she was asleep . . . so we got this lamp . . . and now she's scoffed this bit of peach and . . .

The blank faces win. He dribbles into an embarrassed silence. A long pause.

BARBRA

(*delivered as only she can*)

We're talking about a *turtle?*

JACK

Well, tortoise, yes.

BARBRA

I see.

She doesn't bother saying, 'What? In the middle of a script conference for a multi-million-dollar movie?'

Okay. So we're up to line two . . .

After lines two, three, four, five and six have been queried and argued over and won – by her – it's clear that she's going to go through the entire screenplay, line by line, and expect Jack to take notes, then go home and rewrite the entire film. Yet again.

Now it's Jack who's at the point of no return. A beat, then he gets up, picks up his script and puts it in his briefcase.

JACK

Sorry, Barbra. You don't need a co-writer, you need a secretary. I'm going home now.

And he starts for the door. The lesson from the day Jule Styne lambasted Jack's first draft of the Bar Mitzvah Boy *musical has finally been learnt: if you think you should go, and* say *you're going* – go. *And he does. A bit of bended-knee pleading – from the executives, not Barbra – only delays him getting to the front door by about ten seconds.*

Sadly, although he's kept one promise to himself, he's broken another: that, unlike so many of Barbra's colleagues throughout her career, he'd stay the course, right to the end. And he hasn't. By five days.

He goes.

INT CAR (TRAVELLING) – NIGHT – 1983

Jack drives home through London streets.

He's agreed to work on all the notes given so far and any more that'll be given the next day, and rewrite the screenplay on condition that there are no more script meetings and that Barbra doesn't call him with any additional *notes and that, whatever scene he's in the middle of, he'll finally hang up his pen at 5 p.m. the following Friday.*

He feels a little sad. And happy. And sad.

EXT A STREET – CZECHOSLOVAKIA – DAY – 1983

In peasant costume of 1900, Barbra is peering through the eyepiece of a movie camera, checking a shot in a scene for Yentl.

After all the screenplay traumas, Barbra directs the film expertly and artistically, precisely *as she'd always imagined each shot to be. Which, to Jack, is an admirable, very rarely achieved, achievement.*

Never mind the screenplay, to Jack's mind, the directing of Yentl *never gets the recognition it deserved. There may have been a couple of Golden Globes, but critically it's sniffed at. Probably, firstly, because its first-time director is a woman and, secondly, because the woman is Barbra Streisand.*

INT/EXT ODEON – LEICESTER SQUARE – LONDON – NIGHT – 1983

The Yentl *premiere. VIPs welcome scores of other VIPs over the red carpet into the cinema. Flashbulbs pop, fans cheer behind the police cordons.*

JACK (VO)

Editing *Yentl* proved an arduous process, taking almost as long as writing it. Barbra asked me to stick in my two penn'orth, and I was glad to.

A blip between the co-writers over their credits. Contractually, I had to be given first mention in our shared credit. Barbra disputed it. She wanted *sole* credit – and, if that was out of the question, which it was – she wanted first mention.

There were two telephone conference calls between the arbitrating members of the American Writers' Guild and Barbra, and the same members and me. We both presented our arguments. I mentioned, en passant, that I like Barbara but doubted we'd ever go on holiday together. The arbitration panel reached their conclusion: it's the only *Yentl* argument I won. As per contract, I got first mention.

I *do* like her. Yes, she drove me crazy, yes, she's obsessive, yes, indecisive and, yes, she's a superstar and knows it. Many times, I swore I'd never work with her again. But I did, years later, on *The Prince of Tides*. Our collaboration wasn't filled with laughter, but, then again, it hadn't been a particularly happy time in her life.

Apart from being a superstar, of course, she's also (almost) any woman from Golders Green. Like all of us, she's two – or more – people. And for every superstar minus she clocks up, there's a very human plus. Despite all our battles, all but one of which I lost, I'd have liked to have made her laugh a little more.

Throughout our time together, I resisted plea after plea from the Press to give interviews. Why be interviewed? So's they could knock her as they always do? Why do they? Why knock such a great, unique singer, such a gifted actress and such a talented director? Oh, of course, that's why. Because she *is*.

INT CIRCLE FOYER – ODEON – LEICESTER SQUARE – LONDON – NIGHT – 1983 (CONT)

Barbra, looking her most glamorous, stands in the centre of a long line of her Yentl *colleagues – maybe twenty or thirty technicians and actors. Jack is by her side.*

Maureen's had to decline her invitation; she's working in the theatre. In her place is her mum, Zelma.

Much to his embarrassment, Jack notices that somehow she's evaded (or charmed) the security guards, and she's standing at the end of the line, to his right, about to be introduced, for no logical reason, to the Duchess of Kent and her entourage. He closes his eyes and clenches everything clenchable.

When he opens his eyes again, he's relieved to see that the Duchess has now moved on along the line, shaking hands and chatting . . . to people who do *have a right to be there.*

He then, by chance, glances to his left – and there, at the end of the line, Zelig-like, impatient for her second *royal greeting . . . is Zelma.*

At the end of the film, when the audience gives Barbra a rapturous, standing ovation, Zelma is gracious enough not to elbow her out of the way.

She's rooting in her handbag for a pen in case she's asked for her autograph . . .

EXT 124 DUKE'S AVENUE – MUSWELL HILL – DAY – 1983

A removal van is parked outside the door. Tattooed men lug towards it (among other furniture) the tan leather settee that was perched vertically in the hall, the day the family moved in and Sir Laurence phoned. Jack's word-processor is sitting on it.

JACK (VO)

After almost seven years, we felt we'd like to leave Muswell Hill and go back to Hampstead. (It means 'Homestead', after all.) We pored over the property pages, and leaping out came an ad for an Edwardian 'gentleman's residence' – very spacious, two receptions, five bedrooms, a study, a vast garden with gazebo, a 'motor house', original features. £135,000 on a 90 per cent mortgage. I think the words 'gentleman's residence' swung it for me.

Perfect. Apart from one minor point: it wasn't in Hampstead, it was round the corner in Muswell Hill.

EXT THE GENTLEMAN'S RESIDENCE – MUSWELL HILL – DAY – 1983

The removal men unload (among other furniture) the settee and word-processor from the van and carry them along a drive and front garden into a double-fronted house.

INT KITCHEN – THE GENTLEMAN'S RESIDENCE – MUSWELL HILL – DAY – 1983

Open on a kettle pouring boiling water into twenty mugs standing in a row, a teabag in each of them.

CAM pulls back to reveal the hands are Maureen's. She looks harassed . . .

JACK (VO)

There was a lot to be done – walls to come down, others to go up, door to be moved, pipes to be plumbed, electricity to crackle. This meant twenty workmen – every day.

MONTAGE: DIFFERENT ROOMS – THE GENTLEMAN'S RESIDENCE – MUSWELL HILL – 1983

Through clouds of dust, bricks and plaster crash down to the ground. Picking her way through the rubble comes Maureen with a tray of mugs of tea. Two builders take a couple.

A plumber's hand appears through the gap provided by an uprooted floorboard on the landing, and takes a mug of tea from Maureen.

Maureen reaches with a cup of tea up to a hole in the ceiling, from where an electrician reaches down and takes it.

Maureen clambers over gallon cans of paint to hand a mug of tea to a silver-haired, kindly faced man in his seventies – and in a suit. This is the architect, Sir Roger Walters, who has organised and integrated all the work to perfection.

As an electrician finishes some rewiring and steps back, a plasterer promptly steps foward to repair the chased wall.

JACK (VO)

Within a few weeks, the house was as we wanted. Knowing what we wanted, however, was the customary nervous-breakdown trauma. Sir Roger, our GP and the odd therapist soothed us through.

INT KITCHEN – THE GENTLEMAN'S RESIDENCE – MUSWELL HILL – DAY – 1983

Jack collects now-empty mugs from two tilers, two Gas Board fitters and two burglar-alarm engineers as he treads carefully towards an internal door.

He opens it. On the floor behind it is a trapdoor. He lifts it by its iron handle and reveals a scarily steep staircase down to the cellar. Dangerous, with two young children in the house. What if you opened the door and stepped in and the trapdoor were up*? You'd fall down to . . . Jack trembles at the thought, and ponders what to do about it.*

CU Jack pondering, brow furrowed. Then it gradually un*furrows. He rather smugly whispers, 'Eureka!'*

INT KITCHEN – THE GENTLEMAN'S RESIDENCE – MUSWELL HILL – DAY – 1983

The next day.

Jack opens and closes, opens and closes the cellar door, running through his plan to himself. It's this. If the cellar door is closed, *the trapdoor is down and it's therefore safe to open the door and walk in. If the door is* open, *you can* see *whether the trapdoor is up or down.*

It's a foolproof plan. Except he forgets to mention it to anyone else.

INT KITCHEN – THE GENTLEMAN'S RESIDENCE – MUSWELL HILL – DAY – 1983

Later.

Jack rather complacently approaches the cellar door. It's closed. He opens it and walks cockily in.

And, yes, Sod's Law – the trapdoor is up.

INT CELLAR – THE GENTLEMAN'S RESIDENCE – MUSWELL HILL – DAY – 1983 (CONT)

Jack hurtles the twelve feet or so down to the concrete floor of the cellar. He lands, not *metaphorically, on his feet.*

INT LIVING ROOM – THE GENTLEMAN'S RESIDENCE – MUSWELL HILL – DAY – 1983

Jack propels himself into the room in a wheelchair. Lucky not to have broken his neck, it's probable that the fall will have momentarily concertina'd his bones and that, in a few years' time, it'll lead to an arthritic hip and a titanium replacement.

He zooms his wheelchair over to the ornate fireplace, hidden behind a few years' worth of coats of white paint, brakes in front of it and starts stripping off the paint, to expose the marble beneath.

He scrubs harder and harder, like a Dervish in a time trial, with a ball of wire wool. Then, abruptly, howls in pain – he's given himself tennis elbow. He transfers the wire wool to his left hand and continues frenziedly scrubbing. And gives himself a second tennis elbow.

He is now unable to walk or use either arm. On the mantelpiece, before his eyes, is a greetings card reading 'Good Luck in your New Home'.

EXT A BALCONY – NIGHT – 1983

In the moonlight it's uncertain whether we're in Verona or Muswell Hill.

Or whether, in the street below, in doublet and hose, on one knee, it's Romeo – or Don Black; and whether, on the balcony, in a muslin shift and blond ringlets, it's Juliet – or Jack.

CU Romeo – ah, now we see, behind the specs and Beatle-haircut, it's actually Don.

CU Juliet – and, yes, the glasses and five o'clock shadow are dead giveaways. It's really Jack.

JACK (VO)

For over a year, I resisted Don's wooing, pursuing and blandishing to become involved in another musical. The songs, *good* songs, were already written, with witty lyrics by Don and melodic music by Geoff Stephens, the amiable and enthusiastic composer of, among other hits, 'There's a Kinda Hush', 'The Crying Game' and 'Winchester Cathedral'.

But still I said no. Don said it'd be different from the *Bar Mitzvah Boy* musical flop. This one'd be a hit. As the months went by and Don's pleas became more ardent, I weakened. And finally yielded.

'Romeo' stands up and blows 'Juliet' a kiss. 'She' blows one back, then tucks up the skirt, clambers over the balcony and shins down the drainpipe into his arms.

JACK

Yes!

After the Jule Styne lesson ('If you think you should walk away – walk away!'), comes another: 'If you know you should say no – don't say yes.'

INT CAMBRIDGE THEATRE – LONDON – DAY – 1983

Dear Anyone *is in rehearsal.*

In the pit, the orchestra is playing 'I'll Put You Together Again'. On stage, the chorus are being put through their choreographed paces, in front of a massive, transparent globe extending up to the roof, bisected by a floor. This is Ralph Koltai's bewildering set. Can the globe be derived from the fact that some of the action takes place in a newspaper office called the Daily Globe?

Don, Geoff and Jack sit watching in the stalls with the director, David Taylor. Out of the four lower lips, one is being chewed . . .

JACK (VO)

I'd had qualms about the book from the outset, which is why I'd spent so long saying no. It's a story about an Agony Aunt – and the only story I could dream up was the obvious cliché of the Agony Aunt who can solve everyone's problems but her own. It had already been definitively and successfully done by Maureen in her TV comedy series *Agony*.

Don didn't feel the qualms. He had some producer status on the show, but understandably, was more at ease wrestling with the few minutes of the emotional narrative of a song than with the dramatic dynamics of a two-hour play. And David seemed happy. So was Geoff.

On stage,'I'll Put You Together Again' comes to an end, and another number is rehearsed. This is 'Gotta Come Down from This Mountain' – written in some panic just before opening night. The singer is Stubby Kaye, the erstwhile star of Guys and Dolls. *The song is intended to be a show-stopper, and, in feel, it's an overt, unashamed steal of his 'Guys and Dolls' hit, 'Sit Down You're Rocking the Boat'. (The critics notice and aren't amused.) To further mystify the audience, Stubby sings 'Gotta Come Down from This Mountain' while walking* up *a staircase.*

EXT CAMBRIDGE THEATRE – LONDON – DAY – 1983

The Dear Anyone *display posters are being taken down.*

JACK (VO)

Sadly – particularly for Stephens and his lovely music, complementing Don's clever and psychologically perceptive lyrics – Don's prognosis that the fate of *Dear Anyone* would be different from that of the *Bar Mitzvah Boy* musical proved ironically correct. Instead of closing in ten weeks, it closed in eight.

Even so, it was far too late for Juliet to stuff her skirts in her knickers and scuttle back *up* the drainpipe. In the dark.

EXT THE GENTLEMAN'S RESIDENCE – MUSWELL HILL – DAY – 1983

Jack clutching a stack of scripts to his chest carries them to his Honda Accord and loads them into the boot. During this:

A telephone ringing tone. A click as the receiver is picked up, then:

JACK (OS)

Hello?

MAN (OS)

(*American accent*)

Mr Jack Rosenthal?

JACK (OS)

Speaking.

MAN (OS)

Well, hi. Good to talk to you. My name's David Susskind, TV producer, impresario, show-host, interviewer, presenter, you name it, 200 million Americans can't be wrong.

JACK (OS)

Oh. Right.

DAVID SUSSKIND (OS)

You may have heard of me. Most people have. Nothing bad, I hope!

(*he laughs; then grows 'serious' again*)

Now, I'd like us to meet up. I think we could do great things together. I want to commission some TV drama.

JACK (OS)

(*now enthusiastically*)

Oh, right!

DAVID SUSSKIND (OS)

I'm in London for four days. Let's do lunch. Claridge's. Tomorrow, twelve noon, okay?

JACK (OS)

Okay, thank you.

DAVID SUSSKIND (OS)

Bring everything you've done.

JACK (OS)

What? Everything?

DAVID SUSSKIND (OS)

How many scripts have you written?

JACK (OS)

Um . . . going on for two hundred.

DAVID SUSSKIND (OS)

(*beat*)

Bring ten.

A telephonic click as he hangs up.

Jack gets into the car and drives off.

INT FOYER – CLARIDGE'S HOTEL – LONDON – DAY – 1983

Receptionists at work at their desks, guests milling about, greeting each other, heading towards the restaurant or lifts or other rooms. For all the world like a chorus in a musical.

Jack is in an armchair, the ten scripts in his lap. He's checking his watch, in some consternation. It reads twenty to one.

Suddenly, a silver-haired, middle-aged ball of fire whirls manically in at the front entrance. It hurtles towards Jack, hand outstretched, and speaks.

DAVID SUSSKIND

Hi! Knew it was you by the pile of paper! I'm David.

They shake hands. He sits down in a facing armchair, acknowledging greetings from passing American tourists who recognise him.

DAVID SUSSKIND

Sorry I'm late. Technical hitch beyond our control. Lunch'll have to wait.

JACK

(*hungry but polite*)

That's perfectly –

DAVID SUSSKIND

(*interrupting*)

The thing is I need to help Poppa. Poppa is an Iranian pal of mine, escaped when the Ayatollah took over, and came to the US, penniless. *Penniless*. All he has is this antique business in New York and another in France.

(*beat*)

Now. I always help Poppa buy his cars. It's kinda traditional. I'm pretty much a maven with cars. And I only have this lunchtime to do that. So, what I'm suggesting is we go now to Jack Barclay's showrooms in Berkeley Square, meet Poppa there, pick him a horseless carriage, then back here for lunch. How's that for a schedule?

JACK

Um . . . absolutely –

DAVID SUSSKIND

(*interrupting*)

Great. Let's go.

He whirls off, returning American waves of recognition, towards the exit. Jack follows, clutching his scripts.

INT/EXT JAGUAR SALOON (TRAVELLING) – DAY – 1983

The hired car, driven by a chauffeur, slinks its way through West End streets. David, Jack and the pile of scripts sit in the back.

JACK

(*whispering, to David*)

What's your driver's name?

DAVID SUSSKIND

Gordon.

JACK

(*to the chauffeur*)

Gordon, can I ask you a question?

GORDON

Certainly, sir.

JACK

If I traded in my Honda for a secondhand Jag, what's the oldest model I should go for? Before it, you know, becomes a load of trouble.

GORDON

(*whistles through his teeth*)

Hard to say, sir. Depends. Three years, maybe four. If you're lucky p'raps even –

DAVID SUSSKIND

(*to Jack*)

You like the car?

JACK

Sorry?

DAVID SUSSKIND

This Jag?

JACK

It's beautiful.

DAVID SUSSKIND

You want it, it's yours. I go back to New York, Friday. Friday, it's yours. Gordon'll deliver it to your home. How's that?

Jack stares at him.

JACK

Um . . . How much would it –

DAVID SUSSKIND

'How much' isn't in the equation. 'How much' is dialogue deleted. It's *free*. A gift from me to you.

Jack stares all the more.

JACK

The Jag?

DAVID SUSSKIND

The very same.

JACK

David, you don't know me! We only met ten min–

DAVID SUSSKIND

Listen. We're going to do great shows, you and I. I'll know you like family. You like the vehicle, take it, enjoy, have fun.

INT BARCLAY'S CAR SHOWROOM – BERKELEY SQUARE – LONDON – DAY – 1983

David and Poppa – plumpish, tastefully groomed, middle-aged – carefully inspect the blindingly polished Rolls-Royces. Jack strolls behind them, trying to look as though wandering round Rolls-Royce showrooms is a slightly boring habit of his. He succeeds. A salesman, say six foot five, and every inch of them an ex-Guardsman, toothbrush-moustached, approaches him, bowing just perceptibly.

SALESMAN

May I be of assistance, sir?

Jack's Mancunian accent is suddenly crunched under a ton or two of cut glass . . .

JACK

Actually, I'm with those two gentlemen, actually.

SALESMAN

(*an understanding inclination of the head*)

Very good, sir.

David seems to be plumping for either one of two secondhand Rolls-Royces. One is black, with a matt black stripe around the entire body and white leather upholstery. The other is a white convertible with black leather upholstery. They each cost £50,000. A difficult choice, you'll agree.

Poppa thinks hard. David sighs gravely. Then abruptly, impulsively, penniless Poppa yells his decision:

POPPA

I'll take them *both*!

(*to the salesman*)

The black one to my Paris address by tomorrow midday, the white one to my address in Antibes tomorrow 7 p.m.

JACK (VO)

Which, as anyone who's ever bought a car knows, is impossible. It takes at least a week to sort out the payment and the registration and the insurance and the –

SALESMAN

(*to Poppa*)

Certainly, sir. Our pleasure.

INT RESTAURANT – CLARIDGE'S – LONDON – DAY – 1983

David and Jack (now wearing a tie borrowed from the men's room) are at the table. The pile of scripts sits on a chair beside them. Jack picks embarrassedly at his lunch while David screams vitriolic insults at the waiters and modestly signs autographs from passing fans. Almost at the same time.

DAVID SUSSKIND

So, friend and colleague, you made your mind up yet? You want the Jaguar?

INT BEDROOM – THE GENTLEMAN'S RESIDENCE – MUSWELL HILL – DAY – 1983

It's two days later. Friday. 7.30 a.m.

The bedside phone rings. Jack's hand and pyjama'd arm snake out of the bedclothes. He takes the phone, whispering so's not to wake Maureen.

JACK

(*into phone*)

Hello?

(*beat; sighs*)

No, David, I *told* you . . . It only does about twenty to the gallon, I couldn't even affo–

(*beat*)

David. It's very kind of you. Very. Incredibly. But I can't accept a present worth thousands of pounds from a virtually complete –

(*beat*)

David . . .

(*beat*)

David! He mustn't!

(*beat*)

No, David, *please*. Please don't have Gordon delivering it here in half an hour!

(*beat*)

David?

He replaces the receiver, lies back and stares at the ceiling.

MAUREEN

(*in her sleep*)

What colour would it have been?

Jack knows – and others confirm – that accepting the car would mean being at David's command for ever, supplying drama ideas and scripts for free. He decides that when he gets up he'll take the Honda to the car-wash.

He and David never get round to working together. Years later they bump into each other in an office in LA. David gallantly pretends to remember him and gives him a cordial hug. Jack's later told that a New York judge has impounded David's cars until he coughs up the alimony owing to his ex-wife. His cars – with an 's'. His thirteen *cars.*

EXT STREETS – OLDHAM – DAY – 1984

Jack is walking along the busy main street, past the inexplicably, but joyously named pub 'Dr Syntax', towards the Coliseum Theatre.

JACK (VO)

Back in Oldham. Here it is, 1984, and Big Brother is so busy watching everybody else, he neglects to keep half an eye on *me* . . . so here I am involved in *another* sort of musical. I know. I know. But there are mitigating circumstances – it's not *really* a musical, not even a play with music, just a play with a few songs right at the end . . .

Jack reaches the theatre and passes a display poster advertising Our Gracie. *It's the story of desperately unhappy happy-go-lucky Gracie Fields, once Britain's highest showbiz earner, from rags to riches, from misery to more misery . . . through three loveless, insulting marriages to three spongeing, abusing husbands.*

JACK (VO)

Her last one, Boris, adept at clattering her round the house, even forbade her – one of the most famous singers in the world – to sing in it. The house was her villa in Capri, which, according to Denis Pitt's taped interview with her, on which part of my play is based, was in hock to the Mafia to pay off Boris's debts.

Luckily for everyone, *Our Gracie* was only scheduled to run for two weeks. The play wasn't what Oldham's senior-citizen audience wanted: they'd come to hear Gracie's songs for two hours not ten minutes. And they were as bemused as its author by the director having all the sets painted pillar-box red and all the characters wheeling shopping trolleys.

EXT HOTEL SACHER – VIENNA – EVENING – 1984

Jack sits outside, gorging himself on Sachertorte.

JACK (VO)

From the home of the 'Latics football team to the home of the Holy Roman Habsburgs . . .

I was researching a three-hour TV film adaptation of a novel, *The Devil's Lieutenant* for Channel 4. Unfortunately, it was bedevilled by being a European co-production – which meant a multinational cast uncomfortably speaking English and all thinking they're playing Hamlet.

The honourable exception was Ian Charleson, who was perfect in the role of the lieutenant.

A WIDE-SHOT, from Jack's POV, of hundreds of evening-dressed opera-goers filing out of the Opera House, opposite the Hotel Sacher, and setting off clockwise round the building to stretch their legs in the interval.

'Clockwise' is the unwritten rule. The tradition. Very possibly, the First Law of Nature.

Should the glitterati be suddenly faced by any rebellious spirits stretching their blue-denimed legs anti-*clockwise, their Nazi blood, never far below the surface in Vienna, would be at boiling point almost at once.*

Jack pays the waiter, gets up from his chair and starts limping away.

JACK (VO)

One year after my fall down the cellar, the first twinges of an arthritic hip. And so began a long-running, long-*limping* saga . . .

EXT LONDON AIRPORT – DAY – 1984

Concorde gracefully, powerfully takes off, its Pinocchio nose twitching towards New York.

INT CONCORDE (IN FLIGHT) – DAY – 1984

Elbows pinned to their ribs in the narrow seats, Jack and the rest of the passengers are eating breakfast. Apart from one – David Frost, who had hoisted himself aboard seconds before the plane started taxiing to take-off and has been fast asleep ever since, across the tiny aisle from Jack.

JACK (VO)

I had two appointments in New York. One with the cultured producers of *Masterpiece Theater,* and the other with the two producers of a proposed TV film of Hitler's boyhood and early years. Nothing came of the first – maybe I didn't come up with an idea; and nothing happened with the second because, interestingly, they ran out of money minutes before they were due to pay me for the script I'd written and delivered.

EXT SKIES – DAY – 1984

As Concorde flies on, three hours or so later:

STEWARD (OS)

Would all passengers please return your seats to the upright position, fold away your trays and kindly fasten your seatbelts for landing? Thank you.

JACK (VO)

At which point –

INT CONCORDE (IN FLIGHT) – DAY – 1984 (CONT)

JACK (VO)

– David Frost finally surfaced.

As Jack and the rest of the passengers busily comply with the steward's request, David awakes and stops a stewardess as she passes, checking seatbelts.

DAVID FROST

Excuse me.

STEWARDESS

Yes, sir?

DAVID FROST

A little breakfast, good girl.

No chance. Breakfast finished an hour or two ago and the plane is about to start its descent. On the other hand, David Frost is Concorde's most regular and celebrated passenger – three flights a week, there and back.

STEWARDESS

Of course, sir.

JACK (VO)

No doubt if he'd asked for the plane to land in Paris at midday and Antibes at 7 p.m., it could've been arranged.

Jack smiles and says, 'Hi, Dave.' After all they did work together, week after week, on That was the Week That Was *in the early sixties. David bares his teeth vaguely, trying in vain to remember who this unfamiliar, over-familar creep is.*

EXT WEST 44TH STREET – NEW YORK – DAY – 1984

Jack carries his suitcase hurriedly down the street. Hurriedly because a hobo with a worse limp than his is hobbling quickly across the street towards him. But not hurriedly enough. The hobo stops in front of him, barring his way.

HOBO

Gimme fifty dollars.

JACK

I haven't any dollars. Only travellers' cheques.

HOBO

(*disappointed*)

How about cents and dimes?

Jack roots in his pocket, pulls out loose change and counts it.

JACK

One dollar thirty-five.

HOBO

(*pocketing the money*)

How long you been in New York?

JACK

Just off the plane. Just now.

The hobo shakes his head, sympathetically.

HOBO

And the first thing that happens, you get mugged. Terrible world we live in.

He hobbles away. Thinking it's also sometimes quite a wonderful world, Jack goes into the Algonquin Hotel.

INT RECEPTION – ALGONQUIN HOTEL – NEW YORK – DAY – 1984 (CONT)

Jack checks in, leaning backwards to pinch the odd, sly peek at the famous Round Table, straining every brain-cell to try and imagine Dorothy Parker et al seated around it being brilliant.

His reverie's suddenly broken by a tall, blonde, Swedish beauty squeezing in at the door, struggling to balance pieces of matching luggage, handbag and computer. Every man within ten yards leaps to help her. Jack's roughly three men too late.

INT CORRIDOR – ALGONQUIN HOTEL – NEW YORK – DAY – 1984 (CONT)

Jack turns the key in his lock and starts to haul his case inside.

As he does so, a bellhop wheeling the matching luggage, handbag and computer leads the Swedish beauty to the room next door. She and Jack swap a brief, polite smile.

They go into their respective rooms. So they're to be next-door neighbours.

And thereby, of course, hangs a tale . . .

INT BEDROOM – ALGONQUIN HOTEL – NEW YORK – DAY – 1984 (CONT)

It's small and pokey, faded wallpaper on its paper-thin walls.

Jack is unpacking from his suitcase, open on the bed.

From the adjacent room he hears his Swedish neighbour snapping rapid, staccato instructions down the phone, icily, impatiently. She ends the call and begins another. Just as busy and businesslike. Not just a blonde bimbo, then. A no-nonsense tycoon.

He finds himself hanging his jacket in the wardrobe very quietly so's not to disturb her while she's running Wall Street.

EXT MANHATTAN SKYLINE – NIGHT

A panorama of skyscrapers, their illuminated windows gradually being extinguished.

EXT WEST 44TH STREET – NEW YORK – NIGHT (CONT)

The hobo mugger is hanging around the Algonquin entrance, limping his beat. He finally decides to call it a night and hobbles off. A yellow cab drives past and stops at the hotel. Jack gets out, pays, over-tips and goes into the hotel.

INT BEDROOM – ALGONQUIN HOTEL – NEW YORK – NIGHT – 1984

In the half-light, Jack asleep in bed.

Suddenly, there's a searing cry from the next room. Jack's eyes spring open. Another cry – and Jack snaps bolt-upright. He hears muffled noises, apart from his thumping heart, then another voice, muted, menacing and male. More noises, then another cry – female. Then another – male.

Jack jerks a wild-eyed look at the window. A burglar or rapist or serial killer wouldn't find it too hard to climb up – and in. Another bayonet-sharp cry, and Jack decides he must act at once to save his helpless neighbour. Whatever the danger to himself. At the same time, of course, he must remember he's British. A certain dignity, a certain reserve is called for. And so:

JACK
(*calling through the wall*)

Can I help you?

There's an abrupt silence from next door.

I say. Hello? Can I help you?

He can't help but notice how stiff-upper-lip British his accent has become all on its own. Not only the accent, the timbre. It's so far-back it could be coming from West 45th Street.

Then, from the other side of the wall – the sound of a man and woman laughing. Louder and louder, more and more. In great, helpless, hysterical whoops.

Jack sinks down and covers his head with the bedclothes.

JACK (VO)

The next morning, as I was going into the dining room for breakfast, I saw the Swedish beauty wolfing waffles with some burgling serial killer or other. I did a swift about-turn and had breakfast at a deli down the street.

INT FOYER – CLARIDGE'S – LONDON – DAY – 1984

Jack lounges in an armchair, humming happily to himself.

JACK (VO)

Claridge's again. For what promised to be a massive turning-point in my career – on what promised to be certainly the most financially profitable day of my life.

It was a Monday. The previous Friday, the truly great film director Martin Scorsese had had delivered to my house a copy of *The Threepenny Opera,* a tape of the songs and a note: would I introduce myself to him on Sunday at the

BAFTA Awards, where he had been nominated for his movie, *The King of Comedy*?

I read the play, listened to the songs and shook hands with him at the ceremony. He asked me to come to Claridge's, 2 p.m. on Monday.

A porter leaves reception and approaches Jack.

PORTER

Mr Rosenthal, Mr Scorsese says would you please go up now. Room 519.

INT LIFT – CLARIDGE'S – LONDON – DAY – 1984 (CONT)

Jack stands in the lift, as it rises through the floors. Still humming, though now, since he's alone, a little more loudly.

JACK (VO)

A true wheeler-dealer, of course, would fret about nothing happening Monday *morning*. No need. At the weekend, Sam Wanamaker, the tireless, fiercely passionate, eventual resurrector of the Globe, had asked me to meet him on Monday morning for coffee. I did, and he asked me would I like to write a film about Daniel Mendoza, the eighteenth-century bare-knuckle pugilist champion. 'I would,' I said. 'Good,' he said, 'I'll talk to your agent.'

The lift stops at the fifth floor.

INT CORRIDOR – CLARIDGE'S – LONDON – DAY – 1984 (CONT)

Jack approaches room 519, takes a couple of nerve-settling deep breaths and knocks. The door opens at once. The great man is there – short, wiry, wiry steel-grey hair, wiry black eyebrows, big smile. They greet each other again, shake hands and Martin Scorsese ushers Jack in.

INT ROOM 519 – CLARIDGE'S – LONDON – DAY – 1984 (CONT)

As Martin closes the door behind Jack, before they've even sat down:

MARTIN SCORSESE

So? What's the verdict? Would you like to adapt it for a movie, *The Threepenny Opera*?

JACK

Absolutely. I imagine you'd like it to be made contemporary, a contemporary version? I've already plotted a –

MARTIN SCORSESE

No, no. Exactly as the original. Historical.

JACK
(*surprised*)
Oh. Okay.

MARTIN SCORSESE
So, if you'd like to do it, it's all yours.

JACK
(*another deep breath*)
Well . . . thank you.

MARTIN SCORSESE
You're welcome. I'm taking a trip to China right now. In the meantime, my lawyers'll get things mobile. When I get back, you'll maybe have the first draft figured out.

JACK
Absolutely. Well, thanks again.

MARTIN SCORSESE
My pleasure. Thanks for dropping by.

They shake hands again and Jack leaves. They never do get round to sitting down.

JACK (VO)
The meeting lasted less than two minutes. But I suppose lots of earth-shattering events take even less. The Big Bang, for example.

INT/EXT BUS (TRAVELLING) – DAY – 1984

The bus is lumbering along through Kentish Town.

Jack is seated, feet up, on the front upper-deck seat. He can barely contain his excitement.

JACK (VO)
Two film offers in one day. Two exciting subjects. One interesting producer, one fascinating director. One pretty big pay-packet, one Hollywood-size massive one. The sun shone all the way home . . .

INT LIVING ROOM – THE GENTLEMAN'S RESIDENCE – MUSWELL HILL – DAY – 1984

Jack paces round in a small, agitated circle, phone in hand . . .

JACK (VO)
. . . then, once home, it not only stopped shining, it slipped with a mocking laugh into a passing black hole. Twice.

First, Peggy Ramsay called to tell me Sam Wanamaker's offer – no commissioning money. Just a share of the profits. Which, for writers, traditionally amounts to no money at all. Ever.

Second, Martin Scorsese's lawyers rang. *The Threepenny Opera* was off. Martin had also offered it to another writer who'd dropped by five minutes after me – and who'd also suggested a contemporary version, which Martin had this time okayed. The lawyers apologised for Martin's 'naughtiness'.

JACK
(*into phone*)
Don't mention it.

He replaces the phone. He flops into a chair, sighs, sips a mug of tea and begins to laugh. Philosophically, he thinks. To the casual observer it looks more like heartbrokenly.

JACK (VO)
From eleven o'clock till two minutes past two, I'd been potentially the busiest, richest writer in the land. All the Rolls-Royces I could've bought . . . black with white upholstery, white with black and my own, legitimate secondhand Jag for slumming in.

(*beat*)
Neither film was made. But it was a nice day out.

EXT RHODES AVENUE PRIMARY SCHOOL – MUSWELL HILL – DAY – 1984

A babel of young squeaking voices. It's dinner-break and kids are swarming all over the playing field in front of the building; playing with (or without) plastic balls, dashing about like loony lemmings, climbing, fighting or – girls only – meandering along, arms linked, four abreast, inseparable best friends, gossiping out of the sides of their mouths, all at the same time.

There's one exception. A loner. One kid, oblivious to the rest, shuffling slowly round the perimeter of the field, muttering quietly and earnestly to herself. The occasional hand gesture or sudden animated facial expression shows she's not simply talking to herself – she's acting. *Playing all the characters in a play she's concocting as she shuffles along. Amy, now aged ten and a bit.*

At the far end of the field, Adam, now eight, is in the middle of a ruck of wildly kicking, hacking, jostling (i.e. fouling) boys, trying to kick the ball, when appropriate, with his left foot, as brainwashed by his dad.

INT LIVING ROOM – THE GENTLEMAN'S RESIDENCE – MUSWELL HILL – EVENING – 1984

Amy and Adam are eating their spaghetti bolognaise. Maureen and Jack sit opposite them, looking concerned. A family conference in progress . . .

Neither child is doing well at school. Every day, the same question –

MAUREEN

What did you learn at school today?

– brings, of course, the same answer:

AMY/ADAM

Nothing.

Although this is every schoolchild's usual answer, in the case of our two it's true. Amy, so literate almost from birth, has trouble adding one and one. Adam, a bit the other way round.

After weeks of sickening heart-searching, reluctantly and guiltily, Maureen and Jack betray their Socialist principles and decide to take their kids out of Haringey's state-school system and put them into private schools.

JACK (VO)

The obvious choice for Amy was King Alfred's in Golders Green. Liberal and *laissez-faire,* it was famous for welcoming the most academically challenged kids so long as their parents were in showbusiness. One appearance on *The Bill* got you a discount on the term's fees.

EXT KING ALFRED'S SCHOOL – GOLDERS GREEN – DAY – 1984

Maureen and Jack, left eyebrows raised a little smugly, take Amy through the gates into the school.

JACK (VO)

The daughter of an actress and writer, we ushered her in for her English and Maths test.

EXT KING ALFRED'S SCHOOL – GOLDERS GREEN – DAY – 1984

Maureen and Jack, eyebrows now glowering, propel Amy out *of the school and back through the gates.*

JACK (VO)

The daughter of the actress and the writer failed – and unbelievably was consequently refused admission! Unheard of! It created a King Alfred's precedent, a school record. Half the members of Equity and the Writers' Guild lost their faith in human nature.

EXT QUEEN'S COLLEGE – HARLEY STREET – LONDON – DAY – 1984

Jack's Honda draws up. Amy gets out and dashes up to a group of girls going into the school, babbling away, and goes in with them – also babbling away.

JACK (VO)

She finally went – happily and fruitfully – to Queen's College. Nineteen years later, just as happily, she's back there, supplementing her playwriting earnings as a drama teacher.

EXT ST ANTHONY'S SCHOOL – HAMPSTEAD – DAY – 1984

Adam trudges into school, along with other blue blazered boys.

JACK (VO)

Although it was the day after St Anthony's had supposedly finalised their intake, Adam went for *his* entrance exam. At Rhodes Avenue, he'd been top of the class in Maths. Here he failed – and some of our guilt for taking him out of Rhodes Avenue lifted. His English result and the pleas of one of the other boys' fathers got him accepted. The boy was his pal, David Shindler. His father was *our* pal, Colin, TV producer and writer – later to achieve fame with, among other books and films, *Manchester United Ruined My Life*.

Adam, too, flourished at his new school, with its eccentric, effing and blinding headmaster, Tim Patten.

One morning, one of the new boys' mothers who hadn't yet met Tim saw him outside the school; with his straggly hair and beard, his jeans and trainers and bottle of Guinness. She gave him a pound.

EXT FOOTBALL PITCH – REGENT'S PARK – LONDON – DAY – 1984

It's Sunday morning. A gaggle of ten sleepy, slightly bored boys and one girl, all in white shirts and black shorts, take the field. They include David Shindler and Adam Rosenthal. These are the Little Londoners, playing in a local junior league. Although, to David's dad and Adam's dad, they're not. They're the England team playing in the World Cup Final, possibly in Brazil.

The two dads are their embarrassingly fanatical coaches. Jack is the more embarrassing of the two. While the Little Londoners saunter about the pitch, dreaming of their half-time oranges, their coaches harangue them with vein-bulging screams from the touchline . . .

COLIN

Keep your shape in midfield!

JACK

Press on in the final third!

COLIN

Use your overlapping full-backs!

JACK

Hard shots!

COLIN

Their goalie's only little – just kick it over his head!

One of the stalwarts in central defence is the lone girl, Emily, but the real hero is Anthony, a silent, wispy-thin, white-faced lad who turns up every Sunday and stands motionless in the middle of the field for the entire match, never kicking the ball, never running after it, seemingly oblivious to its whereabouts or even existence.

The Little Londoners win the league and the Cup Final, without much caring. Their coaches, however, punch the air in ecstatic triumph –

COLIN AND JACK

Yes!

– and hug each other. Via a proxy England team via a proxy schoolboy team, their roles as fathers have been vindicated and they've won the Jules Rimet Trophy. The expressions 'Sad bugger' and 'Get a life' are, unfortunately, not yet in common currency.

EXT CENTURY CITY – LOS ANGELES – DAY – 1985

A huge, tree-lined forecourt in which you could lose the whole of Wardour Street leads to twenty or thirty steps sweeping up to the entrance of a massive white-stone building housing the offices of various independent film producers.

Jack, limping a little more these days, climbs up. He has an idea for an American movie and he's here seeing as many executives as possible in a week. This appointment is for 6.45 p.m.

INT CORRIDOR – CENTURY CITY BUILDING – LOS ANGELES DAY – 1985 (CONT)

The building is deserted. This being the movie industry, everyone's apparently gone home – early dinner, early to bed, ridiculously early to rise the next day.

Jack walks with echoing footsteps down the empty corridor towards a room some miles away at the end. As he nears the room, he hears through the open door the end of a phone conversation:

FILM PRODUCER (OS)

That's fine, sweetheart. Get in the car now, you'll be here in, say, twenty, twenty-five minutes, then we'll shoot off for dinner.

(*beat*)

Sure I'll be through by then. I'll be through in five minutes. I just have this shmock from England to see. Make that four minutes.

We hear the phone replaced. Jack knocks on the open door.

FILM PRODUCER (OS)

Come in!

INT FILM PRODUCER'S OFFICE – LOS ANGELES – DAY – 1985 (CONT)

The customary designer-designed producer's office. Posters of unheard-of hit films on the walls, two TV sets, half a dozen phones, plants, seemingly brand-new furniture.

Jack comes in. The producer lobs him an uninterested glance and waves him to a chair.

FILM PRODUCER

You're Jack, right?

JACK

Right. The shmock from England.

The uninterested glance freezes into an embarrassed grimace. But, being a film producer, he doesn't stay embarrassed for long. Jack sits down.

FILM PRODUCER

I saw your TV movie today, *Ready When You Are, Mr McGill* . . .

JACK

(*hopes rising*)

Oh, yes?

FILM PRODUCER

(*already bored*)

Not a bad little effort. Quite charming in its own little way. No Oscar winner, but heck, what *is*? I quite enjoyed it. Kind of. In a sense.

Jack's hopes sink with each half-brick of faint praise being tied round its ankles. Then:

So, tell me, what was the last thing you wrote?

JACK

Yentl.

The film producer jerks out of his boredom, stiffens and stares.

FILM PRODUCER

You wrote Yentl?

JACK

Co-wrote. With Miss Streisand.

FILM PRODUCER

(*excitedly and moved*)

You wrote Yentl?! Listen, your TV movie, *Ready When You Are, Mr Whatever* – what a great movie! Fantastic. Tremendous. A truly stupendous movie. I loved it. Who wouldn't?

(*beat; then reverently*)

So you wrote *Yentl* . . .

Jack eventually manages to start pitching the idea he's come here for. The film producer thinks it's wonderful, terrific, marvellous, and promises to think about it. His dinner-date arrives and has to wait, with a lot of loud sharp intakes of breath, in an outer office while her boyfriend practises his superlatives about the TV film he didn't like twenty minutes earlier.

EXT ABC TV BUILDING – LOS ANGELES – DAY – 1985

Jack makes his way into another unnecessarily magnificent building. Another day, another executive.

INT TV EXECUTIVE'S OFFICE – ABC TV – LOS ANGELES – DAY – 1985 (CONT)

Jack sits facing the Head of Drama lolling in his leather chair behind his mahogany desk, mentally paring his fingernails. He looks about fifteen years old. He tries to summon up a little interest . . .

HEAD OF DRAMA

So . . . Have you written anything before?

JACK

(*thrown*)

Um . . . did you read my list of credits?

HEAD OF DRAMA

Haven't seen it. Sorry.

JACK

It's *there*!

(*he points*)
On the desk. In front of you. Albeit upside down.

HEAD OF DRAMA
Oh. That's it, is it? Uh-huh.

He grants it a long-distance, half-second glance – still upside down. Then, suddenly animated:

Okay. Let me acquaint you with our operation here. *Movie of the Week*. Our flagship. Going great. Terrific ratings, terrific audience reaction, very happy sponsor. Which is terrific.

(*beat*)
Now, my creative input, which – though far be it from me to sing my own praises –

(*sings out*)
Hallelujah!

(*laughs at his little joke*)
– is as follows: 'High Concept'.

This is a label unknown in Muswell Hill. The Head of Drama smugly recognises the blank expression on his listener's face.

HEAD OF DRAMA
'High Concept' means any subject that can be described in ten words. For the TV guides, you understand. For example, 'Mother of twins has cancer but bravely wins through.'

JACK
That's nine, isn't it?

HEAD OF DRAMA
Nine, ten, same difference. So, what *kind* of High Concept, you ask. Okay.

He pauses for dramatic, even melo*dramatic effect.*

Heart, Stomach and Groin. Heart is love stories; Stomach, horror stories; Groin, sexploitation.

*He beams as though he's solved Einstein's dream of the Theory of Everything. Jack tries to smile back or, at least, look impressed, but can do neither. All he wants is to get out into the air-*unconditioned *street.*

JACK
(*beat*)
Right.

(*beat*)
I'm afraid I don't do Heart, Stomach *or* Groin.

(*beat*)

I only do Elbow.

The teenage drama monster squints at him. A long, highly charged pause.

HEAD OF DRAMA

You do *Elbow*?

JACK

That's all.

He gets up, offers a handshake.

But thanks for seeing me. Bye.

EXT HOTEL – LOS ANGELES – NIGHT – 1985

Jack stands, impatiently looking up and down the street. He's being picked up and taken back home for dinner by Michael Grade, now running Embassy Films in LA, and can't wait to see him and tell him about Heart, Stomach and Groin.

Finally Michael's car draws up. Michael lowers his window.

MICHAEL

Jump in.

INT MICHAEL GRADE'S CAR (TRAVELLING) – NIGHT – 1985 (CONT)

Michael drives. Jack immediately launches into his adventure story.

JACK

I went to see this bloke this afternoon. He told me he only does High Concept movies. I said, 'Like what?' And he said –

MICHAEL

'Heart, Stomach and Groin.'

Jack's face falls.

JACK

How did you know?

MICHAEL

I assume you were at ABC TV?

Jack nods.

That's what he always says. And everyone always throws up. He used to work for me. I fired him six months ago.

But the episode isn't quite over . . .

INT HOTEL BEDROOM – LOS ANGELES – DAY – 1985

The following morning. The bed's dishevelled and empty. The bedside phone starts to ring. Jack pads out of the shower in a towelling robe. He takes the phone.

JACK

Hello?

INT WILLIAM MORRIS AGENCY – LOS ANGELES – DAY – 1985 (CONT)

Beth Swofford, Jack's American agent, young, sweet-faced, cuddly-plump but tough as they come, is at her desk.

BETH
(*into phone*)

Hi. Beth.

INTERCUT between the hotel bedroom and Beth's office:

JACK
(*into phone*)

Blimey. It's only five to nine.

BETH
(*into phone*)

I know. I thought I'd let you sleep in. I've had three calls about you already. The first at seven thirty.

JACK
(*into phone*)

Who from?

BETH
(*into phone*)

All the same person. You were a big hit yesterday.

JACK
(*into phone*)

Was I? Where?

BETH
(*into phone*)

ABC TV. What the hell's this Elbow thing about?

JACK
(*into phone*)

What?

BETH
(*into phone*)

He wants you to write Elbow. All he wants is Elbow. He's going crazy for Elbow. He'd leave his wife and kids for Elbow. What the hell is it?

JACK
(*into phone, smiles*)
I was hoping *you* might know . . .

INT ALAN PARKER'S OFFICE – LONDON – DAY – 1985

A creative meeting in progress. Being creative are Alan Parker (who has become, since his The Evacuees *debut, a masterful and massively successful feature film director), Paul Weiland, Alan Marshall, Patsy Pollock and Jack.*

Alan has asked Jack to adapt two of Tom Sharpe's South African novels, Riotous Assembly *and* Indecent Exposure, *into a single feature film. Alan is to produce it with Alan Marshall; Paul – a bright and talented director of TV commercials – is to direct it; and Patsy, a casting director, is there to . . . well, gently stick her oar in now and then.*

And Alan Parker does a remarkable thing. In Jack's experience, a truly amazing thing. He starts circling the floor and, scarcely pausing for breath or to work out his next thought, verbally structures the entire film, scene by succeeding scene, off the top of his Islington barnet. It's an absolutely virtuoso tour de force. *Jack scribbles away, gratefully copying down every word. When he eventually comes to write the screenplay, it has almost exactly the same structure.*

On the surface it seems that Paul and Jack would make a good team, a simpatico writer/director partnership. But somehow they get off on the wrong foot. Over the years, the wrong foot twists its ankle, then stubs its toe, sprains its Achilles tendon and pulls a hamstring. A decade later, on another proposed project, they're at crutches at dawn. It's a shame. Somehow it could all have been . . . might've been . . . could conceivably . . . Who knows?

EXT SKIES ABOVE THE ATLANTIC – DAY – 1985

A jumbo jet en route to Los Angeles, from right of frame to left.

JACK (VO)
Alan read my screenplay – entitled *Non-White Comedy* – on a plane, and was disappointed.

EXT SKIES ABOVE THE ATLANTIC – DAY – 1985

The jet is making the reverse trip – from left of frame to right.

JACK (VO)
He read it again – and hated it.

INT CAR (TRAVELLING) – LONDON – DAY – 1985

Alan is hunched up in the back seat of a chauffeur-driven film unit car, engrossed in Non-White Comedy.

JACK (VO)

Later he read it again and, third time lucky, this time he loved it. Now he thought it was brilliant. So he went to pitch it to a studio executive at Columbia.

DISSOLVE TO:

INT OFFICE – COLUMBIA PICTURES – LOS ANGELES – DAY – 1985

The executive sits gently swivelling in his chair, just possibly – though it can't, of course, be guaranteed – deep in thought. The swivelling takes him from gazing blankly out of the window to gazing, still blankly, at Alan, who's hopping impatiently from foot to foot on the other side of the desk.

ALAN PARKER

Well?

COLUMBIA EXECUTIVE

No.

ALAN PARKER

No what?

COLUMBIA EXECUTIVE

No, I don't buy it. A satire about apartheid? I don't think so.

ALAN PARKER

It'll be terrific!

COLUMBIA EXECUTIVE

Dead in the bathtub.

Whereupon Alan leaps across the desk and socks the executive on the jaw. It doesn't help to get the film made, but it does make everybody feel that bit better. P'raps not the executive.

Years pass, and the wind of change finally blows apartheid away – and, with it, the topical relevance of Non-White Comedy.

EXT THE WAILING WALL – JERUSALEM – DAY – 1986

Maureen, Jack, Amy and Adam are crossing the enormous plaza to the Wall in head-hammering, lung-squeezing heat. They're on holiday. To Jack, anywhere except Ibiza, Spain and Portugal, and maybe Florida, is a good holiday: this particular spot, of course, is God-given. And it's here that Amy or Adam, or maybe both, utter what, to us anyway, achieves classic status:

AMY/ADAM

Do we *have* to keep going to interesting places?

EXT HAWORTH – DAY – 1986

From Jack's POV, a sweeping panoramic shot of Haworth from high above the exquisite town lying in its valley.

JACK (VO)

Another place of interest. Lumb Bank in Yorkshire, in the heart of Brontë Country.

CAM pans with Jack as he turns and makes his way into a black, stone house.

INT COMMUNAL LIVING ROOM – LUMB BANK – DAY – 1986

Jack is addressing a group of twenty or so would-be writers; men, women, young, old, potentially promising or better off learning chiropody. They're lounging in chairs or on sofas or squatting on the floor, making notes while slurping tea and wolfing bacon sarnies. This is the week-long Arvon Writer's Course and Jack is a tutor.

As he lectures . . .

JACK (VO)

By now I had three more TV plays either written or produced or a twinkle in my eye: *Mrs Capper's Birthday,* adapted from Noël Coward's short story, compassionately directed by the lovely Mike Ockrent; *Fools on the Hill* – which brought me the worst reviews I've ever had – telling the story of the birth of television at Alexandra Palace (round the corner from the Gentleman's Residence) in 1936; and *A Day to Remember*.

***A Day to Remember* – superbly starring George Cole, as Wally, and Ron Cooke, as Graham – was based on a true story starring my father-in-law as himself and me as me . . .**

Wally (the fictional Maurice Lipman), in his sixties, is staying in London for Xmas with his wife, Hilda, his daughter, Judy, and his son-in-law, Graham (the fictional Jack).

Like Maurice, Wally's suffered for eight years from the loss of his immediate memory. Out of his home environment he's completely disorientated – he doesn't know how long he's been away or when he's going back or where Hilda and Judy have gone (Christmas shopping).

Like Maurice, even at home, he doesn't know if he had breakfast ten minutes ago or two hours ago or at all, and no idea where he was yesterday or even today. If he's halfway

through the front door in his overcoat, he's unsure whether he's coming in or going out.

Like Maurice, he reads items in the newspaper over and over again – and each time it's news to *him.*

Like Maurice, all he knows is – he knows nothing. And it's terrifying. And, despite his son-in-law's vows of saintly patience, it's driving Graham pot-shop.

DISSOLVE TO:

FILM EXCERPT: *A Day to Remember*

INT KITCHEN – GRAHAM'S HOUSE – DAY

Open on two eggs being broken on the edge of a frying pan, then dropped in. Graham is at the stove doing the frying. The table is set for a light lunch, knife and fork already erect in Wally's hands. As he waits, he's singing happily to himself, to the tune of 'Red Sails in the Sunset' . . .

WALLY

Fried eggs in the sunset
In a sandwich for me
Fried eggs in my belly
Da-da-da-da-dee
Fried eggs up in London
With a dollop of HP
Fried eggs with young Graham
Da-da-da-da-dee.

Graham throws him an amused glance.

GRAHAM

Doesn't take much, does it?

WALLY

Sorry?

GRAHAM

To cheer you up. Half a dozen hens in your backyard you'd be the happiest man in Southend.

WALLY

(*grins*)

It's being so cheerful as keeps me going.

Gradually Graham's reciprocatory smile begins to fade. His expression grows tense. Wally's smile also fades as he registers this.

WALLY

What's up?

Graham's thoughts are racing. His tenseness erupts into excitement.

GRAHAM

Experiment!

WALLY

(*scared*)

How do you mean?

GRAHAM

In the interests of medical science.

WALLY

What is?

GRAHAM

Where did we go last night, you and me?

WALLY

(*more scared*)

I'm worse when you test me ...

GRAHAM

No, no! You're happy, right? At this moment, you're *happy*! So all I'm trying to – Come on! Last night! You and me! In a big hall watching something!

WALLY

Won't my eggs burn?

Graham flicks off the gas, then wheels round to face him again.

GRAHAM

Think, Wally!

Wally looks blank.

Alright. Different tack. Where's Hilda and Judy gone?

WALLY

Um ...

GRAHAM

Concentrate, Wally!

WALLY

Out.

GRAHAM

More. More. Out where?

WALLY
(*at a loss*)
Well, they won't have gone to a wrestling match, I think I can vouch for that.

Graham stares at him, intrigued incredulously.

What've I said?

Graham sits at the table, deeply pensive.

GRAHAM
Now *that* ... *that* ... has more to it than meets the whatsit ...

WALLY
(*helpfully*)
The eye.

GRAHAM
(*working through his thoughts*)
In a way, you've ... It's all in there somewhere ... But jumbled up ... it just needs organising.

WALLY
What does?

GRAHAM
Got it!

He leaps up and races to a drawer. He snatches writing paper and pencil from it. Wally watches, uncomprehending.

GRAHAM
Eu-bloody-reka, my son!

He plonks himself down at the table, pushes the pencil and paper towards Wally and smiles at him.

That's it.

WALLY
What's what?

GRAHAM
Wally, your memories are all there.

WALLY
They're not, Graham, I don't remember them.

GRAHAM
The wrestling was there.

WALLY
What wrestling?

GRAHAM

From now on you carry a little writing pad ... not like this, smaller ... and everything you do, everything you need to remember, you *write down*. Like last night, when we got home –

WALLY

(shakes his head)

Graham ...

GRAHAM

– you'd have written down: 'December 18th, Fairfield Hall with Graham. To see the wrestling. Big Daddy and Cyanide Cooper', then you'd –

WALLY

Graham, listen ...

GRAHAM

– look at it this morning and *remember*! Then you'd write: 'December 19th, Hilda and Judy gone shopping' ... Then whenever you weren't absolutely 100 per cent sure where they were, you just look in your little writing pad and –

WALLY

It wouldn't work, Graham. I'd *forget* to write it down. I'd need a billboard in front of my face, tied round my neck, *telling* me to do it. Either that or a whatsit, that I could *feel* in my pocket, heavy ... one of them dictaphone jobs ... cassette things ... so's I could feel it there ...

Graham stares at him as though at a revelation. A musical beat now begins, gathering momentum throughout the rest of the scene. By the end it has accelerated and built in volume, ending in a triumphant climax. Wally fidgets apprehensively in the face of Graham's staring.

WALLY

What?

GRAHAM

(*reverently*)

Oh, my God ...

WALLY

(*frightened*)

What?

GRAHAM

That's it!

WALLY

What is?

GRAHAM

A cassette-recorder! Even better! Perfect! You don't have to do *anything* later! You speak into it *while* things are happening to you! *At the time*! Oh, Jesus, Wally, we've only gone and done it! Don't say, 'Done what?'

WALLY

(*who was just about to*)

Um . . . no . . .

GRAHAM

(*gravely, quietly*)

Wally, we've brought you back to life.

WALLY

(*awed*)

Have we?

GRAHAM

(*shaking with emotion*)

What we've done, Wally, in this little house, unknown to the world, what we've done is a minor bloody miracle.

WALLY

I haven't *got* a cassette-recorder, Graham . . .

Graham smiles at him beatifically, overflowing with Christian charity.

GRAHAM

Not *yet* you haven't . . . Merry Christmas, Wally.

INT HALLWAY – GRAHAM'S HOUSE – DAY (CONT)

Graham is helping Wally into his overcoat.

WALLY

Graham, I can't let you . . .

GRAHAM

You'll press a button and you'll talk to your memory. You'll press another – your memory'll talk to *you*. Bingo.

Wally is now quaking – with fear and gratitude, but mostly with hope that the impossible is about to happen.

WALLY

(*in tears*)

Oh, mate . . .

GRAHAM

(*nobly*)

What's it feel like – being brought back to life?

WALLY

Nice. Except the emotion wells up on me when I'm not looking.

Graham puts his own coat on and leads him reverently to the front door. Wally suddenly stops in his tracks.

WALLY

You didn't have your fried eggs!

GRAHAM

They were yours. I don't eat eggs.

WALLY

I *had* mine. They were lovely. Enjoyed them.

GRAHAM

No, you didn't, Wally. I'd only just started fry–

He decides it's wiser to let it go.

Look, when we get back, I'll do your fried eggs.

WALLY

No, no, I'm satisfied with those I had. I've no egg-yolk on my chin, have I?

He juts his chin out for inspection. Graham chucks him under the chin, indulgently.

GRAHAM

One miracle a day, eh, Wally?

He ushers him through the front door, then follows him out.

DISSOLVE TO:

INT LIVING ROOM – GRAHAM'S HOUSE – DAY – SOME HOURS LATER

We hear the front door open and close and Hilda and Judy enter, weighed down with Christmas shopping, ready to drop, more than ready for a cup of tea.

Graham races towards them, beside himself with excitement. He burbles joyously about bringing Wally's memory back, saying they should have champagne instead of tea.

HILDA

What are you rambling about?

GRAHAM

(*points to recorder*)

That.

HILDA

What's that got to do with his memory?

GRAHAM

It *is* his memory, Hilda! Every day, he'll record whatever he's –

Hilda's shoulders slump. She turns and starts towards the kitchen.

HILDA

(*to Judy*)

I'll put the kettle on.

GRAHAM

Hilda! Didn't you hear what I –

HILDA

He'll never use that, you twerp. He's *got* one. He's had it for years. It sits on the mantelpiece at home, year in, year out. He forgets to use it.

She and Judy exit to kitchen. Graham, white-faced, stares at Wally. A long pause, then he yells at him at the top of his voice.

GRAHAM

Why didn't you tell me, you silly sod!

WALLY

(*blankly*)

Tell you what?

DISSOLVE TO:

INT LIVING ROOM – THE GENTLEMAN'S RESIDENCE – MUSWELL HILL – NIGHT – 1986

A TV screen is showing the last moments of the previous scene, a CU of Wally's face.

Jack is watching from an armchair. He sighs and sadly shakes his head.

JACK (VO)

Poor Maurice. Poor Zelma. Poor Maurice.

EXT A RAILWAY TRACK MONTAGE – U.S.A. – DAY – 1986

As in the traditional cinema-cliché, a speeded-up train hurtles along the track and over CAM, whistles blowing, wheels spinning . . . while through the track a sign zooms out at us reading 'Dallas!' It clears frame, to be replaced by another reading 'Washington!' And that's replaced by a third, reading 'Chicago!'

INT EXHIBITION HALL – CHICAGO – DAY – 1986

A toy manufacturers' convention is in progress. Around the massive space are extravagant stalls of merchandise – varying from the most embarrassing kitsch to some rather tasteful replica bronzes of Frederic Remington cowboys and Indians.

In the body of the hall sit hundreds of manufacturers and salespersons listening to a keynote speaker on the platform, flanked by baton-twirling, white-booted, miniskirted blondes and accompanied by swelling background music.

At the back of the hall, Jack is scribbling notes on everything he sees and hears. A young, harassed-looking, fair-haired woman squeezes along the row, apologising as she goes and sits down beside him. This is Jackie Zambrano.

ZAMBRANO

I got you four interviews for tonight –

SALESMAN

Ssshh!

Zambrano gives him the finger and continues.

ZAMBRANO

– and eight for tomorrow if you survive tonight's.

Zambrano is a researcher with Universal Pictures, assigned to Jack. She's tough, efficient and hard-working when she's not too busy planning her wilder-by-the-day wedding to her boyfriend back in LA.

Jack has pitched an idea to the studio: a film about the American convention of conventions, a satire on one of America's most sacred traditions and – though hard to believe – pleasures.

Zambrano and Jack are travelling from city to city attending as many conventions as possible. Now they're in Chicago for two days.

INT CORRIDOR – HOTEL – CHICAGO – NIGHT – 1986

Zambrano and Jack appear from a grand, sweeping staircase and trudge exhaustedly along towards their rooms. After covering three conventions during the day and two in the evening, they can hardly keep their eyes open.

Then suddenly, Jack's eyes pop wide *open. Then screw up in disgust.*

There, coming towards him, he sees a man in his fifties, overweight, his jacket and trousers straining across his paunch, non-Gentile nose, shuffling along like an old man – with a young, bouncy blonde beside him.

JACK

Look at that. Ought to be ashamed of himself. Dirty old bugger. He's old enough to be her father.

Zambrano seems a little puzzled at this. She and Jack walk on towards the dirty old bugger and his nymphette walking towards them.

A few more paces and Jack realises he and Zambrano are walking towards a full-length mirror.

EXT A RAILWAY TRACK MONTAGE – USA – DAY – 1986

With a jarring scream of brakes, the speeded-up train suddenly starts to slow down, its wheels shooting sparks as they scrape and slide to a stop.

JACK (VO)

Despite Jon Amiel (of Denis Potter's *The Singing Detective* fame and now Hollywood's flavour-of-the-year) wanting to direct the screenplay, Universal turned the *Conventions* screenplay down. On the fairly understandable grounds that either no one would go and see it or it'd lead to riots in the streets. Americans *love* conventions; sacred cows are to be patted, not slaughtered.

DISSOLVE TO:

EXT OLD TRAFFORD FOOTBALL GROUND – MANCHESTER – DAY – LATE 1960S

Along with 50,000 others, Jack is standing on the terraces watching a footballer cheekily dance and sway and sashay like a will-o'-the-wisp through the lunging, flailing tackles of defenders.

Slight of build, but lithe and strong, he's 22 years old, almost impossibly athletic, his film-star good looks topped by a flowing Beatle black mop of hair.

He scores a superb goal. Thousands of fists punch the air and thousands of voices begin a rhythmic, insistent, haunting chant – two syllables in an eerie, dying fall: 'Georgie, Georgie, Georgie.'

During this:

JACK (VO)

Eighteen years later, Columbia Pictures had this bright idea. A film about the most charismatic footballer in the game. The best. *George* Best. But not about George the footballer. About George the lover (and eventual husband) of Angie.

They labelled it *The Greatest Love Story Ever Told* – which it wasn't. It was simply *The Usual Story of George Getting His*

***End Away*. I tried to tell Columbia this, but they were adamant. Accordingly . . .**

DISSOLVE TO:

EXT HEALTH FARM – ENGLAND – DAY – 1986

Eighteen years later.

Three cars draw up and stop outside the entrance. Out of the first comes George, heavier, of course, and bearded. Out of the second comes Angie, now George's ex-*wife. Out of the third comes Jack.*

They all greet each other and haul their suitcases from the car boots.

INT LOUNGE – HEALTH FARM – ENGLAND – DAY – 1986

Angie, George and Jack sit round a table with glasses of fruit juice or water. Angie is talking animatedly. Jack is taking notes. George is silent and fed up, occasionally twisting his glass of water round and round as though trying to strangle it.

JACK (VO)

Columbia's second bright idea was that the three of us should spend a weekend together, when George and Angie would confess to me all the steamy secrets of The Greatest Love Story Ever Told.

We decided on a health farm because George was under medical orders to keep on the wagon. Angie did all the talking – not that there was much to tell apart from a hot three minutes in a poolside changing room in California, on a spiky rubber mat.

ANGIE

My arse finished up looking like a colander.

JACK (VO)

George sometimes muttered, 'Yes,' sometimes, 'No,' but mostly shrugged.

INT BILLIARD ROOM – HEALTH FARM – ENGLAND – NIGHT – 1986

George, Angie and Jack are playing snooker. Suddenly George looks at his watch, puts his cue back in the rack and starts for the door.

GEORGE

See you.

ANGIE

Where are you going?

GEORGE

Out.

ANGIE

Not for a drink, George! You're not allowed!

GEORGE

You know, that's very similar to the rumour *I* heard. Funny old world. Don't wait up.

He goes, throwing himself head-first off the wagon as soon as it rattles alongside the nearest pub.

INT STAIRS AND LANDING – HEALTH FARM – ENGLAND – NIGHT – 1986

Walking up the stairs and along the landing to the bedrooms are Angie with her current young man; George, burping slightly, with his latest girlfriend (also called Angie); and Jack with his notepad and pen. They swap 'Goodnights'. The two couples peel off into adjacent bedrooms. Jack limps into his.

INT JACK'S BEDROOM – HEALTH FARM – ENGLAND – NIGHT 1986

Lit by the bedside lamp, Jack is skimming through his notes.

JACK (VO)

Angie had given me intriguing, personal insights into George's life . . . his painful adolescent failure with girls (yes, George, of all people); his inconsolable heartbreak at the death of his beloved grandad; his mother's secret, amateurish but maybe very influential alcoholism; his poems of love for his mother and pleas for her forgiveness – written after her death.

For all Angie's reminiscences, of course, there was no real love story to tell – but there *was* a truly psychologically revealing, truly dramatic story to be told: that of George's three weeks drying out in an alcoholics' clinic in the Californian desert.

And this became the core of my screenplay . . .

DISSOLVE TO:

FILM EXCERPT: ***The Best***

EXT HAYWARD CLINIC – CALIFORNIA – DAY – 1981

George has successfully completed his three-week stint as a teetotaller – and got a medal from the clinic's director to prove it.

Angie [now the long-suffering Mrs Best] and the coach of the San Jose football team that George wants to join, have insisted on George drying out. To both of them it's George's very last chance.

Angie has arranged to pick him up and take him home – now a reformed and officially cured drunk.

He comes out of the entrance, suitcase in hand, and makes his way to the gate. He puts the case down and leans on the wall with his forearms to wait for Angie.

A truck lumbers along the road and stops opposite the gate. The trucker leans out of his cab window.

TRUCKER
(*Manchester accent*)
Hey, can you direct me to –

He stares at George incredulously.

Jesus! *Are you who I think you are?*

GEORGE
Probably.

TRUCKER
I can't believe it!

GEORGE
I have a little trouble with that, myself, sometimes.

TRUCKER
I'm from Manchester! I used to watch you! Alan Walton. Cheetham Hill Road.

GEORGE
Small world.

TRUCKER
Jesus ...

GEORGE
Where did you want to get to?

TRUCKER
Hayward Village.

GEORGE

About a mile down the road.

TRUCKER

(*shaking his head*)

George Best in the middle of nowhere! Want a beer? I've two hundred crates of beer on here. Some get sort of mislaid. Have a drink on me, Georgie.

He produces a bottle of beer from the cab, whips off the top and hands it down to George.

GEORGE

Cheers.

He drinks. The trucker is still shaking his head in happy bewilderment.

TRUCKER

So what brings you out here, Georgie?

We hear a car approaching. It's Angie's – with Angie at the wheel. CU her face, as from her POV, we see George drinking from the bottle.

Angie stops the car dead. She stares at George at the gate. A long moment.

ANGIE

(*to herself*)

Goodbye, George. That's it.

WIDE SHOT EXT HAYWARD CLINIC: Angie's car slowly approaches George. He smiles, glad to see her, picks up his suitcase, waves goodbye to the trucker and starts towards the car – but Angie reverses it in the driveway, puts her foot down in both senses, and roars off back to LA, leaving George stranded helplessly at the gate.

JACK (VO)

A true story. Columbia Pictures, however, decided not to make the film – 'We've already made an alcoholic movie this year, and, anyway, we really wanted The Greatest Love Story Ever Told.'

(*beat*)

Or, as it would turn out, *never* told . . .

DISSOLVE TO:

INT WARD – VICTORIA HOSPITAL – BLACKPOOL – DAY – 1986

Jack's brother David's wife, Eileen, lies in bed, jaundiced, tearful and frightened. She has cancer.

Amy and Adam stand one on each side of her bed.

EILEEN

I'm going to die. I'm going to die. I'm going to die. I'm going to die.

AMY

You're not.

ADAM

You won't die.

They hold her hands and try to smile comforting smiles. And they stand there for three and a half *hours. David and Jack shamefacedly nip out every now and then for cartons of tea and a fag. But Amy and Adam stay and tell her about school and what they and their pals have been up to. It's the most grown-up thing they've ever instinctively done and Jack's moved to tears of pride.*

JACK (VO)

Eileen died two weeks later. Childless herself, she'd always adored Amy and Adam. Sometimes fiery-tempered, sometimes *very* fiery-tempered, she had a tough childhood herself, in Larne, Northern Ireland.

After marrying David, her almost-religious priority in life was paying off the mortgage. To do it, she hoarded every penny David earned – and, working as a barman or casual labourer-gardener, he never earned much more than one and a half to rub together; she did without comforts let alone luxuries, lived spartanly and died with her mortgage paid off, no debts and a sacrosanct, untouchable £30,000 in the bank.

She had never been genuinely accepted by Lakey, tolerated at best. But, surprisingly, she was accepted by Sam. Except for one Easter, which also happened to fall at Passover time . . .

FLASHBACK TO:

INT THE ROSENTHAL DINING ROOM – BLACKPOOL – NIGHT – MID-1960S

Sam, David, Eileen and Jack are at the table, part-way through the candlelit Seder Night ritual. Before each of them on the blindingly white tablecloth are glasses of wine (and one for the angel, Elijah) and Hagaddahs (the Passover prayer books).

Lakey is serving the traditional dish of cold hard-boiled eggs in salt water. (Delicious, though it doesn't sound it. Refreshing. Why don't we have it on any other night?)

JACK
The soup was terrific, Mum.

LAKEY
Ta.

SAM
(*curtly*)
The best soup comes from Israel.

Everyone looks at him, puzzled.

And meat.

Everyone shares bewildered glances.

And spuds.

Everyone's at the head-scratching stage.

LAKEY
What the hell are you rambling about, you daft bugger?

SAM
And *pullovers*. The best pullovers in the world come from Israel.

JACK (VO)
It finally dawned on me – this was Sam's revenge for Eileen having gone to Mass that morning. Sam, the most irreligious of men, was trying to level the score – Catholics one, Jews one.

(*beat*)
Pullovers, **though . . . ?**

INT FIRE STATION APPLIANCE ROOM – LONDON – DAY – 1986

Bells urgently clang, firefighters slide swiftly down their pole and climb into two fire engines (officially known as 'machines') and change rapidly if awkwardly into firefighting rig as the drivers start the engines.

The fire station's automatic doors concertina open and the machines race out into the street.

During this:

JACK (VO)
The idea for writing ***London's Burning*** **really began years earlier when our Swiss au-pair girl, Ruth, married Les, a London fireman.**

They lived with us for a year, and almost every day Les had adventures to tell us, some heart-rending, some hilarious. All

of them re-creating the unique and uniquely dramatic world of the fire brigade.

EXT STREETS – LONDON – DAY – 1986 (CONT)

Panic-stricken cars swerve onto the pavements, slamming on their brakes to let the two red juggernauts pass, sirens howling, blue lamps flashing.

JACK (VO)

For a firefighter, going to work might mean going into a literal hell of pitch-black, lung-shrivelling smoke and searing infernos – and melted corpses – and often being lucky to come out alive themselves.

INT A FIERCELY-BURNING BUILDING – DAY – 1986 (CONT)

Firefighters, wearing breathing apparatus, battle through engulfing flames.

JACK (VO)

To keep sane – or insane enough to do the job they do – firefighters devote the other half of their brain to inventing what they call 'wheezes'. Practical jokes, to us.

DISSOLVE TO:

FILM EXCERPT: ***London's Burning***

EXT STREET OUTSIDE FIRE STATION – DAY

A small queue stands at the bus stop. Near the feet of the last man in the queue is a £5 note. He glances at the others to see if they've noticed it. Satisfied that they haven't, he bends down as nonchalantly as possible to pick it up.

Just as his fingers are closing over it, it flutters away from him and settles down at the feet of a woman in the queue. As the man goes for it, she bends down to pick it up. It promptly flutters away again.

A youth tries to grab it. It dances away from him – and as they all try to catch it in mid-air, it swoops away and up to a window in the fire station.

The queue watches open-mouthed as the fiver dances into:

INT MESS/KITCHEN – FIRE STATION – DAY (CONT)

Amid schoolboy whoops of glee, the firefighters haul in a thin wire to which the fiver's attached.

JACK (VO)

This double life of extremes – tragedy and farce, heroism and silliness – breeds more opposites: a compassion for the victims of fires – and none at all for each other.

ANGLE ON MORE FIREFIGHTERS, seated round the Mess table eating.

A firefighter, wolfing his statutory (and beloved) cheese and onion roll, wouldn't dream of saying he had a headache or couldn't afford his mortgage or his wife had left him. At best, he'd get half a dozen Coke cans hurled straight at his headache, he'd be told to go and live in a tent and his mates would ask for his wife's new phone number.

INT STUDY – THE GENTLEMAN'S RESIDENCE – MUSWELL HILL – DAY – 1986

Jack is typing at his computer.

JACK (VO)

Over the years, Les told me his stories, and then, in October 1985, the Broadwater Farm riot down the road in Tottenham became their dramatic framework: a fictional centre that could make the fact all the more true.

That centre is Ethnic – a character who is (as many are) both black and a firefighter; who feels loyalty both to his ghetto community and to his fire station community, and who becomes the pivot of extremes and colliding opposites. That's why Ethnic was born – and why, at the end of the film, he dies.

INT MESS/KITCHEN – FIRE STATION – DAY – 1986

The film unit is shooting a scene from London's Burning. *Firefighters eating, drinking, playing cards, winding each other up around the Mess table . . . Bayleaf (played by the subtly superb Jimmy Hazeldine), Vaseline (Mark Arden), Ethnic (Gary McDonald), Charisma (Gerard Horan), Sicknote (Richard Walsh) and Josie (Katherine Rogers).*

The director, Les Blair, stands watching. Jack is beside him . . . but, happily for a change, not beside himself.

JACK (VO)

Throughout the filming it seemed that Les Blair and I could well be a perfect match. Both from similar Manchester backgrounds, we spoke the same language. I thought he was directing beautifully and I really believed I'd found the director for all my future work.

Until, that is . . .

(*sighs*)

Here we go again.

INT EDITING ROOM – LONDON – DAY – 1986

On the Steenbeck editing screen, we see the footage shot in the previous scene – and quietly spoken Les is yelling at the top of his voice. At Jack.

JACK (VO)

. . . until, as usual, we were in editing and I, as usual, gave notes and the director, as usual, went berserk because the writer had the effrontery to voice his comments.

LES BLAIR

No one tells me *how to edit a comedy sequence*!

JACK

Even if you're wrong?

JACK (VO)

On *P'Tang, Yang Kipperbang* with its big-time director, Mike Apted, its very big-time producer, David Puttnam, had paid Jack to sit in editing and shoot his mouth off. However, the otherwise excellent producer of London's Burning and friend of Jack's, Paul Knight, has a different idea: to ban Jack from the editing room. Later, not quite too late, the executive producer, Linda Agran, Jack's great ally, bans Paul from banning.

Then it was *my* turn to go berserk, when Les let slip that he'd never shot what, to me, was one of the most crucial scenes in the film – and maybe its whole *raison d'être*.

Ethnic's character gave me the chance to try and explore the deprivation and bitterness of ghetto life; and to show how they flare into petty street violence, and that violence into cold-blooded, hot-blooded, meaningless murder. To try and understand from both points of view. And to offer the viewers of *London's Burning*, if not an understanding, then, at least the fact that there's something we have to understand and do something about. Or live (or die) to regret it.

The missing scene is this:

DISSOLVE TO:

INT COMMUNITY HALL – BLACK GHETTO – DAY

(A petrol-bomb bottle has been pushed through the letterbox at Ethnic's mother's flat and has burst into violent flame. Ethnic has managed to get

his mum, Beatrice, out of the house, and while he deals with the fire, she has run, tears streaming down her face, to the safety of the Community Hall.)

Beatrice is seated, trembling with shock, at a trestle table, clutching a cup of tea. Seated around her are her friend, Rose, two middle-aged women and an elderly man, in silent sympathy.

At the back of the hall others are playing dominoes.

BEATRICE

Why firemen? Why firemen, Rose?

ROSE

Boys aroun here, a whole heap act crazy sometimes ...

1ST WOMAN

A whole heap aroun de *world* act crazy these days. Go anywhere, all de same.

BEATRICE

But firemen ent policemen. Firemen don't give no one bad time. Jus' put out de fires. Save people. Is bobbylan dey hate.

A pause.

2ND WOMAN

T'ain't *all* hate policeman.

1ST WOMAN

T'ain't *all* policeman give us bad time.

2ND WOMAN

Rest. If you're *youth* an' you're lime in de street, you get bad time. They think they *all* bad.

ROSE

Policeman have his work to do.

2ND WOMAN

Youth have *none*. No work to do. You reason with me? Is one vicious thing.

BEATRICE

Maybe *my* boy hang aroun after this. Maybe I tell him stop being fireman.

ROSE

No, Bea.

BEATRICE

Why firemen? It don't make sense.

ROSE

Not one piece of it make sense.

ELDERLY MAN

Cha! Of course it does! You stick a bunch of rats in a cage, good rats, bad rats, they got nothin to eat, what gonna happen den? They go crazy, they eat each *other*. Them that ain't so crazy get their flesh chewed off first. White rats, black rats, all de same.

(*beat*)

All de same underneath. Same white bones picked clean.

(*beat*)

Either you open de cage, or you throw in some cheese.

(*beat*)

Or maybe . . . they chew through de bars with their sharp white teeth. And what den?

A long, bleak silence.

DISSOLVE TO:

EXT RODEO DRIVE – LA – DAY – 1987

In baking, blinding sunshine, expensive limos, even more expensive sports cars – and their even more expensive owners – cruise along the almost Champs-Elysées-wide street, past boutiques, jewellers' treasure troves, fashion houses and exotic restaurants. A street that makes Bond Street look like Flat Iron Market.

Jack limps along the pavement, pretending not to be impressed.

JACK (VO)

Some people work their way through Hollywood. Some con their way through it. I had a spell *eating* my way through it.

He goes into a restaurant.

INT RESTAURANT – RODEO DRIVE – DAY – 1987 (CONT)

Jack is having lunch, alfresco, with Jane Fonda and her manager. Both the restaurant and Jane are stunningly though understatedly glamorous. Jack and her manager perhaps a little less so.

JANE

I guess what I'm really looking for is a buddy movie. Let's brainstorm for a few days.

JACK

Certainly . . . um . . . Jane.

INT JANE FONDA'S OFFICE – LA – DAY – 1987

Jane is showing Jack display cabinet after display cabinet after display cabinet of the shimmering, sparkling, glittering prizes she's won – from Oscars downwards.

She and Jack get on well together, like a couple of old buddies themselves, but the brainstorming gets nowhere.

INT HOTEL RESTAURANT – LA – DAY – 1987

The next engagement in Jack's eating schedule. He comes into the dining room and is shown to Sally Field's table. They greet each other, Jack sits and they start pre-brainstorming chat.

During this:

JACK (VO)

Eating, of course, began with breakfast. But, this was Sally's *second* business breakfast of the day – and she was scheduled for a third. En route, she was looking for an idea for a movie. *Any* idea, really. Once again, I didn't come up with one.

INT SUBURBAN HOUSE – LA – NIGHT – 1987

Jack is having Friday night dinner in the homely home of Wendy Fineman's mom, pop and siblings. Wendy is a young, seemingly scatty, fair-haired independent movie producer.

JACK (VO)

Wendy would achieve her fifteen seconds of fame some years later when she swept on stage to pick up her Oscar for Best Film (the appalling *Forrest Gump*) – so maybe she wasn't so scatty after all.

We were working on an idea of mine called *Family Matters*. The script was written but, you've guessed it, the film was never made. The dinner was delicious.

EXT VENTURA BOULEVARD – LA – DAY – 1987

Another day, another breakfast. Jack shuffles his way into the Arts Deli at number 12224.

INT ARTS DELI – LA – DAY – 1987 (CONT)

David Puttnam picks uninterestedly at his Canadian bacon, grilled tomato and English muffin, while filling Jack in on the situation he's in. He's here, he hopes, incognito, almost in hiding, almost on the run.

The howitzers of Hollywood's immensely powerful, back-scratching, million-dollar back-handing guardians of the status quo are pointed straight at him. Now at Columbia, he's had the temerity to question the wheeler-dealing and challenge the industry to finance creativity as opposed to agents' and studio executives' Acapulco penthouses.

Consequently, as in any third-rate Tinseltown detective movie, they're having him followed wherever he goes, investigated, to try and find any dirt and run him out of town.

JACK (VO)

They failed. He was Persil-white. And eventually *strolled* out of town of his own accord.

The other reason for our secret breakfast was for him to tell me how much he loved a screenplay he'd commissioned from me, an adaptation of the superb Portuguese novel *Gabriela: Clove and Cinnamon.* It was to be directed by Roland Joffe, who also loved it. As did Columbia.

Unfortunately, after David left Columbia, Universal had the rights – and they *didn't* love it at all. More sort of hated it. But not enough to let it go to another studio

End of same old story . . .

EXT PATRICK MOORE'S GARDEN – SUSSEX – LATE AFTERNOON – 1987

At first sight, it seems populated with Epstein statues. In fact, they're different kinds of telescopes – some old and cherished, others state of the art. This is Patrick Moore's observatory. He's showing Adam round and letting him peer through the lenses at the gradually darkening sky.

JACK (VO)

Adam was much more star-struck than his dad. But by *real* stars. I'd wangled an invitation from Patrick and Adam had the afternoon of his life – tea and biscuits with an astronomy fanatic and a cricket fanatic at the same time.

EXT PATIO – THE GENTLEMAN'S RESIDENCE – MUSWELL HILL – NIGHT – 1987

As opposed to Patrick's garden, on this garden's patio there's one small, amateur telescope on its wonky tripod. Adam is squinting through the eyepiece. Jack stands watching him. Suddenly:

ADAM

(*yelling excitedly*)

I can see the craters on the moon! As though they're only yards away!

Jack's puzzled – but only for a moment. The lad's pointing the telescope not at the moon, but at next-door's wall *– which* is *only yards away, he's right.*

ADAM

All the craters! Hundreds of 'em! It's fantastic!

Next-door's wall is pebbledashed. He's looking at little pebbledash hollows. Well, even Patrick Moore probably started somewhere.

EXT A RESIDENTIAL STREET – LONDON – DAY – 1987

A film unit is shooting the incomparable Warren Mitchell as the gaffer, with his team of removal men playing a scene while (avoiding) humping furniture from their removals van.

Watching it – apart from a group of extras standing to one side, eating bacon baps – is the vastly skilled, vastly experienced director, Jack Gold; the other Jack, of course, at his shoulder.

Warren is playing a character called Bamber, an obsessed but completely incompetent evening-class student of philosophy.

The film – feature film this time – is The Chain, *the story of a gang of removal men clod-hopping their way through a full circle of seven emotional dramas in seven streets; a London* La Ronde *of people moving house, each character leading to the next in a chain of the Seven Deadly Sins, which are the motivating forces behind each move. They take us from Hackney to Tufnell Park to Willesden to Hammersmith to Hampstead to Holland Park to Knightsbridge – and back to Hackney . . .*

DISSOLVE TO:

FILM EXCERPT: *The Chain*

EXT REMOVALS FIRM DEPOT – DAY

It's the end of the working day. Bamber and his team (Nick, Paul and Tornado – so-called because he sleeps through life) leave the depot and start through the yard for home.

Tonight's the night of Bamber's big evening-class exam and Nick has been arm-twisted into testing him from his grubby exercise book of scribbled philosophy notes.

Nick peers at the name on the page.

NICK

I can't pronounce him.

BAMBER

Vico. Giambattista Vico.

NICK

Irishman, was he?

BAMBER

Now, what he's saying, the point he's making, his point is ... is there's birth and growing, then decaying, then what we call rebirth and regrowing again.

PAUL

Well, that's cobblers, innit? Who gets reborn? Who that *we* know?

NICK

(*to Bamber*)

Come on, head down. He sums it up, how?

BAMBER

(*concentrating*)

He sums it up ... like if you leave your doorstep and travel as far as you can, well, all you do is wind up on your own doorstep again, what you started from.

TORNADO

What – even if you travel right round the world?

BAMBER

Well, of course. Bound to, en't you? World's round, innit? What he's getting at, really, is that it takes the whole journey ... all your life and that ... to get to know *yourself*, what you're about.

PAUL

I know what I'll be about tonight, darling. Few Guinness down the pub till leg-over time, then trousers down and –

BAMBER

I don't want to know.

He takes the exercise book from Nick and stuffs it in his pocket. They walk on.

TORNADO

I'll tell you a rum thing. I once knew a bloke called Torvill.

NICK

What?

TORNADO

Vic Torvill. No relation, I don't think. He had all Rosemary Clooney's records and a drooping eyelid.

DISSOLVE TO:

EXT RESIDENTIAL STREET – LONDON – DAY – 1987

The film unit comes to the end of a take.

JACK GOLD

Cut! One more, for luck.

As the crew, actors and extras regroup for another take, the unit's 3rd assistant comes running out of a house, in which the production office is installed, some fifty yards down the street.

3RD ASSISTANT

(*calling*)

Phone call for you, Jack!

JACK GOLD

Okay.

He starts towards the house.

3RD ASSISTANT

(*hastily*)

No, no, not you, Jack. Jack Rosenthal.

Jack, the director, stops and Jack, the writer, starts for the house.

Hang about! Not you, either! The *other* Jack Rosenthal!

Now Jack, the writer, stops. Then one of the extras peels away from his mates.

EXTRA

(*calling*)

Right with you, Precious.

And Jack Rosenthal, the extra, strides off to the production office to take his call.

INT STUDY – THE GENTLEMAN'S RESIDENCE – MUSWELL HILL – NIGHT – 1988

Jack is seated at his desk, beckoning a tortoise to walk across it. It does so . . . um, slowly . . . then clambers over the computer keyboard and into the screen – where it dissolves into a page of typed script.

JACK (VO)

The story of the saving of Zuckerman's life finally became a TV script. I took it to Channel 4, suggesting a series of six plays, of which *Tortoise* would be one, and the rest to be written by five established writers. Channel 4 yelled an enthusiastic, 'Yes!', commissioned them, weren't so enthusiastic about some of them and cancelled the whole project.

The computer screen crashes – just as the virtual image of the tortoise returns into its 3-D reality mode, which slithers out, back down the keyboard and back across the desk.

JACK (VO)

***Tortoise* continued creeping forward and back again throughout the rest of the twentieth century and well into the 21st – now with two other scripts on its back. En route it met a Scouse BBC executive who gave all three a kiss of life (with tongues), then manically jumped on them in hobnailed Doc Martens.**

DISSOLVE TO:

FILM EXCERPT: *Bag Lady*

EXT WEST END STREETS – LONDON – DAY

Meandering a lonely path through the rush-hour commuters shlurries a bag lady. Sixty years old, cocooned in random layers of men's and women's clothes scrabbled from dustbins. Her coat is tied with string. On top of her long, frizzy, grey hair is a once-smart, now ridiculous, dilapidated hat.

She clutches six or seven bags (carrier bags, cloth and plastic) in her mittened hands. She's very dirty and more than a bit deranged.

As she walks, she talks to herself aloud. Occasional outbursts are directed at passers-by. They either ignore her or jerk apprehensively away to dodge past her – and her smell.

During this:

JACK (VO)

After adapting CP Taylor's stage play *And A Nightingale Sang* for television, starring Joan Plowright, I wrote what I thought was the best script I'd ever written — and still do. It was called *Bag Lady,* an episode in Maureen's TV series, *About Face,* in which she played six different, *entirely* different, characters. As the bag lady, she gave a performance even better than the 'best' script, a virtuoso half-hour monologue and a performance of definitive, heart-breaking

brilliance and truth. Certainly, for me, the most unforgettable performance I've ever seen.

During her West End wanderings, bit by bit, in seemingly disconnected dribs and drabs, echoes and non-sequiturs, we piece together how she ever became a bag lady, the events that dragged her from fairly normal normality to near-madness, from a carefree life to an engulfing 28-year-long obsession and every-day-long, year-long, 28-year-long loneliness.

Her obsession is to find her one possession, her bed, put into storage all those years ago. In her addled mind, she believes the Prime Minister has it . . .

EXT WHITEHALL – DAY

She wanders along counting her steps.

BAG LADY

Go and see the Prime Minister now. Made my bed, want to lie in it . . .

The policeman, standing on the other side of the barrier, arms folded, tells her she's got the wrong address and sends her on her way.

I only want my bed back. I get fed up looking. Will you ask the Prime Minister can I please have it back now?

(*helplessly weeping*)

And p'raps the lampshade with the tassels. Or is that being greedy?

EXT SHAFTESBURY AVENUE – EVENING

The bag lady shoulders her way through the theatregoers and commuters on their way home, the evening version of the opening scene.

BAG LADY

I didn't know what Wilfred was on about at first. 'I'm leaving you and marrying her and I'm taking Rosemary 'cos Dr Bullimore says you're not a fit mother and you're not a fit wife since she was born, 'cos you always say no, and you always said yes to your Polish airmen and Yanks and corporals in the Free French.' And I said, 'Who told you that?' And he said, 'And everything's in my name so you get nothing. For mental cruelty.'

(*beat*)

It was Marjorie, I bet. Getting her own back. For me pinching Whatsisname, Stanislav, the Polish airman, off her. Which I didn't. *He* pinched *me*.

(*beat*)

So then what you do is walk round and round, doing what your dad always said: 'Never give up. Always be brave.' Though he did neither. Just cleared off and left us. I still miss my dad. He smelled of warm. Warm and Woodbines. But it's going round in circles really, 'cos you never find the Prime Minister ...

And then she does. Or thinks she does. At the end of an alleyway she spots a van stopped at the traffic lights. On its side are the words: 'MacMillan Furniture Storage, 355 Uxbridge Rd, W12'. She begins to tremble – so that's where the Prime Minister really lives ...

She trudges off to W12, repeating the number of the street with each step.

EXT MACMILLAN STORAGE DEPOT – NIGHT

Still trembling, exhausted, the bag lady presses the night-bell. A young warehouseman, earringed, head-cropped and tattooed, opens the door. She tries to explain – it was July 1961, she hasn't got a ticket any more, but there's a bed and a lamp with tassels in her name, the headboard's walnut, Waring and Gillow.

INT MACMILLAN STORAGE DEPOT – NIGHT

A vast warehouse filled with stacks of stored furniture of all styles and periods, arranged between long aisles and labelled for owner-identification.

In the middle of the stacks is the bag lady, settling down to sleep, snuggled up on a couple of sacks on the bare springs of a walnut bed. A tasselled lampshade stands beside it.

The warehouseman treads softly towards her.

WAREHOUSEMAN

You say nothing to no bugger, alright?

She smiles, eyes closed.

You come back each night and scarper each morning first thing.

She seems asleep.

'Night, then.

He tiptoes away.

BAG LADY

(*drifting into sleep*)

Goodnight, Stanislav.

CAM pulls back . . . Surrounded by acres of furniture, we see the one tiny figure on her bed . . . like the world's last survivor on a raft, in the middle of an endless ocean.

DISSOLVE TO:

EXT SYDNEY HARBOUR – AUSTRALIA – DAY – 1989

Another Maureen performance which is even more, much, much more unforgettable to the great British public – and probably will be as long as the suffix, ''ology', exists – is her role of Beattie in the British Telecom commercials. All 53 of them.

She's now in Sydney, where, in between Mancunian downpours, a film unit is shooting number 54.

EXT SEBEL TOWNHOUSE HOTEL – SYDNEY – DAY – 1989

With Maureen, just for the trip, is the rest of the family. Maureen, Amy and Adam go into the hotel entrance, wincing and grimacing in sympathy with Jack who's wincing and grimacing with each step, now limping more than ever, hip locked, following on behind.

Also staying at the Townhouse are Mike Parkinson (Jack's mate from their Granada days), Roald Dahl – and one other person who, as far as Amy and Adam are concerned, is the only one that matters, possibly in the world, apart from Jason Donovan.

INT CORRIDOR – TOWNHOUSE HOTEL – SYDNEY – NIGHT – 1989

JACK (VO)

And that, of course, was Kylie Minogue.

Amy and Adam are strolling with appallingly badly acted nonchalance past a bedroom door, first one way, then about-turning the other way. Each clutches a sheet of paper and a pen.

JACK (VO)

They lay in wait to ambush her for what seemed like days, not even knowing whether she'd be coming out or going in.

Kylie Minogue comes out of her room.

Ah! Coming out.

Very respectfully, very diffidently but with rather better-acted nonchalance, they ask for her autograph. She grins and obliges. Their cup brimmeth over.

INT HALL – QUEEN'S COLLEGE – HARLEY STREET – LONDON – NIGHT – 1989

A school musical in progress. On stage, grease-painted girls are throwing themselves into Anne of Green Gables. *In the body of the packed hall, kvelling parents smile and nudge each other and mouth the words their daughters are delivering. And who's playing Anne? And whose parents are kvelling more than the rest? Star-struck Amy in red ringlets. The year before she'd been disappointed (for which, read 'heartbroken') at being overlooked for* The Boyfriend. *This year she's landed the lead.*

JACK (VO)

It goes without saying she was terrific. As a singer – maybe . . . possibly – she left a little something to be desired, but as an actress . . .

(*beat*)

I'm saying it just the same. She was terrific.

INT WEST LONDON SYNAGOGUE – LONDON – DAY – 1989

The synagogue is packed like a West End first night with congregants, relatives and friends. On the front row, in the best seats, are Maureen, Jack, Zelma, Amy, David and Maureen's Auntie Rita. Maurice, sadly, is too unwell to be here . . . on probably the proudest day of his life, Adam's big day – his bar mitzvah.

Adam stands on the bimah with the shul's much-loved rabbi, Hugo Gryn. He's chanting his Portion of the Law – and half of Hugo's prayers for good measure – word-perfect, beautifully, with feeling and meaning. Like a grown man.

JACK (VO)

. . . Which was only as it should be, I suppose, since this was the day he traditionally became one.

Adam gives the decade a heartwarming send-off. The kids are growing up. Maureen is growing in fame and stature. And Jack? Maybe growing sort of sideways . . .

POSTSCRIPT

by Maureen Lipman

Those who are near me do not know
That you are nearer to me than they are.
They who speak to me do not know
That my heart is full of your unspoken words.
They who crowd in my path do not know
That I am walking alone with you.
They who love me do not know
That their love brings you to my heart.

Rabindranath Tagore

INT MUSWELL HILL HOUSE – MID-AFTERNOON – AUGUST 2004

Outside the sun shines.

The woman, Maureen, tall, bespectacled, long-necked, chunky-hipped, is standing up from her armchair, tears coursing down her cheeks, fist raised.

MAUREEN
(*shouting*)

Yes!

She is alone in front of the TV. It's 21 August 2004 and the coxless four have just won their gold medal at the Olympics. Maureen couldn't care less about rowing, coxless or – er – coxed, but she is caught up in a rare moment of national pride and empathy with Matthew Pinsett's even rarer moment of tired emotionalism.

It is seven weeks and four days since her husband, Jack Rosenthal, died in the North London Hospice after a two year battle against Multiple Myeloma.

MAUREEN

Stoppit. Just stoppit. You've to toughen up. You can't spend the rest of your life crying. You've to get on.

She makes a funny inward squeak in her throat. She's been doing this a lot lately. It's like a bird asking for food. A phone rings. She answers it.

MAUREEN

Hello. Oh, hi Elaine. Really? It was, wasn't it? It was lovely having both of you. No, actually. It wasn't that hard. I've just finished clearing up and I'm going to start on Jack's book. I know. I keep on talking about it and not doing it and the publisher rang first thing. He just wants me to try to touch on the last decade, you know, the one Jack didn't get to . . . well, he sort of ran out of steam really. I don't know, it could have been the illness – but, I mean, he wrote frantically right through the first year – right through the chemo and the stem-cell transplant. When? Oh God, I think . . . I can't remember when he stopped. Or why. He just sort of lost confidence in it . . . I know, I know. Anyway, listen, I'd best get on. Thanks again for the dessert . . . no, it was a huge pleasure. Talk soon, bye.

She goes back into the kitchen, wipes the surface with a medicated wipe and unstacks the dishwasher of last night's pots. She catches sight of herself in a silver placemat.

MAUREEN (VO)

I look fine. This is a good haircut. Manageable. I don't look old. Fat though. Comfort eating. I should go to the gym each day. I hate it though. The gym is hell; set faces, ugly music. I'll have to go, though. You'd want me to, wouldn't you, darl?

She finishes off last night's aubergine crisps. The phone rings. She hesitates. The machine will answer it. She should pick up Jack's manuscript and get on with it . . . Endless procrastination. She gives in and answers the phone.

MAUREEN

Hello. Oh, hi love. Yes, it was, wasn't it? Thank you. No, thank *you*. No, I've nearly got it all cleared away.

Her voice fades out and we pull back to watch her putting the dishes away, the phone still wedged to her ear.

MAUREEN (VO)

Jack would have unloaded the dishwasher and had the kitchen shipshape three hours ago. I'd have come down at 10.30 in the morning, bleary, and he'd have said 'Alright, love. I've made a start at it. I know it doesn't look like it, but I've shifted a helluva lot. This is the second load.'

MAUREEN

Yeah, I've got to make a start on Jack's book . . . it's really weighing on me that I haven't . . .

MAUREEN (VO)

He loved it when we entertained – never much wanted to go out. 'Jack's idea of a good night out is staying in' was my staple phrase. If I'd depended on him for our social life we'd never have left the front porch. But he was such good value when we got there. Such a wonderfully lively guest. Deadpan comments, self-deprecating stories – I'd interrupt because I'd

remember them differently and wanted them built-up in the way I first heard them. He never minded my contradictions, like some husbands do – no face-darkening, wait-till-we-get-home glowering; he was proud of my vivacity. We were a good couple.

FLASHBACK TO:

INT JACK'S CAR – NIGHT – ANY OLD YEAR

Jack and Maureen are driving home from a party.

JACK

You were on fantastic form tonight.

MAUREEN

Me? What about you?

JACK

Not like you. You lighten the room up. I love it when you do that 'Professor of Logic' joke.

MAUREEN

You don't! Even when you've heard it so many times?

JACK

It doesn't matter. I just love it. Give me your glasses love.

(*He beams at her*)

I don't know how you can see a thing through them.

At the traffic lights, he takes her rimless specs, breathes on them heavily, buffs the lenses with his pocket hanky and hands them back.It's as natural as changing gear. If he doesn't do it, they stay dirty.

MAUREEN (VO)

The thing is, I don't think I believe he's gone. It's just a part I'm playing. The play will end its run soon.

(*beat*)

I was good in it. Everyone said so.

INT HOOP LANE CEMETERY CHAPEL – DAY – 31 MAY 2004

It is a beautiful sun-drenched day. The chapel is packed. Maureen wears a black suit and hat. Amy and Adam sit by her side. A violinist plays Massenet's Meditation *from* Thais, *very much in the middle-European style. Amy and Maureen squeeze each other's hands. They are remembering Jack's late-in-life, self-taught violin playing. He had all the right requisites for a violinist, the Russian heavy-lidded eyes, the soulfulness – he looked like a violinist. He just couldn't help sounding like a violently braking bus. What was enchanting in a five-year-old Suzuki star was hilarious in a furrowed-browed 55-year-old .*

FLASHBACK TO:

INT DUKES AVE – VICTORIAN TERRACED HOUSE – MUSWELL HILL – DAY – 1985

Jack in his study, glasses on head. In front of him is a music stand, on which rests Songs from the First World War. *He opens it to 'Kiss me Goodnight, Sergeant Major' and addresses an unknown spectator.*

JACK

Right then, Zuckerman, what do you fancy now? 'The Sun Has Got His Hat On' or 'There'll be Bluebirds Over . . . ?'

Camera pans down to register Zuckerman, the family tortoise. Headless in an insulated box, surrounded by herrings, apricots out-of-season, and chopped cucumber. She (for it has been discovered by the reptile expert that he, Zuckerman is, in fact, she) is lit overhead by an ultra-violet lamp. Like every February, for many years, she's woken too early with a frozen brain. Jack is trying to revive her interest in life.

INT HOOP LANE CEMETERY CHAPEL – DAY – MAY 2004

AMY

It *feels* a bit like Dod.

MAUREEN

He's nudging her elbow.

Maureen glances down at the Rabbi. He has a huge surgical appliance on his foot, like a ski boot. She'd asked him about it earlier: he said he had a blister on his foot and the boot stopped any pressure being put on it. She'd smiled wanly and said, 'In my day they gave you an Elastoplast.'

MAUREEN (VO)

Between the violinist and the boot I felt strangely light-headed. Almost giggly. I caught the eye of a friend, Linda Agran, and saw her nostrils widen. Some of Jack's levity was in the room. I knew that from now on I'd be looking for signs of his still being around.

(*beat*)

First thing that morning I'd asked him for a sign – to get me through the ceremony. Almost immediately, the phone rang. It was the violinist. I'd asked her to play Jack's favourite piece, Bruch's *Violin Concerto*, the one he'd chosen to take to his Desert Island, and she was ringing to say it really needed a

piano accompaniment. She wondered if there was a piano there?

INT MAUREEN'S BEDROOM – MUSWELL HILL – DAY – MAY 2004

Maureen is in the bedroom, surrounded by a Greek chorus of daughter Amy, ex-housekeeper Esperanza and her daughter Lina, and other, dark-clad, women friends, all pinning her into a black dress and moving feathers from one hat to another. Maureen is on the phone.

MAUREEN

A piano? I don't think so . . . It's a cemetery.

(*beat*)

I beg your pardon? The what instead?

(*beat*)

Massenet's *Meditation* from *Thais*. Oh my G—

(*she sits down on the bed, poleaxed*)

Yes! I'm so happy! Thank you . . . Yes. Play that! Play that!

Maureen puts the phone down and announces excitedly:

If that's not a sign, I don't know what is!

The Greek Chorus exchange worried looks.

MAUREEN (VO)

The violinist was a stranger and not to know that the Massenet was the Act 1 curtain music of Amy's first play *Sitting Pretty*, when shy, overweight Nancy, finds herself, inadvertently, modelling nude in a life-drawing class. In theatres all around the country I'd watched the emotional heat rise, as Nancy transmogrified from a Munch to a Reubens, to the swell of the Massenet *Meditation*.

I knew we'd be alright now. We'd get through it. But Adam and I both knew we wouldn't be able to stand up and speak about him. We couldn't. Amy was the amazing one. Amy, who falls apart if a friend delays returning a text message, quite calmly said 'It's OK, I'll do it.'

INT HOOP LANE CEMETERY CHAPEL – DAY – MAY 2004

Amy stands at the lectern.

AMY

Even as I search for these words it is so unreal that the man who would have helped me to find them isn't here to ask. Isn't here in his usual chair with a cup of what he called 'Reality Coffee' and a square of hazelnut chocolate, looking up as I come in and saying 'Hello Gribbiny'. And I can't stand watching over his shoulder with my usual thrilled trepidation as he, the great writer, begins to read. Knowing that although he might draw a pedantic line under my grammatical errors, at the end he will put down the pages and look up at me, his beautiful melancholy eyes radiating love, and say 'Amela. How do you *know* all this?'

Well, I know all this because of him. My father, my friend, whose guidance and patience and unending, uncritical love has taught me everything I know about anything. Who, when Adam and I were little, got up with us every morning at an ungodly, Dodly, hour to peruse the children's encyclopaedia and tell us the meanings of words. Who instilled in us a love of language and appreciation of beauty from the earliest age. Who would carry me, as a tiny baby, from painting to painting on the walls of our flat in Rosslyn Hill, pointing out the details, teaching me how to look and how to see. I remember that clearly, thirty years on, and I will remember everything.

How he painstakingly guided us through our homework and school projects, rousing us from listless uninterest with his own beaming enthusiasm: 'Right! Let's attack this Trigonometry lark! We're not going to let it beat us! Boom-boom-boom!' How he made packed lunches not just for me but for my school friends, teaching us to spread the butter and the filling right to the edges so that you never get a mouthful of dry bread.

My Dod was a saint, but he was an eccentric saint, an offbeat angel with his feet on the ground and a heart the size of Old Trafford. He was and will always be an example to us, for he showed us how people should be treated, with warmth and compassion and care. His relationship with our exceptional mother, the fun and the friendship they shared and the way they supported each other, in sickness (and *such* sickness) and in health, has taught us what marriage means.

Dod approached his cancer in the same way that he approached my difficulty with Maths. 'We'll crack it. We'll beat it. We'll show it who's boss.' Unfortunately, in both cases, he was wrong. But there was a part of Dod that did beat the cancer, that did show it who was boss. Because his soul was completely healthy, all the way through. Healthy, pure and free of disease. Perfect.

Even – or especially – in her absence, I like to leave the last word to Grandma. 'You'll never meet a man like your Daddy,' she used to say, comfortingly, as I was growing up. 'They broke the mould when they made Jack.' As usual, she was right. They did.

INT MAUREEN'S CAR – DAY – JUNE 2004

Maureen is driving across Waterloo Bridge. The radio starts to play Gershwin's Rhapsody in Blue. *She freezes. The tears drop as she makes the small squeaking in-breath.*

FLASHBACK TO:

INT HIRE CAR – RING OF BEARA – SOUTHERN IRELAND – DAY – AUGUST 2000

Jack is driving, with Maureen beside him. The radio plays Gershwin's Rhapsody In Blue. *The music so perfectly reflects the changes in the scenery. It is immigrant music, so it works anywhere. They exchange fond looks and Jack does his wide-mouthed-frog beam.*

JACK

(*aggressively*)

I luv *you*! You get on me nerves.

MAUREEN

(*Coronation Street style*)

That's as maybe.

FLASHBACK TO:

INT KITCHEN – DUKES AVENUE – MUSWELL HILL – 1983

Maureen is in the kitchen unpacking bags and bags of Costco supermarket shopping. Jack picks up 24 tins of Whiskas.

JACK

Are they all tuna?

MAUREEN

No. Some are chicken.

JACK

'Cos she goes off it if she gets the same each day.

MAUREEN

That's why I got two kinds.

Jack picks up the pack, whistling.

CU Maureen's face. She hates whistling.

Birdseed.

JACK

Pardon?

MAUREEN
(insistently)

Birdseed.

JACK

Sorry.

He puts the pack in the cupboard and returns.

Cup of tea?

MAUREEN

OK.

JACK

Ord? *(ordinary)*

MAUREEN

Just bag. *(herbal)*

Jack puts on the kettle and walks around kitchen jingling coins in his pocket.

CU *Maureen's face. This drives her mad.*

MAUREEN
You're doing *that* now, aren't you?

JACK
(looking baffled)

Doing what?

MAUREEN (VO)
Sometimes I engineered a row out of nowhere, just to shake up the comfort of it all. All that happened was that I felt better and forgot it and he just, quietly, hurt. It wasn't worth it.

A SERIES OF FLASHBACKS SHOW:

Jack coming home – making the familial, braying 'I'm home' noise. Maureen, cooking in the kitchen to the accompaniment of Radio 4, responds in kind.

Maureen, heavily made-up, coming home from performing in the theatre to find a menu on the door which reads:

Starter: *Home-Made Tomato Soup (made in the home of Mr Heinz)*

Main Course: *Lamb Chops à la Maureen/microwave-defrosted*

Mash à la Jack (egg added for extra nourishment and not enough salt)

Dessert: *Fresh fruit/carrot cake/hot liquid of your choice.*

Hot water on for après two-shows bath.

INT SPARE BEDROOM – MUSWELL HILL – DAY – 2000

We discover Jack up to his elbows in wet clay. Newspaper on the floor. Moulding clay on the armature on a rickety mobile stand. The statue is an eighteen-inch model of Manchester United's Ryan Giggs at the moment he tore off his shirt after scoring against Bayern Munich.

MAUREEN (VO)

It was my idea, originally, that he should take up sculpting again after laying off it for some twenty years. Sculpting was just another branch of writing. Detailed, affectionate, a bit obsessive. Invariably he was unable to let it go when it was finished. Come to think of it, that's how he was with the kids too. And me.

Jack is laboriously adding chest hairs one by one to Giggsy's chest.

Enter Maureen, pale faced, struggling into her coat, her mind already drifting towards that day's matinée of Oklahoma.

***Oklahoma* at the National Theatre lasted three hours . . . six on a Thursday and Saturday. It was after all a Trevor Nunn production, and a work of art. I knew Jack would be lost without something to engage his heart on twice-weekly matinée days.**

Jack looks up and smiles on seeing Maureen.

MAUREEN

How is he? I'm off now.

JACK

I'm stopping in a bit. I've overdone the clay – it's gone all spongey.

MAUREEN

The face is great. It's just like him – that expression. How did you get it?

Jack holds up a scrappy clay-stained newspaper photo.

JACK

From this. And sometimes I do his face in the mirror. To get the cheekbones.

He shows her the face of an athlete straining in the mirror. There is clay in his hair and on his nose. He wets his hands in a small grubby bowl of water and adds another rolled up piece of clay hair to Ryan's chest.

JACK

But I'm stopping when I've done this bit. I'm coming down for a cup of tea.

MAUREEN

I'll be late 'cos the Swifts are coming round after the show. We'll have a quick bite at Joe Allens, so don't do me anything.

JACK

OK, love. Have two good ones. Bye. You look very nice. Have I seen that?

MAUREEN

Me? This? Jigsaw. It's ten years old. Bye, love. Ring Zelma for me and find out what day she's coming for Yomtov *(a Jewish festival)*, will you? Bye.

CAM *circles Jack as he swivels the sculpture round, examining all sides.*

MAUREEN (VO)

Jack didn't have a great circle of good men friends. He didn't work at it as you have to. On the whole, we, the family, were his friends, along with a couple of good telephone pals like writer Willis Hall. I could always tell when Willis phoned because Jack started jack-knifing with laughter. Stuck on a script, he usually kicked off with 'I don't know what to *put*, do you? and somewhere down the line 'foreign muck' would be mentioned for any food which wasn't egg and chips.

(*beat*)

Occasionally, I'd come home and he'd still be sitting in the same position working on the same bit of Ryan. Six hours had passed and he'd forgone food, drink, TV and conversation. He was obsessed, obsessive, but quite content. It was a form of meditation, I suppose. It took the place of the life of writing he'd always known. Two-hundred-and-fifty-odd plays. As Mother, God rest her soul, always said: 'When does he ever do it, Maureen? You never see him actually *write*, do you?'

He was so patient with my parents but it was impossible to explain to Zelma that he was writing all the time. Writing as he chopped the onions for his famous salmon fishballs, writing as he walked round the garden shouting at the squirrels, writing as he drove to pick up the kids from school and most of all writing when he was just staring out of the

window, playing with his lip or his beard, if he happened to have one that year.

INT JACK'S STUDY – MUSWELL HILL – DAY – EARLY NINETIES

Jack is sitting at a battered desk beneath a stained-glass window depicting a tortoise and a rhino which Maureen commissioned for his birthday. He's staring out the window. Enter Zelma, his mother-in-law.

ZELMA

Ja-ack. Are you there?

Jack's eyes glaze. It's her third entrance in an hour – the last query was 'Do you rinse off your plates before you put them in the dishwasher?'

JACK

(*sighing*)

Yes, Zelma.

ZELMA

Do you use a tin of pink salmon in with the red when you do the patties? I've used three tall tins so far.

JACK

No, I don't use pink, as I've told you before. Zelma love, I know I don't look as if I'm doing anything but I am actually thinking. I don't mind you interrupting me if it's important but . . . sorry, but can you not ask me stuff if it isn't?

ZELMA

(*somewhat miffed*)

Oh . . . alright . . . I thought you were just . . . Oh, alright then.

Jack gives her a smile and a wave and tries to remember what he'd been writing about.

Angle on the clock, which reads 1.00pm

INT JACK'S STUDY – MUSWELL HILL – DAY

Angle on Jack's clock, half an hour later.

Pull back to see Zelma, now smartly dressed, standing nervously and silently in the doorway.

Jack becomes aware of her presence.

JACK

Yes, Zel . . . Is it important?

ZELMA

(*pause*)

I don't know.

JACK
(*good-naturedly*)
Go on then. What is it?

ZELMA
(*bashful*)
I'm just going to Brent Cross. Does this jumper go with this skirt?

EXT MUSWELL HILL HOUSE – DAY – JULY 2004

It is two months since Jack's death and a taxi is delivering Maureen home late at night. For a moment, from her POV, we see Jack at the front door . . . then he disappears.

Maureen walks in to the darkened house and makes the 'I'm home' sound.

She struggles with the alarm. Sits on the stairs for a very long, silent time. Then goes upstairs to bed.

INT PARKSIDE CLINIC – WIMBLEDON – SPRING 2004

Jack is on a chemo drip. Writing his autobiography, in longhand, on foolscap.

He hardly looks up as Ray Powles, his consultant; grey, spiky hair and track suit, comes – no, bursts, into his room.

RAY
Still at it! You are stunning, absolutely stunning! I don't know how you do it. Tell me something . . . does it just flow or do you have to think about it? It's such an effort for me when I have to write my papers . . . and look at you – page after page . . . stunning!

He shuffles a huge wad of case notes, several of which drop to the floor.

Oops! No worries, just got to . . . tell . . . you what . . . Now . . . when did we extract your bone-marrow?

JACK
Ray, you've got my notes in your hand.

RAY
So I have . . . Now . . . Where's my notes on . . . Jack Rosenthal . . . Jack Rosen . . . Tell you what, I'll just pop back to the office and see if . . . Shan't be a tick. I'm off to a conference in Madrid in twenty minutes, so I want to have a chat before I go and I need your X-rays and . . . Back in a sec . . .

He leaves, throwing back over his shoulder as he races down the corridor and tries to outwit a pair of automatic doors:

Your team did well last night. That header from Scholes! Remarkable . . . I'm gonna put a bet on them to win the double. I was only saying that on Saturday in the director's box at Chelsea . . . hang on . . .

Throughout, Jack continues writing, albeit with the bemused expression he reserves for Ray's eccentricities.

MAUREEN (VO)

In the last ten years Jack wrote thirteen dramas, plays and adaptations. In 1991 he wrote *Sleeping Sickness* about an overworked National Health junior doctor. It was part of my TV series of half-hour character-based plays, *About Face*. Jack wrote two of the twelve plays – (the other was *Bag Lady* which he always regarded as the jewel in his crown.)

In 1994 he wrote *Moving Story,* a spin-off from *The Chain,* his 1987 play about removal men, and adapted *Wide Eyed and Legless* from Deric Longden's book about the slow demise of his wife Diana from M.E. It starred Jim Broadbent and JulieWalters, was nominated for a BAFTA award and won an Emmy in America under the title *The Wedding Gift.* As usual, Jack's empathy was total.

R. D. Laing told us that one can't experience another person's experience. Jack was one-man proof that Laing was two couches short of a surgery. Jack understood only too well why people in hospitals are called 'patients'.

Occasionally though, empathy can work against you. It means you never learn from history. In the same year, 1994, he actually worked for Barbra Streisand again on her film *The Prince of Tides.*

INT JACK'S STUDY – MUSWELL HILL – DAY – 1994

Jack is on the phone to his agent.

JACK

She wants me to rewrite what? Has she got memory loss? I couldn't. I've only got one life. I want to live to see my children pay off their mortgages, please God . . .

Look – tell her I'll give her 42 days and ask for the national debt as a fee . . . she'll never buy it.

He turns to look at Maureen.

Are you sure? Ms. Streisand at my service . . . don't worry. It'll never happen.

EXT MUSWELL HILL HOUSE – DAY – 1994

The postman is staggering down the drive with a parcel the size of a small horse. It is the seventeen versions of the script which Barbra already had commissioned and received. She wants an eighteenth from Jack.

INT BARBRA'S ESTATE – BEVERLEY HILLS – EVENING – 1994

Barbra's famous nails are wound around a phone.

BARBRA

Won't it be great, Jack. You and me. Just like in the old days . . .

INT JACK'S STUDY – MUSWELL HILL – DAY – 1994

CU of Jack opening, then closing his mouth.

MAUREEN (VO)

Jack had been brought in to 'humanize the dialogue.' He didn't think his suggestions made any significant contribution to the final version of the film, and his name doesn't appear in the list of credits, but it wasn't as painful as it could have been. Because it didn't matter to him. He gave her exactly the number of days he said he would. He waited until 6 o'clock then he came home. Job done.

INT KITCHEN – MUSWELL HILL HOUSE – 1994

Jack stands by the oven, sleeves rolled up, glasses on head, chewing nicotine gum.

MAUREEN (VO)

And made chips.

Perfect Chips by Jack Rosenthal.

First. New oil. Sunflower. Basket in deep pan. Heat to boiling point. Chips, peeled, soaked, drained and salted. Maris Pipers cut into medium thick chips – not too thick. Try one chip to test heat – should sizzle. Add the rest and cook for five minutes, then lift basket out and turn heat down. The chips are now blanched. Just before serving heat oil to boiling, turn down and replace basket in oil until chips are golden brown. Remove, drain on rack, then on kitchen paper, pat dry, salt and serve. With 'eggs with a belly on' or 'sunny side up' as our American cousins term them.

We once gave egg and chips to Lord and Lady Puttnam, followed by rice pudding with a skin. I don't think they've ever forgotten it.

INT DINING ROOM – MUSWELL HILL – DAY – 2004

Maureen sits at the dining table, surrounded by papers and kindly accountants in grey suits. She's nodding intelligently, having removed her brain from the conversation some minutes ago.

MAUREEN (VO)

Nurturing was second nature to Jack. Now, as I struggle to understand car insurance and probate and how to bang a picture hook into a wall when I can't be bothered to measure the space properly, I could kick myself for letting him *let* me be so helpless.

Maureen opens a file on the table, spilling cuttings of newspaper obituaries.

Of course, a lot of the obits took the angle: 'Rosenthal was content to stay home and bring up the children while his wife pursued her theatrical ambitions.' I do like the idea that I was always swanning off in a black limo, licking the lip gloss, on my way to dinner on the yacht with Speilberg, yelling back at him 'Don't wait up, dahling, I'll be back when they're teenagers!' It wasn't like that. It was just that Jack had time for everybody. And patience . . .

INT KITCHEN – MUSWELL HILL – DAY – ANY YEAR BETWEEN 1973 AND 2003

Jack is doing letters at table. Zelma, wearing kitchen overalls, pops head round door.

ZELMA

I'm going to make myself that cheese on toast that *you* make. I just fancy some.

JACK

(*looking up from his work*)

Do you want me to do it for you, Zel?

ZELMA

Nooo. I can do it.

Crash, bang, doors open and close.

Do you want some?

JACK

No thanks, love.

ZELMA

Do you use this grill pan or the one with the grooves in it?

JACK

The one that's in the grill. The grill pan.

ZELMA

Oh, I thought so.

(*beat*)

Do you use the cheddar cheese or this one in the Tupperware . . . ?

JACK

Do you want me to do it, Zel, 'cos . . .?

ZELMA

Nooo. I've told you. I just wanted to know which chee . . .

JACK

The cheddar. The cheddar.

ZELMA

One slice or . . . ?

JACK

One. Two. How ever many you w . . .

ZELMA

I always use the processed at home. That's why I'm asking . . .

She cuts a slice of bread then stands by the butter dish for a very long time.

JACK

What is it, Zel? Do you want to know if I put butter on first?

ZELMA

Er – yes, well no, I can't remember – you do, don't you? Or don't you?

JACK

Zel. Go. And sit down. In front of Richard and Judy. And let me make the cheese on ruddy toast.

ZELMA

Why? I'm doing it! I only wondered if . . .

Jack gets out of chair, slowly, still looking at his notes.

No . . . you get on. Honestly.

She goes to put the bread under the grill then stands before the admittedly confusing cooker buttons. Pushes one in – it pops out of its socket – she tries to get it back – fiddles about, clicking things until:

I'll swing for this blooming cooker . . .

JACK

Right. That's it. SIT BLOODY DOWN!

She sits, looking astonished at his attitude. Four minutes later he presents her with a plate of piping hot ('Oooh, I love food when it burns your mouth!') cheese on toast, two slices, finely sliced tomato, HP Sauce, a cup of tea you could stand a spoon up in – with saucer, utensils and napkin.

JACK

Nah! Done! Eat!

ZELMA

(*rhetorically, with a dewy-eyed look at anyone who'll listen*)

Aaaah! In't he marvellous? I say . . . aah – thank you, you're the best son-in-law anyone ever . . .

The food goes in at fantastic rate.

Ooh – do you know? – this is fantastic. Ooh – this is my favourite meal. I say. Do you think I could make this in my flat in Hull?

(*beat*)

How did you do it? Just toast? And cheese? Did you just put the cheese. Straight on the toast? And then what? You put it under the grill – what numero? – Oh, you don't have numeros, do you? 8 or 9? Was it? Oooh, it's just fabulous. The more you have, the more you want. Mmmm.

JACK

(*wiping surfaces and cleaning grill pan*)

Did you want more?

ZELMA

More? Me?

Her tone implies was the question would she like to have her head split open with a scythe?

No! I'm full up to bursting. I couldn't eat another thing. Thank you anyway. But no. I couldn't.

Pause, whilst he replaces grill pan and stacks dishwasher.

Why? 'Ave you got more cheese you want rid of? I don't mind if you have. Just one slice though.

(*beat*)

And a tomato.

INT KITCHEN – MUSWELL HILL – DECEMBER 2003

Jack is hovering around the kettle. He is in severe back pain; the beginning of the end of his remission. Maureen is on the phone to Accident and Emergency of Hull Royal Infirmary.

MAUREEN
(*into phone*)
Yes, Mrs Zelma Lipman. No, not Zelda, Zelma. She's just been admitted to Casualty. Yes, L-i-p-m-a-n. Thank you, yes.

She covers the mouthpiece. To Jack:

I don't get it. When Rosalind rang she said Zelma was just getting ready to go to shule, she was perfectly alright and she suddenly got pains in her chest . . . We'll have to get the train . . .

Oh Yes, Thanks . . . it's her daughter, in London. How is she? Can you give me any more information please?

She stares at Jack. He stares at her. Neither of them sees each other, they are both planning the journey.

Hello, yes . . . Yes that's right, her daughter – Can you tell me how she is?

Long pause.

Sorry . . . She . . . On arriv . . . how? I mean, what . . . ? Did they try to . . . I see. No, of course. Thank you.

She shakes her head at Jack and mouths the words that she never ever thought would apply to her vibrant, funny, unchangingly beautiful mother.

She died.

Jack moves slowly towards her.

MAUREEN (VO)
We clung to each other over the first of ten thousand hot sweet cups of tea, but my main concern was for him. We drove to Hull.

The flat which she so adored was spotless and pristine in pink. Her account books were immaculate. Every phone call she made was listed in diaries. Every time she cleaned the windows or turned the mattress, she wrote down the precise day and time. There were nineteen perfectly-tended scrapbooks of press coverage of my work, Amy's and Jack's work. There was almost nothing for us to do, but kiss her cold forehead and make those blessed arrangements. And sit 'Shiva' (mourning week) for our mother and our Muse.

The loss aged him in an instant and the subsequent maelstrom of hospital, cemetery and Shiva played cruel games with his depleted immune system.

(*beat*)

In a sense, he never got over Zelma's death and neither of us had the time or strength to grieve for her. One thing is certain. The next few months of Jacko's slow demise would have been impossible for Zelma to live through. Although it was a terrible body-blow and the absence of her resounds still, in a sense the manner of her death was as tidy as the manner of her life.

INT BEDROOM – MUSWELL HILL – DAY – OCTOBER 2004

Maureen is putting piles of clothing in bags.

MAUREEN (VO)

Today I unpacked your herringbone overcoat, my darling. The one in the somewhat ghostly shades of grey and white. It has been folded up in a bag since we brought home all the stuff from the Hospice. I've got rid of quite a lot. Adam wears your leather jacket and your jumpers and shirts all the time and I've given choice bits to friends and relatives. Ad wears your new tuxedo jacket, the one I had made for you in Hull and I wear your lilac check shirt all the time.

The coat, though. You wore it every time we went to the Royal Marsden Hospital in Sutton or, subsequently, the Parkside in Wimbledon, after your consultant opened up the new clinic there.

There's a film out called *Wimbledon.* There'll be many more years of lawn tennis to watch at Wimbledon. There are, apparently, Wombles in Wimbledon. But to me, Wimbledon will only ever mean one thing, sadly, and that is pain. Pain and suffering and your phenomenal, beautiful bravery, my boy. When the infections struck you it was generally in the night time. A sudden shift in temperature, the pain rising sharply, and a certain look we came to recognise.

Then, the telephone calls to the Sister in charge and the sad, sorry realization that we couldn't handle this at home and we must dress you and haul you down the stairs. Somehow, after our experience with the private ambulance, we always managed by ourselves. There was no pillow on board, no blanket on board and no water. No *water.* Every bump in the road went through you via me. It was the longest journey of our lives.

I remember how Tony Porter – what a good friend he is – came at midnight and carried you down the stairs like a mannequin, and drove us twenty five miles round the North Circular. Our rueful faces as the staff came to meet us;

'Here we are again. Can't keep us away.'

Then the drip and the finding of the vein and the antibiotics and the oxygen mask and somehow they always pulled you round. One more time. The nurses all loved you; Jo, Carol and brilliant little Nurse Amy, remember how she came in to check on you, on her day off? Then the time would come to bring you home. Just Adam and me this time, wrapping you up, scarf, peaked cap, and ghostly grey coat.

Home again, bome again, tiddly-o-foo,
That's the way for me and you.

Now, as I sit here, weeks after your death, I am giddy with the absence of you. The phone rang and it was Betty Gould, the marvellous ninety-odd-year old, ex Bluebell Girl who sold us the chaise-longue in Highgate? She lost her old man to cancer thirty years ago but we still shed a few tears together.

'But you're like me, dear', she said, 'you'll soldier on. You won't wear a miserable face. Not for long, love. He wouldn't have wanted it. Like *my* Jack. Never had a day's illness in his life. I wouldn't let them touch him. Sat up in a chair by his bedside all night, gave him his morphine. It gets easier, love – it does, but it never goes away.'

Anyway, your coat; I took it out of the bag and shook it out and of course it fell into the particular contours of your body. Your stance . . . was still in it. That fuzzy soft texture – it cost a fortune in Neckline in Muswell Hill and I had to force you to have it – and I knew when I put it to my face that it would still smell of you, and it did. So good. So true. Even when you were filled with seventeen different fucking medicines and morphined up to the brows and your bowels were blocked by the morphine or the reverse . . . you still smelled, beautifully, of you.

I will try to write about the last two years. But not now. The phone keeps ringing, everyone is so sweet and tender, but you know what it's like – sympathy makes me worse. Perhaps I'll put the coat back in your wardrobe. Just for now.

(*long pause*)

Forgive me. I tried. I really tried to write this your way, but it's like I'm in a straitjacket. I must abandon the screenplay format and continue as I know how, in prose. I'll leave the scriptwriting to the rest of the family.

IN PRAISE OF PROSE

For a man with such a heightened sense of the absurd, Jack could be very gullible. On his seventieth birthday he was driving Amy and me home from the opening of her play *Sitting Pretty* in Southampton. Unbeknown to him, I had arranged for all our friends to be in the house for a surprise brunch party on our return. Great secrecy surrounded the event, although his boffin-like sensibility was such that when an old friend rang to accept the invitation, Jack said 'Sorry love, there's no brunch that day, we'll be on our way back from Southampton and I won't have time to go to the deli.'

'Oh dear,' said the friend, 'have I let the cat out of the bag?'

Believe it or not, no alarm-bells went off. I realised I probably could have had 27 simultaneous affairs – some of them *in* the house – and he'd have carried on watching Man United slaughter Arsenal live on Teletext.

On the drive home, we found ourselves making very good time. Too good. We were in danger of arriving at our Gentleman's Residence before our gentle guests. Delaying tactics were called for. Passing a sign for a service station, Amy cried out, 'Can we stop for a coffee, Dod?'

We were only thirty miles from home and Jack was reluctant. 'It'll be horrible, love, but if you want to . . .' Sighing heavily, he parked and bought the coffees. He was right, of course, it was. Horrible. He sat with us as we perched on two vivid plastic toadstools, watching for signs of a drained cup. 'Right then,' he said, 'hit the road, then?' I panicked. 'I'd love a blueberry muffin,' I said. 'I'll have a . . . pear,' said Amy. Then it was the loo; that took up another five minutes. Finally we joined him outside, where he was revving pointedly. In desperation Amy said, 'Would anyone like to play Hide and Seek?'

As we arrived home, turning a blind eye to two good friends frozen in time just outside our drive, our nearest and dearest burst forth and launched into the obligatory chorus. Against all the odds in Ladbrokes, his surprise party completely surprised him.

He was such fun to hoodwink. Once, on a flight to Morocco, he fell asleep after filling in several clues in the *Telegraph* crossword. Scanning my *Guardian* crossword, I observed that the patterns of both were identical, although the clues were different. Painstakingly I transferred all his solutions into *my* crossword and swapped papers. The next five minutes were priceless. It was the world's slowest burn. He awoke, gave me a sheepish smile, glanced at his crossword, focused, blinked, refocused . . . then just stared at it. For ever. Then he put his glasses on his head and brought the paper very close. Then he put the paper on his lap and gazed sightlessly at the ceiling. Then he closed his eyes, and opened them again very wide. With a look that mingled perplexity and panic, he turned to me and said hollowly, 'I think I'm going mad.' I'm afraid I cracked up completely. 'You swine!' he said, not unpleasantly, 'You out-and-out swine!'

Somewhere, I have a blurred photo of Jack at the door of the living room, his hand over his face, shaking with laughter. I'd been trying to find the right voice for a children's tape about a hen. My preoccupation and general clucking did not go unnoticed at home, and snide comments began to emanate from him. 'I hope it won't ruffle your feathers if I ask where my jacket is.' Or 'Shall we meet at the theatre or does it go against the grain?' A peck on the cheek was requested alongside a suggestion that I remove my glasses to take the weight off my beak.

On my return from immortalising Hilda the Hen, Jack was in the kitchen. 'How did it go, love?' I was about to reply when I realised that my husband was circling the kitchen with a basket under his arm, scattering grain on to the floor. He asked if I was at all peckish. Now, I'm not one to harbour a grudge. Not for me the long brooding silence. Never go to sleep on a quarrel, said someone; Louisa May Alcott? Clare Rayner? Idi Amin? Whoever. And we never did. But the following day, for £18, I hired a full chicken costume.

It was a feather balaclava with blue eyelids, an orange beak and a yellow fluffy body, and black tights. I was quite surprised that feet were not included but a pair of yellow rubber gloves seemed to do the trick. I was perched on the garden wall when Adam got off the bus from school. 'Hi Mod,' he intoned. 'I see you're dressed as a chicken. What's for dinner?' When Jack arrived home, I was watching the telly with my rubber gloves up and two hard-boiled eggs beside me on the sofa. When he'd recovered enough to speak, he just said, 'OK, you win.'

Left to his own devices and with a head full of dialogue, Jack loved watering the large rectangular back garden with an ever-dodgy hose. Why could we never get the watering system right? We spent enough money every season on those long, green, chunky bits in local garden centres (the word Hoselock springs to mind) yet there he was, nightly, pottering back and forth to the rusty old tap, adjusting, repairing, replacing – oops, now he's undoing a kink in the tubing, now he's returning to the nozzle at the bottom of the garden where he's dousing the yuccas, now, happily, he's spraying left and right in meditative mode, cigarette in hand, glasses up on head – then a sudden jerk of said head to see why water had stopped flowing, followed by march back to where two sections had sprung apart, and inevitable jamming them both back together without bothering first to switch off the tap fifty yards away.

The result was a triumph of speed, velocity and the power of water over man. Jet of water straight up the chin and down the shirt, he always hopped away from the Hoselock just that tiny bit too late . . . and there he was, sheepish and wet, trying not to notice me, safe, dry, smug and helpless with laughter behind the kitchen window.

He had another memorable look. It was a child's look of pride in achievement, and it always accompanied him into the room where I was cooking with Radio 4, or watching TV, or having my body buffed by teams of Nubian slaves, depending on which paper you read.

The look, eyebrows arched, eyelids lowered, tongue slightly poking out of the corner of the mouth, chin raised and arms slightly swinging, meant he'd fixed something but was too satisfied with himself even to bother to mention it. He'd done some job that men of letters, particularly Jewish ones, weren't supposed to be able to do. He'd changed a high light bulb, or stopped a door from sticking, or especially, done something butch with a hammer and rawlplug.

'You fixed it, didn't you?' I'd croon. He'd look even more casual and fiddle intently with some item of his clothing. 'You got that picture up, didn't you? You did, didn't you?' I'd persevere.

'Might've done.' He'd mutter. 'Might not.'

The last decade, professionally, was often awkward and frustrating. He was writing as effortlessly as ever, but to fewer commissions. It was a situation familiar to all his contemporaries who'd grown up in television. The new, young, commissioning editors, ever mindful of ratings and of 'hooking' the viewers over several nights of the week, had stopped commissioning single plays and were driven by star vehicles (especially ambulance and police vehicles) which were often underpowered or due for an MOT.

Jack had a real go at this in the recent remake of *Ready When You Are, Mr McGill*. It was produced by Working Title films in 2002 and shown, finally, after an inexplicable year on a shelf, unheralded and unreviewed on Sky Movies in September 2004.

It starred Sir Tom Courtenay as the eponymous Mr McGill, an extra on a TV Police drama, who has one line to say at the end of a day of bad weather, technical hitches and extreme frustration. Amanda Holden sent herself up beautifully as TV star Amanda Holden, Stephen Mangan played the unloved writer and Stephen Moore the smarmy TV executive. The director, played with eccentric brio by Bill Nighy, takes out all his frustrations for the day, for the cock-ups and, probably, for his whole life, on the extra, the one person who can't fight back.

The night Sky chose to air *McGill* was Rosh Hashana, the Jewish New Year, and after dinner nine or ten of us sat around the TV and raised a glass to our absent author.

It was an hour and a half of elegantly filmed, beautifully cast, funny, and meticulously well observed television, of the kind we almost never see nowadays. One thinks of the Churchill play with Albert Finney, *The Lost Prince*, and *Conspiracy* with Kenneth Branagh; all single plays, all lauded and prize-winning and all concerned with historic events. Jack didn't much *do* famous historical legends. He did the common man. He was one of the real socialist writers of his generation, though, perhaps, he was never thought of in that light. Through his plays, he elevated the so-called failures, the people whom society rewards with a cup of tea, not a fat-cat bonus. I think he actually changed the public perception of these people, and he did it, like Jane Austen, through his concentration on the specific, the miniature.

I don't believe anybody really understood the Jewish dilemma of keeping up with the Cohens whilst assimilating with the Smiths until Jack's rites-of-passage play *Barmitvah Boy*. Weren't the firemen a bunch of greedy, money-obsessed skivers during the first Firemen's strike and sympathetic, deserving, noble men after sixteen years of *London's Burning*? Did anyone have a good word to say for Vivien Nicholson, the pools-winner, until Jack showed the penury and abuse of her childhood? Or London cabbies until *The Knowledge* showed exactly what mental torment a 'knowledge boy' must go through to achieve that precious Badge of Green? The first *Mr McGill*, 25 years ago, lifted the lid on film-making for a public who, in those innocent days, had no idea that it often took a whole day to shoot a few usable minutes of film, nor that the scores of people who work behind the camera have their own dramas too.

Today, when every family has a video camera and Big Reality has made sophisticates out of Paul the Apprentice and Jade the Big Sister, and anybody who can simmer a roux or is the possessor of fourteen metres of grass and a water feature, it's hard to remember the impact, twenty five years ago, of removing that fourth wall and taking viewers behind the scenes.

2002's *Mr McGill* had a different slant, a more cynical one, which parodied a world where a star actress is sycophantically wooed for her ratings-power and an idea for a series turned down by producers because none of the leading characters were detectives or doctors. It didn't exactly endear itself to the powers that, this year, be, and although Sky have shown it repeatedly at 12.30 or 3.30 in the morning, to date there has been no date given for the transmission on terrestrial television of Jack Rosenthal's final play.

Sir Tom Courtenay said that playing McGill was the best experience in his forty-odd years in the business. Perhaps the ITV schedulers whom Jack gently savaged in the remake of *Mr McGill* had the last word, by simply not airing the play.

Around the time the kids went to University, Jack had a curious dip. He had written at least seven Hollywood screenplays during the preceding few years, all of which ended up in what they call 'turnaround'. This seems to mean three things to the studios: 'We've paid for it; new studio heads no longer want it; and we're buggered if anyone else is going to get it.'

Gabriella, Cloves and Cinnamon was a Brazilian novel which Jack adapted for David Puttnam, then at Warner Bros. It was received with the words 'This is the best script I've ever read.' Weeks later, Puttnam was ousted in a bloody coup and the script has been turning in 'turnaround' ever since. Along with the other six. Point being, I'm told that a paid-for script – even one not made into a film – which is never a 'go' picture, counts as collateral in the accounts of the studio.

I wish I could remember all the reasons why Jack's films stayed in 'turnaround' or, as he wrote in his CV, 'Rotting Gently on Hollywood Shelves': *Why Is This Night?* and *Tales from the Old Testament, The Battle of Cable Street* and *Gypsy and Me, Family Matters, Gabriella Cloves and Cinnamon, Conventions* and the George Best story, *The Best.* His uncredited writing contributions include: *Continental Divide, Everybody's All American, My Life So Far* and *The Prince of Tides.*

In 2002 Jack's adaptation of Kingsley Amis's book *Lucky Jim* was filmed by ITV, starring Stephen Tomkinson and Helen McCrory. After a successful showing in America it lay on an office shelf here for two years before being screened. Incensed by this, Jack, uncharacteristically, wrote a piece for a national newspaper:

> 'Getting a full-length single drama that isn't about cops and robbers on ITV isn't easy. Filming it, once you've got the go ahead, isn't easy either. What you imagine *would* be easy is scheduling it for transmission once it *is* made. Which makes it all the more bewildering to understand the saga surrounding Kingsley Amis's classic novel *Lucky Jim*, which I adapted for television.
>
> When the film was completed, ITV executives professed themselves delighted with it and were intent, they said, on finding a transmission date that would guarantee a big audience; a prestigious date for a prestigious film. Despite extremely good reviews for its transmission in the United States, a year and a half went by. Six dates were then suddenly suggested – then promptly cancelled. ITV is known to be hard up, and balancing the books may well have been a reason for all this. So far, so good . . . and *not* so good.
>
> However. Immediately after the last cancelled date – March 31st – the ITV scheduler finally fixed the date for Friday 11 April. October, November, half of December, January and February are good months for attracting large audiences. April isn't. Nor are Friday nights good for attracting drama lovers. So, we have the wrong night in the wrong month.
>
> The scheduler then split the film's last act into two – in order to make room for another commercial break and extra advertising revenue. This resulted in two very short acts – which illegally contravenes ITC regulations. He then decided on 8.30 as the transmission time. This was announced in the Press and trailed on TV. Two days before transmission, the time was changed to 9.20. Then, without a word to anyone, it was transmitted at 9.05. Wrong night, wrong month, wrong time.
>
> This meant that unless viewers were already watching ITV, they would have missed the first fifteen minutes. As did *I*. And as did anyone who had programmed his or her video recorder to video it.
>
> Throughout all this mess, the scheduler insisted that the viewing figures would be good. They were, in fact, terrible. Four million viewers

for an expensive, 'prestigious' drama of a comic classic is a disgrace.

Lucky Jim, among other things, is a tale of an anti-hero fighting and defeating a bumbling, incompetent, ignorant, arrogant philistine. Unfortunately, we had no real-life anti-hero. Just the bumbling, incompetent, ignorant, arrogant philistine.'

I only remember Jack, sitting in the study, every day, writing on lined paper with a silver biro pen. Hour upon hour, daytime, night-time, weekends, snatched time before social life intruded, 'glancing through it' before bedtime. He was dragged whingeing and moaning into the millennium with a Sony Laptop via something called a Little Brother, and his beloved Olympia retired to the top of the mahogany filing cabinet without so much as a lifetime achievement award.

He gave in to a computer only when his techno-maven, a film buff called Nick, was able to find him one without a 'big fat back' and no large hard-drive unit under his desk. It was slow and cumbersome (I'm typing this on it some years later) and his mistrust of it was total. He didn't want to be in the same room as it and moved lock, stock and longhand pad into the dining room, where he would eventually spend so many of his last months. He commandeered a big cosy wing chair and wrote in longhand on a lap desk, by the window, then transferred to the big mahogany dining table to type up his first draft.

He stopped only for mugs of tea or a sardine/egg/tinned tomatoes (ugh!) on toast lunch or, latterly, to immerse himself in the bliss of a mound of wet clay. He was the living example of George Bernard Shaw's famous maxim, about writing being the art of applying the seat of one's pants to the seat of a chair.

Then he discovered the mahogany bookcase had an elegant pull-down escritoire in it. Out went the favoured dining table and in came the leather shelf with the tiny embossed cubby holes and the secret drawers. He was always uncommonly neat with his work, he hated chaos of any kind. As Adam wrote about his dad in a tribute which he read out during the nights of mourning at our house:

> 'Jack Rosenthal was a one-man war against entropy, against encroaching chaos. He loved order, and he organised our lives and our household in the face of constant ineptitude on our part. Rarely a day went by when something didn't break, something wasn't lost or someone didn't need to take their corset back to Marks & Spencer's by 5.30p.m. Heroically, against all the odds, amid all this, he also managed to write some of the finest social comedy television has seen. This too, for me, is part of his war against chaos. So many impressions, memories, glimpses of people's lives and fleeting moments in history built into something new but true, that will stand the test of time.'

I remember trips to New York, trips to Los Angeles, phone calls at funny hours and ridiculous stories of the traditional Hollywood ritual flattery/humiliation. I remember youthful producers crowing down the line, fast-followed by conference calls revealing how, after he'd completed the few minor changes they'd demanded, everyone loathed the very same script they'd loved. A pecking order where all the peckers are tiny and their owners in permanent fear of castration.

He was never a great reader of popular fiction. He had too much reading to do in the day-job. The newspaper, especially the sports section, and the crossword, could, contentedly, see out his day. Ask me how much remorse I feel about my moral antipathy to satellite dishes and Murdoch-owned stations and I'll tell you there will be no end to it – not until you need sun-block in Siberia and Ann Widdecombe gets into Nicole Kidman's cast-offs.. Why didn't he just say 'I've *ordered* a dish and it's coming on Tuesday and if you don't like it – read a bloody book!'?

He loved those TV nights in his last two years and, dammit, so did I. We were never more tender than on those leisurely evenings when we just ate the most delicious food I could make, drank fresh vegetable and fruit juice and watched the telly. Depending on the state of his health we went upstairs as late as we always did – or he slept in the dining room on a special hospital bed, which we could adjust to ease his current pain. It was hard to leave him, and was even harder to get to sleep without his shoulder beneath my cheek. 'Do you want to lay on my chest darl'?' 'Might. Might not'. Like most long-married couples we had our own peculiar little rituals. In the last months I would read him Alexander McCall Smith's *The First Ladies Detective Agency* in a rubbish Botswana accent and he absolutely adored it. Couldn't wait for the next chapter. Roared with laughter.

Back in the days when television had 'water-cooler factor', i.e. when everyone in the workplace discussed last night's programmes, one of Jack's plays would end and then the phone would ring for the rest of the evening and much of the next day. It doesn't happen any more. People video and forget to watch or they sit down to watch a week later and someone's taped Pro-Celebrity Porno over it.

After his 1994 play *Eskimo Day* it continued to ring for days and was accompanied by sacks and sacks of mail. He'd tapped into an unexplored seam: the empty nest syndrome. Jack had taken Amy to Manchester University and stayed right through Freshers' week. Whilst other kids were joining Film-Soc and learning how to get laid and legless, Amy was dining nightly with her dad at the Midland Hotel. Two years later he was walking another white-faced child, Adam, around the hallowed cloisters of Cambridge. The experience led to *Eskimo Day*, one of his most successful plays.

In the follow up to *Eskimo Day*, entitled *Cold Enough for Snow*, Bevis, the father of our Cambridge lad, comes close to a nervous breakdown. The Empty Nest becomes a chasm. He begins talking to himself, forgetting his routines, laughing and crying inexplicably. He loses his sense of himself, when the focus of his nurturing years is no longer there. It had all happened to Jack.

On his *Desert Island Discs*, first broadcast in 1998 and repeated after his death, Jack talked memorably about walking around Cambridge with Adam, on the day of his three interviews, and watching all the nerve-wracked parents and their blanched offspring, trudging from one tea shop to another.

'Did writing the play help you over your depression, do you think? asked Sue Lawley.

Jack paused, thought about it and said, wryly;

'I suppose it did, now you mention it. Yes, I suppose it must have done.'

'Do you think that's what you've done with many of the crises you've encountered in your life, like being evacuated ... got it out of your system and let it go?'

'Well, er . . . yes. That might well be it. Yes that's probably my version of therapy, who knows?'

Perhaps it was because he was heard and not seen, perhaps it was just the gentle intelligence of Sue Lawley's questions on *Desert Island Discs* that made Jack his most articulate; thing is, Jack was one helluva'n entertainer. For a reserved man he could be remarkably gregarious. His *Omnibus, Jack the Lad* was the nearest you'll get to seeing the real thing. Because he wrote it himself, about himself, it captures his particular dry wit. His delivery is spot on. Not a wrong inflection. His timing exemplary. And he's very funny.

He was always so 'up for it'. In Skibbereen in Ireland, where we went each year to stay with Irene and Richard Beard and a party of friends in their loch-side house, he was quietly the life and soul of the party.

One day, six of the house-party were going off in a 4-wheel-drive for an excursion.

'Did you want to go, love?' asked Jack.

'No, not at all. We can flop about.'

'Great,' he grinned, with some relief. 'I'll be in the lounge with the paper.'

12 seconds later I put my head around the door.

'Shall we dress up as poverty-stricken Ukrainian cleaners to wave them off?'

'Er . . . Do we have to?' he said, and then, as my face fell, 'All right, love, if you like.'

I was already examining the cupboards in the hall and combing the drawers for a pinafore. Jack rolled his trousers up and put on a pair of wellies. Giggling now, I draped a scarf round my head and he put on an old sleeveless anorak. I gave him a flat cap and a bucket, stuffed things down my bra and put on socks and big brown shoes. He found a broom and we wiped muck from dusty corners across our faces for moustaches. His and Hers. We schlepped our buckets and brooms to the front door and appeared there, slopping water on the step, just as the Espace turned into the drive. One by one the passengers saw the 'cleaners' who by now had fags hanging from their lips and were chuntering as they mopped. Jack waved his fist at the passengers: '*Mit der hesen in der shmaltz under der gatkes in der drek!*' By now the guests were collapsing in the back of the van and struggling to find their cameras. Finally, helpless, they left. We got back into our civvies and had a cup of tea. Perfect.

In the late '90s I was booked to give a speech at the Ladies Needlewomen's Guild AGM, at St James's Palace. We were invited, first, to lunch at Clarence House. Jack was looking at the table plan before we went in. He said, 'Bloody 'ell, love, you're not going to believe it. They've put me next to the Queen Mum. What am I going to talk to her about?'

'You'll be fine. Don't worry.' I told him, 'She'll love you.'

He swallowed, white-faced. I watched Jack and the Queen Mum taking their seats on the far side of the beautifully-laid long oval table. The Queen Mum immediately burst out laughing. I relaxed. Several Gin and Dubonnets later, we filed out towards Palace door. The Queen Mum stood waving her guests goodbye. 'So. What did you talk about?' I asked.

'Well, as we sat down, she said "I'm so very happy to be sitting next to you, Mr. Rosenthal." So I said "Let's see if you still think that in half an hour's time, Ma'am."'

I laughed. 'And then what were you saying? I could see you jabbering away like mad.'

He grinned contentedly.

'Sculpture. She loves bronzes too.'

Talking of sculptures, they found the vanished mould of Ryan Giggs. The foundry, I mean; Fiorini's in Fulham. They called me up a couple of months after Jack's death and casually delivered the second-best line I've heard since 'Go on then – marry me'. 'We've been clearing out the works,' said Kevin, 'and we've found Ryan in the wax. You interested at all?' On the dusty shelf marked poignantly 'Jack Rosenthal Shelf', in the Dickensian workshop, was the mould, taken from Jack's original clay model of Ryan Giggs, triumphantly waving his shirt around his head.

Weeks later when I picked up the finished bronze from the foundry, I drove Ryan, wrapped in towels, to Hoop Lane Cemetery and put him by the grave. I fancied I could hear the self-criticism: 'I buggered up the proportion! I can't believe I foreshortened the arms like that! Bloody hell. Chest hairs are good though, aren't they, love?'

So now we have the full oeuvre. Bobby Charlton, Don Bradman, Ryan Giggs and Eric Cantona's noble head, sculpted from memory, whilst the rest of the class was working from a live, nude and decidedly female model. The real Bobby Charlton has the original. Jack said it was the greatest thrill of his life to hear Sir Bobby calling 'Jack!' from the United coach, when they met, as arranged to present Bobby with his model at Old Trafford.

We were a team, but on the whole, people prefer married couples to work separately. The spark isn't there. See Tom and Nicole in Kubrick's *Eyes*

Wide Shut for reference. Prunella Scales and Tim West, and Nanette Newman and Brian Forbes just get away with it; Pauline Collins and John Alderton don't do it often.

The very first time Jack and I worked together was shortly after we met in '68, when he asked me to speak a line of dialogue for the credits of a new series he was writing and producing at Granada. It was called *The Dustbinmen* and my line, delivered in a piping Lancastrian five-year-old's voice, was 'Hey Mam. It's the Dustbinmen'. We hadn't been going out for very long and I was anxious to get the voiceover right. He loved it and I'm afraid we talked in that daft voice to each other for the next thirty-five years.

After playing my own mother-in-law in *The Evacuees* in 1974, and a cameo in *The Knowledge* in 1979, it would be seventeen years before I worked on a Rosenthal film again.

Twenty years later, and it is still rare for me to get into a black cab without a fond discussion of what that play meant to the cabbie whilst he was doing the Knowledge. On my first day of rehearsals for *Aladdin*, before Christmas 2004, I managed to get lost between Waterloo Station and the Old Vic theatre – a distance of five hundred yards. A black cab swung into sight and the driver stuck his head out of the window and yelled 'Come on Maureen – I'll take you . . . where you goin'?'

Shamefacedly I told him.

'Hop in,' he grinned. 'I'm so sorry about your old man. He was a diamond.'

As my tear ducts opened he added,

'I was at the showing of *Mr McGill* at the Screen On The Hill in Hampstead,' (November, Jewish Film Festival, one night only).

'What a cracker that was. He was a gentleman and a genius. Here you are then love. No charge, and thanks for all the pleasure he gave us.'

Several years passed between *The Knowledge* and *The Chain*, in which there was a part I coveted. It was an elderly Greek Cypriot woman, who refuses to leave her home on removal day. Now, we live in an area which is rich in Greek and Turkish culture and the character came about because of my meddling disposition.

We were driving towards our home when I saw a shambolic figure in a black headscarf, pinafore and cardigan who actually fell from a wall towards the road and sat crying on the pavement. When we rushed from the car to help her, although she wasn't hurt, she seemed incapable of speech and couldn't tell us where she lived or what her name was.

We ended up taking her into the local newsagents where somebody recognised her. We took her home to her vociferous middle-aged daughter, who plainly wished we hadn't. She gave both her mother and us an earful. Jack fixed me with a baleful glance – he did bale rather well actually – and I, I'm afraid, talked in 'Mrs Stephanopolides' voice for the rest of the day.

Jack put my name forward to the director Jack Gold when *The Chain* was being prepared, but he saw it differently and cast Billie Whitelaw in the role. She was a very different and rather beautiful Cypriot.

There's a one-liner that goes, 'Did you hear about the dumb blonde actress who went to Hollywood and slept with *THE WRITER*?!'

In 1989 Jack wrote two plays for my series *About Face*. He regarded one of them, *Bag Lady*, as his apotheosis. It was as tender and eccentric a Rosenthal as ever was. Jon Henderson, who directed the twelve half-hour comedy dramas, wrote to me after Jack's death that 'working with Jack on the two scripts to which he contributed was the happiest time of my career.'

'One story you may not even know about him occurred during a very late-night dubbing session on *About Face* when the equipment kept failing and everyone was tired and becoming extremely grumpy. After a time, we noticed that Jack had gone missing; that was until we saw him through the control-room window, sitting in the main studio in semi-darkness listening intently to the dub on a pair of headphones. Not unusual in itself, perhaps, but what was a little different from the norm was that he had collected up eight pairs of headphones and was now wearing a towering construction similar to a Balinese dancer's headdress. Not content merely to have this construction precariously balanced on his head, he was concentrating hard on the sound levels whilst sitting stark naked except for a pair of underpants. If it hadn't been Jack, it would have been certifiable, but his stunt did exactly what he had intended. The laughter he created saw us through that difficult night. We'll never forget Jack.'

The second play in the series, *Mrs Worthington's Daughter*, was written by Astrid Ronning, one of our closest friends. Jack had guided her through the writing process, as he did for so many young writers who sought his advice. Jon Henderson asked him to direct it. It is to my eternal shame that when it became clear what a huge venture it was to shoot the large-cast play in a week, I lost my confidence in Jack as a director and turned to Jon instead. Not a week goes by that I don't relive that cowardly decision. Jack never mentioned it again. He never mentioned many things which hurt him.

I did have to audition for *Eskimo Day*, this time via video. The director was Piers Haggard. When one is a comedienne by nature, it is hard for even the most imaginative of directors to envisage you in a drama. Even a comedy drama.

During the pre-planning stage, Jack played Piers part of the video of my Joyce Grenfell show *Re:Joyce!*. It was a sketch called 'First Flight', and Joyce Grenfell wrote it because she wanted to say something about a kind of goodness that isn't pious or self-aware. Jack loved *Re:Joyce!*, and I don't know what else he said to convince Piers that I could play shy, Northern, working-class Shani, but it worked, and we were all happy with the result. It was elegantly shot, funny, sad, and involved a wicked cameo for Sir Alec Guiness.

One of the last times we worked together was in Robert Young's film *Captain Jack*, a 1998 sea-faring tale penned by Rosenthal, and set in Whitby. Ian Holm came in to read for a smaller part in this true story of a

Whitby sailor who sailed illegally to the Arctic, in an un-seaworthy ship, with a scratch crew of housewives and friends, to put a plaque on an iceberg in memory of Captain Scoresby. Scoresby had been a Whitby man who had previously made the same journey as Captain Cook to the Arctic but according to Captain Jack, received none of the credit.

Ian Holm read his own part and said, 'This is crazy – I should be playing Captain Jack.' They all acknowledged he should . . . but at the time he was a theatre name only and finances were so rickety that they needed a star. Exit Mr Holm and enter Mr Hoskins. A couple of years later Mr Holm was making major movies in Hollywood. This is how the business works. Or doesn't work. I played Captain Jack's loyal secretary. I was probably miscast. Sadie Frost, unseen as yet in the gossip columns, was the cabin boy/love interest and Anna Massey and Gemma Jones were the two squabbling sisters who sailed on the voyage. The film was a bit of a washout.

Tragically, Whitby is the fish and chip centre of the world. I say 'tragically' because Jack and I were on an elimination diet. No yeast, no dairy, no egg-white, no batter, no fun. His face was pure Dostoevsky as he watched plates of crisp maritime magic pass his nose, only to land under the noses of the rest of the cast. 'It's only for three more weeks,' I said.

'By when,' he moaned, 'I'll be at Shepperton where the fish and chips are bloody awful.'

The last time we worked as a team was January 2004, when he was in the middle of Thalidomide treatment after his two-month remission. It was a ten minute playlet which he wrote for a fund-raising dinner in North London, for Chai Cancer Care and it starred George Layton and myself as the parents of a young lad, who must tell his family at Friday night dinner, that he has testicular cancer. I directed it on five successive Sunday mornings in our kitchen. 'I've always longed for someone to analyse every line with the actors, the way you did,' Jack told me. I sighed, 'Me too.' It will always remain the best review I've ever had.

SATURDAY NIGHT – NOVEMBER 2004

I've just watched the first Bridget Jones film, writing pad on lap, surrounded by typed and scrawled pages. How did Jack work so neatly? I started to read back on what I'd written to try to repair the confusion and repetition, but what with Bridget doing solo Karaoke to *All by Myself* and the sheer bloody sadness of remembering all the bits and pieces of him, I just screwed up my face, Bridget-like, and did the silent scream.

I shall go to bed now that Bridget has her nice stiff Mr Darcy. I've learned to say Kaddish for him, just by reading it very slowly, and 48 years of forgetting my Hebrew letters has come back to me. See – some change is for the best. I wake up every couple of hours, put Radio 4 on, have a pee and go back to sleep. Don't feel any the worse for wear.

One weekend I went to the God-parents dinner in Dorset. Amy came too. Since the twins, Rose and Joe, were born, eight years ago, eight couples have been meeting every year, for one weekend. How we've all changed in those eight years. Some partners have moved on, new partners have emerged, there's been a terrible stroke for one of the youngest and a brain tumour in another, relationships have shifted their balance. There was I, still doing the jokes, at my end of the table, with half of my act missing.

Over the course of the weekend I was given sixteen heartfelt condolences and each one cracked me apart. Sod's law of course; if people don't say how sorry they are I sulk and when they do, I blub. How he was loved. And respected. And admired. I wonder if he had any idea.

I *will* write about the last two years, but not now. It's a blur. I can't remember the sequence of everything. I can't talk about it either because sympathy makes me worse and I dread the publicity that will accompany this book for that very reason.

Since his death, almost without exception, my women friends have all told me how much they loved him. He wasn't especially handsome or seductive, in truth he didn't much notice women in the general shifty-glance way of most men. He was just completely himself. In his own skin . . . and droll, and deadpan, and original. 'He spoilt all other men for me,' said Naomi, a friend for many years, and 'My old man's in no doubt how much I love him,' smiled Marilyn, of her husband Geoff, 'but not like I loved Jack.' For over thirty years he shared weekly confidences with Jo Apted, the ex-wife of film director Mike, and in the last months she and her son Paul would come to see him, wherever he was, every week, bringing laughter, nostalgia and his beloved short crust pies from The Maid of Honour bakery in Kew. 'If it weren't for Jack,' she told me recently, 'I wouldn't have had a decent male role model in my whole life.'

On the whole, small talk alarmed him. So did parties where you stood up and made it. The clip-on wine goblet was probably his most reviled object. He was also thoroughly urban and the concept of a walk just for a walk's sake, was beyond his comprehension.

'I'm just going up the street darl,' he'd call out at some point in every afternoon. 'Just cos I haven't been out yet. I'll get a 100 watt bulb.' He'd be back in fifteen minutes. No chatting, no distractions, no armfuls of impulse buys. Just home . . . with the bulb.

Or he'd ask around five o'clock, 'Are we out tonight luv?' 'No, we're in,' brought a grin.

'Yes, we're out to dinner,' required a mental shift and a moment to hide the disappointment. I don't think Jack ever made a social arrangement during our life together. 'I'll put Maureen on,' he'd say, handing me the phone gratefully. Or, he'd say when I came in, 'Marilyn and Geoff rang to see if we'd like to see a movie, and eat with them on Sunday?'

'Did you say yes?'

'I said I'd ask you – and you'd ring her back.'

'We're free aren't we? Did you look in the diary?'
'I did, love. There's nothing in there.'
'So, why didn't you tell her yes?'
'Er . . . I thought you'd like to do that.'

Holidays were, inevitably, a doom-laden prospect for him. He'd start being nervous a couple of weeks before the yearly event and didn't really become himself again until four or five days before we returned. It didn't help that we were renowned for having holiday disasters. As seasoned travellers we were serial whingers. Hurricanes, earthquakes, dung beetles in the minestrone – friends would ring us on our return and ask, solicitously, 'Was *anything* alright?'

We often seemed to be combining holidays with work. I'd be writing a piece about the resort so there'd be deadly dinners with groups of Portuguese couriers, or visits to half-finished hotels. Jack bore this with his usual grace.

In Cornwall, where we've never had a disappointing holiday, he accompanied me to the Cambourne and Falmouth Labour Party headquarters to give a boost to the candidate who had a fat chance of running to victory against Sebastian (now Lord) Coe. The local paper wrote 'Miss Lipman, in cream trouser suit and pendant earrings, was followed at a respectable distance by her husband, Jack Rosenthal, wearing dusty sneakers.'

After years of damp villas in Minorca, atmosphere-free hotels in Paphos and fighting our way through Customs at Miami, we settled on one place which never disappointed us: Ireland. South Africa was forest fires, LA an earthquake, Australia driving rain, but Ireland, beautiful, unspoiled, zany Southern Ireland was home from home.

But still Jack would have to make complicated arrangements with the local NatWest to pick up buff coloured folders with Euros inside. He'd have cancelled the papers and arranged for someone to stay in the house to keep the cat company or to open and close the curtains to mystify burglars. He'd stop the milk and make lists of stuff to do. He'd lay the tickets out, book the mini-cab, Blanco his beloved sneakers, and practise lifting suitcases. Then he'd settle down for some serious worrying. Then he'd worry about the worrying.

What he wouldn't worry about was the only thing I *would* be worrying about. What to pack. First off, he didn't have many clothes. He never shopped. Three or four times a year, and on most national or religious holidays, I bought him clothes. He reacted as he did when anyone bought him anything:

'Aaah . . . it's a shirt . . . is it? It's . . . is it blue? Oh, green, OK. It is . . . lovely. Thank you darl. It's lovely that. (pause) Did I need one?' (Seeing my look) 'I mean . . . I like it. I'll wear it. It's just . . . haven't I got a green shirt already?'

No matter that the other green shirt was a neck size he no longer fitted, nor had irremoveable egg stains and frayed cuffs. It was his green shirt and it would remain so until it crumbled in his hand like a two-day-old moth.

I bought him suits by selecting similar-sized salesmen and making them stand in fish-frying poses. I bought him beautiful Kenzo ties and he always wore the same tie he'd worn the last time he'd worn a tie, which was whenever he couldn't get away without it. He never wore anything if it was 'for best', which meant he kept everything in polythene covers until they were out of fashion. He wore his shirts for two days to get the most out of them and he polished his one pair of black shoes with a proper duster and proper polish and spit.

Once, when we were going to Italy, I said: 'The shoes are marvellous there, darl, you can get some really lovely ones.' He looked at me, puzzled, and said, without irony, 'But I've *got* shoes . . .'

Jack would, for pleasure polish anything. He was a bit of a polisher actually. Give him a a bunch of knobs and some Brasso, an old leather-covered book and some antique wax, or a pair of Sabbath candlesticks and some Silvo and he was a very happy man indeed. He guarded his can of WD40 with his life.

I once bought him a burgundy leather chair and footstool and he looked genuinely upset. 'But what will I do with the chair I've got? . . . I'm very grateful, but I mean . . . where will it go? I don't really use chairs – I mean, I lie on the sofa when I'm—' (as I huffily left the room) '—where you going? I just don't want you to spend all your . . . was it very? . . . and me not to use it.' (Pause) 'Did you keep the bill?'

We didn't need the bill. The chair sat in the corner of his study and he sat in the corner in it, with his feet up whenever he took a break from word bashing. He grew to love it and, like his coat, it grew to take on his shape.

Packing to go away was the nearest we came to mutual irritability. Inevitably I would be running to Brent Cross shopping centre at 5.55 p.m., trying frantically to buy sandals for a man who was uncertain of his shoe size, and swimming trunks for an ex-sailor who couldn't swim. I would return with an impulse linen jacket in yellow or royal blue, which he would wear, to humour me, on the last night of the holiday. Invariably, one of the guests would ask him for another bottle of wine and some toothpicks. Without batting an eyelid he'd ask them smoothly which vintage and pass on their request to the sommelier.

When the rain fell, he would be up before the rest of us staring out of the window, then as we appeared, bleary and disappointed, would burst into his holiday aria to the sun . . .

'Come on you sunshine!
Come on right now.
Come on you sunshine!
Like you know how!'

When the sun finally arrived he never sat in it. He let his own kids and any others around bury him in sand, or he found a place in the shade and did the crossword, or lay across the sofa snoozing with the paper over his face. Then he came home, bronzed as a mahogany chiffonier, while the rest of us, sun-worshippers to a man, sported just the red nose and the flaking skin.

Jack's temper, like his beloved herrings, was generally on a very slow simmer. His replacement hips always embarrassed us at metal detector points. At Toulouse airport once he was stopped as usual: '*C'est mes hanches,*' he explained in flawless Pidgin. '*Ils sont titanium.*' Six Gallic eyes stared blankly at him before one Gallic mouth barked a command to wait behind the barrier for *la police*. Jack looked horror-stricken. Not because he was guilty, naturally.

No, Jack's concern was missing the plane. He had started to breathe in a shallow fashion, and swear, which I knew was to do with his horror of foiled arrangements, but feared customs would interpret it as guilt, so I yelled across the divide, 'Don't worry, love, we can always get a later plane,' which increased his breathing rate to a demi-pant. The police failed to show up and I resorted to outraged Franglais: '*Mais c'est une operation tres populaire, n'est-ce pas? Les hanches?*' *Le douanier* just shrugged. '*En France aussi?*'

Jack was giving me warning looks but I was unstoppable. 'You mean to tell me that *chaque personne qui arrive ici, avec une replacement,* must *attendre pour la police? C'est ridicule.*'

All at once I realised that Jack was going to be searched. I got both nervous and giggly which, combined with his panting, made us look like an elderly Bonnie and Clyde. When the young, armed policeman finally arrived, he swept Jack off into a little cubicle. I pressed my ear to the wall, holding my breath and standing on the balls of my feet in case, in the event of the sound of a snapped rubber glove, I needed to spring him. Happily, the policeman merely wanted to see Jack's scar, which Jack was only too happy to show him.

'Okay,' said the policeman and turned to leave.

'*Non,*' *dit* Jacques imperiously. '*Regarde ici aussi*', which sounds even funnier than it looks. Then, lowering his trousers to the other side, insisted that he look at '*l'autre*' scar. The guy seemed embarrassed. 'Okay!' he kept saying, whilst sidling away from what he no longer took to be a cool smuggler but a hip-flasher. No doubt during all of this, two or three travellers with packets of white stuff up their bums sauntered blithely past, whistling.

Our last holiday together was in the mountain town of Megeve, in the French Alps. It was late summer and the flowers were in bloom. There was a festival of music in the town and most nights we strolled down to listen to the orchestras and choirs. We ate superbly and the small hotel was pine-clad and homesteady. Nothing went wrong. No tornados, no vituperative hoteliers, no twisted ankles or lost passports. Just us. The kids were well on their way now, Amy a published and performed playwright and Adam working in the Darwin Centre at the Natural History Museum. Perhaps holidays could, after all, be a life, if not the other way round.

Jack was a happy man, with a melancholy soul, but there was no better gift in the world than seeing him collapse into Maureen-induced merriment. Like George Burns with Gracie Allen – if you go back that far – he was almost always amused rather than irritated by my dumb-brunette take on life.

Driving to Berkshire one Sunday, he with the radio tuned to the last Test Match in the Caribbean, I realised that he and I were listening to two different languages. His comprehension of the patois was total. Mine was total incomprehension:

'What does he mean, "The night-watchman bishop has just been dismissed"?' I asked him.

Jack looked both amused and superior.

'It means he's out.'

I looked at him, 'Who's out?'

'Bishop.'

'Bishop's a person then, is he?'

'Yes, he's a bowler really.'

'I thought he said he was a night-watchman?'

'He did. He is. He was – last night when the Windies . . .'

'Pardon?'

'Sorry, the West Indians were batting at close of play. They use him 'cos he's a tailender.'

There was a pause while I regrouped myself. 'He's a tailender who they used as a night-watchman?'

'Yes. It means he's an eight or nine – so they put him in, rather than risk losing a three or four in bad light.'

I considered this. It was patently insane. Like putting a terrible warm-up man on stage to make the comic look better. 'So why don't they take people to the West Indies who can bat and bowl?'

'Well, because world class all-rounders are very hard to come by. Boycott couldn't bowl. Bradman couldn't bowl. Atherton, the captain, can't really bowl.'

'He can't bat either by the sound of it. But do you mean in the whole of England they can't find . . .'

'Botham could do it – but mostly they specialise. Even fielders can be best in the slips or in the covers . . .'

I had the WG Grace not to say, 'and dynamite between the sheets.'

'But,' he went on, 'they usually have a couple of rabbits with them . . .'

That did it. 'Rabbits! He's here with his rabbits now! What in all that's sacred . . . ?!'

He's now helpless, shaking at the wheel and a danger to the middle lane.

Meanwhile, the commentator commented on. Apparently, to start with, Tufnell was giving the ball 'just a bit more air', but now it would seem 'he'd flattened out.' The umpire swayed away, which was his way of saying 'not out', and someone else was exploiting the rough. 'He'll have sore fingers tonight,' he chortled knowingly, and his colleague joined in the chortle, adding for good measure, 'Yep – he just floats it up . . .'

Oh. Right then, that's okay then.

I fixed my husband with a baleful look. He beamed back. Men are from Lords and women are just silly mid-off.

Jack's burst of melancholy, after the kids left home, had been easily, if superficially, cleared up. His generation was not one to talk about feelings. He was a 'pull yourself together and get on' sort of chap and it alarmed him when he couldn't do it. It took months of wearing his heaviness lightly for him to come to the realisation that a series of physical symptoms were all related.

He was often incredibly hot. 'Dod's lost his thermostat,' I used to say to the kids when he turned the heating off or threw the bed covers off in the night. He would frequently escape into the street during evenings in restaurants, confounded by the noise and heat. He had skin-rashes and complained that his spectacles no longer corrected his vision. He'd given up smoking, twelve years ago, before his first hip operation, in favour of the odd small cigar, but the odd small cigar escalated into an odd small cigar smoking habit. On more than one occasion I caught him skulking by the garage doors with the dog end of a fag scrunched up painfully in a smouldering hand. He became more set in his ways, his lack of desire to go out became more of a compulsion and his endearing pedantry became more insistent.

I suppose it lasted, in total, about six months and he never, never complained or blamed anyone or anything. Stoically he just stuck it out until it passed.

Had it been me, I would have seen a counsellor, changed my diet, had my feet reflexologised and my chakras checked. Mostly, though, I'd have wept on all my girlfriends and felt unbearably sorry for myself. Come to think of it, that would probably have taken about six months, too, so who's to say whose method was the right one? Horses, of course, for courses.

He handled the multiple myeloma in the same way. 'Tell me what I have to do, I'll do it and I'll get better.' Without bothering anyone. With hindsight, I now realise that the rashes and the over-heating were probably symptoms of the oncoming disease. When the first bone pains in his back started, in 2002, it was diagnosed as arthritis, but it was so excruciating that we were referred to a consultant at University College Hospital and the diagnosis revealed two Plasma Cytomas on his spine.

Multiple Myeloma is a helluva difficult thing to diagnose. It presents itself in so many different ways. In a short film we've recently made for the International Myeloma Foundation, the patients filmed had symptoms as differing as wobbly legs, boils, rashes, severe back pain or failure of one or more organs. Jack's Plasma Cytomas were manifestations of bone marrow cancer on the spine itself, containable through radiotherapy. He had Indolent Myeloma, the kind that simmers but may not ignite.

In April 2002 he had six radiotherapy sessions, bone-growth hormones and a course of chemotherapy tablets. We believed the treatment had worked. When the pain in his ribs exacerbated we were sent to a rheumatism expert in a north London clinic. She examined him and said he clearly wasn't getting enough excercise. How about enrolling in a gym? Eighty pounds and close the door when you're leaving, please. This was another example of the kind of negligence which he'd already faced with Lakey, with me, my father and of course, in the scripts of *Wide-eyed and Legless* and *Sleeping Sickness*.

There was no treatment. It smouldered. You waited. It could lie dormant for years. He was prescribed morphine patches for the pain and in May we packed, somehow without irritation, for a cruise around the Mediterranean called, rather alarmingly, 'Theatre at Sea'.

It was a group of actors, English and American, among whom were Millicent Martin and the now late, always great, Jerry Orbach, Dick Cavett, Patricia Neal and Gena Rowlands. Each of us, along with singers and dancers, were expected to give one night's performance. Spouses were expected to lap up the sun and sparkle over dinner.

Jack boarded that ship a stooped, frail, pallid man and he came off not just rejuvenated but the person everyone wanted to sit next to at breakfast, brunch *and* dinner. When we disembarked we had new friends, new skin tone and a spring in both our steps. Jack went back to a full twelve-hour day on *Ready when You Are Mr. McGill* mark II. In at dawn, first at the catering van, last to leave the editing suite at dusk. Sorted.

In the autumn he relapsed. Suddenly it turned into galloping Multiple Myeloma and it galloped fast. We had changed consultants from University College Hospital to the far-distant Marsden Cancer Hospital in Sutton and we started the weekly trips round the North Circular road for his first sessions of chemotherapy. It was New Year's Day when we went to the Marsden for a consultation with Professor Powles. A world authority on Myeloma. He told Jack that he wanted to start three days of C-Vamp chemo, not just as soon, but sooner than possible. We'd packed a small overnight bag, but Jack was adamant that he was coming home first. On the way to the car park he stopped, turned round and said 'Come on, let's get the bugger over with.'

He reacted well under the intravenous chemotherapy aegis. Some nurses could find veins in one go, some couldn't find them with x-ray vision. Because they discovered a blood clot on his chest, probably a result of the radiotherapy, he was unable to have a Hickman line inserted, which would have saved him the dread of finding a new vein each time. The hair left behind on the pillow, he lived with. The weakness we fought with fresh vegetable juices, fresh organic food, vitamins, filtered water, we were told, no bottled water – too many bacteria, yes, I was shocked too, and no salads. Soft toothbrush and everything double washed with an antibacterial agent. Fine. Let's go.

Colin Shindler was amazing in his absolute devotion to Jack and in the hours he devoted to waiting with us and sharing the prognoses. Adam and

I, and sometimes Colin's cousin Ian shared the driving and we all grew used to the staff, the routine and the other patients, and they to us [Less than nine days after Jack's death, Colin's wife, my dear friend Lynn, home in Santa Barbara to take care of her parents, was felled by a stroke caused by complete kidney failure. It was Multiple Myeloma. The vigil began again. I saw her in rehab when I was in LA and nine months later, by a lake in Ethiopia, I was given the news of her death. She was 59. I threw some jacaranda flowers in Lake Tana and said the Kaddish prayers for her.]

Back in 2003, none of this was known to us. Once home, Jacko rested and slept, took a frightening regime of seventeen pills a day and gave himself daily Fragmin injections to thin his blood. The days hurried by, as the song says, to a precious few, and it was time to face the worst. High-dose chemotherapy and stem cell treatment – dangerous at any age but at 71 a gamble. Still, he was Dod, we reasoned, he looked such a youngster, he always had. Besides, the only choice we had was Hobson's. He went in the day after leading the Passover night service in our dining room with a table full of loved friends around him. 'Why is this night different from all other nights?' was, as it has been for thousands of years, the first question.

He would be in isolation for three weeks. The stem cells would be harvested, cleaned, then fed back into his blood after the high-dose had killed the cancerous cells. That was the plan.

As the high-dose chemo suppressed his immune system, the infections set in. There is no praise high enough for the doctors and nurses in the Royal Marsden's wards and in their Intensive Care Unit. It's the caterers I reserve my distaste for – and of course it's not their fault. They're obeying orders, as Ken Livingstone might say. There has to be a point, though, where the vastly expensive drug-therapy and the vastly demanding human resources are backed up by vastly good sodding vegetables. And soups. And protein. All of the highest quality. Next stop Jamie Oliver. If he can do school dinners on a shoestring he should tackle hospitals. It's life and death we're talking here and I've never been more in the presence of both than in that terrible, wonderful week. The sickness, the sound of his laboured breathing, the diarrhoea and the hallucinations were terrible. One long night of the soul, he told us he couldn't take Saddam Hussein's children on the school run the next day. We sponged his brow and wet his parched lips with tiny sponges and told him it was OK, not to worry, one of the other mums would do it. What was wonderful, though, in spite of everything, was the dedication, the overwhelming love and the fact that he lived through it.

To complicate matters, Jack had never told us that he had Emphysema. He must have known for ages, but he told us he had something called 'airways disease.' Did he make it up? It sounds like something a writer would invent, not a physician. All the 'puffing Billy' jokes we made, and he never told us the truth. 'Breathe from your diaphragm, darl, not your chest,' I'd tell him from the high realms of my Academy of Dramatic Art training. 'Don't hold onto your breath – when you're in the swimming pool – darl – relax into the water.' Well, he couldn't. But he never told us why, so we shouldn't worry. Now, every breath was a struggle and he would have to nebulize through a machine for the rest of his days. It didn't help in the struggle to fight the real villain. Multiple Myeloma.

At this point he hadn't eaten for days and everything ran straight through him. We tried to tempt him with build-up drinks but he was having none of it. He couldn't taste anything. Then one night he called out in a surprisingly 'doing us a favour' tone, 'I'll tell you what I'll have,' We all snapped to attention and flexed our fetching muscles. 'I'll have a Shandy.'

It was pointed out to him as gently as possible that bowel infections, antibiotics, anti-viral pills and steroids probably didn't work with a beer chaser. The craving for beer didn't stop once he was home either. It seemed very out of character. He'd never wanted a beer in the 35 years I'd known him, unless it was the Grand National on a warm day or we'd just shot out of Cork airport in the direction of Skibbereen. I pondered whether, 'I'm going to change a few things' meant I'd wake up one morning next to a fledgling Ricky Tomlinson, sweating and belching on his way down to the Wassailler's Arms to get rat-arsed. 'Where's my piggin' dinner, woman?' he'd bellow as he lurched through the door, 'and get your arse moving 'cos I want me conjugals straight after me rhubarb!' Hmm. Oh, well, 'for better or worse' it said, didn't it?

In September 2003, my lad came back from the wars. He was fragile, with that strange, hollow, hospitalised pallor that follows tasteless food, airless rooms and invasion of all your privacies. But we had him back. It had all been worth it, it seemed and he could be in remission from Myeloma for two to five years. His hat was absurdly large and his belts needed new holes. Every step was an effort and every mouthful a major decision. He was pill popping like a rock star and stuff had to be swabbed and injected at all hours. I had to fatten him up, hold him close and wage war on bacteria. The house was industrially clean and became a repository for Medicated wipes, Zimmer frames, oxygen cylinders, and the odd commode. Jack was exhausted but he was in there somewhere, my heroic boy, dazed and shell-shocked, but he was home and essentially still Jack the Lad.

'When I get home,' he'd whispered, pulling his breathing mask aside at 1.30 a.m. in the gloom of Intensive Care, 'I'm going to change a few things.'

'Oh, yes, love, 'I replied, all scrubbed up and protective-plastic-aproned, from my slumped position at the end of the bed. 'That's nice . . . in what way?'

'Well . . . ' Long pause during which I envisioned the rest of my married life in a French gite, surrounded by truffle pigs and up to my neck in Gauloises.

'Well . . . I'm going to be smarter for one thing.'

I waited. 'I mean,' he continued, painfully, because his breathing was shallow. 'I mean . . . I'm not going to wear the same shirt for two days running to save on laundry. Bugger that for a lark, eh?'

It wasn't the world's most vaunting ambition. In fact it was so achievable that it made me weep.

' . . . and there's more,' he breathed.

'I know darling, but perhaps you shouldn't be talking.'

'I'm going to have a mohair suit made. At a proper tailor's.' He lay back and contemplated the wildness of his ways. 'Have six.' I sniffed.

I'd made the house lovely for him. I'd cleared every surface of every 'chatchka' (nick-nack) just as he'd always wanted. Plants were gone, vases were gone, so were ornaments, anthropomorphic objets, Indian stress balls and month-old messages and magazines, and I'd redone the living room. So when my beloved limped into his sitting room, it looked wider, greener, comfier and not unlike the furniture of his youth, and there in the corner was a wide-screen television with all the channels Mr Murdoch has to offer. Sometimes you have to sup with the devil you know. Yer man Jack was very happy. His hair and his strength began to come back.

We discussed whether I should accept the role of Mrs Meers in the musical *Thoroughly Modern Millie* to open in October at the Shaftesbury Theatre. As always, Jack was the first to encourage me to work. Wrongly, as it happens. It was an adorable musical with amazing choreography and a terrific central performance from Amanda Holden. I loved the show and so did Jack, but we were not out of the water and I began to feel schizophrenic. If he was hospitalised by an infection, then driving from the clinic to dress up as a murderous hotelier disguised as a Chinese laundress ceased to be a distraction and became a teeth-chattering ordeal. 'Sad to be all alone in the world' was my entrance line. It is. I left and Anita Dobson took over the role.

Twice a week I was giving him Caprivan, a serum which came from antibodies in goats. Not yet proven, I believed and still do believe that it is set to become the anti-inflammatory of the age. No matter how immobile Jack was or how frail and weak, five minutes after I injected him he would get up and walk and the colour would come back to his face. The effect lasted for several hours of the day. Thank God, he'd now had a Groschen line inserted in his chest for his frequent blood transfusions and platelets.

It still wasn't enough. Three months later. Three lousy, fucking months later the remission was over. His blood counts were wrong and we were into the next course of preventative treatment. Thalidomide ('But what will happen to Dod's *arms*?' said Amy). When that failed to stop the infections, we progressed to Velcade, the new wonder drug. It was all too much, too late. Help at home was a nightmare, with no downstairs bathroom and nurses turning up, or not, as the feeling took them. Or they phoned at midnight, in impenetrable accents, from a tube station I'd barely heard of saying, 'I'm at Arnos Grove – 'ow do I get to you?'

With the next infection we arranged to take him not to his tried and trusted Parkside, but for ease and convenience to a nearby NHS hospital;

good intentions, major mistake. No one knew him, he was just an old man in a bed. Yes, we could visit him three times a day and bring him the food he needed, but there was no individual attention – how could there be? Worse, more fatally, there was no love. None. After they misread all the painstakingly prepared lists of medication I had gone through with the staff, the shift changed and they gave him twice the bowel medicine prescribed, with inevitable results. 'She's not very nice, this one.' He whispered to me, as an officious nurse swept in. 'She's got a very funny attitude.'

I'm afraid I lost it. For the first time, I did. Irrationally, I wanted to kill her there and then . . . on the ward. '*Do you have any idea who this man is?*' I yelled. '*This man is probably – no, not probably – IS, the finest – the most distinguished – y – you will ever meet in all your – years of nursing.*' I was wailing now like a coyote. '*You will n . . . never, never nurse a better patient . . . or a more wonderful human being! Don't ever, ever, dare to b . . . be anything other than sweet and courteous to this man. You . . . you should be privileged to p p . . . privileged . . .*' Jack was comforting *me* now instead of the other way round. '*Just* GO*!*' I cried, helplessly out of control now, '*Just bloody Go! – And bring me everything I need to make him clean and make him comfy! Go! Do it! Just Go! NOW!*' She went.

The following day we made the decision to take him to the North London Hospice to be made whole again. I'd been working for them as a charity for years and found it the least threatening or doom-laden place in the world. I once witnessed a dear friend's life extend for another year there when he'd practically been given up for dead. We got Jack out of the hospital and into the hospice. I knew it was a place for the living.

He was taken into the warm bosom of the most altruistic people in the land. His room looked out into a pretty courtyard and we stayed with him most of the time. We brought him out of the hospice for Friday-night dinner at home, for trips to the park or to the hospital for blood transfusions and for the Cup Final triumph of Manchester United over valiant little Millwall. '*YES! – The Lads.*' He was surrounded by our most loved friends on Saturday afternoon, all perched on the edge of our new green suite. Man. U.: 2 – Millwall: Eau de nil.

We experienced first-hand the trials of pushing a man in a wheelchair up and down kerbs that were built for the quick and the able. We watched kids play in the park and saw Dennis Potter's blossomest of blossoms from the same viewpoint. We read, we laughed, we stroked and cherished. We said most of what needed to be said. On 28 May, Amy and I slept in an empty bed in an adjacent room and Adam and his fiancée Taina slept, twined around each other, on the window seat in Jack's room. On the morning of 29 May, Colin, Lizzy, Jenny and my cousin Maurice arrived to sit with him as he drifted in and out of sleep.

I had in my wisdom, or not, depending how you view these things, arranged for a healer, Peter, to travel up from Devon to give him some hands-on healing. Five minutes before he arrived at Woodside Park station, Jack sat up, looked at something amazing over all our heads and took his last breath.

When Peter arrived he stood at the door of Jack's room and raised both his hands. 'Ah, he's gone,' he said softly, then he put his hands on those of us who wanted it, then Adam drove him back to the station.

A few days later he rang me. 'It's only happened to me once before,' he said, 'It was a privilege. I saw Jack's soul leave his body. It was surrounded by his guardian Angels.' It was a long time before I spoke: 'What did it look like?' I asked him.

'It was golden,' he told me 'and his angels were blue flames, gathered around as it rose.' I remembered the first present Jack had ever bought me. It was Blake's *Songs of Innocence and Experience*, with those beautiful illuminated illustrations. A good man, a man to whom good came easily.

A few days before, Colin Shindler had decided to go in to see Jack in the Hospice. He wanted to tell him that he loved him. He told me he was going to do this and I wondered how Jack would react to such a declaration. Afterwards I asked Jack what had happened.

'Colin came in today.'

'I know love, how was he?'

'Fine. He told me that he loved me.'

'That's nice, darl. What did you say to him?

'I didn't say anything, really,' said Jack. (*beat*) 'We had sex and he went home.'

BY JACK ROSENTHAL

WRITER'S AWARDS AND HONOURS

1976	British Academy Writer's Award
1976	Royal Television Society Writer's Award
1993	Royal Television Society Hall of Fame
1994	CBE for Services to Drama
1994	Writer's Guild Top British Comedy Writer Award
1994	Hon. M.A. (University of Salford)
1995	Hon. D. Litt. (University of Manchester)
1998	Hon. D. Litt. (University of Sheffield)
2002	Hon. M.A. (Manchester Metropolitan University)

DRAMA AWARDS

1971	***Another Sunday and Sweet F.A.*** (TV Critics' Best Play Award)
1971	***The Lovers*** (Writers' Guild Best Comedy Series Award)
1975	***The Evacuees*** American International Emmy Award British Academy Best Play Award Broadcasting Press Guild Best Play Award)
1976	***Bar Mitzvah Boy*** (British Academy Best Play Award Broadcasting Press Guild Best Play Award)
1977	***Spend, Spend, Spend*** (British Academy Best Play Award)
1981	***Lucky Star*** (Cannes Film Festival Award Best Screenplay, Canadian Academy)

1984 ***Yentl***
(New York Critics' Golden Globe)

1985 ***The Devil's Lieutentant***
(Cine del Luca, Monte Carlo)

1987 ***Ready When You Are, Mr McGill***
(Rio Film Festival Special Jury Award)

1992/93 ***Bye, Bye, Baby***
(Prix Europa Best Play Award)

AWARD NOMINATIONS

1974 ***There'll Almost Always Be an England***
(Writers' Guild Best Play Award)

1976 ***Ready When You Are, Mr McGill***
(British Academy Best Play Award)

1978 ***Spend, Spend, Spend***
(Prix Italia)

1979 ***The Knowledge***
(Prix Italia British Academy Best Play Award)

1983 ***P'tang, Yang, Kipperbang***
(British Academy Best Play Award

1987 ***London's Burning***
(British Academy Best Play Award)

1994 ***Wide-eyed and Legless***
(British Academy Best Play Award)

1994 ***Moving Story***
(Writers' Guild Best Drama Series)

1998 ***Jack: The Lad (Omnibus)***
(British Academy Documentary Award)

ORIGINAL TV PLAYS & FILMS

1963 ***Green Rub*** – Granada TV
1963 ***Pie in The Sky*** – Granada TV
1966 ***The Night before the Morning after*** – ABC TV
1967 ***Compensation Alice*** – ABC TV
1968 ***There's a Hole in Your Dustbin, Delilah*** – Granada TV
1969 ***Your Name's Not God, It's Edgar*** – Granada TV
1971 ***Another Sunday and Sweet F.A.*** – Granada TV
1972 ***And for My Next Trick*** – BBC TV
1974 ***Hot Fat*** – BBC TV Play for Today
1974 ***Polly Put the Kettle On*** – LWT
1974 ***Mr Ellis v the People*** – Granada TV
1974 ***There'll Almost Always Be an England*** – Granada TV
1975 ***Big Sid*** – Granada TV
1975 ***The Evacuees*** – BBC TV Play for Today
1976 ***Ready When You Are, Mr McGill*** – Granada TV

1976 ***Well, Thank You, Thursday*** – Granada TV
1976 ***Bar Mitzvah Boy*** – BBC TV Play for Today
1977 ***Spaghetti Two-step*** – Yorkshire TV
1977 ***Auntie's Niece*** – BBC TV
1977 ***Spend, Spend, Spend*** – BBC TV Play for Today
1979 ***The Knowledge*** – Euston Films
1982 ***P'Tang, Yang, Kipperbang*** – Channel Four
1984 ***The Devil's Lieutenant*** – Channel Four
1986 ***Fools on the Hill*** – BBC TV
1986 ***Day to Remember*** – Channel Four
1986 ***London's Burning*** – LWT
1987 ***The Chain*** – Channel Four
1989 ***Bag Lady*** – Central TV
1991 ***Sleeping Sickness*** – Central TV
1992 ***Bye, Bye, Baby*** – Channel Four
1993 ***Moving Story*** – ABTV/Carlton
1993 ***A Piece of Cake*** **(*Moving Story* sequel)** – ABTV/Carlton
1993 ***Wide-eyed and Legless*** – BBC TV
1996 ***Eskimo Day*** – BBC TV
1997 ***Cold Enough for Snow*** – BBC TV
2002 ***Ready When You Are, Mr McGill*** **(remake)** – WTTV/SKY/ITV

PLAY ADAPTATIONS

1976 ***Hindle Wakes*** – Granada TV: Laurence Olivier Series
1985 ***Mrs Capper's Birthday*** – BBC TV
1989 ***And a Nightingale Sang*** – Tyne-Tees TV
2002 ***Lucky Jim*** – ITV

DRAMA SERIES ORIGINATED

1987 ***London's Burning*** – LWT
1974 ***Red Letter Day*** – Granada TV
1993 ***Moving Story*** – ABTV/Carlton

ORIGINAL COMEDY SERIES

1962 ***Bulldog Breed*** – Granada TV
1969 ***The Dustbinmen*** – Granada TV
1971 ***The Lovers*** – Granada TV
1975 ***Sadie, It's Cold Outside*** – Thames TV

CONTRIBUTION TO OTHER SERIES

1961/69 ***Coronation Street*** – Granada TV: 129 episodes
1962 ***That Was the Week that Was*** – BBC TV: All episodes, first series
1963 ***The Odd Man*** – Granada TV: 2 episodes
1963 ***The Verdict Is Yours*** – Granada TV: 2 episodes

1963 ***Comedy Playhouse*** – BBC TV: 3 episodes
1963 ***The Army Game*** – Granada TV: 1 episode
1964 ***Taxi!*** – BBC TV: 20 episodes
1964 ***The Villains*** – Granada TV: 2 episodes
1965 ***Pardon the Expression*** – Granada TV: 4 episodes
1966 ***Mrs Thursday*** – ATV: 2 episodes
1976/77 ***Duchess of Duke Street*** – BBC TV: 2 episodes

FEATURE FILMS

1973 ***The Lovers*** – British Lion
1981 ***Lucky Star*** – Caneuram
1982 ***P'Tang, Yang, Kipperbang*** – Enigma/Goldcrest
1983 ***Yentl*** (co-written with Barbra Streisand) – UA/MGM
1987 ***The Chain*** – Rank/Quintet
1994 ***The Wedding Gift*** – Island World/Miramar
1997 ***Captain Jack*** – Viva/Granada Films

(Rotting Gently on Hollywood Shelves):

Conventions – Universal
The Best – Columbia
Family Matters – Warner
Gabriela: Clove & Cinnamon – Columbia
Gypsy & Me – Orion

(Uncredited Writing Contributions):

Continental Divide – Universal
Everybody's All-American – Can't even remember
1994 ***The Prince of Tides*** – Columbia
1998 ***My Life So Far*** – Enigma/Miramax

THEATRE

1978 ***Bar Mitzvah Boy*** (musical) – Her Majesty's Theatre
1981 ***Smash*** – Richmond Theatre
1983 ***Dear Anyone*** (musical) – Cambridge Theatre
1984 ***Our Gracie*** – Oldham Coliseum
2000 ***Dreyfus*** (translation) – Tricycle Theatre

TV AUTOBIOGRAPHY

1998 ***Jack the Lad*** **(*Omnibus*)** – BBC TV

Visiting Lecturer in Screenwriting at the Universities of London, Manchester, Oxford, Salford and East Anglia. Maisie Glass Professor of Drama, University of Sheffield.